D1759060

ABCDE
FGHI

Printed in England   (235 - 4N4)

Haynes
THE BOOK

APAA
AUTOMOTIVE
PARTS &
ACCESSORIES
ASSOCIATION MEMBER

Haynes Publishing Group
Sparkford Nr Yeovil
Somerset BA22 7JJ England

Haynes Publications, Inc
861 Lawrence Drive
Newbury Park
California 91320 USA

Acknowledgements

Thanks are due to the Nissan Motor Company Limited of Japan for the provision of technical information and certain illustrations. Castrol Limited supplied lubrication data, and the Champion Sparking Plug Company supplied the illustrations showing the various spark plug conditions. The bodywork repair photographs used in this manual were provided by Lloyds Industries Limited who supply 'Turtle Wax', 'Dupli-Color Holts', and other Holts range products.

Westacre Garage, Wilton Road, Salisbury supplied the Datsun 140J model used as our project car. Keith Vickers, of that establishment was particularly helpful.

Lastly, thanks to all of those people at Sparkford who helped in the production of this manual. Particularly, Brian Horsfall and Les Brazier, who carried out the mechanical work and took the photographs respectively; Ted Frenchum who planned the layout of each page and Rod Grainger the editor.

Introduction to the Datsun 140J, 160J and 710

The models described in this manual include the 140J Mk I and II and 160J saloons, the 160J SSS Coupe and the (North American) 710 series comprising 2 and 4 door sedans, hardtop and station wagon.

The engine used in all versions is of similar 4 cylinder ohc design but varies in capacity through a difference in stroke in the case of the 1428 cc and 1595 cc units and differences in bore and stroke in the case of the 1770 cc and 1952 cc units.

The design and construction of the bodywork and underframe is similar in all models but the 160J SSS incorporates independent rear suspension as opposed to the semi-elliptic leaf spring and rigid axle layout of all other models.

About this manual

Its aim

The aim of this book is to help you get the best value from your car. It can do so in two ways. First it can help you decide what work must be done, even should you choose to get it done by a garage, the routine maintenance and the diagnosis and course of action when random faults occur. But it is hoped that you will also use the second and fuller purpose by tackling the work yourself. This can give you the satisfaction of doing the job yourself. On the simpler jobs it may even be quicker than booking the car into a garage and going there twice, to leave and collect it. Perhaps most important, much money can be saved by avoiding the costs a garage must charge to cover their labour and overheads.

The book has drawings and descriptions to show the function of the various components so that their layout can be understood. Then the tasks are described and photographed in a step-by-step sequence so that even a novice can cope with complicated work. Such a person is the very one to buy a car needing repair yet be unable to afford garage costs.

The jobs are described assuming only normal spanners are available, and not special tools. But a reasonable outfit of tools will be a worthwile investment. Many special workshop tools produced by the makers merely speed the work, and in these cases guidance is given as to how to do the job without them, the oft quoted example being the use of a large hose clip to compress the piston rings for insertion in the cylinder. But on a very few occasions the special tool is essential to prevent damage to components, then their use is described. Though it might be possible to borrow the tool, such work may have to be entrusted to the official agent.

To avoid labour costs a garage will often give a cheaper repair by fitting a reconditioned assembly. The home mechanic can be helped by this book to diagnose the fault and make a repair using only a minor spare part.

The manufacturer's official workshop manuals are written for their trained staff, and so assume special knowledge; detail is left out. This book is written for the owner, and so goes into detail.

Using the manual

The book is divided into thirteen Chapters. Each Chapter is divided into numbered Sections which are headed in bold type between horizontal lines. Each Section consits of serially numbered paragraphs.

There are two types of illustration: (1) Figures which are numbered according to Chapter and sequence of occurrence in that Chapter. (2) Photographs which have a reference number on their caption. All photographs apply to the Chapter in which they occur so that the reference figure pinpoints the pertinent Section and paragraph number.

Procedures, once described in the text, are not normally repeated. If it is necessary to refer to another Chapter the reference will be given in Chapter number and Section number.

When the left or right side of the car is mentioned it is as if looking forward in the normal direction of vehicle movement.

While every care is taken to ensure that the information in this manual is correct, no liability can be accepted by the authors or publishers for loss, damage or injury caused by any errors in, or omissions from, the information given

Contents

Datsun 140J Saloon (UK specification)

Datsun 710 Sedan (USA specification)

Routine maintenance

Maintenance is essential for ensuring safety and desirable for the purpose of getting the best in terms of performance and economy from the car. Over the years the need for periodic lubrication - oiling, greasing and so on - has been drastically reduced if not totally eliminated. This has unfortunately tended to lead some owners to think that because no such action is required the items either no longer exist or will last for ever. This is a serious delusion. It follows therefore that the largest initial element of maintenance is visual examination. This may lead to repairs or renewal.

Jacking and towing

Before carrying out any servicing or repair operations, make sure that you know where to position the jack and axle stands. It is most important to use only the specified points in order to prevent accidents and damage to the vehicle itself.

If the vehicle breaks down or becomes bogged down, a front mounted towing hook is provided to which a tow rope may be attached. No rear hook is provided but a tow rope can be attached if leaf spring type rear suspension is installed. Where independent rear suspension is used, towing other vehicle is not recommended.

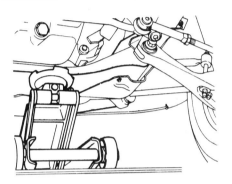

RM.2 Front jacking point

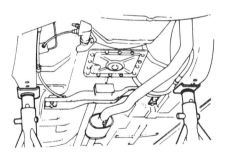

RM.3 Axle stand front support positions

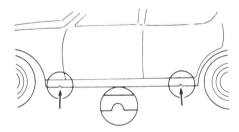

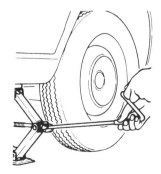

RM.1 Jacking points for use with pantograph type jack supplied with car

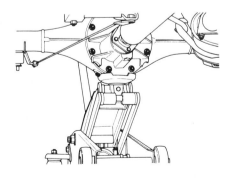

RM.4 Rear jacking point (rigid rear axle)

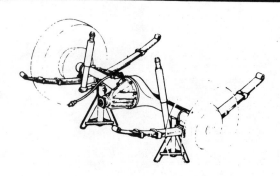

RM.5 Axle stand rear support positions (rigid rear axle)

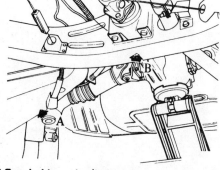

RM.6 Rear jacking point (independent rear suspension) and axle stand support positions (A and B)

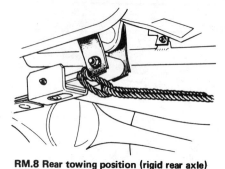

RM.8 Rear towing position (rigid rear axle)

RM.7 Front towing hook

Maintenance schedule

Note: The items in **bold** type affect the owner's safety and are vital; the other items are intended to combat depreciation.

Every 250 miles (400 km) travelled or weekly - whichever comes first

Steering

Check the tyre pressures including the spare
Examine tyres for wear or damage
Is steering smooth and accurate

Brakes

Check reservoir fluid level
Is there any fall off in braking efficiency?
Try an emergency stop. Is adjustment necessary?

Lights, wipers and horns

Do all bulbs work at the front and rear?
Are the headlamp beams aligned properly?
Check windscreen washer fluid level
Do the wipers and horns work?

Engine

Check the sump oil level and top-up if required
Check the radiator coolant level and top-up if required
Check the battery electrolyte level and top-up to the level of the plates with distilled water as needed

3,000 miles (4,800 km)

Every 3,000 miles (4,800 km) or 4 monthly, whichever comes first, or earlier if indications suggest that safety items in particular are not performing correctly.

Steering

Examine all steering linkage rods, joints and bushes for signs of wear or damage

Check front wheel hub bearings and adjust if necessary
Check tightness of steering gear mounting bolts

Brakes

Examine disc pads and drum shoes to determine the amount of friction material left. Renew if necessary. Adjust rear brakes
Examine all hydraulic pipes, cylinders and unions for signs of chafing, corrosion, dents or any other form of deterioration or leaks

Suspension

Examine all nuts, bolts and mountings securing the suspension units, front and rear. Tighten if necessary
Examine the rubber bushes for signs of wear and play

Engine

Change oil
Check distributor points gap (or air gap - transistorized type)
Check and clean spark plugs

Gearbox (manual and automatic)

Check oil level and top-up if necessary

Clutch

Check fluid reservoir level and top-up if necessary

Body

Lubricate all locks and hinges
Check that water drain holes at bottom of doors are clear

6,000 miles (9,600 km)

Check the tension of the engine drive belts
Check the torque of the cylinder head bolts
Check the valve clearances and adjust if necessary
Renew the oil filter
Renew the fuel line filter (if necessary after visual inspection)

Steering
Rotate roadwheels and rebalance if necessary

Brakes
Check pedal free-movement and for oil leakage at cylinders

Clutch
Check pedal free-movement and for oil leakage at cylinders

12,000 miles (19,000 km)

Check crankcase fume emission control system (Chapter 1)
Check fuel storage evaporative emission control system (Chapter 3)
Check exhaust emission control system (Chapter 3)
Fit new spark plugs
Fit new distributor points
Clean carburettor float chamber
Check HT ignition leads for deterioration

Steering
Check wheel alignment

Suspension
Check shock absorber operation

Transmission
Check security of propeller shaft bolts
Check oil level in rear axle and top-up if necessary

24,000 miles (38,000 km) or annually

Engine
Flush cooling system and refill with anti-freeze mixture
Renew air cleaner element
Test operation of brake pressure regulating valve

30,000 miles (48,000 km)

Transmission
Drain manual gearbox and refill with fresh oil
Drain rear axle and refill with fresh oil
Check propeller shaft universal joints for wear and recondition if necessary

Steering
Grease ball joints by removing grease plugs

Headlights
Check beams and adjust if required

Front wheel hubs
Dismantle, clean out old grease and repack with new

48,000 miles (77,000 km)

Brakes
Drain hydraulic system, renew all cylinder seals and refill with fresh fluid. Bleed system. Overhaul vacuum servo unit

Clutch
Drain hydraulic system, renew master and slave cylinder seals, refill with fresh fluid. Bleed system

Additionally the following items should be attended to as time can be spared:

Transmission
Dismantle driveshafts and grease sliding joints (see Chapter 8 160J SSS only).

Rear wheel hubs (160J SSS only)
Dismantle, clean out old grease and repack with new

Spring and autumn

Check position of air cleaner intake flap lever (not automatic temperature controlled type)

Underbody

This should be cleaned by using a high pressure hose or steam cleaner in order to detect rust and corrosion

---

Exhaust system

An exhaust system must be leakproof, and the noise level below a certain maximum. Excessive leaks may cause carbon monoxide fumes to enter the passenger compartment. Excessive noise constitutes a public nuisance. Both these faults may cause the vehicle to be kept off the road. Repair or replace defective sections when symptoms are apparent

1 Remember to check the pressure in the spare tyre

2 Topping-up the engine oil

3 Rear brake adjuster

4 Topping-up the gearbox

5 Oiling door hinges

6 Rear axle oil level and filler plug

7 Air cleaner intake flap control lever

Buying spare parts and vehicle identification numbers

Buying spare parts

Spare parts are available from many sources, for example: Datsun garages, other garages and accessory shops, and motor factors. Our advice regarding spare parts is as follows:

Officially appointed Datsun garages - This is the best source of parts which are peculiar to your car and otherwise not generally available (eg; complete cylinder heads, internal gearbox components, badges, interior trim etc). It is also the only place at which you should buy parts if your car is still under warranty; non-Datsun components may invalidate the warranty. To be sure of obtaining the correct parts it will always be necessary to give the storeman your car's engine and chassis number, and if possible, to take the old part along for positive identification. Remember that many parts are available on a factory exchange scheme - any parts returned should always be clean! It obviously makes good sense to go straight to the specialists on your car for this type of part for they are best equipped to supply you.

Other garages and accessory shops - These are often very good places to buy material and components needed for the maintenance of your car (eg; oil filters, spark plugs, bulbs, fan belts, oils and grease, touch-up paint, filler paste etc). They also sell general accessories, usually have convenient opening hours, charge lower prices and can often be found not far from home.

Motor factors - Good factors will stock all of the more important components which wear out relatively quickly (eg; clutch components, pistons, valves, exhaust systems, brake cylinders/pipes/hoses/seals/shoes and pads etc). Motor factors will often provide new or reconditioned components on a part exchange basis - this can save a considerable amount of money.

Vehicle identification numbers

Modifications are a continuing and unpublished process in vehicle manufacture quite apart from major model changes. Spare parts manuals and lists are compiled upon a numerical basis, the individual vehicle numbers being essential to correct identification of the component required.

140J and 160J SSS models

Vehicle identification plate. This contains the vehicle type, engine capacity, maximum BHP wheel base and engine and vehicle serial numbers and is located on the engine compartment rear bulkhead.

Vehicle serial number. This is stamped on the engine rear bulkhead.

Engine number. This is located just below No. 4 spark plug on the right-hand side of the cylinder block.

Colour code. This is to be found on the radiator supporting crossmember.

710 series models

Vehicle identification plate. Similarly located as for 140J model.

Vehicle serial number. Similarly located as for 140J but number repeated on upper surface of instrument panel.

Engine number. Similarly located as far 140J model.

Colour code. As for 140J model.

Tyre inflation label. Located inside glove compartment lid.

Motor vehicle safety standards (MVSS) label. Located on door edge.

Emission control system labels. Located on upper surface of radiator supporting crossmember.

Exhaust emission test label (California only). This is located on the rear left-hand window.

Automatic choke instructional label. Located inside glove compartment.

Exhaust system catalytic converter precautions label (California). Attached to driver's sun visor.

Starter interlock system instructional label. Affixed to sun visor.

Air conditioner service procedure label. Located on inside of hood lid.

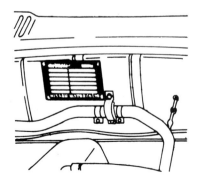

RM.9 Vehicle identification plate (140J and 160J SSS)

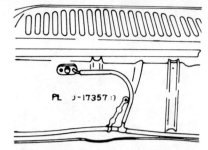

RM.10 Vehicle serial number location

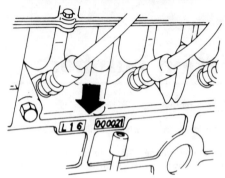

RM.11 Location of engine number

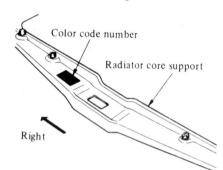

Color code number

Radiator core support

Right

RM.12 Colour code label

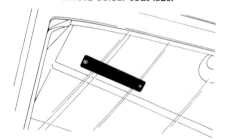

RM.13 Duplicated identification number (North America)

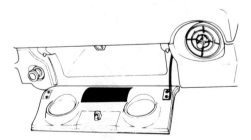

RM.14 Tyre inflation label (710 series)

RM.15 M.V.S.S. label (710 series)

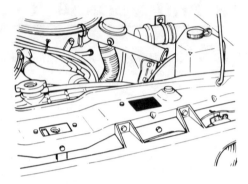

RM.16 Emission control system labels (710 series)

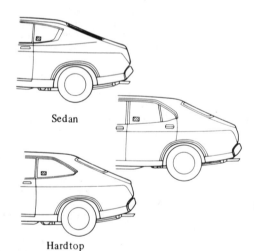

Sedan

Hardtop

RM.17 Exhaust emission test label (710 series - California)

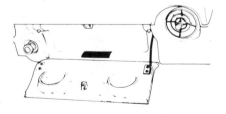

RM.18 Automatic choke instructional label (710 series)

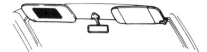

RM.19 Catalytic converter precautionary label (710 series - California)

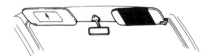

RM.20 Starter interlock system instructional label (710 series)

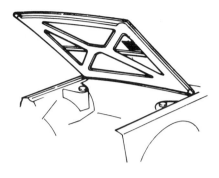

RM.21 Air conditioner service procedure label (710 series)

Recommended lubricants

1	...	...	...	...	...	...	...	Engine	...	...	...	...	... Castrol GTX
2	...	...	...	...	...	...	...	Gearbox:					
								Manual	...	...	...	...	... Castrol Hypoy Light (80 EP)
								Automatic		...	...	...	... Castrol TQ Dexron R
3	...	...	...	...	...	...	...	Rear axle (differential)			...	...	... Castrol Hypoy B (90 EP)
4	...	...	...	...	...	...	...	Front wheel bearings and chassis ...					... Castrol LM Grease

Note: The above are general recommendations. Lubrication requirements vary from territory - consult the operators handbook supplied with your car.

Use of English

As this book has been written in England, it uses the appropriate English component names, phrases, and spelling. Some of these differ from those used in America. Normally, these cause no difficulty, but to make sure, a glossary is printed below. In ordering spare parts remember the parts list may use some of these words:

English	American	English	American
Accelerator	Gas pedal	Leading shoe (of brake)	Primary shoe
Aerial	Antenna	Locks	Latches
Anti-roll bar	Stabiliser or sway bar	Methylated spirit	Denatured alcohol
Big-end bearing	Rod bearing	Motorway	Freeway, turnpike etc
Bonnet (engine cover)	Hood	Number plate	License plate
Boot (luggage compartment)	Trunk	Paraffin	Kerosene
Bulkhead	Firewall	Petrol	Gasoline (gas)
Bush	Bushing	Petrol tank	Gas tank
Cam follower or tappet	Valve lifter or tappet	'Pinking'	'Pinging'
Carburettor	Carburetor	Prise (force apart)	Pry
Catch	Latch	Propeller shaft	Driveshaft
Choke/venturi	Barrel	Quarterlight	Quarter window
Circlip	Snap-ring	Retread	Recap
Clearance	Lash	Reverse	Back-up
Crownwheel	Ring gear (of differential)	Rocker cover	Valve cover
Damper	Shock absorber, shock	Saloon	Sedan
Disc (brake)	Rotor/disk	Seized	Frozen
Distance piece	Spacer	Sidelight	Parking light
Drop arm	Pitman arm	Silencer	Muffler
Drop head coupe	Convertible	Sill panel (beneath doors)	Rocker panel
Dynamo	Generator (DC)	Small end, little end	Piston pin or wrist pin
Earth (electrical)	Ground	Spanner	Wrench
Engineer's blue	Prussian blue	Split cotter (for valve spring cap)	Lock (for valve spring retainer)
Estate car	Station wagon	Split pin	Cotter pin
Exhaust manifold	Header	Steering arm	Spindle arm
Fault finding/diagnosis	Troubleshooting	Sump	Oil pan
Float chamber	Float bowl	Swarf	Metal chips or debris
Free-play	Lash	Tab washer	Tang or lock
Freewheel	Coast	Tappet	Valve lifter
Gearbox	Transmission	Thrust bearing	Throw-out bearing
Gearchange	Shift	Top gear	High
Grub screw	Setscrew, Allen screw	Trackrod (of steering)	Tie-rod (or connecting rod)
Gudgeon pin	Piston pin or wrist pin	Trailing shoe (of brake)	Secondary shoe
Halfshaft	Axleshaft	Transmission	Whole drive line
Handbrake	Parking brake	Tyre	Tire
Hood	Soft top	Van	Panel wagon/van
Hot spot	Heat riser	Vice	Vise
Indicator	Turn signal	Wheel nut	Lug nut
Interior light	Dome lamp	Windscreen	Windshield
Layshaft (of gearbox)	Countershaft	Wing/mudguard	Fender

Safety first!

Professional motor mechanics are trained in safe working procedures. However enthusiastic you may be about getting on with the job in hand, do take the time to ensure that your safety is not put at risk. A moment's lack of attention can result in an accident, as can failure to observe certain elementary precautions.

There will always be new ways of having accidents, and the following points do not pretend to be a comprehensive list of all dangers; they are intended rather to make you aware of the risks and to encourage a safety-conscious approach to all work you carry out on your vehicle.

Essential DOs and DON'Ts

DON'T rely on a single jack when working underneath the vehicle. Always use reliable additional means of support, such as axle stands, securely placed under a part of the vehicle that you know will not give way.

DON'T attempt to loosen or tighten high-torque nuts (e.g. wheel hub nuts) while the vehicle is on a jack; it may be pulled off.

DON'T start the engine without first ascertaining that the transmission is in neutral (or 'Park' where applicable) and the parking brake applied.

DON'T suddenly remove the filler cap from a hot cooling system – cover it with a cloth and release the pressure gradually first, or you may get scalded by escaping coolant.

DON'T attempt to drain oil until you are sure it has cooled sufficiently to avoid scalding you.

DON'T grasp any part of the engine, exhaust or catalytic converter without first ascertaining that it is sufficiently cool to avoid burning you.

DON'T allow brake fluid or antifreeze to contact vehicle paintwork.

DON'T syphon toxic liquids such as fuel, brake fluid or antifreeze by mouth, or allow them to remain on your skin.

DON'T inhale dust – it may be injurious to health (see *Asbestos* below).

DON'T allow any spilt oil or grease to remain on the floor – wipe it up straight away, before someone slips on it.

DON'T use ill-fitting spanners or other tools which may slip and cause injury.

DON'T attempt to lift a heavy component which may be beyond your capability – get assistance.

DON'T rush to finish a job, or take unverified short cuts.

DON'T allow children or animals in or around an unattended vehicle.

DO wear eye protection when using power tools such as drill, sander, bench grinder etc, and when working under the vehicle.

DO use a barrier cream on your hands prior to undertaking dirty jobs – it will protect your skin from infection as well as making the dirt easier to remove afterwards; but make sure your hands aren't left slippery.

DO keep loose clothing (cuffs, tie etc) and long hair well out of the way of moving mechanical parts.

DO remove rings, wristwatch etc, before working on the vehicle – especially the electrical system.

DO ensure that any lifting tackle used has a safe working load rating adequate for the job.

DO keep your work area tidy – it is only too easy to fall over articles left lying around.

DO get someone to check periodically that all is well, when working alone on the vehicle.

DO carry out work in a logical sequence and check that everything is correctly assembled and tightened afterwards.

DO remember that your vehicle's safety affects that of yourself and others. If in doubt on any point, get specialist advice.

IF, in spite of following these precautions, you are unfortunate enough to injure yourself, seek medical attention as soon as possible.

Asbestos

Certain friction, insulating, sealing, and other products – such as brake linings, brake bands, clutch linings, torque converters, gaskets, etc – contain asbestos. *Extreme care must be taken to avoid inhalation of dust from such products since it is hazardous to health.* If in doubt, assume that they *do* contain asbestos.

Fire

Remember at all times that petrol (gasoline) is highly flammable. Never smoke, or have any kind of naked flame around, when working on the vehicle. But the risk does not end there – a spark caused by an electrical short-circuit, by two metal surfaces contacting each other, by careless use of tools, or even by static electricity built up in your body under certain conditions, can ignite petrol vapour, which in a confined space is highly explosive.

Always disconnect the battery earth (ground) terminal before working on any part of the fuel or electrical system, and never risk spilling fuel on to a hot engine or exhaust.

It is recommended that a fire extinguisher of a type suitable for fuel and electrical fires is kept handy in the garage or workplace at all times. Never try to extinguish a fuel or electrical fire with water.

Fumes

Certain fumes are highly toxic and can quickly cause unconsciousness and even death if inhaled to any extent. Petrol (gasoline) vapour comes into this category, as do the vapours from certain solvents such as trichloroethylene. Any draining or pouring of such volatile fluids should be done in a well ventilated area.

When using cleaning fluids and solvents, read the instructions carefully. Never use materials from unmarked containers – they may give off poisonous vapours.

Never run the engine of a motor vehicle in an enclosed space such as a garage. Exhaust fumes contain carbon monoxide which is extremely poisonous; if you need to run the engine, always do so in the open air or at least have the rear of the vehicle outside the workplace.

If you are fortunate enough to have the use of an inspection pit, never drain or pour petrol, and never run the engine, while the vehicle is standing over it; the fumes, being heavier than air, will concentrate in the pit with possibly lethal results.

The battery

Never cause a spark, or allow a naked light, near the vehicle's battery. It will normally be giving off a certain amount of hydrogen gas, which is highly explosive.

Always disconnect the battery earth (ground) terminal before working on the fuel or electrical systems.

If possible, loosen the filler plugs or cover when charging the battery from an external source. Do not charge at an excessive rate or the battery may burst.

Take care when topping up and when carrying the battery. The acid electrolyte, even when diluted, is very corrosive and should not be allowed to contact the eyes or skin.

If you ever need to prepare electrolyte yourself, always add the acid slowly to the water, and never the other way round. Protect against splashes by wearing rubber gloves and goggles.

When jump starting a car using a booster battery, for negative earth (ground) vehicles, connect the jump leads in the following sequence: First connect one jump lead between the positive (+) terminals of the two batteries. Then connect the other jump lead first to the negative (–) terminal of the booster battery, and then to a good earthing (ground) point on the vehicle to be started, at least 18 in (45 cm) from the battery if possible. Ensure that hands and jump leads are clear of any moving parts, and that the two vehicles do not touch. Disconnect the leads in the reverse order.

Mains electricity

When using an electric power tool, inspection light etc, which works from the mains, always ensure that the appliance is correctly connected to its plug and that, where necessary, it is properly earthed (grounded). Do not use such appliances in damp conditions and, again, beware of creating a spark or applying excessive heat in the vicinity of fuel or fuel vapour.

Ignition HT voltage

A severe electric shock can result from touching certain parts of the ignition system, such as the HT leads, when the engine is running or being cranked, particularly if components are damp or the insulation is defective. Where an electronic ignition system is fitted, the HT voltage is much higher and could prove fatal.

General dimensions and capacities

Dimensions

Dimensions	140J	160J SSS	2 Dr. Sedan	4 Dr. Sedan	710 Series Hardtop	Wagon
Overall length	162.2 in. 412.0 cm	162.2 in. 412.0 cm	170.9 in. 434.1 cm	170.9 in. 434.1 cm	169.3 in. 430.1 cm	172.2 in. 437.4 cm
Overall width	62.2 in. 158.0 cm	62.2 in. 158.0 cm	62.2 in. 158.0 cm	62.2 in. 158.0 cm	62.2 in. 158.0 cm	62.2 in. 158.0 cm
Overall height	54.1 in. 137.5 cm	54.1 in. 137.5 cm	55.5 in. 141.0 cm	55.5 in. 141.0 cm	55.5 in. 141.0 cm	55.9 in. 141.7 cm
Track (front)	51.6 in. 131.0 cm	51.6 in. 131.0 cm	51.6 in. 131.0 cm	51.6 in. 131.0 cm	51.6 in. 131.0 cm	51.6 in. 131.0 cm
Track (rear)	52.0 in. 132.0 cm	52.0 in. 132.0 cm	52.4 in. 133.3 cm	52.4 in. 133.3 cm	52.4 in. 133.3 cm	52.4 in. 133.3 cm
Wheelbase	96.5 in. 245.0 cm	96.5 in. 245.0 cm	96.5 in. 245.0 cm	96.5 in. 245.0 cm	96.5 in. 245.0 cm	96.5 in. 245.0 cm
Ground clearance	6.7 in. 17.0 cm	6.7 in. 17.0 cm	6.7 in. 17.0 cm	6.7 in. 17.0 cm	6.7 in. 17.0 cm	6.7 in. 17.0 cm
Turning circle (kerbs)	31.4 ft 9.6 m	31.4 ft 9.6 m	31.4 ft 9.6 m	31.4 ft 9.6 m	31.4 ft 9.6 m	31.4 ft 9.6 m
Kerb weight: Manual	2225 lb 1018 kg	2249 lb 1020 kg	2293 lb 1040 kg	2315 lb 1050 kg	2293 lb 1040 kg	2448 lb 1110 kg
Automatic	–	–	2326 lb 1055 kg	2348 lb 1065 kg	2326 lb 1055 kg	2481 lb 1125 kg

Capacities

Capacities	140J	160J SSS	2 Dr. Sedan	4 Dr. Sedan	710 Series Hardtop	Wagon
Fuel tank: Imp. U.S.	11 gal. 50 litres	12 1/8 gal. 55 litres	13¼ gal.	13¼ gal.	13¼ gal.	*11 7/8 gal.
Cooling system: Imp. U.S.	1 3/8 gal. 6.5 litres	1 3/8 gal. 6.5 litres	1 7/8 gal.	1 7/8 gal.	1 7/8 gal.	1 7/8 gal.
Engine sump: Imp. U.S.	7½ pints 4.3 litres	7½ pints 4.3 litres	4 3/8 qts.	4 3/8 qts.	4 3/8 qts.	4 3/8 qts.
Gearbox (manual): Imp. U.S.	3½ pints 2.0 litres	3½ pints 2.0 litres	4¼ pints	4¼ pints	4¼ pints	4¼ pints
Auto. transmission (U.S.)	–	–	5 7/8 qts.	5 7/8 qts.	5 7/8 qts.	5 7/8 qts.
Rear axle: Imp. U.S.	2¼ pints 1.3 litres	1 3/8 pints 0.8 litres	2¾ pints	2¾ pints	2¾ pints	2¾ pints

except California 13¼ gal.

Chapter 1 Engine

Contents

Specifications

Engine (general)

Engine application:

	Engine code
140J (Violet)	L14
160J and 160JSSS	L16
710 series (up to 1975)	L18
710 series (1975 onwards)	L20B

Engine type ... ...   Four cylinder, in-line, overhead camshaft (OHC)

	L14	L16	L18	L20B
Displacement	87.1 cu.in	97.3 cu.in	108.0 cu.in	119.1 cu.in
	1428 cc	1595 cc	1770 cc	1952 cc
Bore	3.27 in	3.27 in	3.35 in	3.35 in
	83.0 mm	83.0 mm	85.0 mm	85.0 mm
Stroke	2.60 in	2.90 in	3.07 in	3.39 in
	66.0 mm	73.7 mm	78.0 mm	86.0 mm
Maximum bhp @ 6200 rpm ...	80	95	95	105
Max. torque (lb/ft) @ 4200 rpm	82	95	97	108

Compression ratio:	L14	L16	L18	L20B
Single carburettor	9 : 1	8.5:1	8.5 : 1	8.5 : 1
Twin carburettor	-	9.5 : 1	-	-

Oil pressure (warm) @ 2000 rpm ... ...   50 to 57 p.s.i. (3.5 to 4.0 kg/cm^2)
Oil capacity ... ...   4.3/8 US qts, 7½ Imp. pints, 4.3 litres

Crankshaft

Journal diameter (L14, L16, L18)	2.1631 to 2.1636 in (54.942 to 54.955 mm)
Journal diameter (L20B)	2.3599 to 2.3604 in (59.942 to 59.955 mm)
Max. taper or out of round	less than 0.0004 in (0.01 mm)
Crankshaft end-play	0.0020 to 0.0071 in (0.05 to 0.18 mm)
Max. crankshaft end-play	0.0118 in (0.3 mm)
Crankpin diameter	1.966 to 1.967 in (49.961 to 49.974 mm)
Max. taper or out of round	less than 0.0004 in (0.01 mm)
Main bearing thickness (standard)	0.0719 to 0.0722 in (1.827 to 1.835 mm)
Main bearing clearance	0.008 to 0.0024 in (0.020 to 0.062 mm)
Max. main bearing clearance	0.0047 in (0.12 mm)
Max. permissible crankshaft bend	0.0020 in (0.05 mm)

Camshaft

Journal diameter	1.8877 to 1.8883 in (47.949 to 47.962 mm)
Bearing inner diameter	1.8898 to 1.8904 in (48.000 to 48.016 mm)
Journal to bearing clearance	0.0015 to 0.0026 in (0.038 to 0.067 mm)
Max. permissible camshaft bend	0.0007 in (0.02 mm)
Camshaft end-play	0.0031 to 0.0150 in (0.08 to 0.38 mm)

Camshaft lobe lift:
Inlet:
L14 and single carb L16 ... ...   0.2618 in (6.65 mm)
All other engines... ... ...   0.2756 in (7.00 mm)
Exhaust:
L14 engine ... ...   0.2618 in (6.65 mm)
All other engines... ... ...   0.2756 in (7.00 mm)

Pistons

	L14 and L16	L18 and L20B
Piston dia (standard)	3.2671 to 3.2691 in (82.985 to 83.035 mm)	3.3451 to 3.3470 in (84.965 to 85.015 mm)
Piston dia. (oversize 0.0098 in/0.25 mm)	3.2762 to 3.2781 in (83.215 to 83.265 mm)	—
Piston dia. (0.0197 in/0.50 mm)	3.2860 to 3.2880 in (83.465 to 83.515 mm)	3.3648 to 3.3667 in (85.465 to 85.515 mm)
Piston dia. (0.0295 in/0.75 mm)	3.2959 to 3.2978 in (83.715 to 83.765 mm)	—
Piston dia. (oversize 0.0394 in/1.00 mm)	3.3057 to 3.3077 in (83.965 to 84.015 mm)	3.3844 to 3.3864 in (85.965 to 86.015 mm)
Piston dia. (oversize 0.0492 in/1.25 mm)	3.3254 to 3.3274 in (84.465 to 84.515 mm)	—
Piston to bore clearance...	0.0010 to 0.0018 in (0.025 to 0.045 mm)	

Piston ring groove widths:

	L14 and L16	L18 and L20B
Top compression	0.0787 in (2.0 mm)	0.0799 to 0.0807 in (2.030 to 2.050 mm)
Second compression	0.0787 in (2.0 mm)	0.0795 to 0.0803 in (2.020 to 2.040 mm)
Oil control	0.1575 in (4.0 mm)	0.1581 to 0.1591 in (4.015 to 4.040 mm)

Piston rings

	L14 and L16	L18 and L20B
Thickness:		
Top compression	0.0778 in (1.977 mm)	0.0778 to 0.0783 in (1.977 to 1.990 mm)
Second compression	0.0778 in (1.977 mm)	0.0776 to 0.0783 in (1.970 to 1.990 mm)
Clearance in groove:		
Top compression	0.0016 to 0.0031 in (0.040 to 0.080 mm)	0.0016 to 0.0029 in (0.040 to 0.073 mm)
Second compression	0.0012 to 0.0028 in (0.030 to 0.070 mm)	0.0012 to 0.0028 in (0.030 to 0.070 mm)
Piston ring end gap:		
Top compression	0.0091 to 0.0157 in (0.23 to 0.040 mm)	0.0098 to 0.0157 in (0.25 to 0.40 mm)
Second compression	0.0059 to 0.0118 in (0.15 to 0.30 mm)	0.0118 to 0.0197 in (0.30 to 0.50 mm)

Oil control	0.0118 to 0.0354 in (0.30 to 0.90 mm)	0.0118 to 0.0354 in (0.30 to 0.90 mm)

Gudgeon pins

Diameter	0.8265 to 0.8268 in (20.993 to 21.000 mm)

Length
L14 engine ... ... °··	2.8346 to 2.8445 in (72.00 to 72.25 mm)
Other engines	2.8445 to 2.8740 in (72.25 to 73.00 mm)
Pin to piston clearance	0.0001 to 0.0006 in (0.003 to 0.015 mm)
Pin to connecting rod (interference fit)	0.0006 to 0.0013 in (0.015 to 0.033 mm)

Connecting rods

	L14	L16	L18	L20B
Distance between centres of small end and big-end bearings	5.35 in 136.6 mm	5.25 in 133.0 mm	5.132 in 130.35 mm	5.748 in 146.0 mm

Big-end bearing thickness	0.0588 to 0.0593 in (1.493 to 1.506 mm)
Big-end side play	0.0079 to 0.0118 in (0.20 to 0.30 mm)
Big-end bearing clearance	0.0010 to 0.0022 in (0.025 to 0.055 mm)

Valves

Clearance:
Cold:
Inlet	0.008 in (0.20 mm)
Exhaust	0.010 in (0.25 mm)

Warm:
Inlet	0.010 in (0.25 mm)
Exhaust	0.012 in (0.30 mm)

Valve head diameter	L14	L16	L18	L20B
Inlet	1.5361 in (38.00 mm)	1.6535 in (42.00 mm)	1.650 to 1.657 in (41.9 to 42.1 mm)	1.650 to 1.657 in (41.9 to 42.1 mm)
Exhaust	1.2992 in (33.00 mm)	1.2992 in (33.00 mm)	1.378 to 1.386 in (35.0 to 35.2 mm)	1.378 to 1.386 in (35.0 to 35.2 mm)

Valve stem diameter:
Inlet	0.3136 to 0.3142 in (7.965 to 7.980 mm)
Exhaust	0.3128 to 0.3134 in (7.945 to 7.960 mm)

Valve length:
L14 engine:
Inlet	4.551 to 4.562 in (115.6 to 115.9 mm)
Exhaust	4.555 to 4.567 in (115.7 to 116.0 mm)

All other engines:
Inlet	4.524 to 4.535 in (114.9 to 115.2 mm)
Exhaust	4.555 to 4.567 in (115.7 to 116.0 mm)

Valve lift
Inlet:
L14 and single carb L16	0.394 in (10.0 mm)
All other engines	0.413 in (10.5 mm)

Exhaust:
L14	0.394 in (10.0 mm)
All other engines	0.413 in (10.5 mm)

Valve spring free-length (Inlet and exhaust):
Inner	1.766 in (44.85 mm)
Outer	1.968 in (49.98 mm)

Valve spring coil dia:	L14	L16	L18	L20B
Inlet:				
Inner	—	0.862 in (21.9 mm)	0.953 in (24.2 mm)	0.953 in (24.2 mm)
Outer	1.181 in (30.0 mm)	1.150 in (29.4 mm)	1.150 in (29.4 mm)	1.150 in (29.4 mm)
Exhaust:				
Inner	0.862 in (21.9 mm)	0.862 in (21.9 mm)	0.0953 in (24.2 mm)	0.0953 in (24.2 mm)

Outer	1.150 in (29.4 mm)	1.150 in (29.4 mm)	1.150 in (29.4 mm)	1.150 in (29.4 mm)

Valve guide length   ...   .   2.323 in (59.0 mm)
Valve guide height from surface of cylinder head   ...   ...   0.417 in (10.6 mm)
Valve guide inner diameter   ...   .   0.3150 to 0.3154 in (8.000 to 8.018 mm)
Valve guide outer diameter   ...   .   0.4733 to 0.4738 in (12.023 to 12.034 mm)
Valve stem to guide clearance:
  Inlet   ...   .   0.0008 to 0.0021 in (0.020 to 0.53 mm)
  Exhaust   ...   .   0.0016 to 0.0029 in (0.0040 to 0.0073 mm)

Seat width:	L14	L16	L18	L20B
Inlet	0.0709 in 1.8 mm	0.0551 in 1.5 mm	0.0551 to 0.0630 in 1.4 to 1.6 mm	0.0551 to 0.0630 in 1.4 to 1.6 mm
Exhaust	0.0669 in 1.7 mm	0.0512 in 1.3 mm	0.0709 to 0.0866 in 1.8 to 2.2 mm	0.0709 to 0.0866 in 1.8 to 2.2 mm
Seat angle	45°	45°	45° 30′	45° 30′

Valve seat interference fit:
  Inlet   ...   .   0.0032 to 0.0044 in (0.081 to 0.113 mm)
  Exhaust   ...   .   0.0025 to 0.0038 in (0.064 to 0.096 mm)
Valve guide interference fit   ...   .   0.0011 to 0.0019 in (0.027 to 0.049 mm)

Torque wrench settings

	lb/ft	kg/m
Cylinder head bolts	60	8.3
Connecting rod big-end nuts	40	5.5
Flywheel bolts	110	15.2
Main bearing cap bolts	40	5.5
Camshaft sprocket bolt	85	11.8
Sump drain plug	20	2.8
Rocker pivot locknuts	40	5.5
Carburettor mounting nuts	40	5.5
Crankshaft pulley bolt	100	13.8
Clutch housing to engine bolts	35	4.8
Torque connector housing to engine bolts	35	4.8
Driveplate to torque connector...	35	4.8
Clutch to flywheel bolts...	20	2.8
Cylinder block reinforcement plate	24	3.3
Engine front mounting to bracket	20	2.8
Engine front mounting bracket to crankcase	20	2.8
Rear mounting crossmember to bodyframe	20	2.8

1 General description

The engine fitted is of the four cylinder in-line type, with valve operation by means of an overhead camshaft.

The cast iron cylinder block contains the four bores and acts as a rigid support for the five bearing crankshaft. The machined cylinder bores are surrounded by water jackets to dissipate heat and control operating temperature.

A disposable oil filter is located on the right-hand side of the cylinder block and supplies clean oil to the main gallery and various oilways. The main bearings are lubricated from oil holes which run parallel with the cylinder bores. The forged steel crankshaft is suitably drilled for directing lubricating oil so ensuring full bearing lubrication.

To lubricate the connecting rod small end, drillings are located in the big-ends of the rods so that the oil is squirted upwards.

Crankshaft endfloat is controlled by thrust washers located at the centre main bearings.

The pistons are of a special aluminium casting with struts to control thermal expansion. There are two compression and one oil control ring. The gudgeon pin is a hollow steel shaft which is fully floating in the piston and a press fit in the connecting rod little end. The pistons are attached to the crankshaft via forged steel connecting rods.

The cylinder head is of aluminium and incorporates wedge type combustion chambers. A special aluminium bronze valve seat is used for the inlet valve whilst a steel exhaust valve seat is fitted.

Located on the top of the cylinder head is the cast iron camshaft which is supported in four aluminium alloy brackets. The camshaft bearings are lubricated from drillings which lead from the main oil gallery in the cylinder head.

The supply of oil to each cam lobe is through an oil hole drilled in the base circle of each lobe. The actual oil supply is to the front oil gallery from the 3rd camshaft bearing. These holes on the base circle of the lobe supply oil to the cam pad surface of the rocker arm and to the valve tip end.

Two valves per cylinder are mounted at a slight angle in the cylinder head and are actuated by a pivot type rocker arm in direct contact with the cam mechanism. Double springs are fitted to each valve.

The camshaft is driven by a double row roller chain from the front of the crankshaft. Chain tension is controlled by a tensioner which is operated by oil and spring pressure. The rubber shoe type tensioner controls vibration and tension of the chain.

The operations described in this Chapter apply to all engine capacities and any differences in procedure are clearly shown. Reference should be made however to Specifications for precise details of engine application and variations between the different power units.

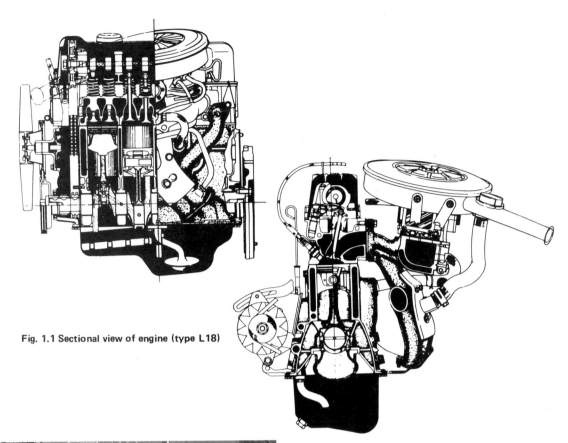

Fig. 1.1 Sectional view of engine (type L18)

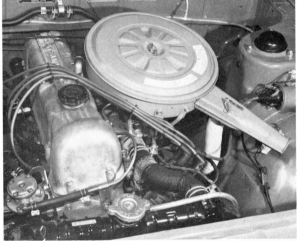

1.1. General view of engine (140J vehicle)

2 Major operations possible with engine in position

1   The following operations can be carried out when the engine is still installed in the vehicle.

(a) Removal and installation of the camshaft: This will require keeping the tension on the timing chain using a hooked piece of wire as the crankshaft sprocket is being removed. Once the sprocket is removed, maintain the tension (using a long wooden wedge if desired to offset the force of the chain tensioner) or the chain may become disconnected from the crankshaft pulley and if this happens, complete retiming will have to be carried out (Section 41).

(b) Removal and installation of the cylinder head: The remarks made in the preceding paragraph regarding the timing chain apply.

(c) Renewal of the engine mountings: The weight of the engine will have to be taken on a hoist or a jack and insulating block placed under the sump before this work can be carried out. (See Section 28).

(d) Removal and installation of the timing cover: This work may be required to renew a faulty timing cover oil seal or to renew one or more of the timing gear or chain components. First remove the radiator. Unscrew the crankshaft pulley wheel bolt but be sure to jam the flywheel starter ring gear to prevent the crankshaft turning.

Take care not to break the sump gasket at its joint with the timing cover. If it does break, cut a fresh section from a new sump gasket and use plenty of gasket jointing compound when refitting.

(e) Removal of the sump and piston/connecting rod assemblies:

It is possible to remove the sump with the engine in the vehicle but certain steering linkage will first have to be removed and the engine hoisted slightly after disconnection of the mountings, to permit removal of sump from above the cross-member.

3 Major operations only possible with engine removed

1   The following operations can only be carried out after the engine has been removed from the vehicle:

   (a) Renewal of the main bearings.

   (b) Removal and installation of the crankshaft

4 Engine - method of removal

1   Although the engine can be removed independently of the transmission unit, it will be found easier to remove the engine/transmission as a combined unit for later separation.
2   Lifting tackle of suitable strength will be required particularly in the case of automatic transmission, as the unit is very heavy.

5 Engine (excluding L20B type) and gearbox - removal

1   Disconnect the lead from the battery negative terminal.
2   Mark the position of the hinge plates on the underside of the bonnet to facilitate refitting and then unbolt the hinges and with the help of an assistant remove the lid. (photo)
3   Drain the coolant, retaining it in a suitable container if required for further use.
4   Drain the engine oil.
5   Disconnect the engine earth strap from the bodyframe.
6   Disconnect the hot air duct from the air cleaner.
7   Disconnect the breather and emission control hoses from the air cleaner and then remove the air cleaner. (photo)
8   Remove the radiator grille. (photo)
9   Disconnect the radiator upper and lower hoses.
10   Remove the radiator shroud.
11   Unbolt the radiator and remove it from the engine compartment. (photos)
12   Disconnect the fuel inlet pipe from the fuel pump.
13   Disconnect the accelerator linkage. (photo)
14   Disconnect the choke control cable from the carburettor (140J) or the automatic choke leads (710 series). (photo)
15   Disconnect the HT lead from the coil. (photo)
16   Disconnect the leads from the starter motor. (photo)
17   Disconnect the leads from the alternator.
18   Disconnect the leads from the reversing lamp switch which is located on the transmission unit. (photo)
19   Disconnect the leads from the oil pressure switch and the water temperature switch.
20   Disconnect the brake servo unit vacuum hose from the inlet manifold.
21   Disconnect the heater flow and return hoses. (photo)
22   Unbolt the clutch hydraulic operating cylinder from the clutch bellhousing and tie it up out of the way. There is no need to disconnect the hydraulic line. (photo)
23   Disconnect the speedometer cable from the rear extension housing. (photo)
24   Remove the centre console and draw the flexible dust excluder up the gearshift lever. Using two spanners, unscrew and remove the gearshift lever from the rubber-bushed socket. (photo)
25   Remove the propeller shaft as described in Chapter 7. (photo)
26   Disconnect the exhaust downpipe from the exhaust manifold. (photo)
27   Support the gearbox on a suitable jack and disconnect the rear mounting from the gearbox and the bodyframe.
28   Attach chains or slings to the engine lifting hooks and take the weight of the engine on the hoist.
29   Disconnect the engine front mounting brackets from the mountings. (photo)
30   Lower the transmission jack and then lift the engine/transmission at a steeply inclined angle from the engine compartment. (photo)
31   *On 710 series vehicle equipped with air conditioning,* before the engine can be removed, the air compressor will have to be removed from its mountings and pushed as far to one side of the engine compartment as its flexible connecting hoses will allow. **On no account disconnect the hoses or pipelines of the system due to the risk of injury from the release of refrigerant gas.** If preferred, have the system evacuated and subsequently charged by a competent refrigeration engineer. Refer also to Chapter 12,

Section 26).
32   Disconnect the vacuum hose and F.I.C.D. actuator (air conditioner), and then remove the actuator from its bracket.

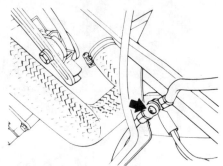

Fig. 1.2 Engine earth strap connection to bodyframe

Fig. 1.3 Air cleaner hose connections (710 series up to 1974)

Fig. 1.4 Remove gearshift control lever

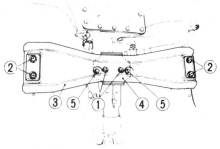

Fig. 1.5 Engine rear mounting

1   *Mounting nut*
2   *Crossmember to bodyframe bolts*
3   *Crossmember*
4   *Insulator*
5   *Insulator to transmission bolt*

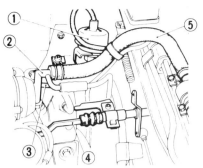

Fig. 1.6 Location of (1) Fast Idle Control Device (F.I.C.D.) for air conditioning system (2) brake servo hose connector (3) vacuum hose for air conditioner (4) throttle shaft (5) brake servo vacuum hose

5.2. Bonnet hinge bolts

5.7. Removing air cleaner (140J)

5.8. Removing radiator grille

5.11A. Radiator securing bolts

5.11B. Removing radiator

5.13. Throttle rod connection at carburettor

5.14. Choke cable connection (140J)

5.15. Coil and connecting leads

5.16. Starter motor connections

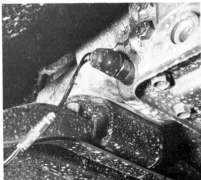

5.18. Reversing lamp switch

5.21A. Heater flow and return hoses

5.21B. Heater flow and return hoses

5.22. Clutch operating cylinder

5.23. Disconnecting speedometer drive cable

5.24. Withdrawing gearshift lever

5.25. Disconnecting propeller shaft from rear axle pinion flange

5.26. Disconnecting exhaust downpipe

5.29. An engine front mounting

5.30 Removing engine/transmission

6 Engine (L20B type) and gearbox - removal

1   The procedure is similar to that described in the preceding Section but the following special operations must be substituted or additionally carried out as appropriate.

2   Remove the hot and cold air ducts from the air cleaner.

3   Release the air cleaner from the carburettor and lift it far enough away to permit disconnection of the following hoses:

   (a) Air pump hose
   (b) Rocker cover hose
   (c) Air control valve hose
   (d) Anti-backfire valve hose
   (e) Vacuum hose

4   Disconnect the fuel pump to filter pipe and disconnect the return pipe on the engine side.

5   Disconnect the fuel evaporative control system carbon canister hose at the engine end.

6   Disconnect the two moulded type connectors. One is located above the right-hand engine mounting bracket and the other is just below the ignition coil.

7   Disconnect the inlet and outlet heater hoses.

8   Remove the heatshield insulators from the front exhaust pipe and catalytic converter (where fitted).

9   Separate the front exhaust pipe from the catalytic converter (where installed) or if one is not fitted, disconnect the front and rear exhaust pipe sections.

10 Unbolt the exhaust downpipe from the manifold.

11 Unbolt and remove the damper which is bolted to some engine rear mounting supports, (see Section 28).

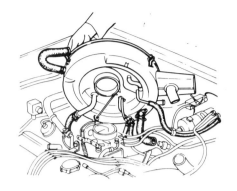

Fig. 1.7 Air cleaner hose connections (710 series 1975 onwards)

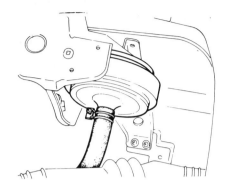

Fig. 1.8 Air pump to air cleaner hose (710 series 1975 onwards)

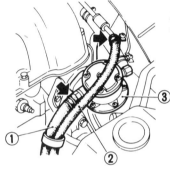

1   Inlet pipe from tank
2   Return pipe
3   Fuel pump

Fig. 1.9 Fuel tank to pump inlet hose and return pipe
(710 series 1975 onwards)

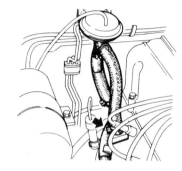

Fig. 1.11 Heater hoses (with air conditioner) - 710 series
1975 onwards

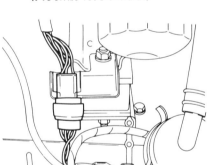

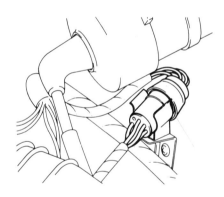

Fig. 1.10 Location of harness connectors (710 series 1975 onwards)

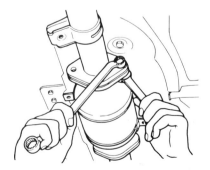

Fig. 1.12 Separating front exhaust from catalytic converter
(710 series 1975 onwards)

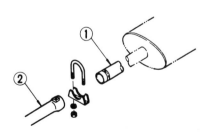

Fig. 1.13 Disconnecting (1) front and (2) rear exhaust sections
on vehicles without catalytic converter (710 series 1975
onwards)

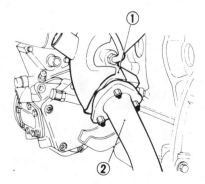

Fig. 1.14 Exhaust downpipe to manifold connection
(710 series 1975 onwards)

1 Downpipe
2 Exhaust manifold

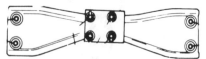

Fig. 1.15 Damper plate fitted to some rear mountings
(1975 onwards)

**7 Engine (excluding L20B type) and automatic transmission -
removal**

1 Carry out operations 1 to 10 given in Section 5.
2 Remove the engine splash shield.
3 Disconnect the hoses from the automatic transmission fluid
cooler which is located at the base of the radiator.
4 Carry out the operations 11 to 21 of section 5.
5 Disconnect the speedometer cable from the rear extension
housing at the transmission unit.
6 Disconnect the leads from the inhibitor switch and from the
downshift solenoid.
7 Disconnect the vacuum tube from the diaphragm.
8 Disconnect the speed selector control rod from the range
selector lever on the side of the transmission casing.
9 Carry out operations 25 to 32 of Section 5.

8 Engine (L20B type) and automatic transmission - removal

1 The procedure is similar to that described in the preceding
Section but with the L20B engine, the special operations
detailed in Section 6 must be substituted or included as
supplementary items.

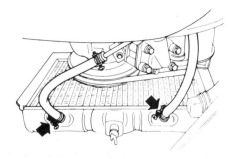

Fig. 1.16 Automatic transmission fluid cooler connections

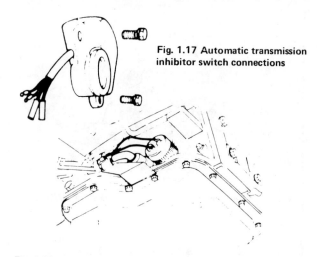

Fig. 1.17 Automatic transmission
inhibitor switch connections

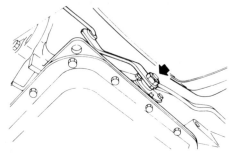

Fig. 1.18 Automatic transmission downshift soleniod and leads

Fig. 1.19 Automatic transmission speed selector rod and range
lever

9 Engine - separation from manual gearbox

1 With the engine and gearbox now removed from the vehicle,
unscrew and remove the bolts which connect the clutch bellhousing to the engine block.
2 Unbolt and remove the starter motor.
3 Pull the gearbox from the engine in a straight line at the same
time supporting the gearbox so that its weight does not hang
upon the primary shaft, even momentarily, whilst the shaft is
still engaged with the clutch mechanism.

10 Engine - separation from automatic transmission

1 Remove the rubber plug from the lower part of the engine
rear plate.
2 Unscrew and remove the bolts which secure the driveplate to
the torque converter. The crankshaft will have to be turned by
means of the pulley bolt so that each driveplate bolt comes into
view in turn.
3 With all the driveplate bolts removed, mark the relative
position of the driveplate to the torque converter. This is best
achieved by placing a dab of coloured paint around one bolt hole
in the driveplate and also on the torque converter hole top
threads.
4 Remove the starter motor and the fluid filler tube support
bolt.
5 Unscrew and remove the bolts which secure the torque
converter housing to the engine.
6 Withdraw the automatic transmission in a straight line and
expect some loss of fluid as the torque converter moves away
from the driveplate.

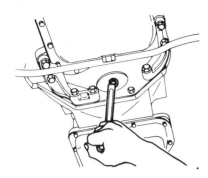

Fig. 1.20 Unscrewing a driveplate to torque converter bolt

11 Engine - dismantling general

1   It is best to mount the engine on a dismantling stand but if one is not available, then stand the engine on a strong bench so as to be at a comfortable working height. Failing this, the engine can be stripped down on the floor.

2   During the dismantling process the greatest care should be taken to keep the exposed parts free from dirt. As an aid to achieving this, it is a sound scheme to thoroughly clean down the outside of the engine, removing all traces of oil and congealed dirt.

3   Use paraffin or a good grease solvent. The latter compound will make the job much easier, as, after the solvent has been applied and allowed to stand for a time, a vigorous jet of water will wash off the solvent and all the grease and filth. If the dirt is thick and deeply embedded, work the solvent into it with a wire brush.

4   Finally wipe down the exterior of the engine with a rag and only then, when it is quite clean should the dismantling process begin. As the engine is stripped, clean each part in a bath of paraffin or petrol.

5   Never immerse parts with oilways in paraffin, i.e. the crankshaft, but to clean, wipe down carefully with a petrol dampened rag. Oilways can be cleaned out with wire. If an air line is present all parts can be blown dry and the oilways blown through as an added precaution.

6   Re-use of old engine gaskets is false economy and can give rise to oil and water leaks, if nothing worse. To avoid the possibility of trouble after the engine has been reassembled **always** use new gaskets throughout.

7   Do not throw the old gaskets away as it sometimes happens that an immediate replacement cannot be found and the old gasket is then very useful as a template. Hang up the old gaskets as they are removed on a suitable hook or nail.

8   To strip the engine it is best to work from the top down. The sump provides a firm base on which the engine can be supported in an upright position. When this stage where the sump must be removed is reached, the engine can be turned on its side and all other work carried out with it in this position.

9   Wherever possible, replace nuts, bolts and washers fingertight from wherever they were removed. This helps avoid later loss and muddle. If they cannot be replaced then lay them out in such a fashion that it is clear from where they came.

12 Ancillary components (engine types L14, L16 and L18) - removal

1   If you are stripping the engine completely or preparing to install a reconditioned unit, all the ancillaries must be removed first. If you are going to obtain a reconditioned 'short' motor (block, crankshaft, pistons and connecting rods) then obviously the cam box, cylinder head and associated parts will need retention for fitting to the new engine. It is advisable to check just what you will get with a reconditioned unit as changes are made from time to time.

2   Remove the fan assembly, noting that the shallow recess of the fan boss faces the radiator. (photo)

3   Remove the right-hand engine mounting bracket.

4   Unscrew and remove the oil filter and discard it. (photo) The use of a chain wrench or similar tool will probably be required to remove the filter.

5   Unscrew and remove the oil pressure switch.

6   Withdraw the engine oil dipstick.

7   Unscrew the crankshaft pulley bolt. To prevent the engine turning during this operation, jam the flywheel starter ring gear by passing a sharp cold chisel or large screwdriver through the starter motor aperture in the engine rear plate.

8   Withdraw the crankshaft pulley. The insertion of two tyre levers behind the pulley will usually extract the pulley but if it is exceptionally tight, use an extractor but take care not to distort the rims of the pulley.

9   Unbolt and remove the clutch assembly from the flywheel, see Chapter 5, Section 8. (photo)

10 Disconnect the HT leads from the spark plugs and then remove the distributor cap complete with leads.

11 Unscrew and remove the spark plugs.

12 Disconnect the crankcase to P.C.V. valve hose. (photo)

13 Disconnect the fuel pump to carburettor hose. (photos)

14 Disconnect the rocker cover to air cleaner hose.

15 Disconnect the two inlet manifold water heater hoses.

16 Remove the exhaust gas recirculation valve (EGR) - 710 series vehicles.

17 Remove the fuel pump.

18 Remove the thermostat housing.

19 Unbolt and remove the manifold assemblies complete with carburettor.

20 Remove the engine left-hand mounting bracket.

21 Remove the water pump.

22 Unscrew and remove the distributor clamp plate bolt from the crankcase and withdraw the distributor from its recess.

23 Remove the rocker cover. (photo)

24 The engine is now stripped of ancillary components and dismantling proper may be carried out as described in Section 14 onwards.

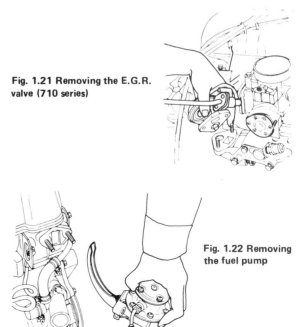

Fig. 1.21 Removing the E.G.R. valve (710 series)

Fig. 1.22 Removing the fuel pump

12.2. Radiator fan assembly

12.4. Removing oil filter

12.9. Removing clutch assembly

12.12. Disconnecting crankcase breather hose

12.13A. Pump to carburettor fuel line (front section)

12.13B. Pump to carburettor fuel line (rear section)

12.23. Interior of rocker cover showing baffle

Fig. 1.23 Removing the thermostat housing

13 Ancillary components (engine type L20B) - removal

1   The procedure is similar to that described in the preceding Section but with the following additional operations.
2   Remove the air pump and idler pulley (emission control system see Chapter 3).
3   Disconnect the P.C.V. valve hose from cylinder block and P.C.V. valve.
4   Disconnect anti-backfire (A.B.) valve to exhaust gas recirculation (E.G.R.) passage hose at the E.G.R. passage.
5   Disconnect the vacuum tube to carburettor hoses (white and yellow in colour) at the vacuum tube.
6   Remove the dashpot bracket from the inlet manifold.
7   Disconnect vacuum hose from the air control valve (if fitted) and remove the air control valve complete with hoses.
8   Disconnect the vacuum pipe from the E.G.R. valve.
9   Remove the check valve from the air gallery pipe.
10 Disconnect E.G.R. tube from the E.G.R. passage and the exhaust manifold.
11 Remove the E.G.R. passage and valve from the inlet. manifold.
12 Remove the cylinder block to P.C.V. valve hose from the cylinder block.
13 The manifold assembly complete with carburettor can now be removed from the cylinder head.

14 Cylinder head - removal

1   From the front of the camshaft, remove the centre bolt and withdraw the fuel pump eccentric cam.
2   Remove the camshaft sprocket complete with chain from the camshaft. Slip the sprocket out of the loop of the timing chain and then support the timing chain with a piece of wire pending

removal of the cylinder head. It is of particular importance when removing the cylinder head with the engine in the vehicle that tension is maintained on the timing chain so that it does not become disengaged from the crankshaft sprocket. A long tapering wooden wedge can also be inserted to overcome the pressure of the chain tensioner. Should the timing chain become disengaged from the crankshaft sprocket, then the timing cover will have to be removed to re-set the chain and sprockets.

3 Unscrew and remove the cylinder head bolts in the sequence shown. **Do not unscrew the camshaft bearing housing bolts by mistake.**

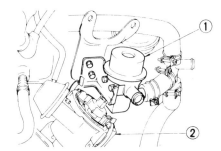

Fig. 1.24 Removing the air control valve   1   *Valve*
(710 series, L20B engine)   2   *Distributor*

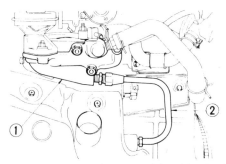

Fig. 1.25 E.G.R. passage (1) and tube (2) - 710 series, L20B engine

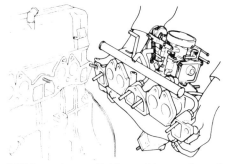

Fig. 1.26 Removing manifold assembly complete with carburettor from cylinder head (710 series, L20B engine)

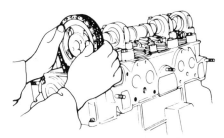

Fig. 1.27 Removing camshaft sprocket

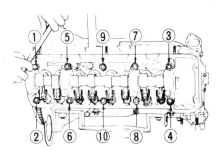

Fig. 1.28 Cylinder head bolt loosening sequence diagram

15 Camshaft - removal

1 Where major engine overhaul is not being carried out, the camshaft can be removed without first withdrawing the cylinder head.

2 Extract the valve rocker springs by lifting them from the rocker arm grooves.

3 Release the pivot locknuts and unscrew the pivots.

4 Compress each valve spring in turn using a large screwdriver and withdraw the rocker arms, taking care to retain the rocker guides. (photo)

5 Remove the camshaft locating plate and withdraw the camshaft, taking care not to damage the bearings as the camshaft lobes pass through them. **On no account unscrew the camshaft bearing housing bolts.** The bearings are in-line bored and alignment will be ruined if they are disturbed.

16 Sump, timing gear and oil pump - removal

1 With the engine upside-down standing on the top face of the cylinder block, unbolt and remove the sump.

2 Unbolt and remove the oil pick-up tube and screen.

3 Unbolt the oil pump and withdraw it complete with drive spindle.

4 Unbolt and remove the timing cover.

5 Unbolt and remove the timing chain tensioner and guide.

6 Remove the timing chain.

7 From the crankshaft front end, remove the oil thrower, the oil pump worm drive gear and then draw off the crankshaft sprocket. (photo)

17 Piston/connecting rod assemblies - removal

1 Examine the big-end bearing caps and connecting rods. They should be match marked from 1 to 4 from the front of the engine. If they are not, dot punch the caps and rods at adjacent points, noting carefully to which side of the engine the numbers or punch marks face so that they can be installed in their same original relative positions.

2 Unbolt No. 1 big-end cap and using the wooden handle of a hammer, carefully tap the piston/connecting rod assembly from the cylinder. It is unlikely that the original shell bearings will be used again but should this be the case, retain them in exact order, identifying them in respect of connecting rod and cap sections.

3 Extract the remaining three piston/connecting rod assemblies.

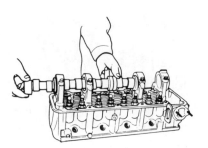

Fig. 1.29 Withdrawing the camshaft

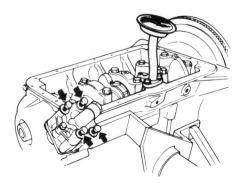

Fig. 1.30 Oil pump and oil pick-up tube/screen

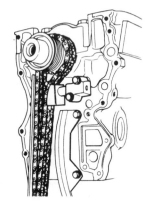

Fig. 1.31 Timing chain tensioner and guide

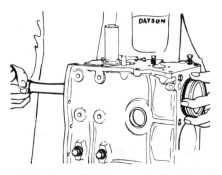

Fig. 1.32 Removing a piston/connecting rod assembly

15.4. Removing rocker arms

16.7. Removing crankshaft sprocket

18 Flywheel (or driveplate - automatic transmission) - removal

1   Mark the position of the flywheel in relation to the crank-shaft flange and unbolt the flywheel.

In order to prevent the flywheel turning while the securing bolts are being unscrewed, wedge one of the crankshaft webs with a piece of wood.

19 Crankshaft and main bearings - removal

1   Examine the main bearing caps for numbers and directional fitting arrows. If they are not marked, dot punch them 1 to 5 from the front of the engine and note which way round the caps are fitted. The centre main bearing incorporates thrust washers.
2   Unbolt and remove each of the main bearing caps. The centre and rear caps may be very tight and will require tapping out or the use of an extractor, a threaded hole being provided for the purpose.
3   Extract the side seals from the rear bearing cap also the crankshaft rear oil seal.
4   Lift the crankshaft from the crankcase. It is unlikely that the original shell bearings will be used again but should this be the

case, retain them in exact order, identifying them in respect of crankcase and cap sections.

5 Remove the baffle plate and mesh block which is part of the crankcase breather system.

20 Piston rings - removal

1 Each ring should be sprung open only just sufficiently to permit it to ride over the lands of the piston body.

2 Once a ring is out of its groove, it is helpful to cut three ¼ in (6.4 mm) wide strips of tin and slip them under the ring at equidistant points.

3 Using a twisting motion this method of removal will prevent the ring dropping into a empty groove as it is being removed from the piston.

21 Gudgeon pin - removal

1 The gudgeon pins are a finger pressure fit (at room temperature) in the pistons but are an interference fit in the connecting rod small end.

2 It is recommended that removal of the gudgeon pin is left to a service station having a suitable press.

3 Where such facilities are available to the home mechanic, the body of the piston must be supported on a suitably shaped distance piece into which the gudgeon pin may be ejected.

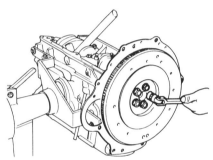

Fig. 1.33 Removing a flywheel bolt

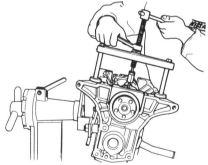

Fig. 1.34 Drawing out the crankshaft rear main bearing cap

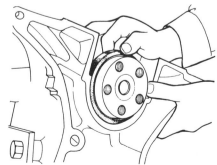

Fig. 1.35 Removing the crankshaft rear oil seal

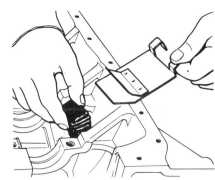

Fig. 1.36 Removing baffle and mesh (crankcase breather system)

Fig. 1.37 Pressing out a gudgeon pin

22 Lubrication system - description

Oil is drawn from the engine sump through an oil strainer by a trochoid type oil pump. This is driven by a spindle which in turn is driven from the crankshaft. The upper end of the spindle drives the distributor. Oil is passed under pressure through a replaceable canister type oil filter and onto the main oil gallery. It is then distributed to all the crankshaft bearings, chain tensioner and timing chain. The oil that is supplied to the crankshaft is fed to the connecting rod big end bearings via drilled passages in the crankshaft. The connection rod little ends and underside cylinder walls are lubricated from jets of oil issuing from little holes in the connection rods.

Oil from the centre of the main gellery passes up to a further gallery in the cylinder head. This distributes oil to the valve mechanism, and to the top of the timing chain. Drillings pass oil from the gallery to the camshaft bearings. Oil that is supplied to number 2 and 3 camshaft bearings is passed to the rocker arm, valve and cam lobe by two drillings inside the camshaft and small drillings in the cam base circle of each arm.

The oil pressure relief valve is located in the oil pump cover and is designed to control the pressure in the system to a maximum of 80 lb sq in (5.6 kg sq cm).

23 Crankcase emission control system

The closed type of crankcase emission control system fitted to models covered by this manual draws air from the air cleaner and passes it through a mesh type flame trap to a hose connected to the rocker cover.

The air is then passed through the inside of the engine and back to the inlet manifold via a hose and regulating valve. This means that fumes in the crankcase are drawn into the combustion chambers, burnt and passed to the exhaust system.

When the car is being driven at full throttle conditions the inlet manifold depression is not sufficient to draw all fumes through the regulating valve and into the inlet manifold. Under these operating conditions the crankcase ventilation flow is reversed with the fumes drawing into the air cleaner instead of the inlet manifold.

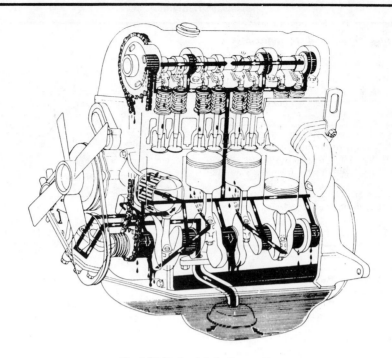

Fig. 1.38 Engine lubrication system

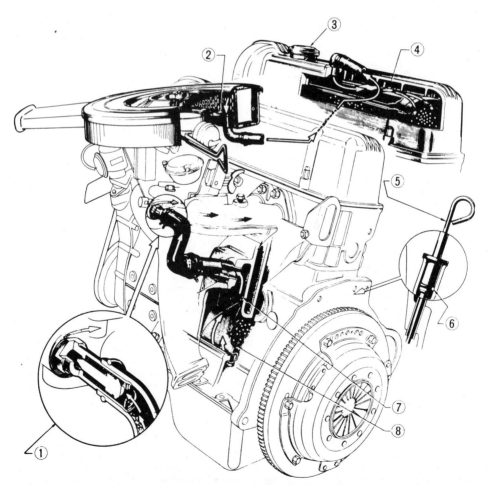

Fig. 1.39 Crankcase ventilation system

| 1 | Control valve | 3 | Oil filler cap | 5 | Dipstick | 7 | Oil separator |
| 2 | Flame trap | 4 | Baffle plate | 6 | 'O' ring seal | 8 | Crankcase baffle |

To prevent engine oil being drawn into the inlet manifold a baffle plate and filter gauze pack is positioned in the crankcase.

Maintenance of the system simply involves inspection of the system and renewal of any suspect parts. Check the condition of the rocker cover to air cleaner hose and the crankcase to inlet manifold hose. Check for blockage, deterioation or collapse should either be evident, new hoses must be fitted.

Inspect the seals on the engine oil filler cap and dipstick. If their condition has deterioated renew the seals.

Operation of the ventilation regulation valve may be checked by running the engine at a steady idle speed and disconnecting the hose from the regulation valve. Listen for a hissing noise from the valve once the hose has been detached. Now place a finger over the inlet valve and a strong depression should be felt immediately as the finger is placed over the valve.

Should the valve prove to be inoperative it must be renewed as it is not practical to dismantle and clean it.

Other symptoms showing a faulty or inoperative valve are:
a) *Engine will not run smoothly at idle speed.*
b) *Smoky exhaust.*
c) *Engine idle speed rises and falls, but engine does not stop.*
d) *Power loss at speeds above idle.*

24 Examination and renovation - general

With the engine stripped and all components thoroughly cleaned, it is not time to examine everything for wear and damage.

Parts and assemblies should be checked and where possible renovated or otherwise renewed as described in the following Sections.

25 Crankshaft and main bearings - examination and renovation

1 Examine the crankpin and main journal surfaces for signs of scoring or scratches. Check the ovality of the crankpins at different positions with a micrometer. If more than 0.001 in (0.03 mm) out of round, the crankpin will have to be reground. It will also have to be reground if there are any scores or scratches present. Also check the journals in the same fashion.
2 If it is necessary to regrind the crankshaft and fit new bearings your local Datsun garage or engineering works will be able to decide how much metal to grind off and the size of new bearing shells.
3 The main bearing clearances may be established by using a strip of Plastigage between the crankshaft journals and the main bearing/shell caps. Tighten the bearing cap bolts to a torque of between 33 and 40 lb/ft (4.6 and 5.5 kg/m). Remove the cap and compare the flattened Plastigage strip with the index provided. The clearance should be compared with the tolerances in Specifications.
4 Temporarily refit the crankshaft to the crankcase having refitted the upper halves of the shell main bearings in their locations. Fit the centre main bearing cap only, complete with shell bearing and tighten the securing bolts to between 33 and 40 lb/ft (4.6 and 5.5 kg/m) torque. Using a feeler gauge, check the endfloat by pushing and pulling the crankshaft. Where the endfloat is outside the specified tolerance, the centre bearing shells will have to be renewed. Enfloat 0.002 to 0.007 in (0.05 to 0.18 mm) maximum 0.012 in (0.3 mm). (photo)
5 Finally examine the primary shaft pilot bush which is located in the centre of the flywheel mounting flange at the rear end of the crankshaft. If it is worn, renew it by tapping a thread in it and screwing in a bolt. Carefully press in the new bush so that its endface will lie below the crankshaft flange surface by between 0.18 and 0.20 in (4.5 and 5.0 mm).

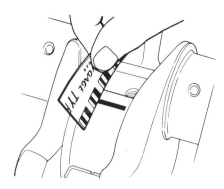

Fig. 1.40 Measuring main bearing clearance

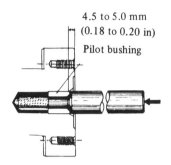

4.5 to 5.0 mm
(0.18 to 0.20 in)
Pilot bushing

Fig. 1.41 Crankshaft pilot bush installation diagram

25.5. Checking crankshaft endfloat

26 Connecting rods and big-end bearings - examination and renovation

1 Big-end bearing failure is indicated by a knocking from within the crankcase and a slight drop in oil pressure.
2 Examine the big-end bearing surfaces for pitting and scoring. Renew the shells in accordance with the sizes specified in Specifications. Where the crankshaft has been reground, the correct undersize big-end shell bearings will be supplied by the repairer.
3 Should there be any suspicion that a connecting rod is bent or twisted or the small end bush no longer provides an interference fit for the gudgeon pin then the complete connecting rod assembly should be exchanged for a reconditoned one but ensure

that the comparative weight of the two rods is within 0.18 oz (5 gr) for the L14 type engine and 0.25 oz (7 gr) for other engines.

4 Measurement of the big-end bearing clearances may be carried out in a similar manner to that described for the main bearings in the previous Section but tighten the securing nuts on the cap bolts to between 33 and 40 lb/ft (4.6 to 5.5 kg/m). The running clearances are given in Specifications.

5 Finally check the big-end thrust clearance which should be between 0.008 and 0.012 in (0.2 and 0.3 mm) with a maximum wear limit of 0.024 in (0.6 mm).

27 Cylinder bores - examination and renovation

1 The cylinder bores must be examined for taper, ovality, scoring and scratches. Start by carefully examining the top of the cylinder bores. If they are at all worn a very slight ridge will be found on the thrust side. This marks the top of the piston ring travel. The owner will have a good indication of the bore wear prior to dismantling the engine, or removing the cylinder head. Excessive oil consumption accompanied by blue smoke from the exhaust is a sure sign of worn cylinder bores and piston rings.

2 Measure the bore diameter just under the ridge with a micrometer and compare it with the diameter at the bottom of the bore, which is not subject to wear. If the difference between the two measurements is more than 0.008 in (0.2 mm) then it will be necessary to fit special pistons and rings or to have the cylinders rebored and fit oversize pistons.

3 The standard clearance between a piston and the cylinder walls is between 0.0010 and 0.0018 in (0.025 and 0.045 mm). The easiest way to check this is to insert the piston into its bore with a feeler blade 0.0016 in (0.04 mm) in thickness inserted between it and the cylinder wall. Attach the feeler blade to a spring balance and note the force required to extract the blade while pulling vertically upwards. This should be between 0.4 and 3.3 lb (0.2 and 1.5 kg). The ambient temperature during this test should be around 68° F (20° C).

4 Where less than the specified force is required to withdraw the feeler blade, then remedial action must be taken. Oversize pistons are available as listed in Specifications.

5 These are accurately machined to just below the indicated measurements so as to provide correct running clearances in bores bored out to the exact oversize dimensions.

6 If the bores are slightly worn but not so badly worn as to justify reboring them, then special oil control rings and pistons can be fitted, which will restore compression and stop the engine burning oil. Several different types are available and the manufacturer's instructions concerning their fitting must be followed closely.

7 If new pistons are being fitted and the bores have not been reground, it is essential to slightly roughen the hard glaze on the sides of the bores with fine glass paper so the new piston rings will have a chance to bed in properly.

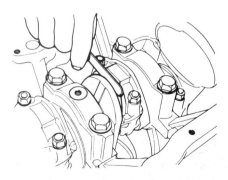

Fig. 1.42 Checking big-end side thrust clearance

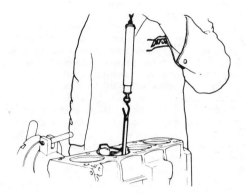

Fig. 1.43 Measuring the piston clearance in a cylinder

28 Crankcase, cylinder block and mountings - examination and renovation

1 Examination of the cylinder block and crankcase should be carried out in conjunction with examination of the cylinder bores. Obviously if any faults or damage are visible, it will be a waste of money having the block rebored.

2 Check for cracks especially between the cylinder bores. Repair of cast iron is a specialized job and it may be more economical to purchase a new assembly or one in good condition from a breakers yard.

3 Examine stud and bolt holes for stripped threads. New spiral type thread inserts can often be used to overcome this problem but the manufacturer's fitting instructions must be strictly observed.

4 Probe all oil and water passages with a piece of wire to ensure freedom from obstruction.

5 Now is the time to examine the engine mountings. Although the mountings can be renewed with the engine still in position in the vehicle by taking its weight on a hoist, now is the best opportunity to check for perished rubber or deformation and to purchase or order new ones from the different types used, according to model.

29 Pistons and piston rings - examination and renovation

1 Where new pistons have been supplied to match the rebore diameter, new sets of piston rings will also be provided but it is worthwhile checking the ring clearances, as described in the following paragraphs.

2 If the original pistons are being refitted, carefully remove the piston rings as described in Section 20.

3 Clean the grooves and rings free from carbon, taking care not to scratch the aluminium surfaces of the pistons.

4 If new rings are being fitted to old pistons (cylinders not rebored) then order the top compression ring to be stepped to prevent it impinging on the 'wear ring' which will almost certainly have been formed at the top of the cylinder bore.

5 Before fitting the rings to the pistons, push each ring in turn down its cylinder bore (use an inverted piston to do this and to keep the ring square) and then measure the ring end gap. The gaps must be as given in Specifications according to engine type and should be measured with a feeler blade.

6 The piston rings should now be tested in their respective grooves from side clearance. The clearances must be as listed in Specifications.

7 Piston ring end gaps can be increased by rubbing them carefully with a file.

8 Where necessary a piston ring which is slightly tight in its groove may be rubbed down holding it perfectly squarely on an oilstone or a sheet of fine emery cloth laid on a piece of plate

glass. Excessive tightness can only be rectified by having the grooves machined out.

9 The gudgeon pin should be a push fit into the piston at room temperature. If it appears slack, then both the piston and gudgeon pin should be renewed.

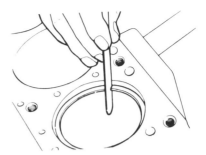

Fig. 1.45 Checking piston ring end gap

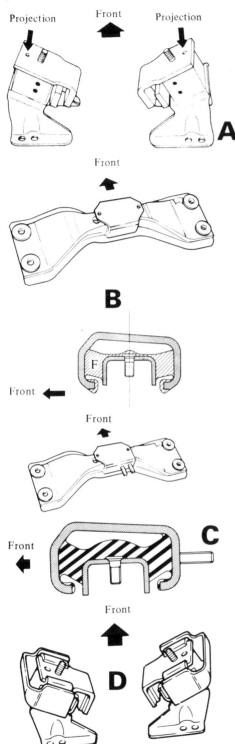

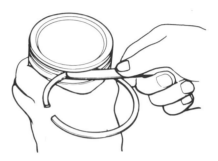

Fig. 1.46 Checking piston ring side clearance

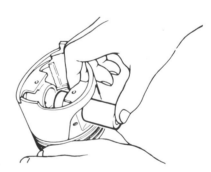

Fig. 1.47 Testing the fit of a gudgeon pin in a piston

Fig. 1.44 Differing types of engine mountings

A Front up to 1974   C Rear 1975 onwards
B Rear up to 1974   D Front 1975 onwards
                              (see also Fig. 1.15)

30 Camshaft and camshaft bearings - examination and renovation

1 Carefully examine the camshaft bearings for wear. If the bearings are obviously worn or pitted then they must be renewed. This is an operation for your local Datsun dealer or local engineering works as it demands the use of specialized equipment. The bearings are removed with a special drift after which new bearings are pressed in, and in-line bored, care being taken to ensure the oil holes in the bearings line up with those in the block.

2 The camshaft itself should show no signs of wear, but, if very slight scoring on the cams is noticed, the score marks can be removed by very gently rubbing down with a very fine emery cloth. The greatest care should be taken to keep the cam profiles smooth.

3 Check the camshaft sprocket for hooked teeth or distortion and renew if evident.

4 When installed, the camshaft endfloat must not exceed between 0.003 and 0.015 in (0.08 and 0.38 mm) or the locating plate will have to be renewed.

31 Timing chain and tensioner - examination and renovation

1   Wear in the timing chain can be compensated for by adjusting the position of the camshaft sprocket as described in the re-assembly operations but if the chain is obviously very badly worn or stretched and a high mileage has been covered, renew it.
2   Check the condition of the chain tensioner and guide and renew them if necessary.

32 Cylinder head and valves - servicing and decarbonising

1   With the cylinder head removed, use a blunt scraper to remove all trace of carbon and deposits from the combustion spaces and ports. Remember that the cylinder head is aluminium alloy and can be damaged easily during the decarbonising operations. Scrape the cylinder head free from scale or old pieces of gasket or jointing compound. Clean the cylinder head by washing it in paraffin and take particular care to pull a piece of rag through the ports and cylinder head bolt holes. Any drit remaining in these recesses may well drop onto the gasket or cylinder block mating surface as the cylinder head is lowered into position and could lead to a gasket leak after reassembly is complete.
2   With the cylinder head clean, test for distortion if a history of coolant leakage has been apparent. Carry out this test using a straight edge and feeler gauges or a piece of plate glass. If the surface shows any warping in excess of 0.0039 in (0.1 mm) then the cylinder head will have to be resurfaced which is a job for a specialist engineering company.
3   Clean the pistons and top of the cylinder bores. If the pistons are still in the block then it is essential that great care is taken to ensure that no carbon gets into the cylinder bores as this could scratch the cylinder walls or cause damage to the piston and rings. To ensure this does not happen, first turn the crankshaft so that two of the pistons are at the top of their bores. Stuff rag into the other two bores or seal them off with paper and masking tape. The waterways should also be covered with small pieces of masking tape to prevent particles of carbon entering the cooling system and damaging the water pump.
4   Before scraping the carbon from the piston crowns, press grease into the gap between the cylinder walls and the two pistons which are to be worked on. With a blunt scraper carefully scrape away the carbon from the piston crown, taking great care not to scratch the aluminium. Also scrape away the carbon from the surrounding lip of the cylinder wall. When all carbon has been removed, scrape away the grease which will not be contaminated with carbon particles, taking care not to press any into the bores. To assist prevention of carbon build-up the piston crown can be polished with a metal polish. Remove the rags or masking tape from the other two cylinders and turn the crankshaft so that the two pistons which were at the bottom are now at the top. Place rag or masking tape in the cylinders which have been decarbonised and proceed as just described.
5   The valves can be removed from the cylinder head by the following method. Compress each spring in turn with a valve spring compressor until the two halves of the collets can be removed. Release the compressor and remove the spring and spring retainer. On L14 engines, a single spring only is used on inlet valves.
6   If, when the valve spring compressor is screwed down, the valve spring retaining cap refuses to free to expose the split collet, do not continue to screw down the compressor as there is a likelihood of damaging.
7   Gently tap the top of the tool directly over the cap with a light hammer. This will free the cap. To avoid the compressor jumping off the valve spring retaining cap when it is tapped, hold the compressor firmly in position with one hand.
8   Slide the rubber oil control seal off the top of each valve stem and then drop out each valve through the combustion chamber.
9   It is essential that the valves are kept in their correct

sequence unless they are so badly worn that they are to be renewed.
10 Examine the heads of the valves for pitting and burning, especially the heads of the exhaust valves. The valve seatings should be examined at the same time. If the pitting on valve and seat is very slight the marks can be removed by grinding the seats and valve together with coarse, and then fine, valve grinding paste.
11 Where bad pitting has occurred to the valve seats it will be necessary to recut them and fit new valves. If the valve seats are so worn that they cannot be recut, then it will be necessary to fit new valve seat inserts. These latter two jobs should be entrusted to the local Datsun agent or engineering works. In practice it is very seldom that the seats are so badly worn that they require renewal. Normally, it is the valve that is too badly worn for replacement, and the owner can easily purchase a new set of valves and match them to the seats by valve grinding.
12 Valve grinding is carried out as follow:
    Smear a trace of coarse carborundum paste on the seat face and apply a suction grinder tool to the valve head. With a semi-rotory motion, grind the valve head to its seat, lifting the valve occasionally to redistribute the grinding paste. When a dull matt even surface finish is produced on both the valve seat and the valve, wipe off the paste and repeat the process with fine carborundum paste, lifting and turning the valve to redistribute the paste as before. A light spring placed under the valve head will greatly ease this operation. When a smooth unbroken ring of light grey matt finish is produced, on both valve and valve seat faces, the grinding operation is completed.
13 Scrape away all carbon from the valve head and the valve stem. Carefully clean away every trace of grinding compound, taking great care to leave none in the ports or in the valve guides. Clean the valves and valve seats with a paraffin soaked rag then with a clean rag, and finally, if an air line is available, blow the valves, valve guides and valve ports clean.
14 Test each valve in its guide for wear. After a considerable mileage, the valve guide bore may wear oval. This can best be tested by inserting a new valve in the guide and moving it from side to side. If the tip of the valve stem deflects by about 0.0080 in (0.2 mm) then it must be assumed that the tolerance between the stem and guide is greater than the permitted maximum.
15 New valve guides (oversizes available) may be pressed or drifted into the cylinder head after the worn ones have been removed in a similar manner. The cylinder head must be heated to 392°F (200°C) before carrying out these operations and although this can be done in a domestic oven, it must be remembered that the new guide will have to be reamed after installation and it may therefore be preferable to leave this work to your Datsun dealer.
16 Finally check the free-length of the valve springs and renew them if they are much less than specified or if they have been in operation for 30,000 miles (48,000 km) or more.

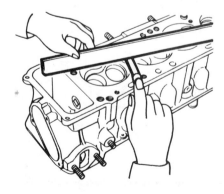

Fig. 1.48 Testing for cylinder head warpage

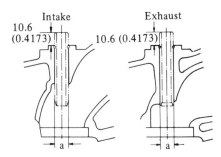

Fig. 1.49 Valve guide installation diagram

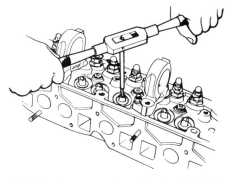

Fig. 1.50 Reaming a new valve guide after installation
Finished bore 0.3150 to 0.3157 in (8.000 to 8.018 mm)

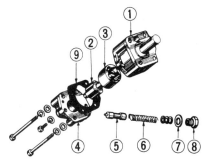

Fig. 1.51 Exploded view of the oil pump

1 Body   5 Regulator valve
2 Inner rotor and shaft   6 Spring
3 Outer rotor   7 Washer
4 Oil pump cover   8 Plug
                           9 Gasket

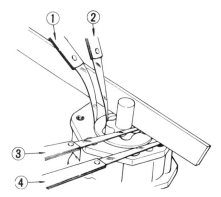

Fig. 1.52 Checking oil pump clearances

1 Outer rotor to body
2 Rotor tip clearance
3 and 4 Side clearance using a straight edge

33 Oil pump - examination and renovation

1 Unbolt the pump cover, remove the gasket and slide out the internal rotors.
2 Remove the regulator valve threaded plug and extract the valve and spring.
3 Clean all components and carry out the following checks for wear using a feeler gauge:
  (a) *Check the clearance between the outer rotor and the oil pump body. This should be between 0.0059 and 0.0083 in (0.15 and 0.21 mm) with a wear limit of 0.020 in (0.5 mm).*
  (b) *Check the clearance between the high points of the inner and outer rotors. This should be less than 0.005 in (0.12 mm) with a maximum of 0.008 in (0.20 mm).*
  (c) *Using a straight-edge, check outer to inner rotor clearance and then pump body to straight-edge gap. Both these clearances should be between 0.0012 and 0.0024 in (0.03 and 0.06 mm).*
4 Where any of the clearances are outside the specified tolerances, either renew the rotors as a matched set or renew the oil pump complete.

34 Flywheel - servicing

1 Examine the clutch driven plate contact area on the flywheel for scoring or cracks. If these are severe or extensive then the flywheel should be renewed. Surface grinding is not recommended as the balance of the crankshaft/flywheel assembly will be upset.
2 If the teeth on the flywheel starter ring are badly worn, or if some are missing then it will be necessary to remove the ring and fit a new one, or preferably exchange the flywheel for a reconditioned unit.
3 Either split the ring with a cold chisel after making a cut with a hacksaw blade between the teeth, or use a soft headed hammer (not steel) to knock the ring off, striking it evenly and alternately at equally spaced points. Take great care not to damage the flywheel during this process.
4 Heat the new ring in either an electric oven to about 392°F (200°C) or immerse in a pan of boiling oil.
5 Hold the ring at this temperature for five minutes and then quickly fit it to the flywheel so the chamfered portion of the teeth faces the gearbox side of the flywheel.
6 The ring should be tapped gently down onto its register and left to cool naturally when the contraction of the metal on cooling will ensure that it is a secure and permanent fit. Great care must be taken not to overheat the ring, indicated by it turning light metallic blue, as if this happens the temper of the ring will be lost.

35 Driveplate - servicing

1 This component, fitted instead of the flywheel in conjunction with automatic transmission should be checked for distortion and elongation of the bolt holes which secure it to the torque converter.
2 Examine the starter ring gear teeth for wear or chipping.
3 Where any of these faults are evident, renew the driveplate complete.

36 Oil seals - renewal

1 At the time of major overhaul, renew the timing cover oil seal and the crankshaft rear oil seal as a matter of routine.
2 Make sure that the lips of the seals face the correct way as shown.
3 Removal and installation of the timing cover oil seal should be carried out using a piece of tubing as a drift. (photo)

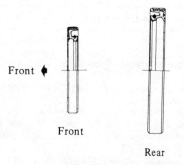

Fig. 1.53 Crankshaft oil seals, installation diagram

36.3. Timing cover oil seal

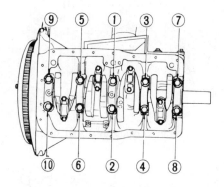

Fig. 1.54 Tightening sequence diagram for main bearing cap bolts

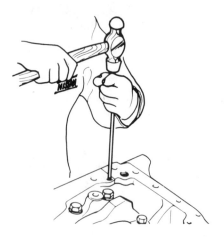

Fig. 1.55 Tapping in a new rear main bearing cap side seal

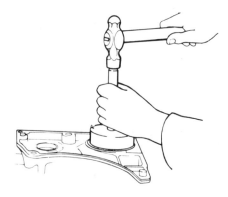

Fig. 1.56 Installing the crankshaft rear oil seal

37 Engine reassembly - general

1   Before commencing reassembly, gather together the necessary tools, gaskets and other small items.
2   Observe absolute cleanliness during reassembly and lubricate each component before installation with clean engine oil.
3   Do not use unnecessary force to fit a part but re-check clearances and tolerances where difficulties are encountered.

38 Crankshaft and main bearings - reassembly

1   Install the upper halves of the main bearing shells into the crankcase and oil them liberally. Note that the centre shell incorporates the thrust washers. Shell bearings (nos. 2 and 4) are similar and interchangeable. The front and rear bearing shells are similar but they are not interchangeable as only the front bearing incorporates an oil hole for the timing chain oil spray. All upper and lower bearing halves of similar type are interchangeable. (photos)
2   If the crankcase breather baffle and mesh were removed, refit them now before installing the crankshaft. (photo)
3   Lower the crankshaft carefully into the crankcase. (photo)
4   Install the main bearing caps complete with shells making sure they go back in their numbered sequence and also the correct way round. (photo)
5   Tighten the main bearing cap bolts to the specified torque, progressively and in the sequence shown. (photo)
6   Smear jointing compound on the new rear main bearing cap side seals and tap them into their recesses. (photo)
7   Install the crankshaft rear oil seal, tapping it into position with a piece of tubing. (photo)

39 Flywheel (or driveplate) - installation

1   Bolt the engine rear plate to the crankcase. (photo)
2   Bolt the flywheel (or driveplate - automatic transmission) to the crankshaft rear mounting flange.
3   Tighten the bolts to the specified torque. (photo)

38.1A. Oiling crankcase bearing shells

38.1B. Main bearing shell incorporating thrust washer

38.1C. Front main bearing with timing chain oil spray hole

38.2. Crankcase breather baffle

38.3. Installing crankshaft

38.4. Installing centre main bearing cap and shell

38.5. Tightening a main bearing cap bolt

38.6. Rear main bearing cap side seal

38.7. Crankshaft rear oil seal

39.1. Engine rear plate

39.3. Tightening flywheel bolts

40.1. Piston directional fitting mark

40 Pistons, rings and connecting rods - reassembly and installation

1   As previously recommended, the pistons will probably have been assembled to their connecting rods by the dealer supplying the new components. When correctly assembled, the notch on the piston crown (on some pistons an 'F' mark is used adjacent to the gudgeon pin boss) must face the front of the engine while the oil hole in the connecting rod will be towards the right-hand side of the engine. (photo)

2   Install the piston rings by reversing the removal procedure described in Section 20. When correctly fitted, the markings on the rings must be facing upwards. The top compression ring is chromium plated while the second compression ring is tapered towards the top. The oil control ring has two rails which can be interchanged and located at top and bottom of the groove. Stagger the piston ring gaps as shown.

3   Install the bearing shells to the connecting rod and big-end cap. (photo)

4   Compress the piston rings with a suitable compressor and then having well lubricated the rings and the cylinder bore with engine oil, tap the piston/connecting rod assembly into the cylinder. (photo)

5   Engage the connecting rod with the crankshaft when the crankpin is at its lowest point of rotational travel. Oil the exposed part of the crankpin.

6   Install the big-end cap complete with shell bearing making sure that the numbers made before dismantling are adjacent and in their correct sequence. (photo)

7   Tighten the big-end nuts to specified torque. (photo)

8   Repeat the operations to install the remaining three piston/connecting rod assemblies.

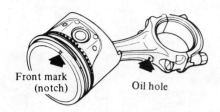

Front mark (notch)   Oil hole

Fig. 1.57 Piston correctly assembled to connecting rod

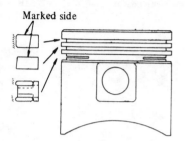

Marked side

Fig. 1.58 Piston ring installation diagram

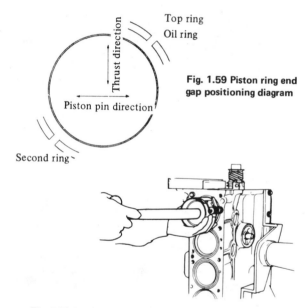

Top ring
Oil ring
Thrust direction
Piston pin direction
Second ring

Fig. 1.59 Piston ring end gap positioning diagram

Fig. 1.60 Installing piston/connecting rod assembly

40.3. Installation connecting rod bearing shell

40.4. Piston installation

40.6. Installing a big-end cap and bearing shell

40.7. Tightening a big-end nut

41 Cylinder head and timing gear - reassembly and installation

1 Insert each valve in turn into its respective guide, applying a little engine oil to the stem. (photo)

2 Fit a new oil seal to the valve stem and with the aid of a spring compressor, assemble the springs (outer spring has close coils nearest cylinder head) retainers and split collets. The latter can be retained in the valve stem cut-out with a dab of thick grease. On L14 engine, inlet valves are fitted with a single spring only. (photo)

3 Oil the camshaft bearings and insert the camshaft carefully into position. (photo)

4 Screw the valve rocker pivots complete with locknuts into the pivot bushes.

5 Fit the rocker arms and guides by depressing the valve springs with a screwdriver.

6 Engage the rocker springs.

7 Fit the camshaft locating plate to the camshaft so that the horizontally engraved line is visible from the front and is positioned at the top of the plate. (photo)

8 Rotate the camshaft until the valve of no. 1 cylinder are fully closed (equivalent to no. 1 piston at TDC) and then turn the crankshaft (by means of the flywheel or driveplate) until no. 1 piston is at TDC.

9 Bolt the two timing chain guides into position. (photo)

10 Clean the mating surfaces of the cylinder block and head and locate a new gasket on the face of the block; do not use gasket cement. (photo)

11 Lower the cylinder head into position and insert the two centre bolts finger-tight only at this stage. (photo)

12 To the front of the crankshaft, fit the sprocket, oil pump - distributor drive gear and the oil thrower. Make sure that the timing marks on the sprocket are visible from the front. (photos)

13 On no account turn the crankshaft or camshaft until the timing chain is installed, otherwise the valves will impinge upon the piston crowns. Fit the chain to the crankshaft sprocket and draw the chain through the opening in the cylinder head.

14 Engage the camshaft sprocket within the upper loop of the timing chain and then engage the chain with the teeth of the crankshaft sprocket and bolt the camshaft sprocket to the camshaft ensuring that the following conditions are met:

    (i) the keyway of the crankshaft sprocket should point vertically.

    (ii) the timing marks ('bright' link plates) on the chain should align with those on the two sprockets and be positioned on the right-hand side when viewed from the front.

On L20B type engines there should be 21 black plates between the two bright plates and on all other engines only 20 black plates between them.

Where a timing chain has stretched, this can upset the valve timing and provision is made for this by alternative dowel holes drilled in the camshaft sprocket.

With no. 1 piston at TDC (compression stroke) check whether the notch in the camshaft sprocket (with chain correctly engaged) appears to the left of the engraved line on the locating plate. If this is the case disengage the camshaft sprocket from the chain and move the sprocket round so that when it is re-engaged with the chain it will locate with the camshaft flange dowel in its no. 2 hole. Where this adjustment does not correct the chain slack, repeat the operation using no. 3 hole of the camshaft sprocket to engage with the flange dowel. Where no 2 or 3 sprocket holes are used then the no. 2 or 3 timing marks must be used to position the chain. Where this adjustment procedure still will not correct or compensate for the slackness in the timing chain then the chain must be renewed. (photos)

15 When the timing is satisfactory, tighten the camshaft sprocket bolt to the specified torque. (photo)

16 Install the chain tensioner so that there is the minimum clearance between the spindle/slipper assembly and the tensioner assembly. (photo)

17 Thoroughly clean the mating faces of the front cover and cylinder block.

18 Locate a new gasket on the front face of the engine, applying gasket cement to both sides of it.

19 Apply gasket cement to the front cover and cylinder block as indicated.

20 Offer up the front cover to the engine and insert the securing bolts finger tight. Take care not to damage the head gasket which is already in position. (photo)

21 The top face of the front cover should be flush with the top surface of the cylinder block or certainly not more than 0.0059 in (1.5 mm) difference in level.

22 Tighten the front cover bolts to the correct torque.

23 Refit the water pump. (photo)

24 Oil the lips of the front cover oil seal and push the pulley onto the crankshaft and tighten its securing bolt to 100 lb/ft (13.8 kg/m). (photo)

25 Insert the remaining cylinder head bolts noting carefully the positions of the longer bolts (A) and the shorter ones (B).

26 Tighten the bolts to the specified torque progressively and in the sequence shown.

Note: Where the cylinder head is being installed with the engine in the vehicle, tension must be applied to the timing chain in an upward direction at all times in order to prevent the chain becoming disengaged from the crankshaft sprocket (see Section 14)

 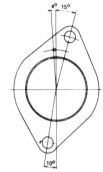

Exhaust   Intake

Fig. 1.61 Valve components   **Fig. 1.62 Installation position for camshaft locating plate**

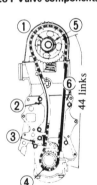 

44 links   42 links

Fig. 1.63 Timing gear installation diagram (L20B engine)   **Fig. 1.64 Timing gear installation diagram (all engines except L20B) For key see Fig. 1.63**

1   *Fuel pump eccentric cam*
2   *Chain guide*
3   *Tensioner*
4   *Crankshaft sprocket*
5   *Camshaft sprocket*
6   *Chain guide*

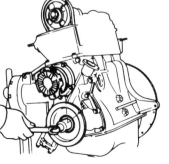

Fig. 1.66 Installing the crankshaft pulley and bolt

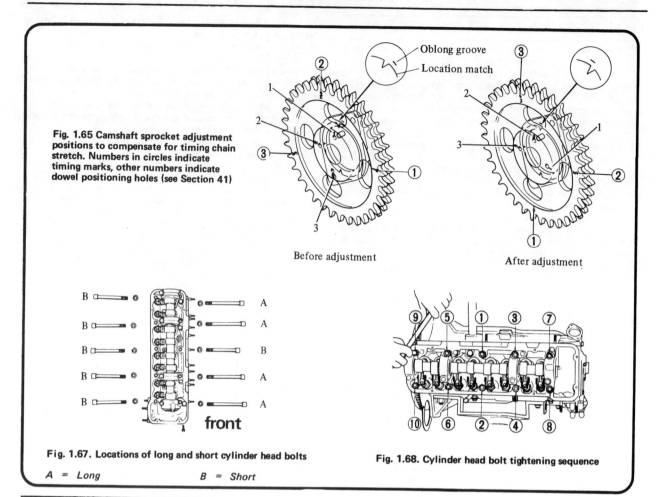

Fig. 1.65 Camshaft sprocket adjustment positions to compensate for timing chain stretch. Numbers in circles indicate timing marks, other numbers indicate dowel positioning holes (see Section 41)

Before adjustment

After adjustment

Fig. 1.67. Locations of long and short cylinder head bolts

A = Long   B = Short

Fig. 1.68. Cylinder head bolt tightening sequence

42 Oil pump and distributor - installation

1 Set the engine so that No. 1 piston is at TDC on its compression stroke.
2 Align the punch mark on the oil pump driveshaft with the oil hole just below the driven gear. (photo)
3 Use a new flange gasket and insert the oil pump into its recess so that as its driveshaft meshes with the drivegear on the crankshaft, the distributor drive tongue will take up a position as shown being at 5° to a line drawn through the centres of the bolt holes of the distributor mounting flange (when viewed from above) and having the smaller segment towards the front of the engine. (photos)
4 Tighten the oil pump securing bolts.
5 Without moving the crankshaft, insert the distributor into its recess so that the large and small segments of the driveshaft engage correctly and then tighten the clamp plate bolt at its original position in the elongated hole. (photo)
6 The ignition timing should be precisely checked and adjusted, as described in Chapter 4.

43 Oil strainer and sump - installation

1 Bolt the oil strainer and pick-up tube assembly to the flange of the crankcase. (photo)
2 Clean the mating surfaces of the crankcase and the sump. Apply gasket cement at the points indicated and then smearing a film of cement to the crankcase flange, stick the sump gasket to the crankcase.
3 Smear the flange of the sump with gasket cement and then bolt it to the crankcase. Do not overtighten these bolts. (photo)

44 Valve clearances - adjustment

1 To adjust the valve clearance, turn the crankshaft until no. 1 piston is at TDC on its compression stroke. In this position the high points of the cam lobes will be furthest from the rocker arms. Check the clearances between the heel of the cam and the rocker arm by inserting the appropriate feeler blade. The blades should be a stiff sliding fit and to adjust the clearance, release the locknut and turn the pivot screw. The valve clearances **cold** are inlet 0.008 in. (0.20 mm); exhaust 0.010 in. (0.25 mm). (photos)
2 As the firing order is 1-3-4-2 it will reduce the amount of the crankshaft rotation required if the valve clearances are adjusted in accordance with the firing order. To obtain a better appreciation of the valve clearance it is recommended that the rocker arm springs are detached. Numbering from the front, the inlet valves are 2-3-6-7 and the exhaust valves 1-4-5-8.
3 When carrying out valve clearance adjustment with the engine in the car, the crankshaft can most easily be turned by engaging top gear and jacking-up and turning a rear roadwheel (manual transmission). On cars fitted with automatic transmission a spanner will have to be applied to the crankshaft pulley bolt which makes the adjustment procedure somewhat more protracted. With either method, the work will be facilitated if the spark plugs are first removed.

45 Ancillary components (engine types L14, L16, L18) - refitting

1 This is essentially a reversal of the removal procedure described in Section 12, but observe the following points.

41.1. Installing a valve

41.2A. Installing valve spring retainer

41.2B. Compressing a valve spring

41.3. Installing camshaft

41.6. Engaging rocker springs with the rocker arms

41.7. Installing camshaft locating plate

41.9. Installing a timing chain guide

41.10. Cylinder head gasket located on block

41.11. Lowering cylinder head into positon

41.12A. Installing crankshaft sprocket

41.21B. Installing oil pump/distributor drive gear

41.21C. Installing crankshaft oil thrower

41.14A. Engaging timing chain with camshaft sprocket

41.14B. Installing camshaft sprocket bolt and fuel pump eccentric

41.14C. Crankshaft sprocket timing mark aligned with chain 'bright' link

41.14D. Camshaft sprocket timing mark aligned with chain 'bright' link

41.15 Tighten the camshaft sprocket bolt to the specified torque

41.16. Installing timing chain tensioner

41.20. Installing front cover

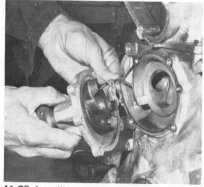
41.23. Installing water pump

41.24. Installing crankshaft pulley

42.2. Oil pump driveshaft alignment marks

42.3A. Installing oil pump

42.3B. Correct positon of distributor drive torque after installation of oil pump

42.5. Installing the distributor

43.1. Oil pick-up tube and strainer installed

43.3. Installing pump

44.1A. Checking an inlet valve clearance

44.1B. Adjusting a valve clearance

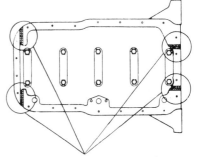
Apply sealant at these points

Fig. 1.69 Crankcase sealant application areas

2   The carburettor flange insulator must be installed on the manifold so that its marking is visible from above.
3   When installing the oil filter, tighten it by hand pressure only.
4   When assembling the clutch mechanism to the flywheel, centralise the driven plate, as described in Chapter 5.

46 Ancillary components (engine type L20B) - refitting

1   This is essentially a reversal of the removal procedure described in Section 13, but observe the following points.
2   When installing the carburettor, make sure to fit the heatshield plate and note that the joint seat duct is inserted into the primary hole in the inlet manifold.
3   When installing the oil filter, tighten it by hand pressure only.
4   When assembling the clutch mechanism to the flywheel, centralise the driven plate as described in Chapter 5.

47 Engine/transmission - installation

1   Reconnect the engine and manual gearbox or engine and automatic transmission by reversing the separation procedure described in Sections 9 or 20.
2   Tighten the securing bolts to the specified torque.
3   Using the hoist and slings, install the engine/transmission in the vehicle by reversing the removal procedure given in Sections 5,6,7 or 8 according to engine type and transmission.
4   When installation is complete, check and adjust the tension of the drive belts to the total deflections shown in the diagnosis according to the equipment fitted to the particular engine.
5   Refill the engine with the correct grade and quantity of oil. Remember to include an extra 1 Imp pint, 1.2 US pints, 0.6 litre

of oil which will be absorbed by the new filter.
6   Refill the cooling system (Chapter 2).
7   Check the levels in the gearbox or automatic transmission and top-up if necessary.

48 Initial start up after major overhaul

1   With the engine installed in the car, make a final visual check to see that everything has been reconnected and that no loose rags or tools have been left within the engine compartment.
2   Turn the idling speed adjusting screw in about ½ turn to ensure that the engine will have a faster than usual idling speed during initial start up and operation.
3   Pull the choke control fully out and start the engine. This may take a little longer than usual as the fuel pump and carburetter bowls will be empty and will require priming.
4   As soon as the engine starts, push the choke control in until the engine will run at a fast tick-over. Examine all hose and pipe connections for leaks.
5   Operate the vehicle on the road until normal engine temperature is reached and then remove the rocker cover and adjust the valve clearances hot to inlet 0.010 in. (0.25 mm) and exhaust 0.012 in. (0.30 mm) as described in Section 44.
6   When the engine has cooled completely check the cylinder head bolt torque settings.
7   Where the majority of engine internal bearings or components (pistons, rings etc) have been renewed than the operating speed should be restricted for the first 500 miles (800 km) and the engine oil changed at the end of this period.
8   Check and adjust if necessary the ignition timing (Chapter 4).
9   Check and adjust the carburettors and all exhaust emission control equipment (Chapter 3).

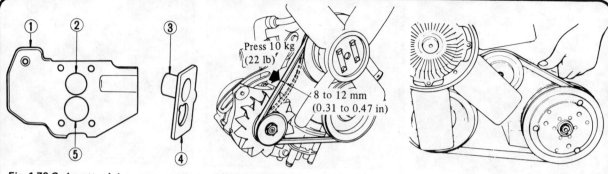

Fig. 1.70 Carburettor joint components (L20B type engine)

1 Heatshield plate
2 Primary hole
3 Duct
4 Joint seat
5 Secondary hole

Fig. 1.71 Drive belt tensioning diagram (alternator only)

Fig. 1.72 Drive belt tensioning diagram (air conditioning compressor - 710 series only)

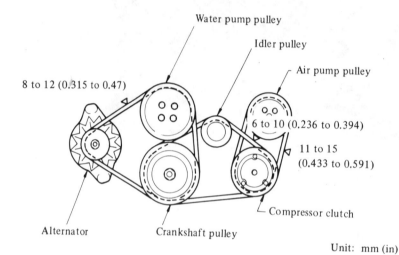

Fig. 1.73 Drive belt tensioning diagram (emission control air pump, alternator and air conditioning compressor - 710 series 1975 onwards)

49 Fault diagnosis - engine

Symptom	Reason/s
Engine will not turn over when starter switch is operated	Flat battery
	Bad battery connections
	Bad connections at solenoid switch and/or starter motor
	Starter motor jammed
	Defective solenoid
	Starter motor defective
Engine turns over normally but fails to start	No spark at plugs
	No fuel reaching engine
	Too much fuel reaching the engine (flooding)
Engine starts but runs unevenly and misfires	Ignition and/or fuel system faults
	Incorrect valve clearances
	Burnt out valves
	Worn out piston rings

Lack of power	Ignition and/or fuel system faults
	Incorrect valve clearances Burnt out valves
	Worn out piston rings
Excessive oil consumption	Oil leaks from crankshaft rear oil seal, timing cover gasket and oil seal, rocker cover gasket, oil filter gasket, sump gasket, sump plug washer Worn piston rings or cylinder bores resulting in oil being burnt by engine Worn valve guides and/or defective valve stem seals
Excessive mechanical noise from engine	Wrong valve to rocker clearances Worn crankshaft bearings Worn cylinders (piston slap) Slack or worn timing chain and sprockets

NOTE: When investigating starting and uneven running faults do not be tempted into snap diagnosis. Start from the beginning of the check procedure and follow it through. It will take less time in the long run. Poor performance from an engine in terms of power and economy is not normally diagnosed quickly. In any event the ignition and fuel systems must be checked first before assuming any further investigation needs to be made.
On later model vehicles pay particular attention to the connections of the emission control system and also refer to the Fault Diagnosis Section in Chapter 3.

Chapter 2 Cooling system

Contents

Specifications

System type	Thermo syphon with pump assistance

Radiator

Type	Corrugated fin
Dimensions:	
140J and 160J	11.0 x 19.2 x 1.5 in. (280.0 x 488.0 x 38.0 mm)
710 series	14.2 x 21.4 x 1.26 in. (360.0 x 544.0 x 32.0 mm)

Radiator cap pressure rating	13 psi (0.9 kg/sq cm)

Thermostat

Opening temperature:	
Standard	180ºF (82ºC)
Cold climates	190ºF (88ºC)
Hot climates	170ºF (76.6ºC)
Full open:	
Standard	203ºF (95ºC)
Cold climates	212ºF (100ºC)
Hot climates	194ºF (90ºC)

Fan fluid coupling capacity (early type only)	11.5 cc
Fluid specification	Silicone oil 700 CTS

Coolant capacity	L14 and L16 (140 and 160J)	L18 710 series to 1974	L20B 710 series 1975 on
Without heater	1 3/4 U.S. gal, 1 3/8 Imp. gal, 6.5 litres	1 1/2 U.S. gal	1 3/4 U.S. gal
With heater	1 7/8 U.S. gal, 1 1/2 Imp. gal, 6.8 litres	1 7/8 U.S. gal	1 7/8 U.S. gal

1 General description

The cooling system comprises the radiator, top and bottom water hoses, water pump, cylinder and block water jackets, radiator cap with pressure relief valve and flow and return heater hoses. The thermostat is located in a recess at the front of the cylinder head. The principle of the system is that cold water in the bottom of the radiator circulates upwards through the lower radiator hose to the water pump, where the pump impeller pushes the water round the cylinder block and head through the various cast-in passages to cool the cylinder bores, combustion surfaces and valve seats. When sufficient heat has been absorbed by the cooling water, the engine has reached an efficient working temperature, the water moves from the cylinder head past the now open thermostat into the top radiator hose and into the radiator header tank.

The water then travels down the radiator tubes when it is rapidly cooled by the in-rush of air, when the vehicle is in forward motion. A multi-bladed fan, mounted on the water pump pulley, assists this cooling action. The water, now cooled, reached the bottom of the radiator and the cycle is repeated.

When the engine is cold the thermostat remains closed until the coolant reaches a pre-determined temperature (see Speci-

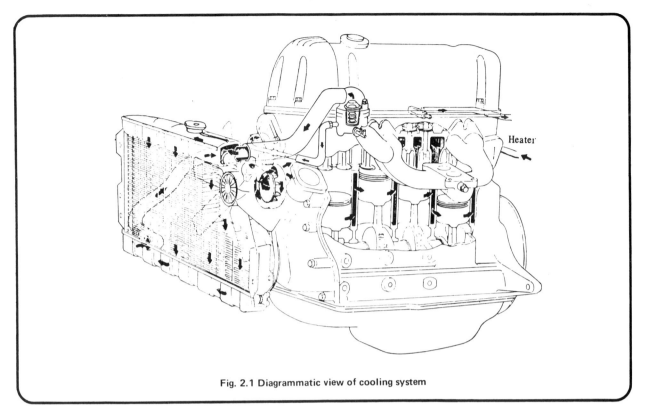

Fig. 2.1 Diagrammatic view of cooling system

fications). This assists rapid warming-up.

An electrosensitive capsule located in the cylinder head measures the water temperature.

The cooling system also provides the heat for the car interior heater and heats the inlet manifold.

On vehicles equipped with automatic transmission, the transmission fluid is cooled by a cooler attached to the base of the radiator.

On cars equipped with air conditioning systems, a condenser is placed ahead of the radiator and is bolted in conjunction with it.

On early models equipped with air conditioning and on all later model vehicles, the radiator fan is of fluid coupling type and by its limited slip characteristic, keeps the fan speed to 3000 rpm or below which at high engine speeds helps to reduce power loss and noise. On early models, the special oil in the fluid coupling can be replenished but on later versions, the unit is sealed.

2 Cooling system - draining

1 Should the system have to be left empty for any reason both the cylinder block and radiator must be completely drained, otherwise with a partly drained system corrosion of the water pump impeller seal face may occur with subsequent early failure of the pump seal and bearing.

2 Place the car on a level surface and have ready a container having a capacity of two gallons (9.0 litres) which will slide beneath the radiator and sump.

3 Move the heater control on the facia to 'HOT' and unscrew and remove the radiator cap. If hot, unscrew the cap very slowly, first covering it with a cloth to remove the danger of scalding when the pressure in the system is released.

4 Unscrew the radiator drain tap at the base of the radiator and then when coolant ceases to flow into the receptacle, repeat the operation by unscrewing the cylinder block plug located on the righthand side of the engine. Retain the coolant for further use, if it contains antifreeze.

3 Cooling system - flushing

1 The radiator and waterways in the engine after some time may become restricted or even blocked with scale or sediment which reduces the efficiency of the cooling system. When this condition occurs or the coolant appears rusty or dark in colour the system should be flushed. In severe cases reverse flushing may be required as described later.

2 Place the heater controls to the 'HOT' position and unscrew fully the radiator and cylinder block drain taps.

3 Remove the radiator filler cap and place a hose in the filler neck. Allow water to run through the system until it emerges quite clean and clear.

4 In severe cases of contamination of the coolant or in the system, reverse flush by first removing the radiator cap and disconnecting the lower radiator hose at the radiator outlet pipe.

5 Remove the top hose at the radiator connection end and remove the radiator as described in Section 6.

6 Invert the radiator and insert the hose in the bottom outlet pipe. Continue flushing until clear water comes from the radiator top tank.

7 To flush the engine water jackets, remove the thermostat as described later in this Chapter and place a hose in the thermostat location until clear water runs from the water pump inlet. Cleaning by the use of chemical compounds is not recommended.

4 Cooling system - filling

1 Place the heater control to the 'HOT' position.

2 Screw in the radiator drain tap and close the cylinder block drain tap.

3 Pour coolant slowly into the radiator so that air can be expelled through the thermostat pin hole without being trapped in a waterway.

4 Fill to the correct level which 1¼ in. (31.8 mm) below the radiator filler neck and replace the filler cap.

5 Run the engine, check for leaks and recheck the coolant level.

5 Antifreeze mixture

1 The cooling system should be filled with antifreeze solution in early autumn. The heater matrix and radiator bottom tank are particularly prone to freeze if antifreeze is not used in air temperatures below freezing. Modern antifreeze is not used in air temperatures below freezing. Modern antifreeze solutions of good quality will also prevent corrosion and rusting and they may be left in the system to advantage all year round, draining and refilling with fresh solution each year.

2 Before adding antifreeze to the system, check all hose connections and check the tightness of the cylinder head bolts as such solutions are searching. The cooling system should be drained and refilled with clean water as previously explained, before adding antifreeze.

3 The quantity of antifreeze which should be used for various levels of protection is given in the table below, expressed as a percentage of the system capacity.

Antifreeze volume	protection to	Safe Pump circulation
25%	$-26^{o}C\ (-15^{o}F)$	$-12^{o}C\ (\ 10^{o}F)$
30%	$-33^{o}C\ (-28^{o}F)$	$-16^{o}C\ (\ \ 3^{o}F)$
35%	$-39^{o}C\ (-38^{o}F)$	$-20^{o}C\ (-\ 4^{o}F)$

4 Where the cooling system contains an antifreeze solution any topping-up should be done with a solution made up in similar proportions to the original in order to avoid dilution.

6 Radiator - removal, inspection and refitting

1 Unscrew the radiator drain plug and drain the coolant into a suitable container. Retain the coolant if it contains antifreeze mixture. There is no need to drain the cylinder block when removing the radiator.

2 Disconnect the radiator upper and lower hoses.

3 *On cars equipped with an air conditioning system,* remove the bolts which secure the lower shroud and withdraw the shroud downwards.

4 Unbolt the radiator, taking care to support the air conditioning system condenser mounted ahead of the radiator and then withdraw the radiator upwards together with the upper shroud section.

5 *On cars equipped with automatic transmission* the inlet and outlet pipes which connect with the fluid cooler at the base of the radiator must also be disconnected.

6 Inspect the radiator for leaks, if evident it is recommended that the repair is left to a specialist or the radiator is exchanged for a reconditioned one.

7 Whenever the radiator is removed, take the opportunity of brushing all flies and accumulated dirt from the radiator fins or applying air from a tyre air compressor in the reverse direction to normal airflow.

8 The radiator pressure cap should be tested by a service station and if it leaks or its spring has weakened, it must be renewed with one of specified pressure rating.

9 Refitting the radiator is a reversal of removal. Refill the cooling system as described in Section 4.

7 Thermostat - removal, testing and refitting

1 Partially drain the cooling system (about ½ gal./2.2 litres drawn off through the radiator drain plug will be sufficient).

2 Disconnect the radiator upper hose from the thermostat elbow on the left-hand side of the cylinder head.

3 Unscrew and remove the two bolts from the thermostat housing cover and remove the cover and the gasket. (photo)

4 Extract the thermostat. Should it be stuck in its seat cut round its rim with a sharp pointed knife and on no account attempt to lever it out.

5 To test whether the unit is serviceable, suspend the thermostat on a piece of string in a pan of water being heated. Using a thermometer, with reference to the opening and closing temperature in Specifications, its operation may be checked. The thermostat should be renewed if it is stuck open or closed or it fails to operate at the specified temperature. The operation of the thermostat is not instantaneous and sufficient time must be allowed for the movement during testing. Never replace a faulty unit - leave it out if no replacement is available immediately.

6 Replacement of the thermostat is a reversal of the removal procedure. Ensure the mating faces of the housing are clean. Use a new gasket with jointing compound. The word "Top" which appears on the thermostat face must be visible from above. (photo)

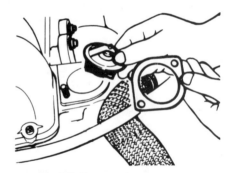

Fig. 2.3. Extracting the thermostat

7.3 Removing the thermostat housing cover

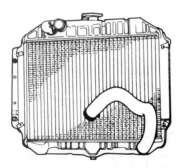

Fig. 2.2. Radiator (manual gearbox type)

7.6 Correct installation of thermostat.
Note bypass hose hole pin

8 Water pump - removal and installation

1 Drain the cooling system, retaining the coolant for further use.
2 Unbolt the shroud from the radiator.
3 Loosen the alternator mounting and adjustment bolts and push the alternator in towards the engine so that the driving belt can be slipped off the alternator and fan pulleys.
4 Unbolt and remove the fan blade/pulley assembly from the water pump hub.
5 Unscrew evenly and then remove the bolts which secure the water pump to the engine front cover. If the water pump is stuck tight, do not lever it off but tap it gently with a hammer and hardwood block to break the gasket seal.
6 Where there is evidence of a leaking seal or severe corrosion of the impeller blades has occurred, do not attempt to repair the water pump but renew if for a reconditioned exchange unit.
7 Installation is a reversal of removal but always use a new sealing gasket and then adjust the fan belt tension, as described in Chapter 1, Section 47. Refill the cooling system.

9 Fluid coupling (early type) - servicing

1 On early type fan fluid couplings (later models are sealed units) any failure or malfunction may be due to deterioration or thickening of the fluid.
2 Remove the screws which secure the two halves of the coupling together, separate the half sections and drain the oil.
3 Clean the internal surfaces and then examine the condition of the seal and bearing. If these are blackened or worn, renew the coupling assembly complete.
4 If the components are in good condition, reassembly and then using a syringe, inject silicone oil (11.5 cc), through the filler plug hole. Inject the oil slowly in order to allow any trapped air to escape.

10 Water temperature thermal transmitter and gauge

1 The testing and removal of these components is described in Chapter 10, to which reference should be made.

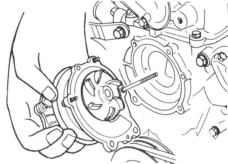

Fig. 2.4. Removing the water pump from engine front face

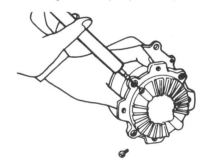

Fig. 2.5. Recharging an early type fan coupling with fluid

Chapter 2 Fault diagnosis overleaf

11 Fault diagnosis - cooling system

Symptom	Reason/s
Heat generated in cylinder not being successfully disposed of by radiator	Insufficient water in cooling system Fan belt slipping (accompanied by a shrieking noise on rapid engine acceleration) Radiator core blocked or radiator grille restricted Bottom water hose collapsed, impeding flow Thermostat not opening properly Ignition advance and retard incorrectly set (accompanied by loss of power and perhaps misfiring) Carburettor incorrectly adjusted (mixture too weak) Exhaust system partially blocked Oil level in sump too low Blown cylinder head gasket (water/steam being forced down the radiator overflow pipe under pressure) Engine not yet run-in Brake binding
Too much heat being dispersed by radiator	Thermostat jammed open Incorrect grade of thermostat fitted allowing premature opening of valve Thermostat missing
Leaks in system	Loose clips on water hoses Top or bottom water hoses perished and leaking Radiator core leaking Thermostat gasket leaking Pressure cap spring worn or seal ineffective Blown cylinder head gasket (pressure in system forcing water/steam down overflow pipe) Cylinder wall or head cracked

Chapter 3 Carburation; fuel, exhaust and emission control systems

Contents

Specifications

Carburettor (140J models)

	Primary	Secondary
Type ... ... Downdraught, dual barrel, fixed jet		
Diameter of outlet	1.1024 in (28.0 mm)	1.2598 in (32.0 mm)
Diameter of venturi	0.8268 in (21.0 mm)	1.1024 in (28.0 mm)
Main jet	96	165
Main air bleed	60	60
1st slow air bleed	0.0394 in (1.0 mm)	-
2nd slow air bleed	220	100
Slow economizer	0.0630 in (1.6 mm)	-
Power jet	50	
Main nozzle	0.0866 in (2.2 mm)	0.0984 in (2.5 mm)
Idling speed	600 rpm	

Carburettor (160J models)

	Primary	Secondary
Type ... ... Downdraught, dual barrel, fixed jet		
Diameter of outlet	1.10 in (28 mm)	1.26 in (32 mm)
Diameter of venturi	0.87 in (22 mm)	1.14 in (29 mm)
Main jet	102	165
Main air bleed	60	60
1st slow air bleed	0.039 in (1.0 mm)	
2nd slow air bleed	180	100
Slow economizer	0.063 in (1.6 mm)	
Power jet	45	
Main nozzle	0.091 in (2.3 mm)	0.098 in (2.5 mm)
Idling speed	600 rpm	

Carburettors (160J SSS models)

Type	Twin variable jet (S.U. type)
Number	HJT38W-7
Diameter of outlet	1.50 in (38.0 mm)
Diameter of inlet	1.409 in (35.8 mm)
Maximum piston lift	1.14 in (29.0 mm)
Jet needle	M—87
Nozzle jet diameter	0.0921 in (2.34 mm)
Fuel inlet needle valve	0.059 in (1.5 mm)
Damper oil viscosity (S.A.E)	IOW — 30
Idling speed	650 rpm

Carburettors (710 models to 1975)

Type	Downdraught, dual barrel, fixed jet
Number:	
Manual transmission	DCH340 — 10
Automatic transmission	DCH340 — 11

	Primary	Secondary
Diameter of outlet	1.18 in (30.0 mm)	1.34 in (34.0 mm)
Diameter of venturi	0.906 in (23.0 mm)	1.181 in (30.0 mm)
Main jet	100	170
Main air bleed	60	60
Slow jet	45	90
Slow air bleed	145	100
Slow economizer	0.071 in (1.8 mm)	
Power jet	41	
Main nozzle	0.098 in (2.5 mm)	0.098 in (2.5 mm)
Internal diameter		
Idling speed:		
Manual transmission	800 rpm	
Automatic transmission	650 rpm (in D)	
CO level	1.5 %	

Carburettor (710 models 1975 onwards)

Type	Downdraught, dual barrel, fixed jet
Number:	
Manual transmission	DCH340-43
Automatic transmission	DCH340-44
Californian models:	
Manual transmission	DCH340-41
Automatic transmission	DCH340-42

	Primary	Secondary
Diameter of outlet	1.181 in (30.0 mm)	1.341 in (34.0 mm)
Diameter of venturi	0.945 in (24.0 mm)	1.220 in (31.0 mm)
Main jet:		
DCH340-43	97	160
DCH340-44	97	160
DCH340-41	99	160
DCH340-42	99	160
Main air bleed	70	60
Slow jet:		
DCH340-43	48	100
DCH340-44	48	100
DCH340-41	48	80
DCH340-42	48	80
Power valve:		
DCH340-43	48	
DCH340-44	48	
DCH340-41	43	
DCH340-42	43	

Idling speed:
    Manual transmission   ...   .   750 rpm
    Automatic transmission   ...   .   650 rpm (in D)
CO level 2%

Fuel tank capacities

140J ...   .   11 Imp gals (50 litres)
160JSSS   ...   .   12.1/8 Imp. gals (55 litres)
710 series (except wagon) ...   .   13¼ U.S. gals.

Torque wrench settings

	lb/in	kg/cm
Anti-dieseling solenoid valve	156 to 304	180 to 350
B.C.D.D.	17.4 to 347	20 to 40

1 General description

All models are equipped with a rear mounted fuel tank, a mechanically operated fuel pump and a carburettor with the necessary pipe lines.

The type of carburettor depends upon the engine type and vehicle model.

All vehicles have crankcase emission systems but only the 710 series has full exhaust emission control and this equipment becomes more complex and sophisticated, the later the date of production and especially on models designed for operation in California.

2 Air cleaner (140J and 160J SSS)

Dual barrel carburettor type air cleaner

1 This type of air cleaner is fitted to engines not having full emission control systems.

2 The element is of disposable, paper type and it should be renewed at 24,000 miles (38000 km) intervals by unscrewing and removing the butterfly type bolts and lifting the air cleaner lid. (photo)

3 Wipe out the interior of the air cleaner body and check that the rubber sealing rings are in good order. Refit the lid and the securing bolts.

4 This type of air cleaner is fitted with an idle compensator. This is a thermostatic valve which opens under conditions of high under-bonnet temperatures and admits extra air to the inlet manifold. This compensates for over-rich mixture and maintains smooth idling.

Twin carburettor type air cleaner

5 Access to the element in this type of air cleaner is obtained in a similar way to that just described.

6 The baseplate of the cleaner may be removed after unbolting it from the carburettor flange. An idle compensator is not fitted to the twin carburettor type air cleaner.

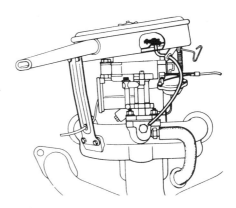

Fig. 3.2 Idle compensator and connecting pipe

Fig. 3.3 Air cleaner (160J SSS type)

Fig. 3.1. Air cleaner (140J type)

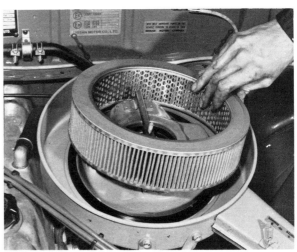

2.2. Removing air cleaner element

3 Air cleaner (automatic temperature control - 710 series)

1   This type of air cleaner is fitted to all 710 series models which are equipped with a full emission control system.

2   The air cleaner incorporates a sensor and valve device which 'mixes' the air being drawn in to the carburettors to maintain the air temperature at a predetermined level thus preventing icing of the carburettor, reduction of exhaust emission and reduced condensation within the rocker box cover.

3   Hot air is drawn from the interior of a deflector plate attached to the exhaust manifold.

4   When the engine is operating under full load, a vacuum diaphragm connected to the inlet manifold opens the control valve fully to exclude hot air and override the sensor 'mixing' device.

5   Renewal of the paper type element is carried out by unscrewing the three butterfly type bolts and removing the air cleaner lid (still with all connecting hoses attached).

6   If the air cleaner assembly is to be removed complete, then disconnect the following:

   (a) Main air inlet hose
   (b) Hot air inlet hose
   (c) Sensor to inlet manifold vacuum hose
   (d) Sensor to vacuum capsule hose
   (e) Idle compensator to inlet manifold hose
   (f) Air pump to air clenaer hose
   (g) Flame trap to air cleaner hose
   (h) Carburettor to air cleaner.
   (j) Air cleaner to rocker cover blow-by hose

7   Unbolt the air cleaner from its supports.

8   In the event of a fault developing which may be reflected in poor idling, increased fume emission or carburettor icing, or the formation of condensation within the rocker box, carry out the following checks:

9   Inspect all air cleaner hose connections for security and correct location.

10   Run the engine until normal operating temperature is reached and then allow the engine to idle for a few minutes with the bonnet closed. Switch off the engine and with the aid of a mirror inspect the position of the air control valve within the air cleaner intake nozzle. The valve should be closed against exhaust manifold

heated air. Conversely with the engine cold and under bonnet temperature below 100° F (38° C) the valve should be open to exhaust manifold heated air.

11   Where these tests prove the sensor unit to be faulty, flatten the retaining clips and disconnect the hoses by pulling them from their nozzles. Note the relative positions of the two hoses.

12   Remove the sensor but leave the gasket which is bonded to the air cleaner body.

13   A dual idle compensator is installed in the base of the air cleaner body. The idle compensator is essentially a thermostatic valve operated by bi-metallic strips.

14   The twin valves of the idle compensator operate at different temperatures:

   No. 1 begins to open 140° F (60° C); fully open 158° F (70° C)

   No. 2 begins to open 158° F (70° C); fully open 194° F (90° C)

15   A faulty idle compensator may be suspected if idling becomes erratic.

16   To test the compensator valve, ensure that the ambient temperature is below the opening level and blow and suck through the connecting hose. Any escape of air will mean that the compensator must be renewed.

17   Access to the compensator is obtained after removing the air cleaner cover.

18   Refitting the air cleaner element and component parts is a reversal of removal.

Fig. 3.5 Checking position of air cleaner deflector valve with a mirror

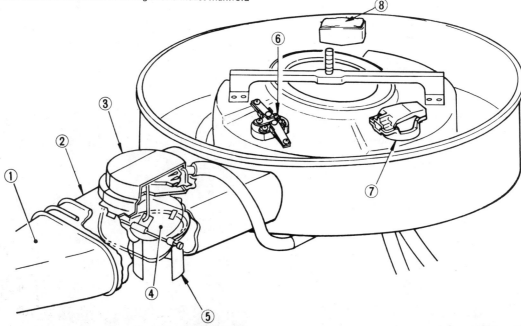

Fig. 3.4 Air cleaner (710 series type

1 Air inlet	3 Vacuum capsule	5 Hot air inlet	7 Sensor
2 Duct	4 Air deflector valve	6 Idle compensator	8 Filter

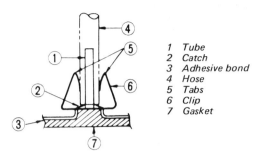

1 Tube
2 Catch
3 Adhesive bond
4 Hose
5 Tabs
6 Clip
7 Gasket

Fig. 3.6 Sensor connecting hose attachment

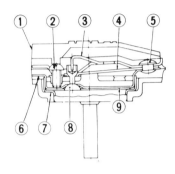

1 Cover	5 Rivet
2 Screw	6 Valve seat
3 Adjustable frame	7 Lower frame
4 Bi-metal strip	8 Air bleed
	9 Gasket

Fig. 3.7 Sectional view of the air cleaner temperature sensor

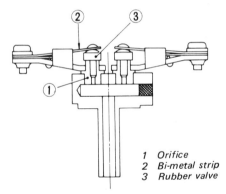

1 Orifice
2 Bi-metal strip
3 Rubber valve

Fig. 3.8 Sectional view of the idle compensator

4 Fuel line filter - renewal

1 The filter is of cartridge, disposable type and should be renewed at intervals not greater than 24000 miles (40000 km).
2 The condition of the element can be seen through its transparent bowl.
3 The filter is located adjacent to the mechanical fuel pump and is removed and replaced simply by disconnecting the hoses from it and then pulling it from its retaining clip.
4 It is recommended that the filter fuel lines are not disconnected when there is a high level of fuel in the tank. In any event, the supply hose from the tank should be raised and plugged immediately it is removed from the fuel filter.

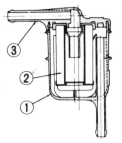

1 Body
2 Element
3 Cover

Fig. 3.9 Sectional view of the fuel line filter

5 Fuel pump - description and testing

The fuel pump is actuated by the movement of its rocker arm on a camshaft eccentric. This movement is transferred to a flexible diaphragm which draws the fuel from the tank and pumps it under pressure to the carburettor float chamber. Inlet and outlet valves are incorporated to control the flow of fuel irrespective of engine speed.

Presuming that the fuel lines and unions are in good condition and that there are no leaks anywhere, check the performance of the fuel pump in the following manner: Disconnect the fuel pipe at the carburettor inlet union, and the high tension lead to the coil, and with a suitable container or a large rag in position to catch the ejected fuel, turn the engine over on the starter motor solenoid. A good spurt of fuel should emerge from the end of the pipe every second revolution.

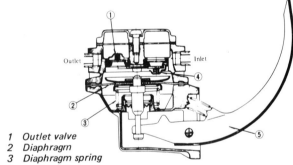

1 Outlet valve
2 Diaphragm
3 Diaphragm spring
4 Inlet valve
5 Rocker arm

Fig. 3.10 Sectional view of the fuel pump

6.2. Removing fuel pump

6 Fuel pump - removal and installation

1   Disconnect the hoses from the pump inlet and outlet nozzles. It is recommended that the fuel lines are not disconnected when the fuel tank is fairly full and in any event the supply pipe from the tank should be raised above the level of fuel in the tank and plugged as soon as it is removed from the pump.
2   Unscrew and remove the securing nuts from the fuel pump flange and remove the pump. Note the sequence of gaskets and spacer. (photo)
3   Refitting is a reversal of removal.

7 Fuel pump - dismantling, inspection and reassembly

1   Remove the five cover securing screws; remove the cover and the gasket.
2   Scratch a mark across the edges of the upper and lower body flanges so that they can be replaced in the same relative positions.
3   Unscrew and remove the screws from the body flange.
4   Unscrew and remove the inlet and outlet elbows.
5   Unscrew and remove the two screws from the valve retainer and remove the two valves.
6   Unhook the diaphragm pushrod from the fork at the end of the rocker arm by depressing the diaphragm against the action of its spring and then tilting the diaphragm/rod assembly until the bottom of the rod can be felt to touch the inside of the pump body.
7   Take care not to damage the oil seal as the diaphragm and pushrod are released.
8   If necessary, the rocker arm pivot pin can be driven out with a small drift.
9   Examine all components for wear or cracks and the diaphragm for porosity or deterioration and renew as appropriate.
10 Reassembly is a reversal of dismantling but use new gaskets and other components from the appropriate repair kit.
11 Grease the rocker arm and pivot before assembly.
12 When the pump is complete, place a finger over the inlet port and depress the rocker arm fully. A strong suction noise should be heard which indicates that the pump is operating correctly.

8 Carburettor (140J type) - description

The carburettor is of downdraught dual-barrel type with manually-operated choke. The primary throttle valve is mechanically operated while the secondary one is vacuum operated by a diaphragm capsule which is actuated by the vacuum in the carburettor venturi. (photos)
The cold starting device comprises a butterfly valve which closes one of the venturi tubes and is so synchronized with the primary valve plate that the latter opens sufficiently to provide a rich mixture and an increased slow-running speed for easy starting.

For idling and slow running, the fuel passes through the slow running jet, the primary slow air bleed and the secondary slow air bleed. The fuel is finally ejected from the by-pass and idle holes.

The accelerator pump is synchronized with the throttle valve. During periods of heavy acceleration, the pump which is of simple piston and valve construction, provides an additional metered quantity of fuel to enrich the normal mixture. The quantity of fuel metered can be varied according to operating climatic conditions by adjusting the stroke of the pump linkage.

The secondary system provides a mixture for normal motoring conditions by means of a main jet and air bleed. The float chamber is fed with fuel pumped by the mechanically operated pump on the crankcase. The level in the chamber is critical and must at all times be maintained as specified.

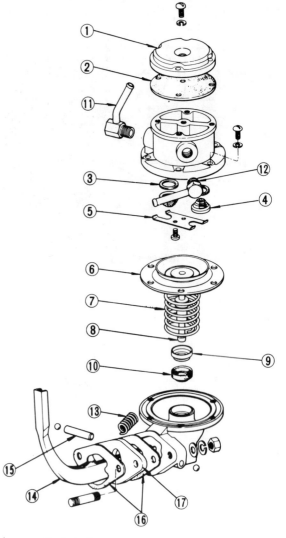

Fig. 3.11 Exploded view of the fuel pump

1 Cover	10 Seal
2 Gasket	11 Inlet union
3 Valve packing	12 Outlet union
4 Valve assembly	13 Rocker arm spring
5 Valve retainer	14 Rocker arm
6 Diaphragm	15 Pivot pin
7 Diaphragm spring	16 Gaskets
8 Pull rod	17 Insulator
9 Seal	

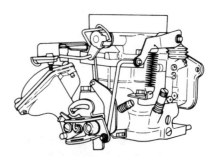

Fig. 3.12 Carburettor (140J type)

8.0A. View of 140J type carburettor

8.0B. View of 140J type carburettor

8.0C. View of 140J type carburettor

9 Carburettor (140J type) - slow-running adjustment

1　The following adjustment can be made without dismantling the carburettor. Other adjustments can only be carried out after removing and dismantling the unit and they are therefore included in the next Section.

2　Run the engine until normal operating temperature is reached and then set the throttle speed screw so that the idling speed is 600 rpm.

3　Now turn the mixture control screw in, or out, until the engine runs smoothly at its highest speed.

4　Re-adjust the idling speed to specification by unscrewing the throttle speed screw.

5　Alternative and more precise adjustment methods are: (a) to connect a vacuum gauge to the inlet manifold and to adjust the mixture control screw until the highest vacuum reading is obtained; (b) to use a device such as a Colortune in accordance with the manufacturer's instructions.

6　If the carburettor has been dismantled or the mixture control screw has been removed, the basic setting position for the screw is to screw it in gently with it seats and then unscrew it 2¼ turns.

10 Carburettor (140J type) - removal, servicing and refitting

1　Remove the air cleaner.

2　Disconnect the fuel inlet pipe from the carburettor.

3　Disconnect the distributor vacuum pipe from the carburettor, also the throttle control linkage. (photo)

4　Disconnect the choke cable from the carburettor.

5　Unscrew and remove the four nuts which secure the carburettor to the inlet manifold. (photo)

6　Lift the carburettor from the inlet manifold, discard the old gasket and clean the mating surfaces.

7　Clean the external surfaces of the carburettor by brushing with fuel or a solvent.

8　Unscrew and remove the main and slow jets. These can be unscrewed from outside the carburettor without any need to dismantle. Do not probe the jets with wire but blow any dirt from them using pressure from a tyre pump. It is worthwhile comparing the jet calibration numbers with those specified in case a previous owner has substituted any jets of incorrect size for the standard jets.

9　Remove the choke chamber after disconnecting the connecting rod, pump link, return spring, stop pin and three securing screws.

10 Withdraw the primary and secondary emulsion tubes after removing the main air bleeds.

11 Dismantle the accelerator pump if necessary after removing the pump arm. Do not lose the check ball.

12 Remove the throttle chamber from the float chamber by removing the diaphragm link rod and unscrewing the three chamber securing screws. It is not recommended that the valve butterfly plates are dismantled. If the valve spindles or bushes are worn it is much better to renew the complete carburettor.

13 Remove the float chamber cover and extract the float and needle valve assembly.

14 Remove the diaphragm (three screws) and then dismantle the unit after detaching the cover screws.

15 With the carburettor completely dismantled, clean and examine all components for wear. Obtain a repair kit which will contain all the necessary gaskets and other renewable items.

16 Reassembly is a reversal of dismantling but carry out the following checks and adjustments.

Float level

17 With the fuel inlet pipe attached to the carburettor turn the engine over on the starter motor so that the fuel pump operates and check that the fuel level is in alignment with the mark on the sight glass of the float chamber. If the fuel level is too high, or too low, bend the float arm as necessary. When the fuel level is correct, then check the stroke of the float arm which should

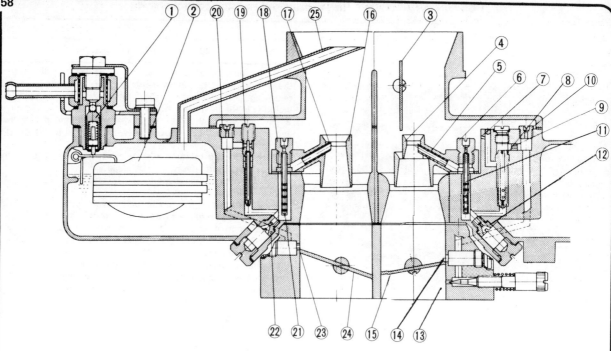

Fig. 3.13 Sectional view of 140J type carburettor

1 Fuel inlet valve	8 Slow jet	14 By-pass	20 Air bleed
2 Float	9 Slow economizer jet	15 Primary throttle valve	21 Secondary emulsion
3 Choke valve plate	10 2nd. slow air bleed	16 Secondary small venturi	tube
4 Primary (small) venturi	11 Primary emulsion tube	17 Secondary main nozzle	22 Secondary main jet
5 Primary main nozzle	12 Primary main jet	18 Secondary main air bleed	23 Bleed hole
6 Primary main air bleed	13 Idle nozzle	19 Bleed jet	24 Secondary throttle valve
7 1st. slow air bleed			25 Fuel vent

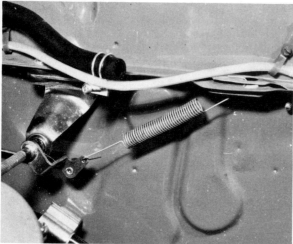

10.3. Throttle control rod return spring

10.5. Removing carburettor from manifold

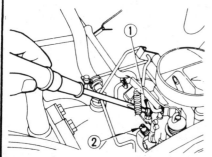

1 Throttle speed screw
2 Mixture screw

Fig. 3.14 Adjusting 140J type carburettor

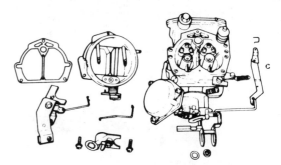

Fig. 3.15 Choke chamber components (140J carburettor)

be 0.040 in (1.0 mm). Correct this if necessary by bending the stop.

Fast idle

18 Hold the choke butterfly valve plate in the fully closed position with the fingers. Using a twist drill or rod, check the clearance between the edge of the throttle valve plate and the carburettor wall. This should be 0.06 in (1.4 mm). If necessary, bend the connecting rod to achieve this.

Primary/secondary interlock adjustment

19 When the primary throttle valve plate opens through 50°, if the interconnecting linkage is correctly adjusted, then the secondary system will be about to actuate. The simplest way to check the adjustment is to open the primary throttle valve plate until the connecting link (2) is at the end of the slot in the throttle arm (A). Now check the gap (G) between the edge of the primary throttle valve plate and the carburettor chamber wall. This should be 0.25 in (6.3 mm) otherwise bend the connecting link.

20 Installation is a reversal of removal but use a new gasket and check that the choke cable has a small amount of slack to ensure that the valve plate is fully open when the control knob is pushed in.

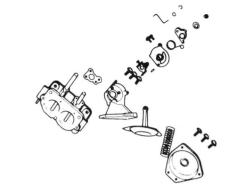

Fig. 3.19 Diaphragm dismantled (140J carburettor)

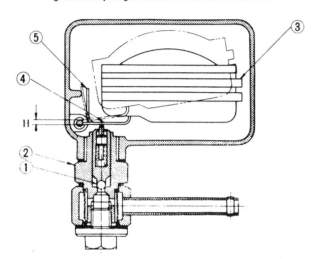

Fig. 3.20 Float adjustment diagram (140J carburettor inverted H is float stroke 0.040 in - 1.0 mm)

1   Ball valve
2   Valve seat
3   Float
4   Float arm
5   Stop

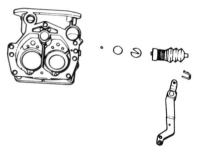

Fig. 3.16 Accelerator pump components (140J carburettor)

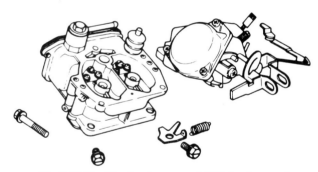

Fig. 3.17 Throttle chamber removal (140J carburettor)

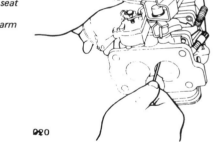

Fig. 3.21 Checking fast idle setting of throttle valve plate (140J)

Fig. 3.18. Float chamber components (140J carbuettor,

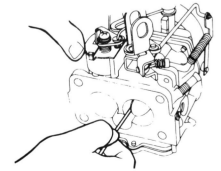

Fig. 3.23 Checking throttle interlock primary valve plate opening (140J)

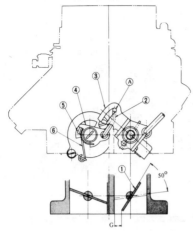

Fig. 3.22 Throttle valve interlock adjustment diagram (140J carburettor)

1 *Primary throttle valve plate*
2 *Link rod*
3 *Throttle arm*
4 *Rocking arm*
5 *Secondary throttle arm*
6 *Return spring*

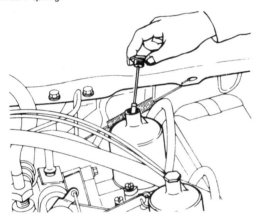

Fig. 3.24 Checking the damper oil (160J SSS carburettor)

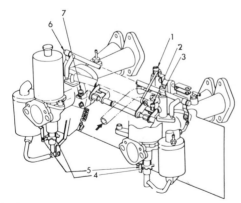

Fig. 3.25 Twin carburettor installation (160J SSS)

1 *Throttle speed screw*
2 *Balance screw*
3 *Mixture screw*
4 *Jet adjusting nut*
5 *Adjusting nut limiter*
6 *Balance tube*
7 *Throttle stop screw*

11 Carburettors (160J SSS type) - description

1 The twin carburettor installation comprises horizontally mounted units of variable jet (SU) type. The choke control is manually operated.
2 Periodically unscrew and remove each of the damper rods. Inspect the oil level which should be between the high and low marks on the rod. Top-up as necessary with SAE 10-30 engine oil.
3 Apply a few drops of oil to the accelerator linkage.

12 Carburettors (160J SSS) - slow-running adjustment

1 Run the engine until normal operating temperature is reached.
2 Set the throttle speed screw so that the engine idles at 650 rpm.
3 Switch off the engine and remove the air cleaner assembly.
4 Re-start the engine and have an assistance depress the accelerator pedal and hold the engine speed steady at 1500 rpm.
5 Using an air flowmeter balance the carburettors. Press the flowmeter against the air cleaner mounting flange of the front carburettor and note the meter reading. If the meter has an adjustment screw, turn it until the float is at the middle position on the scale.
6 Now press the flowmeter against the air cleaner mounting flange of the rear carburettor and adjust the balance screw (on the carburettor) until the reading on the flowmeter is the same as that previously recorded for the front carburettor. Do not touch the flowmeter adjustment screw (if fitted).
7 Allow the engine to return to idling speed and refit the air cleaner.
8 Now adjust the mixture control screw within the range of the limiter cap until the fuel/air ratio is correct. This can be determined either by using a device such as a Colortune or a CO meter (rate 3%). Turning the screw clockwise enrichens the mixture and turning it anticlockwise weakens it. If the adjustment operations continue for more than three minutes with the engine idling, rev the engine to prevent the spark plugs fouling and then let the engine resume its idling speed again for a few seconds before continuing the adjustment. On no account disturb the setting of the jet adjusting nut at the base of the carburettor.

13 Carburettors (160J SSS) - removal, servicing and refitting

1 Remove the air cleaner assembly.
2 Disconnect the choke and throttle controls.
3 Disconnect the fuel inlet pipe and the distributor vacuum tube.
4 Unbolt the two carburettors from the inlet manifold and remove them.
5 Do not dismantle the carburettor unnecessarily. With the carburettors removed, unscrew and remove the damper pistons and raise each of the suction pistons about ½ in (12.5 mm) by inserting the finger through the hole in the air cleaner mounting flange. Release the pistons and check that they drop smoothly without any tendency to stick and are heard to seat with a definite metallic 'clunk'. Where this is not the case, unscrew the two securing screws and lift the suction chamber from the carburettor body.
6 Withdraw the piston, spring and needle assembly.
7 Any discoloration or deposits should be removed from the piston or chamber surfaces with solvent or metal polish, do not use abrasive materials.
8 Do not disturb the needle or jet assembly as these are preset in production.
9 Remove the float chamber cover, extract the float and arm and clean any sediment from the bowl.
10 Should it be necessary to dismantle the linkage or control

rods and levers, mark or sketch the positions of the components to ensure exact replacement.

11 Reassembly is a reversal of dismantling but check and adjust if necessary the float level. To do this, the drain plug will have to be removed from the float chamber and a special gauge installed. Alternatively, a nozzle with a piece of plastic tubing can be substituted. With the carburettors in position on the inlet manifold, turn the engine over on the starter until the float chambers are filled and then read off the fuel level on the gauge or plastic tube (held vertically). The distance between the float chamber cover mating face and the surface of the fuel should be 0.98 in (25.0 mm) for the front carburettor.

12 For the rear carburettor, the distance should be 0.79 in (20.0 mm).

13 Where adjustment is required, remove the float chamber cover and bend the float arm.

14 Refitting is a reversal of removal but use new flange gaskets.

14 Carburettor (710 series) - description

The carburettor is of downdraught dual barrel type. There are slight differences between the units used on vehicles equipped with manual or automatic transmission (see Specifications Section).

The carburettor incorporates an econonizer device which smooths the changeover from steady throttle openings to acceleration or deceleration during periods of light engine loading. An electrically heated automatic choke is used and an anti-dieseling (run-on) solenoid valve cuts off the fuel supply as soon as the ignition is switched off in order to prevent running-on of the engine. A vacuum-operated power valve ensures smooth high speed operation. A boost control deceleration device (B.C.D.D.) reduces the emission of noxious exhaust gas during periods of deceleration. Vehicles equipped with automatic transmission built up to 1975 and all 710 seroes vehicles produced thereafter, incorporate a dashpot to smooth out deceleration while eliminating any tendency for the engine to stall.

On models destined for operation in California, an altitude compensator is installed to vary the fuel/air mixture ratio according to the prevailing atmospheric pressure.

15 Carburettor (710 series) - adjustments with carburettor installed

The following checks and adjustments can be carried out with the carburettor in-situ.

Slow-running adjustment

1 Run the engine until the normal operating temperature is attained. On 1975 models, disconnect the hose between the three-way connector and the air check valve and plug the hose.

2 Adjust the throttle speed screw until the engine idling speed is:

	Up to 1975	1975 onwards
Manual transmission	800 rpm	750 rpm
Automatic transmission (in 'D')	650 rpm	650 rpm

3 Using a CO meter, adjust the mixture control screw to give a CO reading of 1.5% for models built up to 1975 and 2% for vehicles produced thereafter.

4 Re-adjust the throttle speed screw if necessary to bring the idling speed within that specified and re-check the CO reading.

5 A limiter cap is fitted to the mixture control screw and this should not be removed but the screw only adjusted within the limits of the cap. Should the cap have been broken or inadvertently removed, proceed as described in the preceding paragraphs 1 to 4. With the slow-running correctly adjusting, fit the cap so that it can only be turned 1/8th of an inch in the 'RICH' direction before meeting the stop.

Dashpot adjustment

6 Run the engine to normal operating temperature and check that the slow-running adjustment is correct.

7 Release the dashpot locknut and then adjust the position of the dashpot so that it just touches the stop plate when the engine is running at between 1900 and 2100 rpm for manual transmission and between 1650 and 1850 rpm for vehicles equipped with automatic transmission ('N' or 'P'), with the throttle linkage held open with the hand.

8 Retighten the locknut without moving the dashpot.

9 Raise the engine speed to about 2000 rpm and suddenly release the accelerator. The engine speed should be reduced to 1000 rpm in approximately three seconds otherwise the adjustment has been incorrectly carried out or the dashpot is faulty.

Boost controlled deceleration device (B.C.D.D.) - adjustment

It is very unusual for this operation to be required but if new components have been installed or performance is suspect proceed in the following manner.

10 A tachometer and Bourdon type vacuum gauge will be required.

11 Run the engine until normal operating temperature is reached and then connect the vacuum gauge by inserting a tee-piece into the air cleaner vacuum capsule pipe. Connect the tachometer in accordance with the maker's instructions.

12 Disconnect the vacuum control solenoid valve.

13 Raise the engine speed to between 3000 and 3500 rpm and then suddenly release the throttle. The manifold vacuum pressure will gradually decrease to indicate the B.C.D.D. operating pressure which should be:

Manual transmission - 19.69 in Hg (500 mm Hg)
Automatic transmission - 18.90 in Hg (480 mm Hg)

14 If the presure indicated on the gauge is higher than that specified, turn the adjusting screw on the valve in an anti-clockwise direction, if lower, turn the screw clockwise. Repeat the testing procedure.

Choke cover adjustment

15 The normal position of the automatic choke bi-metal cover is for the mark on the cover to be opposite to the centre mark of the choke housing index. Where there is a tendency to over choke on starting up, turn the cover in a clockwise direction by not more than one division.

16 In cold climates if the starting mixture is not sufficiently rich, turn the cover slightly in an anticlockwise direction.

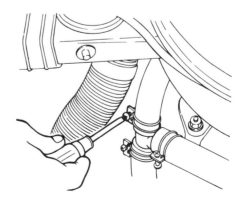

Fig. 3.26 Disconnecting hose from air check valve (710 series carburettor)

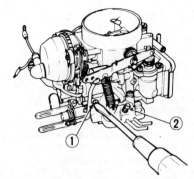

Fig. 3.27 Carburettor adjustment screws (710 series)

1 *Throttle speed screw*
2 *Mixture screw*

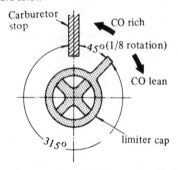

**Fig. 3.28 Mixture control screw limiter cap installation diagram
(710 series carburettors)**

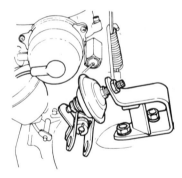

Fig. 3.29 Location of dashpot (710 series carburettors)

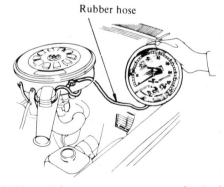

**Fig. 3.30 Method of connecting vacuum gauge for checking
B.C.D.D. (710 series vehicles)**

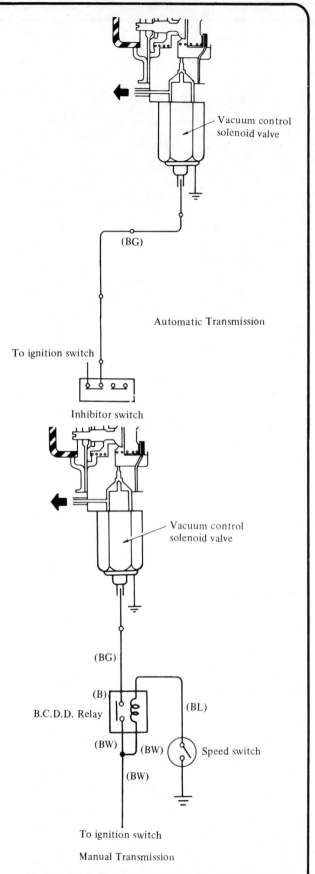

**Fig. 3.31 B.C.D.D. vacuum control valve and connections
(710 series)**

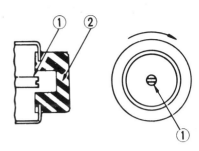

Fig. 3.32 B.C.D.D. valve adjusting screw (1) and cover (2)

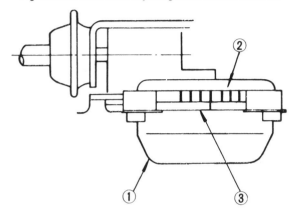

Fig. 3.33 Automatic choke (710 series)

(1) Cover
(2) Housing
(3) Setting index

---

16 Carburettor (710 series) - removal, servicing and refitting

1   Remove the air cleaner (see Section 3).
2   Disconnect the fuel and vacuum pipes from the carburettor, also the leads to the automatic choke and anti-dieseling solenoid valve.
3   Disconnect the throttle linkage from the carburettor.
4   Unscrew the four securing nuts and remove the carburettor from the inlet manifold.
5   Clean any dirt from the external surfaces of the unit with solvent or fuel.
6   From the primary side of the carburettor, remove the throttle return spring, pump lever and rod and the cam link rod.
7   Remove the automatic choke cover (three screws).
8   Remove the choke chamber (four screws) and detach the throttle return spring from the secondary side of the carburettor.
9   Remove the float chamber (four screws).
10 Remove the diaphragm chamber and gasket, the fast idle cam, the cam spring and the lever.
11 Remove the hollow bolt, the banjo union and the filter and stop plate.
12 Dismantle the accelerator pump and outlet valve taking care not to lose the ball and weight.
13 Remove the ventures, main air bleeds and emulsion tubes from the primary and secondary sides of the carburettor.
14 Remove the slow jet and slow air bleed, primary and secondary main jets.
15 If necessary, the fuel level gauge and float can be removed from the float chamber.
16 Remove the power valve.
17 Remove the return plate, sleeve, fast idle lever, spring hanger and throttle lever.
18 Unscrew the antidieseling valve by unscrewing it from the carburettor body.

19 The B.C.D.D. unit can be removed after unscrewing the securing screws.
20 Clean and examine all components for wear. If the throttle plates or spindles or bushes are worn, it is recommended that the carburettor is renewed complete.
21 Obtain a repair kit which will contain all the necessary gaskets and other items requiring renewal.
22 Only clean jets by blowing through them with air from a tyre pump, never probe them with wire. It is worth checking their calibrations against those listed in Specifications in case a previous owner has substituted jets of incorrect size for the standard jets.
23 Reassembly is a reversal of dismantling but the following special procedures and adjustments must be carried out.
24 Apply jointing compound to antidieseling solenoid threads before installing it. If possible leave it overnight for the sealant to set before fuel is allowed into contact with it.

Float level adjustment
25 The fuel level, when viewed through the sight glass of the float chamber should be 0.91 in (23.0 mm) below the chamber top flange. Where the level is incorrect, invert the float chamber and bend the float arm as necessary to provide the dimension 'H' as shown in the diagram. Now check that the stroke of the float arm (h) is between 0.051 and 0.067 in (1.3 and 1.7 mm). If necessary, bend the stop to achieve this.

Fast idle adjustment
26 When the automatic choke is fully closed for cold starting, the fast idle cam opens the throttle by a predetermined amount to provide a fast idle setting of:

Manual transmission	1900 to 2100 rpm
Automatic transmission	2300 to 2500 rpm

Minor adjustments to the fast idle speed can be made by turning the fast idle screw in, or out, as necessary.
27 If the carburettor has been completely dismantled or new components have been fitted, before installing the carburettor, set the fast idle screw on the second step of the cam and adjust the screw so that the dimension 'A' between the edge of the throttle valve plate and the carburettor is as follows:

Manual transmission	0.040 to 0.048 in (1.01 to 1.21 mm)
Automatic transmission	0.048 to 0.052 in (1.23 to 1.33 mm)

Use a twist drill or rod of suitable diameter to carry out the measuring. A further minor adjustment can be made to the fast idle screw when the carburettor is installed and the engine is running under cold start conditions.

Vacuum break adjustment
28 This arrangement opens the choke valve plate after the engine has been started to provide the correct fuel/air ratio of the mixture under the prevailing engine operating conditions.
29 The correct setting should be checked and any adjustment carried out in the following manner. Close the choke valve plate completely with the fingers and retain the valve plate in this position using a rubber band.
30 With a pair of pliers, grip the end of the vacuum diaphragm capsule operating rod and withdraw it as far as it will go without straining it. Now bend the connecting rod to provide a clearance between the edge of the choke valve plate and the carburettor of 0.065 in (1.65 mm).
31 Refitting the carburettor to the manifold is a reversal of removal.

---

17 Altitude compensator (710 series vehicles - California)

---

1   Any malfunction of the compensator can only be rectified by renewal of the complete unit.
2   To check for a faulty unit, attach a length of tubing to the inlet and outlet hoses and suck and blow as appropriate. If there is no restriction during these operations then either the inlet, or outlet, valve will have failed.

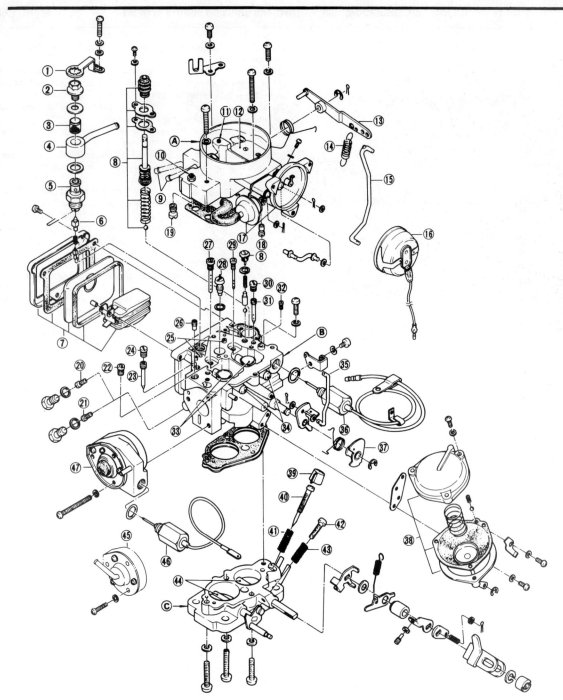

Fig. 3.34 Exploded view of carburettor (710 series, 1975 onwards)

A Choke chamber
1 Lockplate
2 Bolt
3 Filter
4 Banjo union
5 Fuel inlet needle valve body
6 Needle valve
7 Float and sight glass
  components
8 Accelerator pump
9 Altitude compensator
  connecting pipes
  (California 1975 onwards)
10 Coating air bleed
  adjusting screw
11 High speed air
  bleed (enricher)

B Centre body
12 Choke valve plate
13 Accelerator pump lever
14 Throttle return spring
15 Accelerator pump rod
16 Automatic choke cover
17 Automatic choke housing
18 Enriching jet
19 Coating air bleed
20 Primary main jet
21 Secondary main jet
22 Secondary slow air bleed
23 Secondary slow jet
24 Plug
25 Pressed in metering hole

C Throttle chamber
26 Coating jet
27 Secondary main air bleed
28 Power valve
29 Primary main air bleed
30 Plug
31 Primary slow jet
32 Primary slow air bleed no. 2
33 Primary and secondary
  small venturis
34 Venturi stop screw
35 Choke connecting rod
36 Anti-dieseling
  solenoid valve
37 Fast idle cam

38 Diaphragm chamber
39 Mixture screw limiter cap
40 Mixture adjusting screw
41 Spring
42 Throttle speed screw
43 Spring
44 Primary and secondary
  throttle valves
45 B.C.D.D. assembly
  (California only)
46 Vacuum control
  solenoid valve
47 B.C.D.D. assembly (except
  (California)

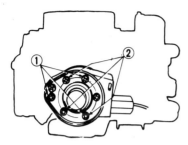

Fig. 3.35 B.C.D.D. securing screws (1) and body assembly screws (2)

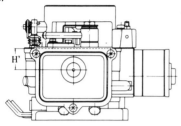

H' = 23 mm (0.91 in)

Fig. 3.36. Fuel level diagram (710 series carburettor)

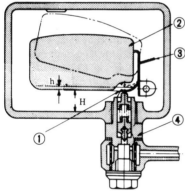

Fig. 3.37 Float adjustment diagram (710 series carburettor, inverted)

1 Float arm   4 Fuel inlet needle valve
2 Float   H = 0.283 in (7.2 mm)
3 Stop   h = 0.051 to 0.067 in (1.3 to 1.7 mm)

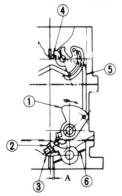

Fig. 3.38. Fast idle adjustment diagram (710 series carburettor)

1 Fast idle cam   5 Link rod
2 Locknut   6 Throttle valve plate
3 Fast idle adjustment screw A see text
4 Choke valve plate

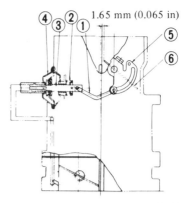

1.65 mm (0.065 in)

Fig. 3.39. Vacuum break adjustment diagram (710 series carburettor)

1 Operating rod
2 Spring
3 Piston
4 Diaphragm capsule
5 Lever
6 Choke valve plate

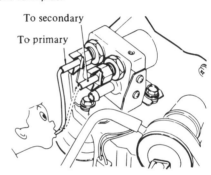

To secondary

To primary

Fig. 3.40. Altitude compensator (California models)

18 Emission control system - description and application

The complexity of the system used varies with the vehicle model and date of production. All vehicles are equipped with a crankcase emission control system (see Section 23, Chapter 1).

710 series vehicles built up until 1975 incorporate:

(i) *Exhaust gas recirculation (EGR) system.* This system returns some of the exhaust gas to the combustion chamber which lowers the combustion temperature and helps to reduce the nitrogen oxide content in the exhaust gas.

(ii) *Fuel evaporative emission control system.* The system comprises a non-vented fuel tank, a separator, a vent line and a flow guide valve.

When the engine is not operating, the system is filled with fuel vapour produced by the fuel in the tank. When the pressure of this vapour reaches a predetermined level, the vapour actuates the flow guide valve and passes into the crankcase.

As soon as the engine is started, the fuel vapour in the crankcase, air cleaner and the inlet manifold are drawn into the combustion chamber and ignited.

Whenever the pressure of vapour in the fuel tank falls (due to reduction in the fuel contents) and a condition of vacuum could prevail within the tank, the flow guide valve opens to admit air to the tank and this is drawn in through the air cleaner.

710 series vehicles built from 1975 onwards incorporate:

(iii) *Exhaust gas heated hotspot valve* This is simply a valve controlled by a bi-metal spring which deflects the gases entering the exhaust manifold to heat the fuel vapour passing through the inlet manifold. As the engine warms up, the bi-metal spring opens the valve and the exhaust gases are no longer deflected.

(iv)   *Spark timing control system* The system overrides the normal distributor vacuum advance and retard movement under certain periods of engine operation in order to reduce excess emissions of noxious exhaust gas. The device is not fitted to Saloon and Hardtop models destined for operation in California.

(v)   *Air injection system.* This is a method of injecting air (generated in an external compressor) into the exhaust ports in order to dilute the combustion gases before they are emitted from the exhaust system. The system when fitted to models destined for operation in California includes an air control valve and an emergency air relief valve.

(vi)   *Catelytic converter.* Installed in the exhaust system of vehicles destined for California, this device speeds up the chemical reaction of the hydrocarbons and carbon monoxide present in the exhaust gases so that they change into harmless carbon dioxide and water. Air for the chemical process is supplied by the air compressor pump.

(vii)   *Exhaust gas recirculation (EGR) system.* This is similar to the system used on earlier 710 series vehicles.

(viii)   *Evaporative emission control system.* This system comprises a non-vented fuel tank, a separator, a vent line, carbon canister and a vacuum signal line.

Fuel vapour is emitted from the fuel tank and is stored in the canister (which is filled with activated carbon) during periods when the engine is not running.

As the throttle is opened, vacuum increases in the vacuum signal line and opens the purge control valve to admit vapour through the main valve port and thence to the inlet manifold.

In addition to the foregoing systems, the Boost Control Deceleration Device (B.C.D.D.) and the Altitude Compensator can be considered as essential parts of the emission control system and reference should be made to Sections 15 and 17 of this Chapter.

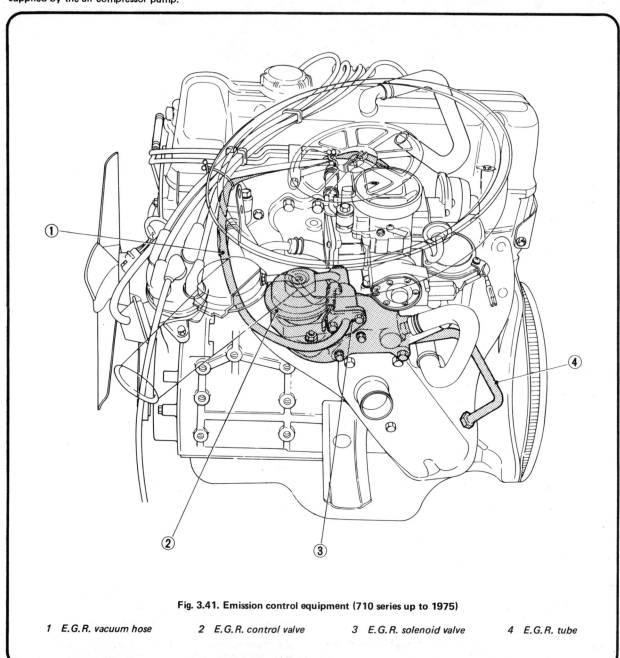

Fig. 3.41. Emission control equipment (710 series up to 1975)

1 E.G.R. vacuum hose   2 E.G.R. control valve   3 E.G.R. solenoid valve   4 E.G.R. tube

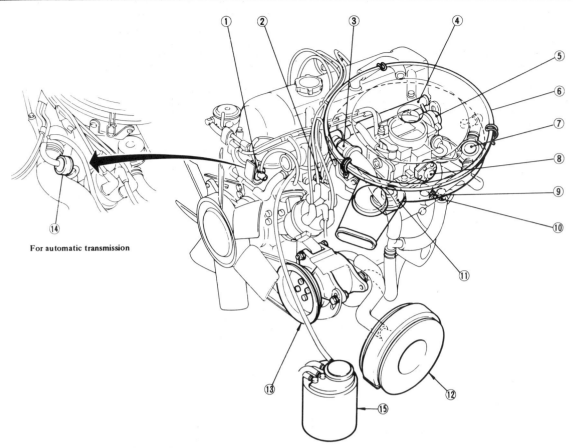

Fig. 3.42. Emission control equipment (710 series, 1975 onwards except California)

For automatic transmission

1 Vacuum switching valve	5 Automatic choke	9 P.C.V. valve	13 Air pump
2 Thermal vacuum valve	6 Air cleaner	10 Air relief valve	14 Spark delay
3 Check valve	7 Anti-backfire valve	11 E.G.R. control valve	valve
4 Air gallery	8 B.C.D.D.	12 Air pump air cleaner	15 Carbon canister

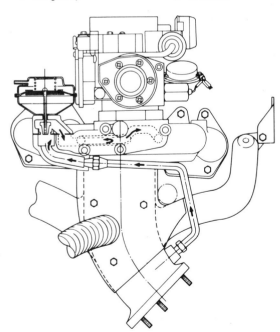

Fig. 3.44. Exhaust gas recirculation (E.G.R.) control system up to 1975

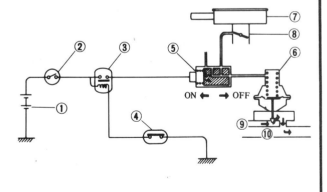

Fig. 3.45. Layout of E.G.R. control system

1 Battery	6 E.G.R. control valve
2 Ignition switch	7 Aur cleaner
3 E.G.R. control relay	8 Throttle valve plate
4 Water temperature switch	9 Exhaust passage
5 E,G,R, solenoid valve	10 Inlet manifold

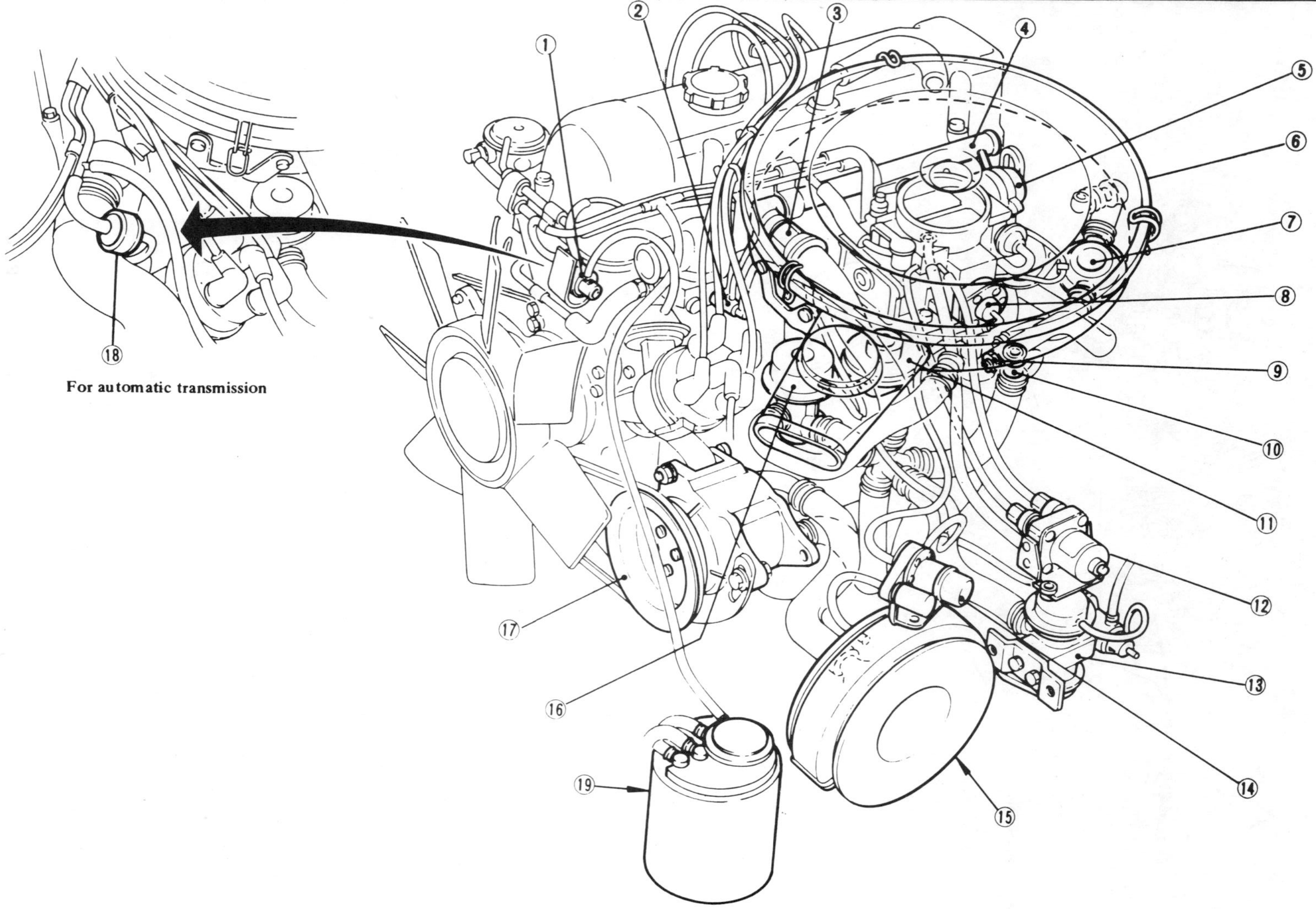

Fig. 3.43. Emission control equipment (710 series, 1975 onwards California)

For automatic transmission

1 Vacuum switching valve
2 Thermal vacuum valve
3 Check valve
4 Air gallery
5 Automatic

6 Air cleaner
7 Anti-backfire valve
8 Boost controlled deceleration device
9 Positive crankcase ventilation valve

choke
10 Air relief valve
11 Exhaust gas recirculation control valve

control valve
12 Altitude compensator
13 Emergency air relief valve

14 Boost controlled deceleration device valve assembly
15 Air pump air cleaner

16 Air control valve
17 Air pump
18 Spark delay valve
19 Carbon canister

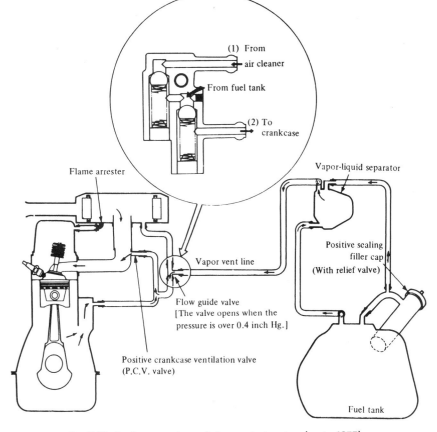

Fig. 3.46. Fuel evaporative emission control system (up to 1975)

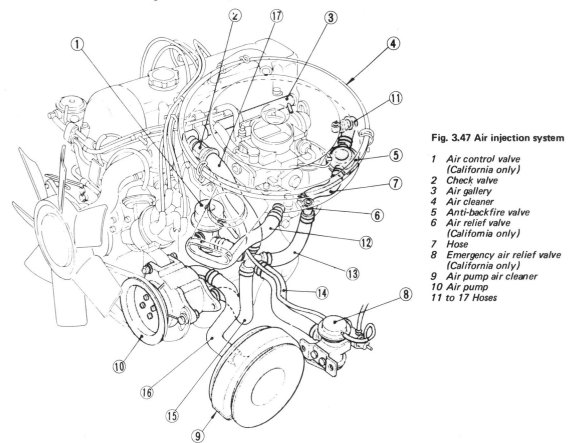

Fig. 3.47 Air injection system

1 Air control valve
  (California only)
2 Check valve
3 Air gallery
4 Air cleaner
5 Anti-backfire valve
6 Air relief valve
  (California only)
7 Hose
8 Emergency air relief valve
  (California only)
9 Air pump air cleaner
10 Air pump
11 to 17 Hoses

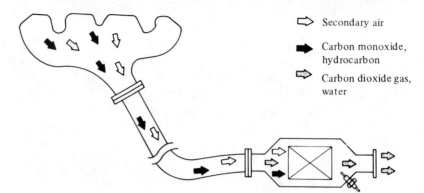

Fig. 3.48. Location of catalytic converter in exhaust gas stream

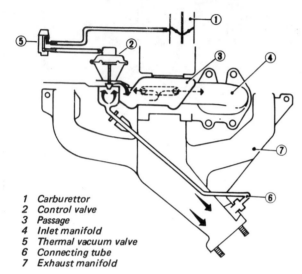

1 Carburettor
2 Control valve
3 Passage
4 Inlet manifold
5 Thermal vacuum valve
6 Connecting tube
7 Exhaust manifold

Fig. 3.49 Exhaust gas recirculation (E.G.R) control system,
1975 onwards

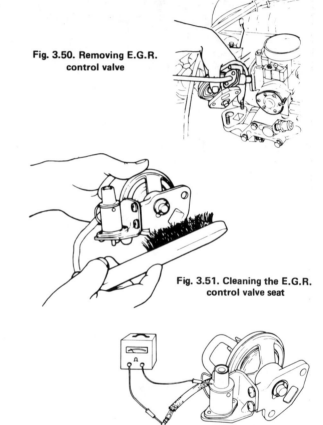

Fig. 3.50. Removing E.G.R.
control valve

Fig. 3.51. Cleaning the E.G.R.
control valve seat

Fig. 3.52. Checking the E.G.R. solenoid valve with an ohmmeter

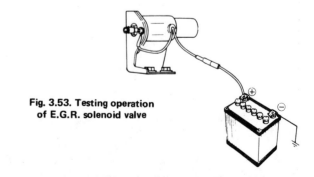

Fig. 3.53. Testing operation
of E.G.R. solenoid valve

19 E.G.R. system (up to 1975) - maintenance and testing

1   Check the complete system for insecure or damaged hoses.
Tighten or renew as appropriate.
2   Periodically, remove the E.G.R. control valve and clean its
seat with a wire brush.
3   The control valve can be checked for correct vacuum
operation by connecting a piece of hose to it and sucking with
the mouth. The valve should move into its fully extended
position and retain this attitude for at least 30 seconds after the
vacuum ceases.
4   To check the E.G.R. valve solenoid, first connect it to an
ohmmeter as shown. If the meter needle deflects, then the
solenoid is electrically sound. Now connect the solenoid directly
to a battery. Make and break the connection intermittently. If
the solenoid valve clicks then it is in good condition.
5   The only other component which is likely to give trouble is
the thermal switch. To test this, partially drain the engine
cooling system and unscrew the switch from the cylinder head
(adjacent to cooling system water temperature switch).
6   Connect the switch to an ohmmeter and then suspend the
switch in a beaker of water being heated. Start with the water
temperature below 77° F (25° C) and the switch should be open
(reading infinity). As the water is heated, the ohmmeter reading
should drop to zero between a water temperature of between 88
and 106° F (31 and 41° C) and remain there as the temperature
climbs.

Fig. 3.55. E.G.R. warning system

1   *Detector drive counter*   2   *Warning lamp*   3   *odometer*

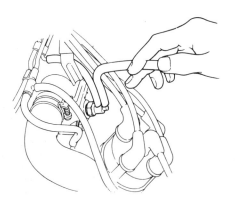

Fig. 3.54. Testing E.G.R. system thermal switch (up to 1975)   **Fig. 3.56. Testing E.G.R. system thermal vacuum valve (1975 onwards)**

20 E.G.R. system (1975 onwards) - maintenance and testing

1 The procedure is similar to that just described for earlier models but the following additional or modified components should be noted.

2 The system has a warning circuit. Check that the warning lamp lights when the ignition switch is turned to 'START'. If it does not illuminate, check the wiring, connections and bulb.

3 If the detector drive counter has not reached 50,000 counts, the warning lamp should be out but when it exceeds 50,000 the lamp should light, indicating that the E.G.R. system needs checking and maintenance. Reset ohmmeter to zero by inserting a screwdriver in the hole provided in the detector drive counter. The hole is normally sealed with a grommet. This device is not installed on vehicles destined for California or Canada.

4 A thermal type vacuum valve is used in place of the thermal switch used in earlier models. To test its operation, unscrew it from the cylinder head and then immerse it in a beaker of water, first having fitted the valve with two lengths of tubing to prevent water entering. Suck the end of the tube to apply vacuum to the valve while heating the water in the beaker and note that the vacuum passage should only open at a temperature between 134 and 145° F (57 to 63° C) and remain open as the temperature climbs.

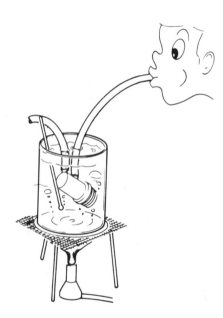

Fig. 3.57. Checking temperature function of thermal vacuum valve

21 Fuel evaporative emission control system (up to 1975) - maintenance and testing

1 Inspect the condition and security of all connecting hoses and renew any that have deteriorated.

2 If the flow guide valve is suspected of being faulty disconnect all hoses from it and then apply air pressure to the upper nozzle. The valve should open at an air pressure of 0.4 in Hg (10 mm Hg), if it does not operate correctly, renew it.

3 Check the operation of the filler cap pressure relief valve by sucking it with the mouth. An initial slight resistance followed by the valve making a clicking noise will indicate that it is in good order.

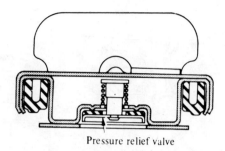

Pressure relief valve

Fig. 3.58. Sectional view of the fuel tank filler cap

22 Fuel evaporative emission control system (1975 onwards) - maintenance and testing

1 Check the security and condition of the connecting hoses.

2 To check the operation of the carbon canister purge control valve, disconnect the hose (which runs between the 'Tee' connector and the canister diaphragm cover) at the tee connector. Suck the end of the hose to verify that there is no leak. If there is, renew the diaphragm.

3 Periodically, renew the filter at the base of the carbon canister.

4 Check the filler cap relief valve, as described in the preceding Section.

23 Exhaust gas heated hotspot valve - inspection

1 Periodically inspect the operation of the heat control valve. On starting with the engine cold, the counterweight should be in its extreme anticlockwise position.

2 During engine acceleration (engine still cold) the counterweight will rotate in a clockwise direction.

3 When the engine reaches normal operating temperature, the counterweight will have moved fully clockwise.

4 External components of the device can be renewed but as the internal valve plate is welded to the operating shaft, any fault or wear in these items will necessitate renewal of the complete manifold assembly.

24 Spark timing control system - maintenance and testing

Manual transmission

1 Check the condition and security of all electrical leads and vacuum hoses.

2 Connect a stroboscope (see Chapter 4 - Ignition), start the engine (already at normal operating temperature) and hold the engine speed at a steady 1800 rpm.

3 Depress the clutch pedal and move the gearshift lever to top, third and neutral while an assistant observes the ignition timing marks. The control system is functioning correctly if the crankshaft pulley timing mark appears to be 5° advanced in top and neutral compared with third gear. If the alteration in timing is not apparent, renew one or both switches as necessary.

Automatic transmission

4 The system incorporates a valve which delays the ignition advance during periods of rapid acceleration.

5 To check the operation of the valve, remove it and then blow into it from the carburettor connecting side. The flow of air should be much greater than when blowing in the reverse direction.

6 Renew the valve assembly every 24,000 miles (38000 km).

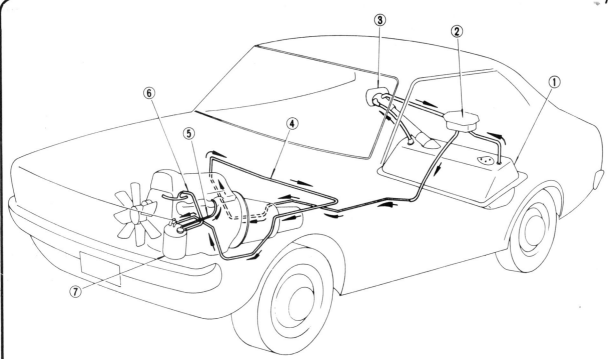

Fig. 3.59. Layout and location of components of fuel evaporative emission control
system (710 series saloon and hardtop 1975 onwards)

1 Tank   vapour separator)   4 Vapour vent line   6 Vacuum signal line
2 Reservoir tank (liquid/   3 Filler cap   5 Carbon canister purge line 7 Carbon canister

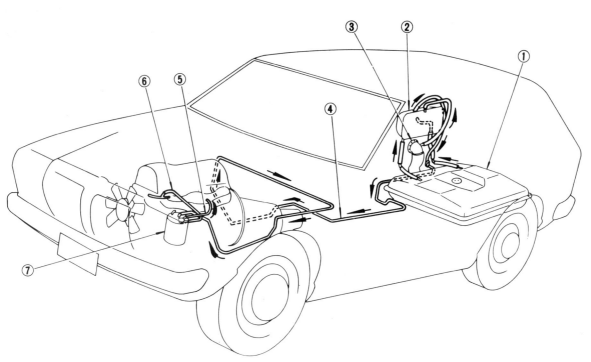

Fig. 3.60. Layout and location of components of fuel evaporative emission control
system (710 series wagon 1975 onwards)

1 Tank   separator)   4 Vapour vent line   6 Vacuum signal line
2 Reservoir tank (liquid/   3 Filler cap   5 Carbon canister purge line 7 Carbon canister

Fig. 3.61. Checking carbon canister purge control valve for split diaphragm

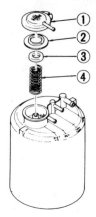

1 Cover
2 Diaphragm
3 Retainer
4 Spring

Fig. 3.62. Components of the carbon canister purge control valve

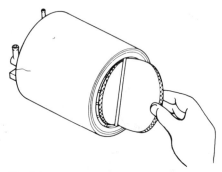

Fig. 3.63. Renewing the carbon canister filter

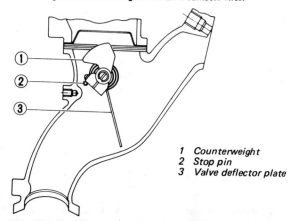

1 Counterweight
2 Stop pin
3 Valve deflector plate

Fig. 3.64. Position of exhaust gas heated hotspot valve with engine cold

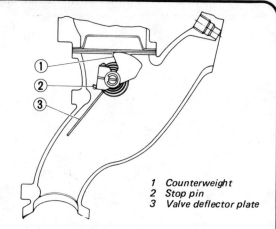

1 Counterweight
2 Stop pin
3 Valve deflector plate

Fig 3.65. Position of exhaust gas heated hotspot valve with engine hot

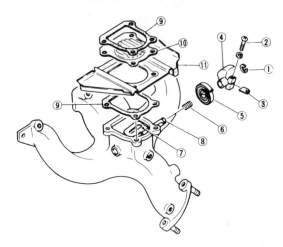

Fig. 3.66. Exploded view of the exhaust manifold and hotspot valve

1 Circlip
2 Pinch bolt
3 Key
4 Counterweight
5 Bi-metal spring
6 Spring
7 Valve deflector plate
8 Shaft
9 Gasket
10 Heat transfer plate
11 Heat shield

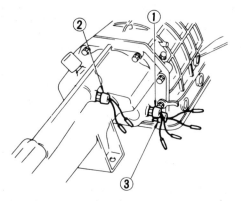

Fig. 3.67. Location of neutral and top gear switches (manual transmission)

1 Top gear switch
2 Neutral switch
3 Reversing lamp switch

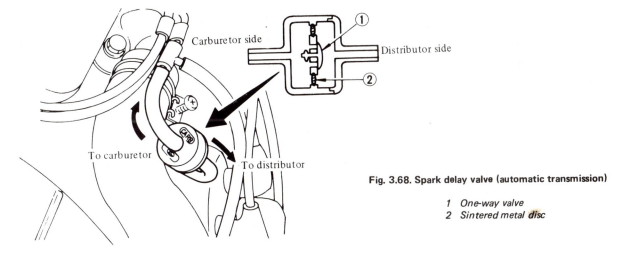

Fig. 3.68. Spark delay valve (automatic transmission)

1 One-way valve
2 Sintered metal disc

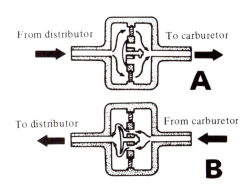

Fig. 3.69. Spark delay valve flow pattern   *A Less flow*
                                             B Greater flow

25 Air injection system - maintenance and testing

1 Check all hoses, air gallery pipes and nozzles for security and condition.
2 Check and adjust the air pump drivebelt tension (refer to Chapter 1, Section 47).
3 With the engine at normal operating temperature, disconnect the hose leading to the non-return valve.
4 Run the engine at approximately 2000 rpm and then let it return to idling speed, all the time watching for exhaust gas leaks from the valve. Where these are evident, renew the valve.
5 Check the operation of the air pump relief valve by first disconnecting the hoses from the non-return valve and then removing the air control valve from the hose connector. Plug the connector.
6 Run the engine at a steady 3000 rpm and place the hand on the air outlet of the air pump relief valve. A good air pressure should be felt but if it is not, renew the valve.
7 To check the air control valve, let the engine idle at normal operating temperature and disconnect the hose from the outlet nozzle of the valve. Place the hand over the nozzle and check for air pressure. If none is evident, renew the valve.
8 Now pull the vacuum hose from the air control valve. If air ejection ceases from the outlet nozzle, the valve is in good condition but if it persists, renew the valve which must be faulty.
9 The anti-backfire valve (flame-trap) can be checked, when the engine is at normal operating temperature, by disconnecting the hose from the air cleaner and placing a finger over the end of the hose. Run the engine at about 3,000 rpm and then return it to idling. During this action, a strong suction effect should be

felt on the finger which indicates that the valve is in good order.
10 Every 12,000 miles (19,000 km), renew the air pump air cleaner element. The assembly is located on the side of the engine compartment close to the air pump. The element and cleaner lower body are disposable being an integral unit. A faulty or worn air pump should be renewed on an exchange basis.

26 Catalytic converter - maintenance and testing

1 Check all hoses and electrical leads for security.
2 Only certain tests can be carried out without the use of special instruments and testing equipment. These are described in the following paragraphs.
3 To check the emergency air relief valve place the gearshift lever in neutral or the speed selector (automatic transmission) in 'P' and allow the engine to idle.
4 Pull the hose (5) from the valve and make sure that air is not being discharged from it. Reconnect it.
5 Pull off the connectors 'A' and 'B' and check that air is not being discharged from the air cleaner. If air is being ejected, during either of the preceding tests, switch off the engine and disconnect tubes (1) and (4). Connect terminals 'A' and 'B' directly to a 12v battery and blow through the tube (4) checking that air comes out of (2) but not from (1). Now disconnect the battery and blow into the tube (4) again. Air should now be ejected from (1) but not from (2). Where the correct pattern of operation is not evident, renew the solenoid valve, the relief valve or the complete assembly.
6 To check the operation of the catalytic converter, let the engine idle and using a CO meter measure the exhaust gases at the end of the exhaust tail pipe. The percentage must be below 0.3%. If it is above, renew the converter.
7 Should the catalyzer temperature rise abnormally, a warning light will come on. Whenever the ignition switch is turned to the start position, the lamp comes on (to verify the serviceability of the bulb) but goes out as soon as the engine fires. If the lamp comes on during normal running, the over heating of the catalyzer may be due to faults in the fuel or ignition systems or in the catalyzer hold relay or switching module. The latter components should be tested by your Datsun dealer.
8 A supplementary warning device is installed in conjunction with the catalytic converter. This is a floor temperature warning system comprising, lamp, sensor unit and relays. The sensor will actuate the warning lamp whenever the floor temperature, as a result of heat emitted from the catalytic converter, rises above 239° F (115° C). It is normal for the warning lamp to come on during periods of hard driving or climbing gradients for long periods in low gears. Any malfunction of the system should be rectified by having your Datsun dealer test the components.

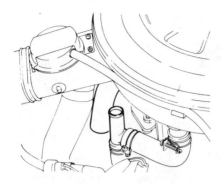

Fig. 3.70. Air injection system non-return valve and connecting hoses

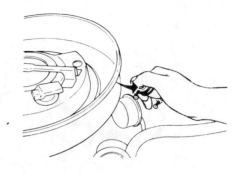

Fig. 3.73. Checking the anti-backfire valve

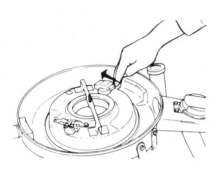

Fig. 3.71. Checking air pump relief valve (air injection system)

Fig. 3.74. Renewing air pump air cleaner element

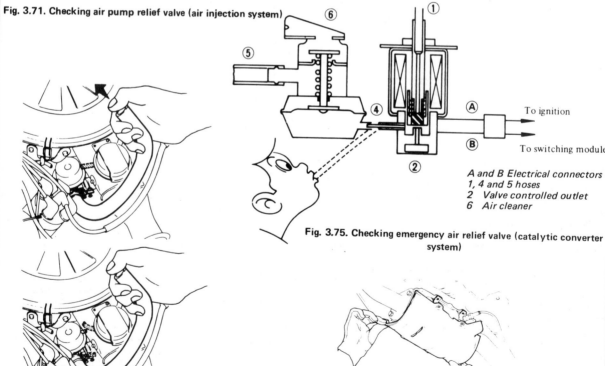

A To ignition

B To switching module

A and B Electrical connectors
1, 4 and 5 hoses
2 Valve controlled outlet
6 Air cleaner

Fig. 3.75. Checking emergency air relief valve (catalytic converter system)

Fig. 3.72. Checking air control valve

Fig. 3.76. Removing catalytic converter from exhaust system

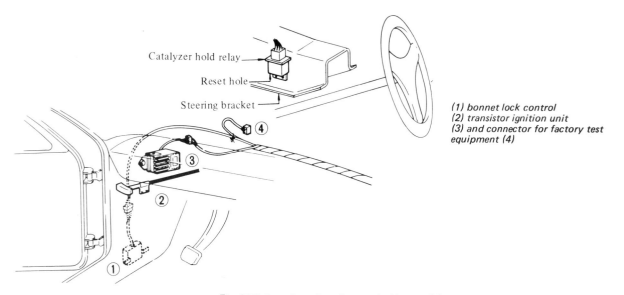

(1) bonnet lock control
(2) transistor ignition unit
(3) and connector for factory test equipment (4)

Fig. 3.77. Location of catalyzer switching module

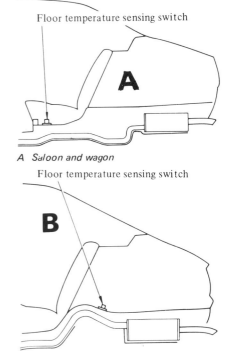

A Saloon and wagon

B Hardtop

Fig. 3.78. Location of floor temperature sensing switch used in conjunction with catalytic converter system

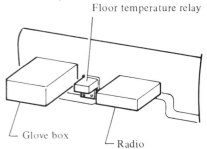

Fig. 3.79 Location of floor temperature relay

27 Fuel tank (140J and 160J SSS) - removal and installation

1   The fuel tanks used and the connecting pipe lines differ slightly between the two models.
2   To remove the tank from either model, first disconnect the lead from the battery negative terminal.
3   Remove the trim panel from the front of the luggage boot.
4   Remove the spare wheel.
5   Unscrew and remove the drain plug and drain the contents of the tank into a suitable contrainer. (photo)
6   Disconnect the filler and breather hoses and the fuel outlet hose from the tank.
7   Disconnect the fuel transmitter unit electrical leads. (photo)
8   Remove the rear seat cushion and seat back.
9   Unscrew and remove the tank mounting bolts and lift the tank from its location.
10 Never be tempted to solder or weld a hole or split in a fuel tank. Leave it to the professionals or better still renew the tank.
11 The tank transmitter can be removed from the tank by turning it in an anticlockwise direction using a screwdriver as a lever.
12 Installation is a reversal of removal but use a new 'O' ring when fitting the transmission unit and renew the sealing mastic around the tank mounting flange to ensure a waterproof seal.

28 Fuel tank (710 series up to 1975) - removal and installation

1   The fuel storage arrangement includes the main tank and a reservoir anxiliary tank which is used in conjunction with the fuel evaporative emission control system (see Section 21).
2   To remove the fuel tank, withdraw the front trim panel from the luggage boot. Remove the spare wheel.
3   Drain the fuel into a suitable container.
4   Disconnect all hoses from the fuel tank.
5   Disconnect the electrical leads from the fuel tank transmitter unit.
6   Remove the rear seat and the seat back.
7   Unbolt and remove the main fuel tank.
8   To remove the reservoir tank, unclip and detach the rear parcels shelf trim and then disconnect the three breather pipes. Unbolt the tank.
9   Refer to paragraphs 10 to 12, of the preceding Section.

27.5. 140J fuel tank

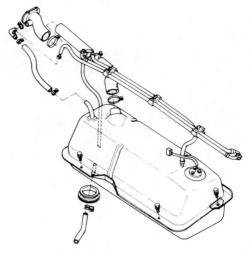

Fig. 3.81. Fuel tank (160J SSS)

27.7. Fuel tank transmitter unit

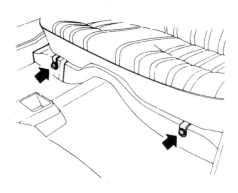

Fig. 3.82. Seat cushion securing bolts

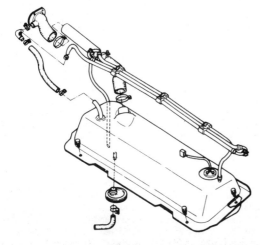

Fig. 3.80. Fuel tank (140J)

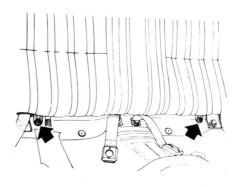

Fig. 3.83. Seat back securing bolts

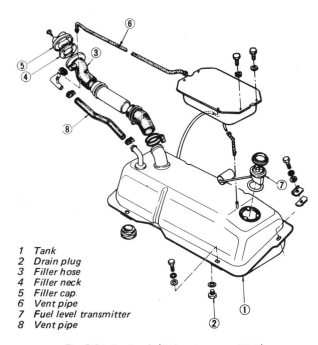

1 Tank
2 Drain plug
3 Filler hose
4 Filler neck
5 Filler cap.
6 Vent pipe
7 Fuel level transmitter
8 Vent pipe

Fig. 3.84. Fuel tank (710 series up to 1975)

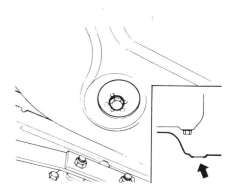

Fig. 3.85. Fuel tank drain plug

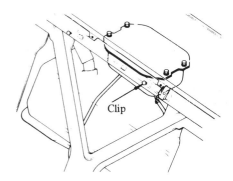

Clip

Fig. 3.86. Location of reservoir tank (710 series up to 1975)

29 Fuel tank (710 series 1975 onwards) - removal and installation

1 The fuel storage system varies according to model and operating territory.
2 On saloon and hardtop versions, the removal of the main and reservoir tanks is similar to the operations described in Section 28.
3 On wagon versions, the leads to the tank transmitter unit must be disconnected after removing the inspection cover from the floor of the luggage area.
4 On wagons destined for operation in California, the reservoir tank (part of the fuel evaporative emission control system, see Section 22) can be removed after withdrawal of the right-hand trim panel from the luggage area. Unscrew the two upper retaining screws, lift the tank and disconnect it from its lower latches.
5 Refer to paragraphs 10 to 12, of Section 27.

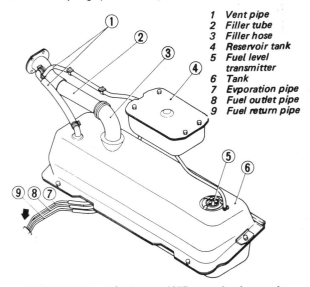

1 Vent pipe
2 Filler tube
3 Filler hose
4 Reservoir tank
5 Fuel level
   transmitter
6 Tank
7 Evporation pipe
8 Fuel outlet pipe
9 Fuel return pipe

Fig. 3.87 Fuel tank (710 series 1975 onwards saloon and hardtop)

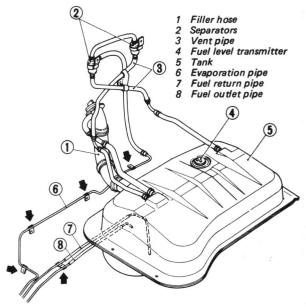

1 Filler hose
2 Separators
3 Vent pipe
4 Fuel level transmitter
5 Tank
6 Evaporation pipe
7 Fuel return pipe
8 Fuel outlet pipe

Fig. 3.88. Fuel tank (710 series wagon 1975 onwards - except California)

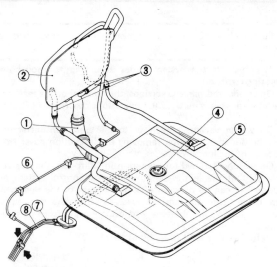

Fig. 3.89. Fuel tank (710 series wagon 1975 onwards - California)

1 Filler hose
2 Reservoir tank
3 Vent pipe
4 Fuel level transmitter
5 Tank
6 Evaporation pipe
7 Fuel outlet pipe
8 Fuel return pipe

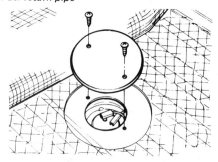

Fig. 3.90. Fuel tank transmitter unit inspection cover

30 Accelerator and choke controls

1 The accelerator linkage on all models is of rod, lever and balljoint type, differing slightly in detail.

2 Every 6,000 miles 910,000 km) apply multi-purpose grease to the joints and moving surfaces.

3 The linkage should be adjusted by means of the threaded rods to provide closure of the throttle butterfly valve plate when the accelerator pedal is released and full opening of the valve plate when the pedal is fully depressed. In order to avoid straining the carburettor throttle components beyond the fully open position, the floor mounted stop bolt must be correctly adjusted to restrict the downward travel of the pedal.

4 The choke control on 140J and 160J SSS models is of cable operated type. Connect the choke cable at the carburettor end so that when the choke valve plate is fully open, there is a little free-movement at the knob to give slight slackness in the cable.

5 On 710 series vehicles (1975 onwards), equipped with air conditioning, a fast idle control device is installed which raises the normal engine idling speed when the air conditioning system is in operation.

6 To adjust the device, first run the engine to normal operating temperature and check that the engine idling speed is as specified with the air conditioning system off.

7 Now switch the air conditioning system on, and adjust the fast idle actuator to give an idling speed of 800 rpm (manual transmission in neutral automatic transmission in 'N').

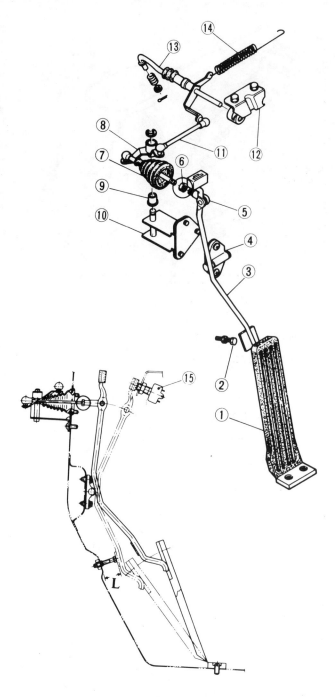

Fig. 3.91. Accelerator linkage (710 series up to 1975)

1 Accelerator pedal
2 Stop bolt
3 Arm
4 Bracket
5 Balljoint
6 Locknut
7 Boot
8 Bellcrank
9 Bush
10 Bracket
11 Balljoint link rod
12 Shaft support
13 Shaft
14 Return spring
15 Kickdown switch (auto. transmission)

Fig. 3.92. Choke control knob (140J and 160J SSS)

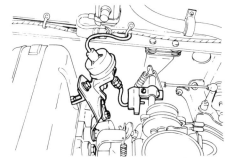

Fig. 3.93. Location of the fast idle actuator (710 series 1975 onwards with air conditioning)

31 Exhaust systems

1 The design of the exhaust system varies according to vehicle model and date of production: the differing design of the components can be seen in the illustrations.

2 The system is mounted on rubber rings or blocks. (photo)

3 On models fitted with a Catalytic converter, remember to disconnect and remove the sensor unit before commencing to dismantle.

4 Examination of the exhaust pipe and silencers at regular intervals is worthwhile as small defects may be repairable when, if left they will almost certainly require renewal of one of the sections of the system. Also, any leaks, apart from the noise factor, may cause poisonous exhaust gases to get inside the car which can be unpleasant, to say the least, even in mild concentrations. Prolonged inhalation could cause sickness and giddiness.

5 As the sleeve connections and clamps are usually very difficult to separate it is quicker and easier in the long run to remove the complete system from the car when renewing a section. It can be expensive if another section is damaged when trying to separate a bad section from it.

6 To remove the system first remove the bolts holding the tail pipe bracket to the body. Support the rear silencer on something to prevent cracking or kinking the pipes elsewhere.

7 Disconnect the rubber mountings or suspension rings and unbolt the downpipe flanges from the exhaust manifold. Withdraw the complete system from below and to the rear of the vehicle. If necessary, jack-up the rear of the vehicle to provide more clearance.

8 When separating the damaged section which is to be renewed, cut away the bad section from the good one rather than risking damage to the good section by attempting to drive the components apart with a hammer or by twisting them free.

9 If small repairs are being carried out it is best, if possible, not to try and pull the sections apart.

10 Refitting should be carried out after connecting the two sections together. De-burr and apply sealant to the connecting socket and make sure that the clamp is in good conditon and slipped over the front pipe but do not tighten it at this stage.

11 Connect the system to the manifold and connect the rear support strap. Now adjust the attitude of the silencer so that the tension on the two rubber support rings will be equalized when fitted.

12 Tighten the pipe clamp, the manifold flange nuts and the rear suspension strap bolts. Check that the exhaust system will not knock against any part of the vehicle when deflected slightly in a sideways or upward direction. (photos)

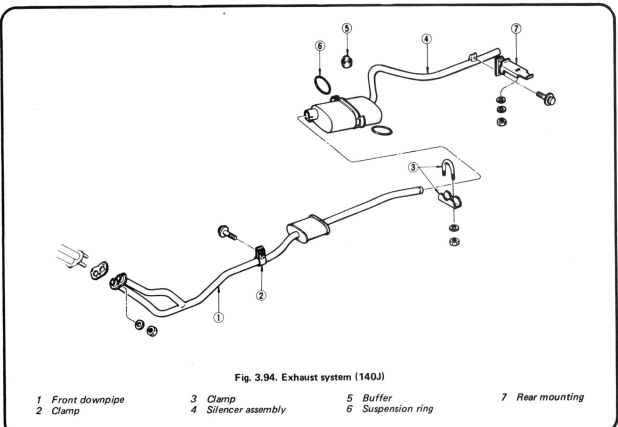

Fig. 3.94. Exhaust system (140J)

1 Front downpipe	3 Clamp	5 Buffer	7 Rear mounting
2 Clamp	4 Silencer assembly	6 Suspension ring	

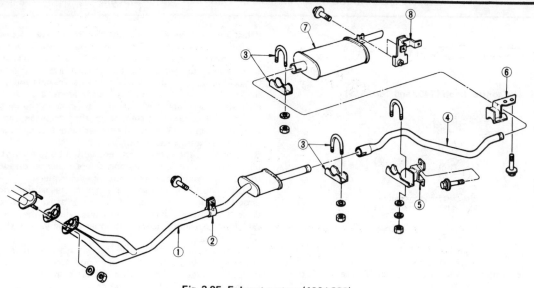

Fig. 3.95. Exhaust system (160J SSS)

1 Front downpipe
2 Clamp
3 Clamp
4 Tailpipe
5 Flexible mounting
6 Flexible mounting
7 Silencer
8 Rear mounting

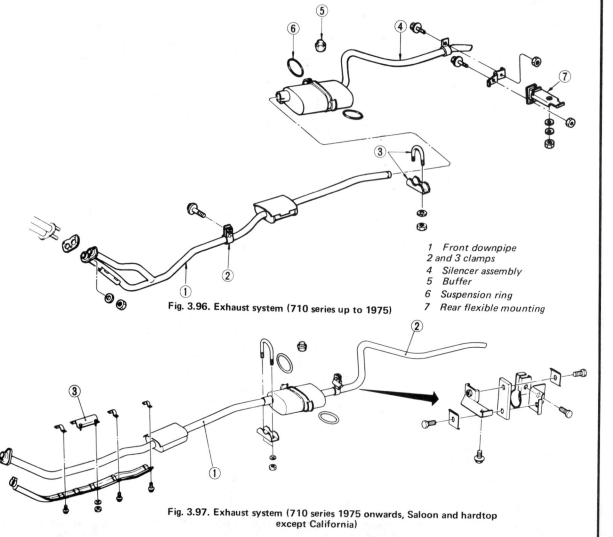

1 Front downpipe
2 and 3 clamps
4 Silencer assembly
5 Buffer
6 Suspension ring
7 Rear flexible mounting

Fig. 3.96. Exhaust system (710 series up to 1975)

Fig. 3.97. Exhaust system (710 series 1975 onwards, Saloon and hardtop except California)

1 Downtube and expansion box
2 Tailpipe/silencer section
3 Heat insulator (automatic transmission only)

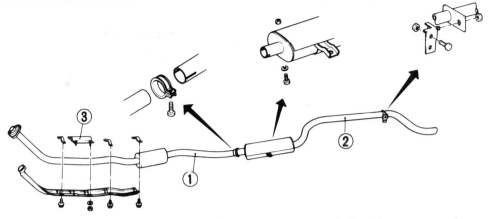

Fig. 3.98. Exhaust system (710 series wagon except California)

1   Downtube and
    expansion box

2   Tailpipe/silencer
    section

3   Heat insulator
    (automatic transmission)

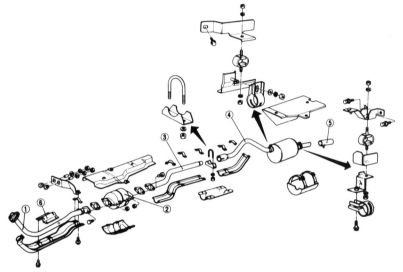

Fig. 3.99. Exhaust system (710 series saloon and hardtop — California)

1   Downtube
2   Catalytic converter

3   Central exhaust
    section

4   Silencer section
5   Trim

6   Heat shield

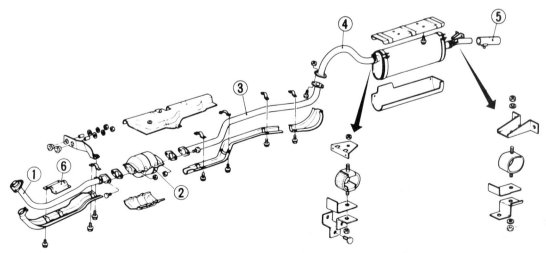

Fig. 3.100. Exhaust system (710 series wagon — California)

1   Downtube
2   Catalytic converter

3   Central exhaust
    section

4   Silencer section
5   Trim

6   Heat shield

31.2. Exhaust support ring

31.12A. Exhaust manifold and gaskets (140J)

31.12B. Inlet manifold showing air cleaner supports and brake booster hose right-angled connection (140J)

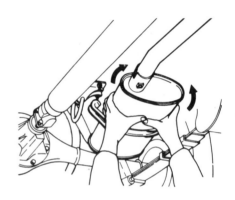

Fig. 3.101 Adjusting attitude of exhaust silencer before tightening clamp bolts

32 Fault diagnosis - Carburation; fuel and emission control systems

Symptom	Reason/s
Fuel consumption excessive	Air cleaner choked and dirty giving rich mixture
	Fuel leaking from carburettors, fuel pumps, or fuel lines
	Float chambers flooding
	Generally worn carburettor
	Distributor condenser faulty
	Balance weights or vacuum advance mechanism in distributor faulty
	Carburettors incorrectly adjusted, mixture too rich
	Idling speed too high
	Contact breaker gap incorrect
	Valve clearances incorrect
	Incorrectly set spark plugs
	Tyres under-inflated
	Wrong spark plugs fitted
	Brakes dragging
	Emission control system faulty (see later in this Section)
Insufficient fuel delivery or weak mixture due to air leaks	Partially clogged filters in pump and carburettors or fuel line
	Incorrectly seating valves in fuel pump
	Fuel pump diaphragm leaking or damaged
	Gasket in fuel pump damaged
	Fuel pump valves sticking due to fuel gumming
	Too little fuel in fuel tank (prevalent when climbing steep hills
	Union joints on pipe connections loose
	Split in fuel pipe on suction side of fuel pump
	Inlet manifold to block or inlet manifold to carburettor gaskets leaking
	Fuel tank relief valve stuck closed
Power reduced	Clogged main jets
	Accelerator linkage requires adjustment
	Fuel filter blocked
	Air cleaner blocked
	Carburettor diaphragm damaged
	Power valve faulty
Erratic idling	Slow jet clogged
	Secondary throttle valve operating incorrectly
	Worn throttle valve shafts
	Broken carburettor flange gasket
	Incorrectly adjusted B.C.D.D.
Flat spot or hesitation	Clogged jets
	Emulsion tube clogged
	Secondary throttle valve operating incorrectly
Engine will not start	Fuel level too high
	Lack of fuel
	Incorrect setting of mixture screw
	Faulty anti-dieseling solenoid
	Incorrect fast idle adjustment

Emission control system faults

Symptom	Reason/s
Erratic idling	Faulty anti-backfire valve (flame trap)
	Carbon canister purge line disconnected
	Exhaust gas heated hotspot valve stuck
	Faulty E.G.R. valve
Power reduced	Faulty spark timing control valve
	Faulty altitude compensator (California)
	Faulty E.G.R. valve
	Exhaust gas heated hotspot valve stuck

Chapter 4 Ignition system

Contents

Specifications

System type	12 volt, battery and coil

Distributors

	L14	L16	L18	L20B
Make	Hitachi	Hitachi	Hitachi	Hitachi
Code:				
Manual gearbox	D411-63	D411-58K (160J) or D411-54K (160JSSS)	D4A2-01	D4A4-04
Automatic transmission	-	-	-	D4A4-06
Transistor type	-	-	-	D4F4-03
Ignition timing (at idle)	8°BTDC	10° BTDC	12° BTDC	TDC

All distributors

Rotational direction	Counter clockwise
Dwell angle	49 to 55°
Condenser capacity	0.20 to 0.24 u F
Contact breaker gap (mechanical)	0.018 to 0.022 in. (0.45 to 0.55 mm)
Air gap (transistor)	0.008 to 0.016 in. (0.2 to 0.4 mm)

Coil

	140J	160J & SSS	710 series up to 1975	710 series 1975 on
Make	Hitachi	Hitachi	Hanshin	Hitachi or Hanshin
Number:				
Mechanical breaker	6R-200	6R-200	H5-15-1	C6R-607 or H5-15-10
Transistor type	—	—	—	CIT-17 or STC - 10
Primary voltage	12	12	12	12
Primary resistance @ 68°F	1.5 to 1.7 Ω	1.5 to 1.7 Ω	1.17 to 1.43 Ω	1.17 to 1.43* Ω
Secondary resistance @ 68°F	9.5 to 11.6 Ω	9.5 to 11.6 Ω	11.2 to 16.8 Ω	11.2 to 16.8** Ω
Resistor	1.6 Ω	1.6 Ω	1.3 to 1.7 Ω	1.5 *** Ω

*Transistor type 0.45 to 0.55 Ω
**Transistor type 8.5 to 12.7K Ω
***Transistor type 1.3 Ω

Spark plugs

	L14	L16	L18	L20B
Make	NGK	NGK	NGK	NGK
Type	BP-5ES	BP-6ES	B-6ES	BP-6ES or L45-PW
Gap	0.031 to 0.035 in. (0.8 to 0.9 mm)	0.031 to 0.035 in. (0.8 to 0.9 mm)	0.028 to 0.031 in. (0.7 to 0.8 mm)	0.031 to 0.035 in. (0.8 to 0.9 mm)

Torque wrench setting

	lb/ft	kg/m
Spark plug	20	2.8

1 General description

In order that the engine can run correctly it is necessary for an electrical spark to ignite the fuel/air mixture in the combustion chamber at exactly the right moment in relation to engine speed and load. The ignition system is based on feeding low tension (LT) voltage from the battery to the coil where it is converted to high tension (HT) voltage. The high tension voltage is powerful enough to jump the spark plug gap in the cylinders many times a second under high compression pressures, providing that the system is in good condition and that all adjustments are correct.

The ignition system is divided into two circuits: the low tension circuit and the high tension circuit.

The low tension (sometimes known as the primary) circuit consists of the battery lead to the control box, lead to the ignition switch, lead from the ignition switch to the low tension or primary coil windings (terminal SW), and the lead from the low tension coil windings (coil terminal CB) to the contact breaker points and condenser in the distributor.

The high tension circuit consists of the high tension or secondary coil windings, the heavy ignition lead from the centre of the coil to the centre of the distributor cap, the rotor arm, and the spark plug leads and spark plugs.

The system functions in the following manner. Low tension voltage is changed in the coil into high tension voltage by the opening and closing of the contact breaker points in the low tension circuit. High tension voltage is then fed via the carbon brush in the centre of the distributor cap to the rotor arm of the distributor cap, and each time it comes in line with one of the four metal segments in the cap, which are connected to the spark plug leads, the opening and closing of the contact breaker points causes the high tension voltage to build up, jump the gap from the rotor arm to the appropriate metal segment and so via the spark plug lead to the spark plug, were it finally jumps the spark plug gap before going to earth.

The ignition is advanced and retarded automatically, to ensure the spark occurs at just the right instant for the particular load at the prevailing engine speed.

The ignition advance is controlled both mechanically and by a vacuum operated system. The mechanical governor mechanism comprises two weights, which move out from the distributor shaft as the engine speed rises due to centrifugal force. As they move outward they rotate the cam relative to the distributor shaft and so advance the spark timing. The weights are held in position by two light springs and it is the tension of the springs which is largely responsible for correct spark advancement.

The vacuum control consists of a diaphragm, one side of which is connected via a small bore tube to the carburettor, and the other side to the contact breaker plate. Depression in the inlet manifold and carburettor, which varies with engine speed and throttle opening, causes the diaphragm to move, so moving the contact breaker plate, and advancing or retarding the spark. A fine degree of control is achieved by a spring in the vacuum assembly.

On vehicles equipped with a full emission control system a spark timing control system is employed. The system varies between vehicles equipped with manual or automatic transmission but basically is designed to advance or retard the ignition timing in accordance with the prevailing engine operating conditions in order to reduce the emission of noxious exhaust fumes particularly during periods of deceleration. Reference should be made to Chapter 3 for full details of this and the other emission control devices.

A resistor is incorporated in the ignition circuit so that during starting with the engine being cranked by the starter motor, full battery voltage is applied at the coil to maintain a good spark at the plug electrodes which would not be the case should a drop in voltage occur. On vehicles built for operation in certain North American territories from 1975 onwards, a transistorized ignition system is used. The essential difference between this and the mechanical type is that the mechanical type 'make-and-break' contact points are replaced by a reluctor and coil which carries out the function electronically by interruption of a magnetic field and signal generation.

Distributor models vary with the particular engine type and car and reference should be made to Specifications for relevant details and application, especially when ordering spares it is advisable to quote the exact distributor reference number.

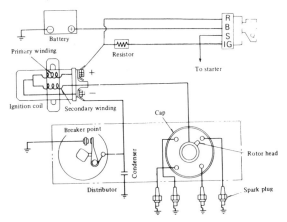

Fig. 4.1 Ignition circuit (mechanical type contact breaker)

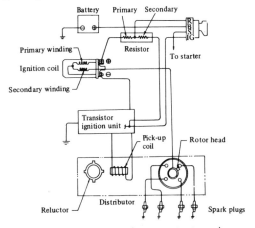

Fig. 4.2 Ignition circuit (transistorized type)

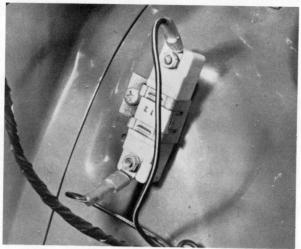

1   Resistor, located within engine compartment

The descriptions throughout this Chapter apply to all relevant model assemblies but detail differences will be apparent in the particular components according to vehicle model and year of production. This is especially the case with distributors.

2   Contact breaker (mechanical type) - adjustment

1   To adjust the contact breaker points to the correct gap, first pull off the two clips securing the distributor cap to the distributor body, and lift away the cap. Clean the cap inside and out with a dry cloth. It is unlikely that the four segments will be badly burned or scored, but if they are the cap will have to be renewed.

2   Inspect the carbon brush contact located in the top of the cap - see that it is unbroken and stands proud of the plastic surface.

3   Check the rotor arm. It must be clean and on the cam shoulder.

4   Gently prise the contact breaker points open to examine the conditions of their faces. If they are rough, pitted or dirty, it will be necessary to remove them for resurfacing, or for replacement points to be fitted.

5   Presuming the points are satisfactory, or that they have been cleaned and replaced, measure the gap between the points by turning the engine over until the heel of the breaker arm is on the highest point of the cam.

6   An 0.018 to 0.022 in. (0.45 to 0.5 mm) feeler gauge should now just fit between the points.

7   If the gap varies from this amount slacken the contact plate securing screw.

8   Adjust the contact gap by inserting a screwdriver in the screw located in the cut-out of the breaker plate. Turn clockwise to increase and anticlockwise to decrease the gap. When the gap is correct tighten the securing screw and check the gap again.

9   Making sure the rotor is in position replace the distributor cap and clip the spring blade retainers into position.

3   Contact breaker points - removal and refitting

1   Slip back the spring clips which secure the distributor cap in position. Remove the distributor cap and lay it to one side, only removing one or two of the HT leads from the plugs if necessary to provide greater movement of the cap.

2   Pull the rotor from the distributor shaft.

3   Unscrew the setscrews just enough to be able to slide out the primary (LT) lead terminals.

4   Unscrew and remove the two contact breaker securing screws and detach the end of the earth lead. Pull the contact breaker assembly outwards and upwards to remove it. Remove the pivot circlip to dismantle.

5   Inspect the faces of the contact points. If they are only lightly burned or pitted then they may be ground square on an oilstone or by rubbing a carborundum strip between them. Where the points are found to be severely burned or pitted, then they must be renewed and at the same time the cause of the erosion

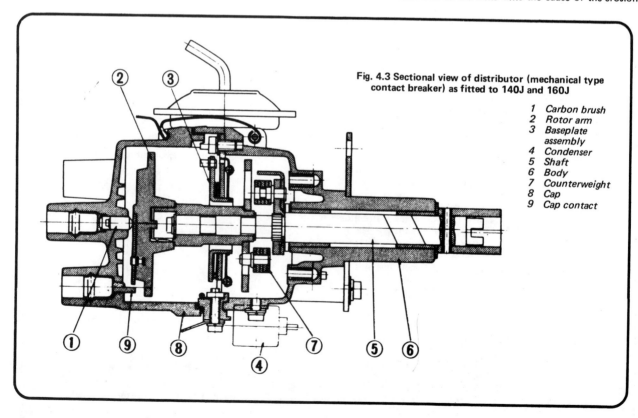

Fig. 4.3 Sectional view of distributor (mechanical type contact breaker) as fitted to 140J and 160J

1   Carbon brush
2   Rotor arm
3   Baseplate assembly
4   Condenser
5   Shaft
6   Body
7   Counterweight
8   Cap
9   Cap contact

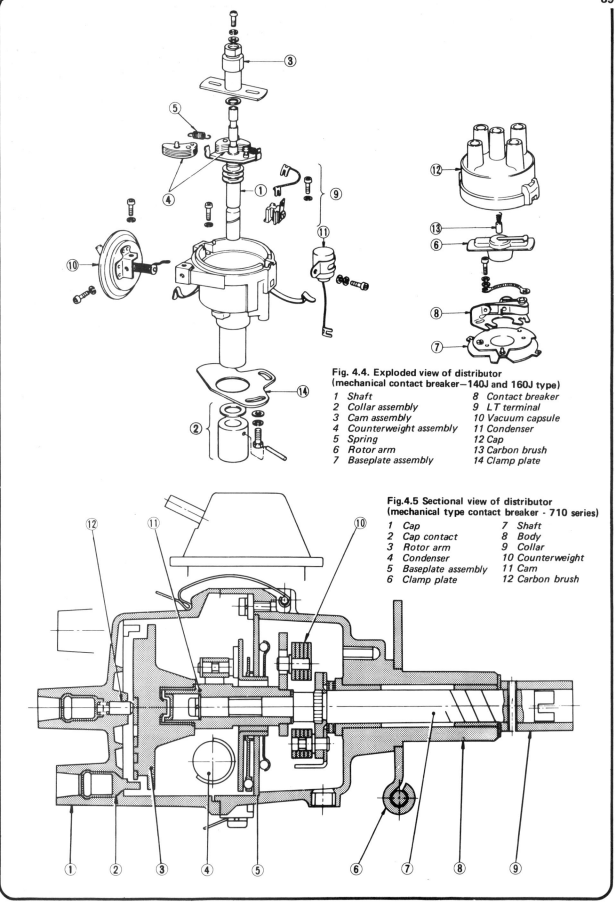

Fig. 4.4. Exploded view of distributor
(mechanical contact breaker—140J and 160J type)

1	Shaft	8	Contact breaker
2	Collar assembly	9	LT terminal
3	Cam assembly	10	Vacuum capsule
4	Counterweight assembly	11	Condenser
5	Spring	12	Cap
6	Rotor arm	13	Carbon brush
7	Baseplate assembly	14	Clamp plate

Fig.4.5 Sectional view of distributor
(mechanical type contact breaker - 710 series)

1	Cap	7	Shaft
2	Cap contact	8	Body
3	Rotor arm	9	Collar
4	Condenser	10	Counterweight
5	Baseplate assembly	11	Cam
6	Clamp plate	12	Carbon brush

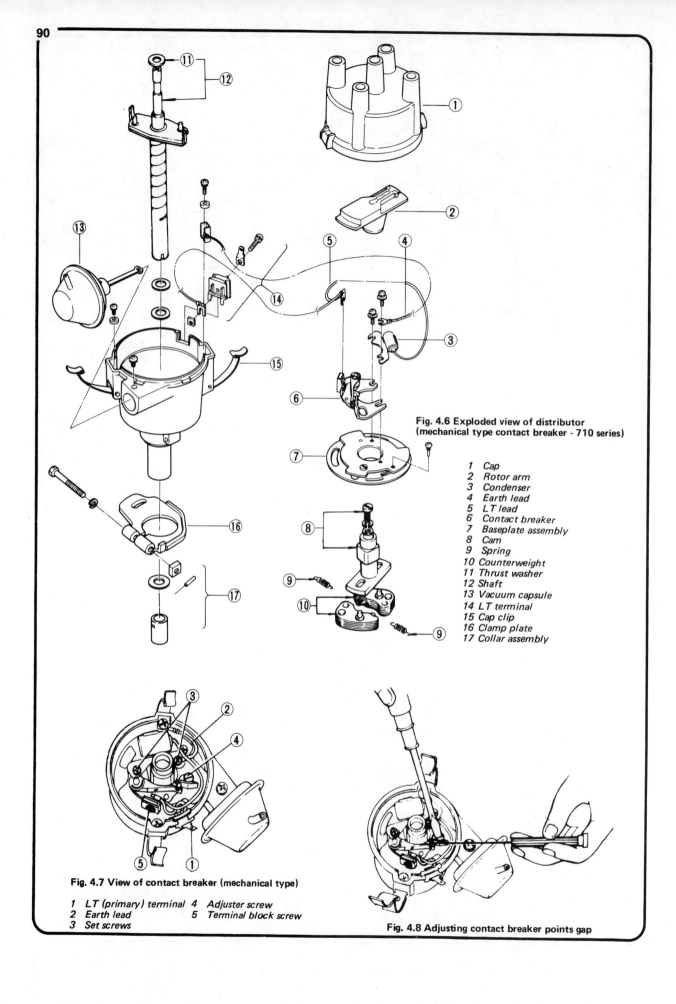

Fig. 4.6 Exploded view of distributor (mechanical type contact breaker - 710 series)

1 Cap
2 Rotor arm
3 Condenser
4 Earth lead
5 LT lead
6 Contact breaker
7 Baseplate assembly
8 Cam
9 Spring
10 Counterweight
11 Thrust washer
12 Shaft
13 Vacuum capsule
14 LT terminal
15 Cap clip
16 Clamp plate
17 Collar assembly

Fig. 4.7 View of contact breaker (mechanical type)

1 LT (primary) terminal   4 Adjuster screw
2 Earth lead   5 Terminal block screw
3 Set screws

Fig. 4.8 Adjusting contact breaker points gap

of the points established. This is most likely to be due to poor earth connections from the battery negative lead to body earth or the engine to earth strap. Remove the connecting bolts at these points, scrape the surfaces free from rust and corrosion and tighten the bolts using a star type lock washer. Other screws to check for security are: the baseplate to distributor body securing screws, the condenser securing screw and the distributor body to lockplate bolt. Looseness in any of these could contribute to a poor earth connection. Check the condenser (Sec 4).

6 Refitting the contact breaker assembly is a reversal of removal and when fitted, adjust the points gap as described in the preceding Section and apply a smear of grease to the high points of the cam.

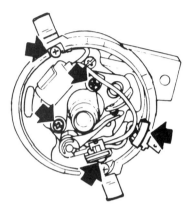

Fig. 4.9 Removal points for contact breaker assembly

4 Condenser (capacitor) - removal, testing and refitting

1 The condenser ensures that with the contact breaker points open, the sparking between them is not excessive to cause severe pitting. The condenser if fitted in parallel and its failure will automatically cause failure of the ignition system as the points will be prevented from interrupting the low tension circuit.
2 Testing for an unserviceable condenser may be effected by switching on the ignition and separating the contact points by hand. If this action is accompanied by a blue flash then condenser failure is indicated. Difficult starting, missing of the engine after several miles running or badly pitting points are other indications of the faulty condenser.
3 The surest test is by substitution of a new unit.
4 Removal of the condenser is by means of withdrawing the screw which retains it to the distributor. Replacement is a reversal of this procedure.

5 Distributor - removal and installation

1 To remove the distributor complete with cap from the engine, begin by pulling the plug lead terminals off the spark plugs. Free the HT lead from the centre of the coil to the centre of the distributor by undoing the lead retaining cap from the coil.
2 Pull off the rubber pipe holding the vacuum tube to the distributor vacuum advance and retard take off pipe.
3 Disconnect the low tension wire from the coil.
4 Undo and remove the bolt which holds the distributor clamp plate to the crankcase and lift out the distributor.
5 Installation of the distributor is fully described in Section 42, of Chapter 1.

6 Ignition timing (distributor with mechanical contact breakers)

1 Turn the engine until No 1 piston is rising on its compression

stroke. This may be checked by removing No 1 spark plug and placing a finger over the plug hole to feel the compression being generated or alternatively, removing the distributor cap and observing that the rotor arm is coming up to align with the position of No 1 contact segment in the distributor cap.
2 There is a notch on the rim of the crankshaft pulley and a scale on the timing cover. Continue turning the crankshaft until the notch on the pulley is opposite the approriate static ignition setting mark on the scale. Refer to specifications for this setting as it varies between engine and model types. (photo)
3 Slacken the distributor clamp plate bolt.
4 Connect a test lamp between the LT terminal of the distributor and a good earth and switch on the ignition.
5 Turn the distributor body to the position where even the slightest further movement will illuminate the test bulb.
6 Tighten the distributor clamp plate bolt, remove the test lamp and switch off the ignition.
7 An alternative method of ignition timing is to use a stroboscope, as described in Section 9 of this Chapter.

6.2. Ignition timing scale on engine front cover

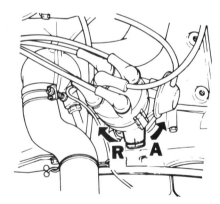

Fig. 4.10 Distributor advance and retard movement

7 Distributor (mechanical contact breaker type) - dismantling and reassembly

1 Remove the cap and pull off the rotor.
2 Unscrew and remove the two screws which secure the vacuum capsule to the distributor body. Tilt the capsule slightly to disengage the actuating rod from the pivot of the movable baseplate. Withdraw the vacuum capsule.
3 Remove the contact breaker assembly as described in Section

4 Unscrew and remove the securing screws from the baseplate assembly and lift out the assembly.

5 If the movable and fixed baseplates are to be separated, remove the securing screws but take care not to lose the balls which are sandwiched between the two components.

6 Knock out the pin from the collar at the base of the distributor shaft using a suitable drift.

7 The shaft and counterweight assembly may now be withdrawn through the upper end of the distributor body.

8 Where it is necessary to remove the cam from the top of the distributor shaft, first mark the relative position of the cam to the shaft and then unscrew and remove the screw from the cam recess.

9 Where the counterweights and their springs are to be dismantled, take care not to stretch the springs.

10 Check all components for wear and renew as appropriate.

11 Grease the counterweight pivots and reassemble by reversing the dismantling procedure but ensure that the rotor positioning flat on the cam is towards the circular hook and also that the circular and rectangular ended springs are correctly located.

Fig. 4.11 Distributor vacuum capsule and securing screw

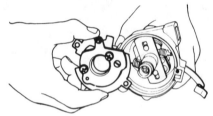

Fig. 4.12 Removing the fixed and moveable baseplate assembly

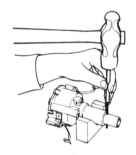

Fig. 4.13 Driving out the shaft collar retaining pin

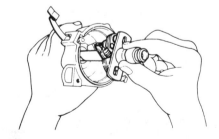

Fig. 4.14 Withdrawing distributor shaft/cam assembly

Fig. 4.15 Removing the cam to shaft securing screw

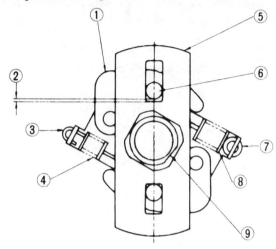

Fig. 4.16 Cam and counterweight spring setting diagram

1 Counterweight	6 Pivot pin
2 Clearance	7 Circular shaped spring end
3 'U' shaped spring end	8 Counterweight spring
4 Counterweight spring	9 Rotor positioning flat
5 Cam plate	

8   Distributor (transistor type) - air gap adjustment

1 This type of distributor employs a reluctor at the top of the shaft and a pick-up coil.

The pick-up coil comprises a magnet and coil and whenever one of the projections on the reluctor is in alignment with the pole piece of the coil, the magnetic path between them is instrumental in generating the signal in the pick-up coil. This signal is relayed to the transistor ignition unit which in turn breaks the primary circuit and so generates high voltage in the secondary winding.

2 On this type of distributor the air gap between the projection of the reluctor and the pole piece of the pick-up coil must be maintained at between 0.008 and 0.016 in. (0.2 to 0.4 mm). Check with feeler blades and adjust if necessary after slackening the pick-up coil screws.

3 Apply grease to the top of the distributor shaft and refit the rubber plug.

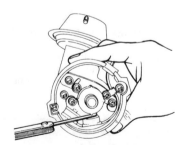

Fig. 4.17 Checking the air gap on a transistor type distributor

9 Ignition timing (transistor type distributor)

1 Mark the notch on the crankshaft pulley with chalk or white paint.
2 Mark in a similar manner the appropriate line on the timing cover scale (see Specifications for static timing figure according to engine and vehicle type).
3 Disconnect the vacuum pipe (which runs from the vacuum capsule on the distributor to the carburettor. Disconnect the pipe from the distributor end and plug the pipe.
4 Connect a stroboscope in accordance with the maker's instructions (usually interposed between No 1 spark plug and HT lead).
5 Start the engine (which should previously have been run to normal operating temperature) and let it idle slowly (see recommended speeds in Specifications) otherwise the mechanical advance mechanism will operate and give a false ignition timing.
6 Point the stroboscope at the ignition timing marks when they will appear stationary and if the ignition timing is correct, in alignment. If the marks are not in alignment, loosen the distributor clamp plate screw and turn the distributor.
7 Switch off the ignition, tighten the distributor clamp plate screw and remove the stroboscope.
8 Unplug and reconnect the vacuum pipe.

10 Distributor (transistor type) - dismantling and reassembly

1 Remove the distributor cap and rotor.
2 Remove the two screws which secure the vacuum capsule, tilt it slightly to disengage the operating rod from the baseplate pivot.
3 Unscrew and remove the screws which hold the pick-up coil and remove it.
4 Using two bars as levers, prise the reluctor from the distributor shaft and then remove the tension pin.
5 Unscrew and remove the screws which secure the baseplate

and lift off the baseplate.
6 Drive out the pin from the lower end of the shaft, remove the collar and then withdraw the upper counterweight assembly and shaft from the top of the distributor.
7 Unscrew and remove the screw from the recess at the end of the shaft and then remove the camplate, counterweight assembly.
8 Where the counterweights and springs are dismantled, take care not to stretch the springs.
9 Renew any worn components.
10 Reassembly is a reversal of dismantling but ensure that the following conditions are met:

(a) *The reluctor is correctly orientated on the distributor shaft with regard to the positions of the flat and the tension pin. Note that the slot in the tension pin must face outwards.*
(b) *If the contactor has been disturbed, adjust the cam to contactor clearance to 0.012 in. (0.3 mm) on reassembly*
(c) *Grease the counterweight pivots and install the reluctor so that its flat is towards the circular counterweight spring hook making sure that the circular and rectangular ended springs are correctly installed in a similar way to that shown in Fig. 4.17*

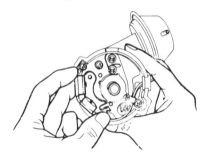

Fig. 4.19 Removing the pick-up coil (transistor type distributor)

1 Cap
2 Rotor arm
3 Tension pin
4 Reluctor
5 Pick-up coil

6 Contactor
7 Baseplate assembly
8 Lubricating felt
9 Cam plate
10 Counterweight spring

11 Counterweight
12 Shaft
13 Cap locator
14 Vacuum capsule

15 Body
16 Clamp plate
17 'O' ring seal
18 Collar

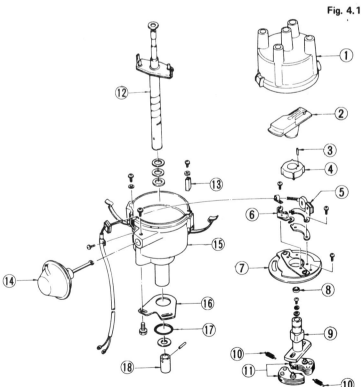

Fig. 4.18 Exploded view of transistor type distributor

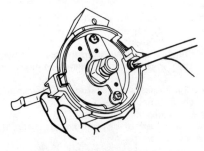

Fig. 4.20 Removing baseplate securing screws (transistor type distributor)

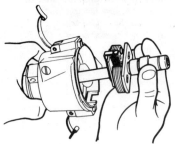

Fig. 4.21 Withdrawing shaft/counterweight/cam assembly (transistor type distributor)

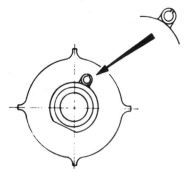

Fig. 4.22 Reluctor setting diagram (transistor type distributor)

0.3 mm (0.012 in)

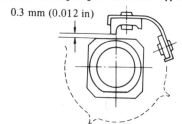

Fig. 4.23 Cam to contactor clearance setting diagram (transistor type distributor)

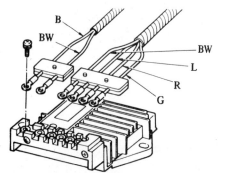

Fig. 4.24 Transistorized ignition unit and connections

11 Transistorized ignition unit

1   The unit is located below the left-hand side of the fascia panel within the vehicle.
2   It performs the following functions:
   (a) It 'makes' and 'breaks' the current in the primary circuit of the ignition coil.
   (b) Sets and maintains the make-and-break cycle according to engine speed.
   (c) Incorporates a delayed cut-out to disconnect the primary current within a period not exceeding ten seconds if the ignition is left switched on with the engine not running.
3   A fault in the transistorized ignition system can only be checked and traced using an oscilloscope and this work should therefore be left to an auto-electrician.
4   Any fault occuring in the unit itself will require a new unit as the original cannot be repaired.
5   To renew a unit, disconnect the lead from the battery negative terminal.
6   Disconnect the wiring harness from the unit.
7   Unscrew and remove the securing setscrews and lift the unit from its location.
8   Installation is a reversal of removal but take great care to connect the wiring harness correctly.

12 Coil - descrpition and polarity

1   High tension current should be negative at the spark plug terminals. To ensure this, check the LT connections to the coil are correctly made.
2   The LT wire from the distributor must connect with the negative (−) terminal on the coil.
3   The coil positive (+) terminal is connected to the ignition-/starter switch.
4   An incorrect connection can cause as much as a 60% loss of spark efficiency and can cause rough idling and misfiring at speed.
5   The type of coil fitted is dependent upon the engine and vehicle type and date of production. Refer to Specification section for precise application.
6   Where a CIT-17 or STC-10 coil is used, do not disconnect a spark plug lead when the engine is running.

13 Spark plugs and high tension (HT) leads

1   The correct functioning of the spark plugs is vital for the correct running and efficiency of the engine. The plugs fitted as standard are listed on the Specifications page.
2   At intervals of 3,000 miles (4,800 km) the plugs should be removed, examined, cleaned and, if worn excessively, renewed. The condition of the spark plug will also tell much about the overall condition of the engine.
3   If the insulator nose of the spark plug is clean and white, with no deposits, this is indicative of a weak mixture, or too hot a plug. (A hot plug transfers heat away from the electrode slowly - a cold plug transfers it away quickly).
4   If the top and insulator nose is covered with hard black looking deposits, then this is indicative that the mixture is too rich. Should the plug be black and oily, then it is likely that the engine is fairly worn, as well as the mixture being too rich.
5   If the insulator nose is covered with light tan to greyish brown deposits, then the mixture is correct and it is likely that the engine is in good condition.
6   If there are any traces of long brown tapering stains on the outside of the white portion of the plug, then the plug will have to be renewed, as this shows that there is a faulty joint between the plug body and the insulator, and compression is being allowed to leak away.
7   Plugs should be cleaned by a sand blasting machine, which will free them from carbon more thoroughly than cleaning by

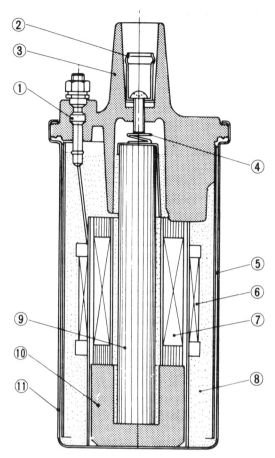

Fig. 4.25 Sectional view of coil fitted to 140J and 160J vehicles and to earlier 710 series

1 LT primary terminals
2 HT (secondary) terminals
3 Cap
4 Spring
5 Core
6 Primary winding
7 Secondary winding
8 Insulating oil
9 Centre core
10 Insulator
11 Casing

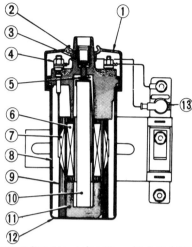

Fig. 4.27 Coil fitted in conjunction with transistor type distributor (710 series 1975 onwards)

1 Rubber bore
2 HT (secondary terminal)
3 Cap
4 LT (primary terminal)
5 Spring
6 Secondary winding
7 Primary winding
8 Core
9 Insulating oil
10 Centre core
11 Insulator
12 Casing
13 Terminal rubber cap

hand. The machine will also test the condition of the plugs under compression. Any plug that fails to spark at the recommended pressure should be renewed.

8 The spark plug gap is of considerable importance, as, if it is too large or too small the size of the spark and its efficiency will be seriously impaired. The spark plug gap should be set to between 0.031 and 0.035 in. (0.8 and 0.8 mm) for the best results.

9 To set it, measure the gap with a feeler gauge, and then bend open, or close, the outer plug electrode until the correct gap is achieved. The centre electrode should never be bent as this may crack the insulation and cause plug failure, if nothing worse.

10 When replacing the plugs, remember to use new plugs washers and replace the leads from the distributor in the correct firing order 1-3-4-2 number 1 cylinder being the one nearest the radiator.

11 The plug leads require no attention other than being kept clean and wiped over regularly.

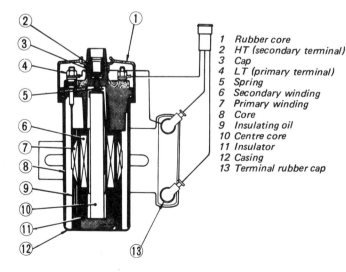

1 Rubber core
2 HT (secondary terminal)
3 Cap
4 LT (primary terminal)
5 Spring
6 Secondary winding
7 Primary winding
8 Core
9 Insulating oil
10 Centre core
11 Insulator
12 Casing
13 Terminal rubber cap

Fig. 4.26 Coil fitted in conjunction with mechanical type contact breaker distributor (710 series 1975 onwards)

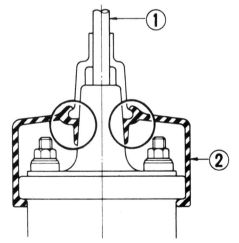

Fig. 4.30 Method of sealing HT lead (1) to late type coil cap (2)

14 Ignition system (mechanical contact breaker) - fault symptoms

Engine fails to start

1 If the engine fails to start and the car was running normally when it was last used, first check there is fuel in the fuel tank. If the engine turns over normally on the starter motor and the battery is evidently well charged, then the fault may be in either the high or low tension circuits. First check the HT circuit. Note: if the battery is known to be fully charged; the ignition light comes on, and the starter motor fails to turn the engine check the tightness of the leads on the battery terminals and also the secureness of the earth lead to its connection to the body. If is quite common for the leads to have worked loose, even if they look and feel secure. If one of the battery terminal posts gets very hot when trying to work the starter motor this is a sure indication of a faulty connection to that terminal.

2 One of the commonest reasons for bad starting is wet or damp spark plug leads and distributor. Remove the distributor cap. If condensation is visible internally, dry the cap with a rag and also wipe over the leads. Replace the cap.

3 If the engine still fails to start, check that current is reaching the plugs by disconnecting each plug lead in turn at the spark plug end, and hold the end of the cable about 3/16th (5 mm) away from the cylinder block. Spin the engine on the starter motor.

4 Sparking between the end of the cable and the block should be fairly strong with a regular blue spark. (Hold the lead with rubber to avoid electric shocks). If current is reaching the plugs, then remove them and clean and regap them. The engine should now start.

5 If there is no spark at the plug leads take off the HT lead from the centre of the distributor cap and hold it to the block as before. Spin the engine on the starter once more. A rapid succession of blue sparks between the end of the lead and the block indicate that the coil is in order and that the distributor cap is cracked, the rotor arm faulty, or the carbon brush in the top of the distributor cap is not making good contact with the spring on the rotor arm. Possibly the points are in bad condition. Clean and reset them as described in this Chapter.

6 If there are no sparks from the end of the lead from the coil check the connections at the coil end of the lead. If it is in order start checking the low tension circuit.

7 Use a 12v voltmeter or a 12v bulb and two lengths of wire. With the ignition switch on the points open test between the low tension wire to the coil (it is marked SW or +) and earth. No reading indicates a break in the supply from the ignition switch. Check the connections at the switch to see if any are loose. Refit them and the engine should run. A reading shows a faulty coil or condenser, or broken lead between the coil and the distributor.

8 Take the condenser wire off the points assembly and with the points open, test between the moving points and earth. If there now is a reading, then the fault is in the condenser. Fit a new one and the fault is cleared.

9 With no reading from the moving point to earth take a reading between earth and the negative terminal of the coil. A reading here shows a broken wire which will need to be replaced betweem the coil and distributor. No reading confirms that the coil has failed and must be replaced, after which the engine will run once more. Remember to refit the condenser wire to the points assembly. For these tests it is sufficient to separate the points with a piece of dry paper while testing with the points open.

Engine misfires

10 If the engine misfires regularly, run it at a fast idling speed. Pull off each of the plug caps in turn and listen to the note of the engine. Hold the plug cap in a dry cloth or with a rubber glove as additional protection against a shock from the HT supply.

11 No difference in engine running will be noticed when the lead from the defective circuit is removed. Removing the lead from one of the good cylinders will accentuate the misfire.

12 Remove the plug lead from the end of the defective plug and hold it about 3/16th inch (5 mm) away from the block. Restart the engine. If the sparking is fairly strong and regular the fault must lie in the spark plug.

13 The plug may be loose, the insulation may be cracked, or the points may have burnt away giving too wide a gap for the spark to jump. Worse still, one of the points may have broken off. Either renew the plug, or clean it, reset the gap, and then test it.

14 If there is no spark at the end of the plug lead, or if it is weak and intermittent, check the ignition lead from the distributor to the plug. If the insulation is cracked or perished, renew the lead. Check the connections at the distributor cap.

15 If there is still no spark, examine the distributor cap carefully for tracking. This can be recognised by a very thin black line running between two or more electrodes, or between an electrode and some other part of the distributor. These lines are paths which now conduct electricity across the cap thus letting it run to earth. The only answer is a new distributor cap.

16 Apart from the ignition timing being incorrect, other causes of misfiring have already been dealt with under the section dealing with the failure of the engine to start. To recap - these are that:
 a) the coil may be faulty giving an intermittent misfire;
 b) there may be damaged wire or loose connection in the low tension circuit;
 c) the condenser may be short circuiting;
 d) there may be a mechanical fault in the distributor (broken driving spindle or contact breaker spring).

17 If the ignition timing is too far retarded, it should be noted that the engine will tend to overheat, and there will be a quite noticeable drop in power. If the engine is overheating and the power is down, and the ignition timing is correct, then the carburettor should be checked, as it is likely that this is where the fault lies.

15 Ignition system (transistor type) - testing and fault finding

1 Expensive and special equipment is required to test the transistor unit. It is therefore recommended that the unit, which is located on the facia panel within the car interior, should be removed and tested by a competent automobile electrician.

2 Apart from this, check the security of all HT and LT leads and examine the distributor cap for cracks.

3 The testing procedure described in the preceding Section will apply except in respect of the contact breaker which of course should be ignored. The air gap between the reluctor and the pick-up coil should however be checked as described earlier in this Chapter (Section 8).

Measuring plug gap. A feeler gauge of the correct size (see ignition system specifications) should have a slight 'drag' when slid between the electrodes. Adjust gap if necessary

Adjusting plug gap. The plug gap is adjusted by bending the earth electrode inwards, or outwards, as necessary until the correct clearance is obtained. Note the use of the correct tool

Normal. Grey-brown deposits, lightly coated core nose. Gap increasing by around 0.001 in (0.025 mm) per 1000 miles (1600 km). Plugs ideally suited to engine, and engine in good condition

Carbon fouling. Dry, black, sooty deposits. Will cause weak spark and eventually misfire. Fault: over-rich fuel mixture. Check: carburettor mixture settings, float level and jet sizes; choke operation and cleanliness of air filter. Plugs can be re-used after cleaning

Oil fouling. Wet, oily deposits. Will cause weak spark and eventually misfire. Fault: worn bores/piston rings or valve guides; sometimes occurs (temporarily) during running-in period. Plugs can be re-used after thorough cleaning

Overheating. Electrodes have glazed appearance, core nose very white — few deposits. Fault: plug overheating. Check: plug value, ignition timing, fuel octane rating (too low) and fuel mixture (too weak). Discard plugs and cure fault immediately

Electrode damage. Electrodes burned away; core nose has burned, glazed appearance. Fault: pre-ignition. Check: as for 'Overheating' but may be more severe. Discard plugs and remedy fault before piston or valve damage occurs

Split core nose (may appear initially as a crack). Damage is self-evident, but cracks will only show after cleaning. Fault: pre-ignition or wrong gap-setting technique. Check: ignition timing, cooling system, fuel octane rating (too low) and fuel mixture (too weak). Discard plugs, rectify fault immediately

Chapter 5 Clutch

Contents

Specifications

Type	Single dry plate, diaphragm spring, sealed ball type release bearing, hydraulic operation

Clutch driven plate friction lining

Outside diameter	7.87 in. (200.0 mm)
Inside diameter	5.12 in. (130.0 mm)
Thickness	0.138 in. (3.5 mm)
Number of torsion springs	6

Clutch pedal height from floor	7.1 in. (180.0 mm)

Free-movement at pedal pad	0.04 to 0.20 in. (1.0 to 5.0 mm)

Master cylinder diameter	5/8 in. (15.87 mm)

Operating cylinder diameter	¾ in. (19.05 mm)

Torque wrench settings

	lb/ft	kg/m
Clutch housing to engine bolts	35	4.8
Clutch to flywheel bolts	20	2.8
Operating cylinder securing bolts	30	4.1
Withdrawal lever ball pivot stud	36	5.0

1 General description

The clutch assembly is similar on all models but the design detail of some components varies according to model and date of manufacture. This in no way effects the procedure described in the Sections of this Chapter.

Major components comprise a pressure plate and cover assembly, diaphragm spring and a driven plate (friction disc) which incorporates torsion coil springs to cushion rotational shock when the drive is taken up.

The clutch release bearing is of sealed ball type and clutch actuation is hydraulic.

Depressing the clutch pedal moves the piston in the master cylinder forwards, so forcing hydraulic fluid through the clutch hydraulic pipe to the slave cylinder.

The piston in the slave cylinder moves forward on the entry of the fluid and actuates the clutch release arm by means of a short pushrod.

The release arm pushes the release bearing forwards to bear against the release plate, so moving the centre of the diaphragm spring inwards. The spring is sandwiched between two annular rings which act as fulcrum points. As the centre of the spring is pushed in, the outside of the spring is pushed out, so moving the pressure plate backwards and disengaging the pressure plate from the clutch disc.

When the clutch pedal is released the diaphragm spring forces the pressure plate into contact with the high friction linings on the clutch disc and at the same time pushes the clutch disc a fraction of an inch forwards on its splines so engaging the clutch disc with the flywheel. The clutch disc is now firmly sandwiched between the pressure plate and the flywheel so the drive is taken up.

On all models, the specified free-movement must be maintained between the face of the clutch release bearing and the pressure plate diaphragm spring fingers. This is carried out by first checking the pedal height and then screwing the master cylinder pushrod in, or out, as necessary and as described in the next Section.

On all models, this free-movement, once set, is maintained by a special type of operating cylinder which is self-adjusting to compensate for wear on the driven plate friction linings.

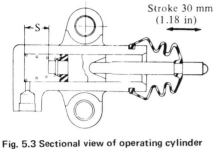

Stroke 30 mm
(1.18 in)

Fig. 5.3 Sectional view of operating cylinder

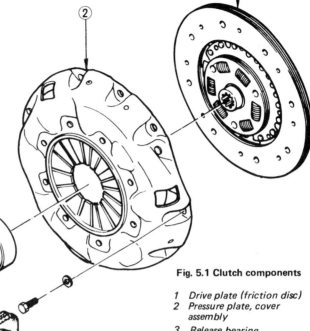

Fig. 5.1 Clutch components

1 Drive plate (friction disc)
2 Pressure plate, cover assembly
3 Release bearing
4 Release bearing hub
5 Withdrawl lever
6 Pivot

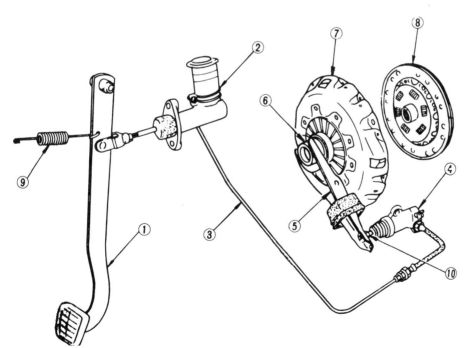

Fig. 5.2 Hydraulic operating system

1 Clutch pedal	4 Operating cylinder	7 Cover	9 Pedal return spring
2 Master cylinder	5 Withdrawl lever	8 Drive plate	10 Pushrod
3 Hydraulic line	6 Release bearing		

2 Clutch - adjustment

1 Measure the height of the clutch pedal pad upper surface from the floor. This should be 7.1 in. (180.0 mm) and if necessary, adjust by releasing the locknut and turning the stop bolt in or out.
2 Now adjust the pushrod so that there is a free-movement of between 0.04 and 0.20 in. (1.0 and 5.0 mm) when the pedal pad is depressed with the fingers.
3 Retighten all locknuts.

3 Master cylinder - removal and installation

1 Disconnect the master cylinder pushrod from the pedal arm.
2 Disconnect the fluid line from the master cylinder and drain the fluid into a suitable container.
3 Remove the master cylinder flange mounting bolts and withdraw the unit from the engine compartment rear bulkhead.
4 Installation is a reversal of removal, but check the pedal height and free-movement as previously described in this Chapter and bleed the hydraulic system (Sec 7).

4 Master cylinder - servicing

1 Unscrew and remove the reservoir cap and drain any fluid.
2 Peel back the dust excluder and extract the circlip.
3 Withdraw the pushrod and the piston assembly.
4 Remove the valve assembly and return spring.
5 Wash all components in clean hydraulic fluid or methylated spirit and examine the surface of the piston and the bore of the cylinder for scoring or 'bright' wear areas. Where these are evident, renew the master cylinder complete.
6 Where the components are in good condition, discard the rubber seals and obtain a repair kit. The end of the valve stem can be released from the 'keyhole' in the spring seat by first compressing the return spring and pulling the spring seat to one side.

7 Dip the new seals in clean hydraulic fluid and manipulate them into position using the fingers only. Check that their lips and chamfers face the correct way.
8 Reassembly is a reversal of dismantling, use all the parts supplied in the repair kit.
9 Check that the vent holes in the reservoir cap are clear by probing them with a piece of wire.

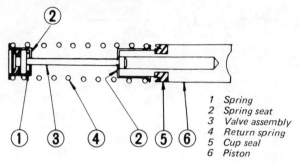

1 Spring
2 Spring seat
3 Valve assembly
4 Return spring
5 Cup seal
6 Piston

Fig. 5.5 Sectional view of the master cylinder piston assembly

5 Operating cylinder - removal and refitting

1 Unscrew and remove the two bolts which secure the slave cylinder to the clutch bellhousing. Withdraw the slave cylinder extracting the end of the pushrod from the clutch withdrawal lever at the same time.
2 Without straining or twisting the hydraulic hose (hold its end fitting securely in a spanner) unscrew the slave cylinder from the end fitting of the hose and then plug the end fitting, to prevent loss of fluid. An alternative method, to prevent loss of fluid, is to remove the reservoir cap and place a piece of polythene sheeting over the open reservoir. Screw on the cap and thus create a vacuum which will stop the fluid running out of the open hose.
3 Installation is a reversal of removal but bleed the hydraulic system (Section 7) and check the clutch pedal free-movement.

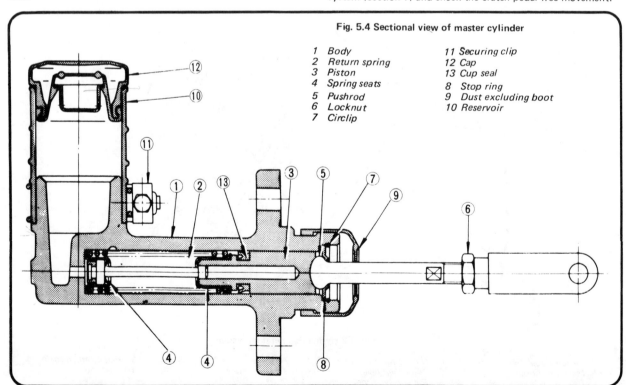

Fig. 5.4 Sectional view of master cylinder

1 Body	11 Securing clip
2 Return spring	12 Cap
3 Piston	13 Cup seal
4 Spring seats	8 Stop ring
5 Pushrod	9 Dust excluding boot
6 Locknut	10 Reservoir
7 Circlip	

6 Operating cylinder - servicing

1 Withdraw the pushrod and dust cover from the end of the cylinder body.
2 Extract the piston and the piston spring. If these components are difficult to remove, apply air pressure from a tyre pump at the fluid entry port on the cylinder body.
3 Wash all components in clean hydraulic fluid or methylated spirit and then examine the surfaces of the piston and cylinder bore. If these are scored or any 'bright' wear areas are evident, renew the slave cylinder complete.
4 If the components are in good order, discard the seal and obtain a repair kit.
5 Manipulate the new seal into position, ensuring that its lip faces the correct way.
6 Reassembly is a reversal of dismantling but take care not to nip the piston seal as it enters the cylinder bore. Alway dip the piston assembly in clean hydraulic fluid before commencing to assemble it.

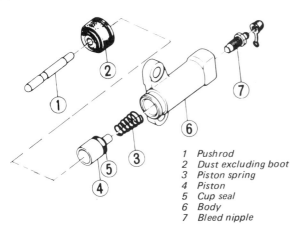

1 Pushrod
2 Dust excluding boot
3 Piston spring
4 Piston
5 Cup seal
6 Body
7 Bleed nipple

Fig. 5.6 Exploded view of the clutch operating cylinder

7 Hydraulic system - bleeding

1 The need for bleeding the cylinders and fluid lines arises when air gets into them. Air gets in whenever a joint or seal leaks or a part has to be dismantled. Bleeding is simply the process of venting the air out again.
2 Make sure the reservoir is filled and obtain a piece of 3/16 inch (4.8 mm) bore diameter rubber tube about 2 to 3 feet (0.6 to 0.8 mm) long and a clean glass jar. A small quantity of fresh, clean hydraulic fluid as also necessary.
3 Detach the cap (if fitted) on the bleed nipple and surrounding area. Unscrew the nipple ¼ turn and fit the tube over it. Put about ½ inch (12.7 mm) of fluid in the jar and put the other end of the pipe in it. The jar can be placed on the ground under the car.
4 The clutch pedal should then be depressed quickly and released slowly until no more air bubbles come from the pipe. Quick pedal action carries the air along rather than leaving it behind. Keep the reservoir topped up.
5 When the air bubbles stop tighten the nipple at the end of a down stroke.
6 Check that the operation of the clutch is satisfactory. Even though there may be no exterior leaks it is possible that the movement of the pushrod from the clutch cylinder is inadequate because fluid is leaking internally past the seals in the master cylinder. If this is the case, it is best to replace all seals in both cylinders.
7 Always use clean hydraulic fluid which has been stored in an airtight container and has remained unshaken for the preceding 24 hours.

8 Clutch - removal

1 Remove the engine/gearbox as a unit as fully described in Chapter 1, or alternatively 'drop' the gearbox as described in Chapter 6.
2 Separate the gearbox from the engine by removing the clutch bellhousing to crankcase securing bolts.
3 The pressure plate need not be marked in relation to the flywheel as it can only be fitted one way due to the positioning dowels.
4 Unscrew the clutch assembly securing bolts a turn at a time in diametrically opposite sequence until the tension of the diaphragm spring is released. Remove the bolts and lift the pressure plate assembly away.
5 At this stage, the driven plate (friction disc) will fall from its location between the pressure plate and the flywheel.

9 Clutch - inspection and renovation

1 Due to the slow-wearing qualities of the clutch, it is not easy to decide when to go to the trouble of removing the gearbox in order to check the wear on the friction lining. The only positive indication that something needs doing is when it starts to slip or when seqealing noises on engagement indicate that the friction lining has worn down to the rivets. In such instances it can only be hoped that the friction surfaces on the flywheel and pressure plate have not been badly worn or scored.
  A clutch will wear according to the way in which it is used. Much intentional slipping of the clutch while driving - rather then the correct selection of gears - will accelerate wear. It is best to assume, however, that the friction disc will need renewal every 35,000 miles (56,000 km) at least and that it will be worth replacing it after 25,000 miles (40,000 km). The maintenance history of the car is obviously very useful in such cases.
2 Examine the surfaces of the pressure plate and flywheel for signs of scoring. If this is only light it may be left, but if very deep the pressure plate unit will have to be renewed. If the flywheel is deeply scored it should be taken off and advice sought from an engineering firm. Providing it may be machined completely across the face of overall balance of engine and flywheel should not be too severely upset. If renewal of the flywheel is necessary the new one will have to be balanced to match the original.
3 The friction plate lining surfaces should be at least 1/32 in. (0.8 mm) above the rivets, otherwise the disc is not worth putting back. If the lining material shows signs of breaking up or black areas where oil contamination has occured it should also be renewed. If facilities are readily available for obtaining and fitting new friction pads to the existing disc this may be done but the saving is relatively small compared with obtaining a complete new disc assembly which ensures that the shock absorbing springs and the splined hub are renewed also. The same applies to the pressure plate assembly which cannot be readily dismantled and put back together without specialised riveting tools and balancing equipment. An allowance is usually given for exchange units.

10 Clutch release bearing - renewal

1 The sealed, ball bearing type release bearing, although designed for long life, is worth renewing at the same time as the other clutch components are being renewed or serviced.
2 Deterioration of the release bearing should be suspected when there are signs of grease leakage or the unit is noisy when spun with the fingers.
3 Remove the rubber dust excluder which surrounds the withdrawal lever at the bellhousing aperture.
4 Disconnect and remove the spring from the release bearing hub. (photos)

5 Disconnect the withdrawal lever from the release bearing hub.

6 Withdraw the release bearing/hub assembly from the front cover of the gearbox.

7 Remove the release bearing from its hub using a two or three legged puller and a bridge piece across the end-face of the hub.

8 Press on the new bearing but apply pressure only to the centre track.

9 Reassembly is a reversal of dismantling but apply high melting point grease to the internal recess of the release bearing hub.

10 Also apply similar grease to the pivot points of the clutch withdrawal lever.

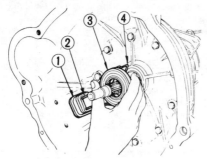

Fig. 5.7 Removing clutch release mechanism

1 Grommet
2 Withdrawl lever
3 Release bearing
4 Retaining spring

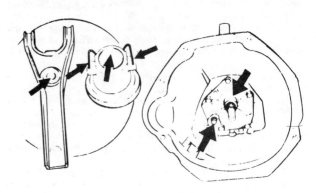

Fig. 5.11 Grease application points for clutch release and withdrawal lever components

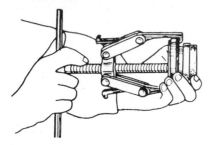

Fig. 5.8 Extracting clutch release bearing from its hub

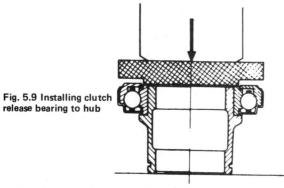

Fig. 5.9 Installing clutch release bearing to hub

10.4A Clutch release bearing and withdrawal lever

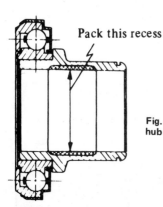

Pack this recess

Fig. 5.10 Clutch release bearing hub grease packing diagram

10.4B Release bearing to withdrawal lever retaining springs

11 Clutch - installation

1 Clean the face of the flywheel and the pressure plate.
2 On early models, apply a little high melting point grease to the spigot bush in the centre of the flywheel. On later vehicles, this need not be done as the bush is self-lubricating. Apply grease also to the splines of the input shaft.
3 Locate the driven plate against the flywheel so that its larger projecting boss is furthest from the engine.
4 Position the pressure plate assembly on the flywheel so that the positioning dowels engage.
5 Screw in each of the pressure plate bolts finger tight and then centralise the driven plate. This is accomplished by passing an old input shaft or stepped dowel rod through the splined hub of the driven plate and engaging it in the spigot bush. By moving the shaft or rod in the appropriate directions, the position will be established where the centralising tool can be withdrawn without any side pressure from the driven plate, proving that the driven plate is centralised.
6 Without disturbing the setting of the driven plate, tighten the pressure plate bolts, a turn at a time, in diametrically opposite sequence to the specified torque.
7 Refit the gearbox to engine (Chapter 6) when, if the driven plate has been correctly centralised, the input shaft of the gearbox will pass easily through the splined hub of the driven plate to engage with the spigot bush in the centre of the flywheel. Do not allow the weight of the gearbox to hang upon the input shaft while it is passing through the clutch mechanism or damage to the clutch components may result.

12 Clutch pedal - removal and installation

1 Detach the return spring.
2 Withdraw the split pin and the clevis pin and disconnect the master cylinder pushrod from the pedal arm.
3 Remove the pivot bolt and withdraw the clutch pedal assembly.
4 Installation is a reversal of removal but apply multi-purpose grease to the pivot bolt and bushes.

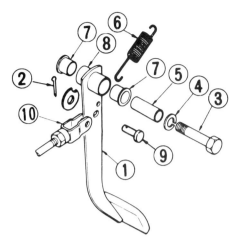

Fig. 5.13 Exploded view of the clutch pedal assembly

1 Pedal   6 Pedal return spring
2 Split pin   7 Bush
3 Pivot bolt   8 Boss
4 Lock washer   9 Clevis
5 Sleeve   10 Master cylinder pushrod

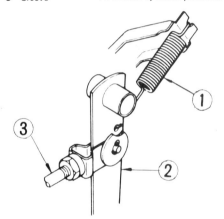

Fig. 5.14 Pushrod to pedal arm assembly (early type)

1 Return spring   3 Pushrod
2 Pedal assembly

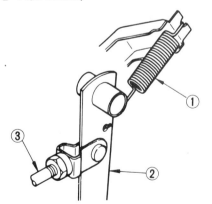

Fig. 5.15 Pushrod to pedal arm assembly (later type)

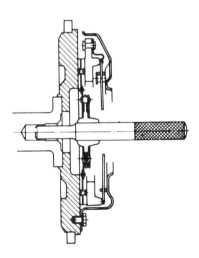

Fig. 5.12 Centralising the clutch driven plate

Fault diagnosis is given overleaf

13 Fault diagnosis - clutch

Symptom	Reason/s
Judder when taking up drive	Loose engine or gearbox mountings Badly worn friction surfaces or contaminated with oil Worn splines on gearbox input shaft or driven plate hub Worn input shaft spigot bush in flywheel
Clutch spin (failure to disengage) so that gears cannot be meshed	Incorrect release bearing to diaphragm spring finger clearance Driven plate sticking on input shaft splines due to rust. May occur after vehicle standing idle for long period Damaged or misaligned pressure plate assembly
Clutch slip (increase in engine speed does not result in increase in vehicle road speed - particularly on gradients)	Incorrect release bearing to diaphragm spring finger clearance Friction surfaces worn out or oil contaminated
Noise evident on depressing clutch pedal	Dry, worn or damaged release bearing Insufficient pedal free travel Weak or broken pedal return spring Weak or broken clutch release lever return spring Excessive play between driven plate hub splines and input shaft splines
Noise evident as clutch pedal released	Distorted driven plate Broken or weak driven plate cushion coil springs Insufficient pedal free travel Weak or broken clutch pedal return spring Weak or broken release lever return spring Distorted or worn input shaft Release bearing loose on retainer hub

Chapter 6 Part 1: Manual gearbox

Contents

Specifications

Gearbox type	F4W63L - four forward speeds and reverse. Synchromesh on all forward speeds

Ratios

1st	3.382 : 1
2nd	2.031 : 1
3rd	1.312 : 1
4th	1.000 : 1
Reverse	3.365 : 1

Speedometer gear ratio	16/5

Final drive ratio

140J and 160J.SSS	3.900
710 series	3.700

Endfloat

1st gear	0.0126 to 0.0165 in. (0.32 to 0.42 mm)
2nd gear	0.0087 to 0.0126 in. (0.22 to 0.32 mm)
3rd gear	0.0020 to 0.0059 in. (0.05 to 0.15 mm)
Reverse idler	0.0039 to 0.0118 in. (0.10 to 0.30 mm)

Backlash (all gears)	0.0020 to 0.0079 in. (0.05 to 0.20 mm)
Countershaft assembly endfloat	0.0020 to 0.0059 in. (0.05 to 0.15 mm)
Baulk ring to gear cone clearance	0.047 to 0.063 in. (1.2 to 1.6 mm)
Oil capacity	3½ Imp. pts, 4¼ U.S. pts, 2.0 litres

Torque wrench settings	lb/ft	kg/m
Clutch bellhousing to engine bolts	35	4.8
Clutch operating cylinder bolts	30	4.1
Crossmember to bodyframe bolt	20	2.8
Mainshaft nut	80	11.1
Reverse lamp switch	22	3.0
Neutral switch	22	3.0
Top gear switch	22	3.0
Filler plug	25	3.5
Drain plug	25	3.5

1 General description

The gearbox fitted to all models is of four-speed and one reverse type with synchromesh on all forward gears.

The forward gears are of a helical gear formation and the reverse gear a sliding mesh type using spur gears.

The main driveshaft gear is meshed with the counter drive gear. The forward speed gears on the countershaft are in constant mesh with the main gears. Each of the main gears rides on the mainshaft on needle roller bearings, rotating freely.

When the gearchange lever is operated the relevant coupling sleeve is caused to slide on the synchronizer hub and engages its inner teeth with the outer teeth formed on the mainshaft gear. The synchronizer hub is splined to the mainshaft so enabling them to rotate in unison.

Moving the gearchange lever to the reverse gear position moves the mainshaft reverse gear into engagement with the reverse idler gear.

The gearbox casing comprises two major parts, the main casing which contains all the gear and shaft assemblies and the rear extension housing.

The gear selector mechanism is controlled from a floor mounted lever. Movement of the lever is transferred through a striking rod to dogs on the ends of the selector rods and then through the medium of shift forks which are permanently engaged in the grooves of the synchro. unit sleeves.

2 Gearbox - removal and installation

1 Disconnect the lead from the battery negative terminal and drain the oil from the gearbox. (photo)

2 On certain 710 series North American vehicles, disconnect the catalyzer sensor wiring harness and remove the harness shield.

3 Preferably place the vehicle over an inspection pit but if one is not available, raise the vehicle and support is securely on axle stands making sure that there is sufficient clearance below the bodyframe to enable the largest diameter of the clutch bellhousing to pass through during the removal operations.

4 From inside the vehicle, remove the centre console.

5 Using two open-ended spanners, remove the gearshift control lever. (photo)

6 On certain North American 710 series vehicles, remove the shield from the lower side of the catalytic converter and disconnect the exhaust pipe from the converter.

7 On all other models, disconnect the exhaust downpipe from the exhaust manifold and from the rest of the exhaust system.

8 Disconnect the leads from the reversing lamp switch and then disconnect the speedometer drive cable.

9 Disconnect the leads from the top gear switch.

10 Disconnect the leads from the neutral switch.

11 Unbolt the clutch operating cylinder from the clutch bellhousing and tie it up out of the way. There is no need to dis-

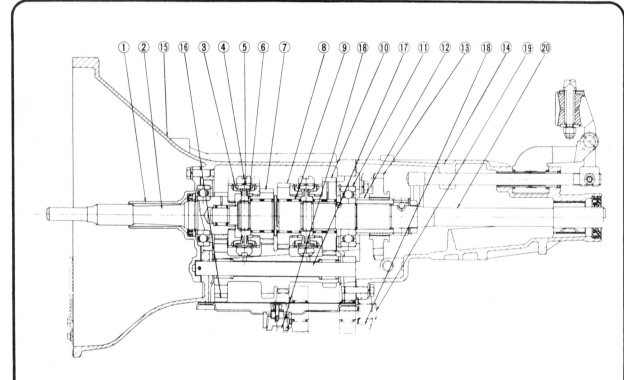

Fig. 6.1 Sectional view of four-speed manual gearbox

1 Front cover	components of 3rd. /4th.
2 Input shaft	synchro.)
3 Baulk ring	7 3rd. gear
4 Synchro. sleeve	8 2nd. gear
5 Shift key	9 Needle bearing
6 Syncho. hub (3 to 6	10 1st. gear

11 Mainshaft rear bearing
12 Reverse gear hub
13 Reverse gear
14 Rear extension housing
15 Casing

16 Countergear
17 Countershaft
18 Reverse idler gear
19 Reverse idler shaft
20 Mainshaft

connect the hydraulic system.

12 Disconnect the propeller shaft and remove it, as described in Chapter 7. There may be some loss of oil from the rear end of the extension housing and to prevent this, slide a small plastic bag over the end of the extension housing and secure it with a rubber band as soon as the propeller shaft is withdrawn. (photo)

13 Support the engine under the sump by using a jack and wooden insulating block to prevent damaging the sump pan.

14 Remove the rear mounting both from the transmission casing and from the bodyframe.

15 Unbolt and remove the starter motor.

16 Unbolt and remove the two rear reinforcement plates.

17 Unscrew and remove the bolts which secure the clutch bell-housing to the engine.

18 Carefully lower the jack until the gearbox can be withdrawn to the rear from below the vehicle. The use of a trolley type jack placed under the gearbox will facilitate this operation as it is most important that the weight of the gearbox does not hang upon the input shaft while the latter is still engaged with the clutch assembly otherwise the clutch may be seriously damaged. (photo)

19 Installation is a reversal of removal but first apply a smear of high melting point grease to the input shaft splines.

20 When installation is complete, check the clutch pedal adjustment (Chapter 5) and refill the gearbox with the correct grade and quantity of oil.

2.12 Withdrawing propeller shaft from gearbox

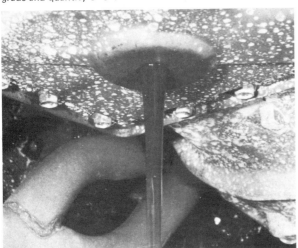

2.1 Draining the gearbox

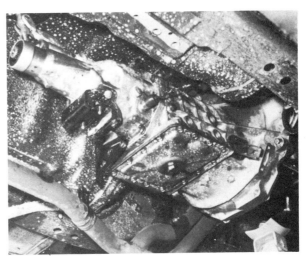

2.18A Gearbox ready for removal

2.5 Gearshift lever retaining nut viewed from below

12.18B View of clutch and flywheel, gearbox withdrawn

Fig. 6.2 Removing gearshift lever

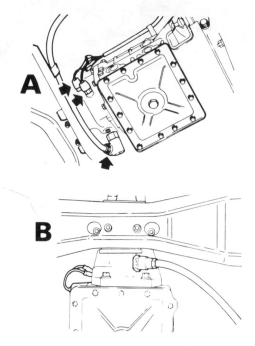

Fig. 6.3 Reversing lamp switch leads and speedometer cable connection

A 1975 model for California
B All other models

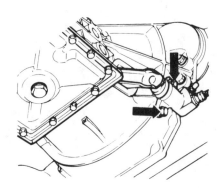

Fig. 6.4 Clutch operating cylinder securing bolts

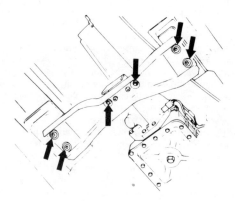

Fig. 6.5 Rear mounting and crossmember bolts

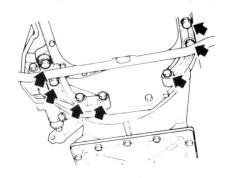

Fig. 6.6 Reinforcement plates and bolts

3 Gearbox - dismantling into major assemblies

1 Before work commences, clean the external surfaces with paraffin or a water soluble solvent.
2 Drain the oil (unless this was done before removal).
3 With the unit secure on the bench, unscrew and remove the speedometer pinion and housing assembly. (photos)
4 Remove the dust excluding boot from the clutch bellhousing and then extract the clutch withdrawal lever and release bearing.
5 Unbolt and remove the front cover.
6 Unbolt and remove the transmission lower cover plate, noting the internal magnet which should be wiped clean. (photo)
7 Unscrew and remove the reversing lamp, neutral and top gear switches. (photo)
8 Make sure that the gears are set in the neutral position and then withdraw the pin from the remote control rod. (photos)
9 Unscrew and remove the six bolts which secure the rear extension housing to the transmission casing. (photo)
10 Tap off the extension housing using a soft-faced or wooden mallet. (photo)
11 Remove the remote control rod.
12 Unscrew the detent ball plugs and extract the springs and balls.
13 Drive out the tension pins which secure the shift forks to the selector rods.
14 Withdraw each of the selector rods and remove the shift forks taking care to retrieve the interlock plugs. (photo)
15 Using a screwdriver, move the synchronizer sleeves so that the gears engage and lock up the mainshaft.
16 Straighten the lockwasher tab and release the mainshaft end nut. Return the synchronizer sleeves to their neutral positions.
17 Using a piece of rod of suitable diameter, tap out the countershaft towards the front of the gearbox. Lift out the countergear together with thrust washers and needle bearings.
18 Prise off the circlip which retains the reverse idler gear in

3.3A Speedometer gear and retainer

3.3B Withdrawing speedometer gear

3.6 Interior of gearbox bottom cover showing magnet for collecting metal particles

3.7 Removing reversing lamp

3.8A Gearshift control rod pin circlip

3.8B Withdrawing control rod pin

3.9 Removing extension housing bolts. Note exhaust bracket

3.10 Removing extension housing

3.14A Removing reverse selector rod and fork

3.14B Removing 3rd./4th. selector rod and fork

3.14C Removing 1st./2nd. selector rod and fork

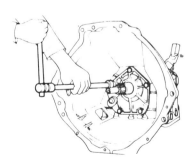
Fig. 6.7 Unbolting gearbox front cover

position. The circlip is located at the front end of the shaft.
19 Withdraw the idler gear shaft from the rear of the gearbox casing.
20 Unscrew and remove the bolts which secure the mainshaft rear bearing retainer.
21 Withdraw the mainshaft assembly from the rear of the gearbox casing.
22 Extract the pilot bearing which is located between the mainshaft and the input shaft.
23 Using the wooden handle of a hammer as a drift, tap out the input shaft from the front of the gearbox casing.
24 The gearbox is now completely dismantled into its major components but further operations should not be undertaken unless the facilities of a press or extractors are available.

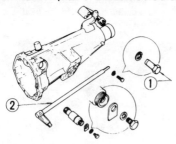

Fig. 6.8 Gear selector remote control rod pin (1) and rod (2)

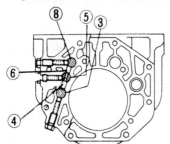

3   1st./2nd. selector rod
4   Interlock plunger
5   3rd./4th. selector rod
6   Interlock plunger
8   Reverse selector rod

Fig. 6.9 Sectional view of gear selector interlock mechanism

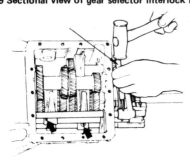

Fig. 6.10 Using drift (arrowed) to remove shift fork retaining pin

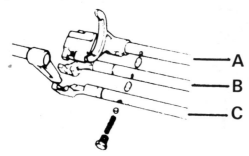

Fig. 6.11 Selector rods and interlock plungers

A   Reverse selector rod
B   3rd./4th. selector rod
C   1st./2nd. selector rod

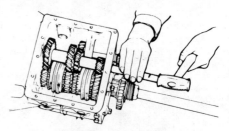

Fig. 6.12 Removing countershaft

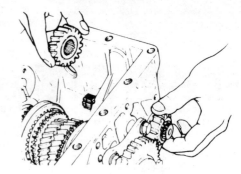

Fig. 6.13 Removing reverse idler gears and shaft

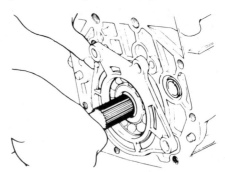

Fig. 6.14 Withdrawing the mainshaft assembly

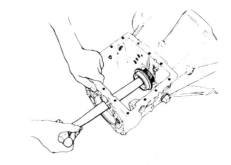

Fig. 6.15 Removing input shaft assembly

---

4   Mainshaft - servicing

---

1   Extract the circlip from the front end of the mainshaft.
2   Withdraw 3rd/4th synchro. unit and 3rd gear.
3   The mainshaft end nut will have already been released (see paragraphs 15 and 16, of the preceding Section). Now unscrew and remove it and withdraw reverse gear, reverse gear hub and the speedometer drive gear. Make sure that the speedometer gear locking ball is retained.
4   Draw off 1st gear, ball bearing and retainer from the rear end of the mainshaft. This may be carried out by using a puller having its legs engaged behind the front face of 1st. gear or

otherwise supporting first gear and pressing the mainshaft from the gear, bearing and retainer. Do not use 2nd gear front face as a pressure area during these operations or the mainshaft 1st gear spacer may collapse. Extract the thrust washer and locking ball which is located between the bearing and 1st gear.

5 In a similar manner to that just described in the preceding paragraph, either draw off 1st/2nd gear synchro. and 2nd gear or press the mainshaft from them.

6 Extract the circlip and drive the mainshaft rear bearing from its retainer.

7 The synchro. hubs are only too easy to dismantle - just push the centre out and the whole assembly flies apart. The point is to prevent this happening, before you are ready. Do not dismantle the hubs without reason and do not mix up the parts of the two hubs.

8 It is most important to check backlash in the splines between the outer sleeve and inner hub. If any is noticeable the whole assembly must be renewed.

9 Mark the hubs and sleeve so that you may reassemble them on the same splines. With the hub and sleeve separated, the teeth at the end of the splines which engage with corresponding teeth of the gear wheels, must be checked for damage and wear.

10 Do not confuse the keystone shape at the ends of the teeth. This shape matches the gearteeth shape and it is a design characteristic to minimise jump-out tendencies.

11 If the synchronising cones are being renewed it is sensible also to renew the sliding keys and springs which hold them in position.

12 Place each baulk ring in turn on its gear cone and then, using a feeler blade, measure the baulk ring to cone clearance. This should be as specified otherwise renew the baulk ring.

13 Reassemble the synchro. units by placing the hub into its sleeve and insert the shift keys.

14 Install the springs so that they engage in the shift keys and the open sections of the springs are not in alignment but 180° apart.

15 It is assumed that the gearbox has been dismantled for reasons of excessive noise, lack of synchromesh action on certain gears or for failure to stay in gear. If anything more drastic than this (total failure, seizure or main casing cracked) it would be better to leave it alone and look for a replacement, either secondhand or an exchange.

16 Examine all gears for excessively worn, chipped or damaged teeth. Any such gears should be renewed. Check the endfloat and backlash is in accordance with specification.

17 All ball race bearings should be checked for chatter and roughness after they have been flushed out. It is advisable to renew these anyway even though they may not appear too badly worn. (photo)

18 Circlips which are all important in locating bearings, gears and hubs should be checked to ensure that they are undistorted and undamaged. In any case a selection of new circlips of varying thicknesses should be obtained to compensate for variations in new components fitted, and wear in old ones. The specifications indicate what is available.

19 Needle roller bearings between the input shaft and mainshaft and in the laygear are usually found in good order, but if in any doubt replace the needle rollers as necessary.

20 Commence reassembly by installing 2nd gear needle roller bearing, 2nd gear and 2nd gear baulk ring. (photo)

21 Install 1st/2nd synchro. unit checking that it is fitted the correct way round. (photo)

22 Drive on 1st. gear spacer using a piece of brass tubing. (photo)

23 Install 1st gear baulk ring, the needle bearing, 1st gear, locking ball and the thrust washer. (photos)

24 Press on the mainshaft bearing. (photo)

25 Install 3rd gear needle roller bearing, 3rd gear and baulk ring. (photo)

26 Install 3rd/4th synchro. unit checking that it is fitted the correct way round. (photo)

27 Fit a circlip from the thicknesses available:
> 0.0551 to 0.0571 in. (1.40 to 1.45 mm)
> 0.0571 to 0.0591 in. (1.45 to 1.50 mm)
> 0.0591 to 0.0610 in. (1.50 to 1.55 mm)
> 0.0610 to 0.0630 in. (1.55 to 1.60 mm)
> 0.0630 to 0.0650 in. (1.60 to 1.65 mm)

which will provide the mimimum clearance between the endface of the synchro. hub and the circlip groove. (photo)

28 To the rear end of the mainshaft, fit the reverse gear, locking ball and speedometer drive gear, lockplate and mainshaft nut. Do not tighten the nut fully at this stage. (photos)

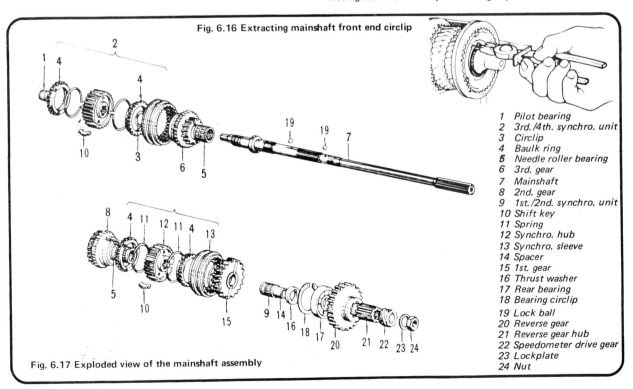

Fig. 6.16 Extracting mainshaft front end circlip

1 Pilot bearing
2 3rd./4th. synchro. unit
3 Circlip
4 Baulk ring
5 Needle roller bearing
6 3rd. gear
7 Mainshaft
8 2nd. gear
9 1st./2nd. synchro. unit
10 Shift key
11 Spring
12 Synchro. hub
13 Synchro. sleeve
14 Spacer
15 1st. gear
16 Thrust washer
17 Rear bearing
18 Bearing circlip
19 Lock ball
20 Reverse gear
21 Reverse gear hub
22 Speedometer drive gear
23 Lockplate
24 Nut

Fig. 6.17 Exploded view of the mainshaft assembly

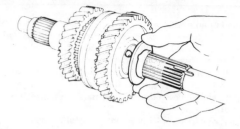

Fig. 6.18 Mainshaft thrust washer and lock ball

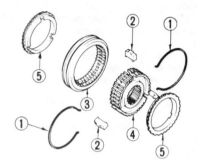

Fig. 6.19 Exploded view of a synchro. unit

1 Springs
2 Shift key
3 Sleeve
4 Hub
5 Baulk ring

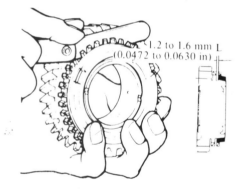

Fig. 6.20 Measuring synchro. baulk ring to gear cone clearance

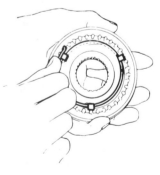

Fig. 6.21 Installing synchro. unit springs

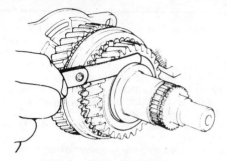

Fig. 6.22 Checking gear endfloat

Fig. 6.23 Using a dial gauge to measure gear backlash

Fig. 6.24 Checking a bearing for wear and roughness

4.17 Mainshaft rear bearing retaining circlip

4.20 Installing needle roller bearing, 2nd. gear and baulkring to mainshaft

4.21 Installing 1st./2nd. synchro. unit to mainshaft

4.22 Installing 1st. gear spacer to mainshaft

4.23A Installing 1st. gear baulkring and needle roller bearing to mainshaft

4.23B Installing 1st. gear and thrust washer locking ball to mainshaft

4.23C 1st. gear thrust washer secured to mainshaft by locking ball

4.24 Bearing ready for pressing onto mainshaft

4.25 Installing 3rd. gear, baulkring and needle roller bearing to front end of mainshaft

4.26 Installing 3rd./4th. synchro. unit to mainshaft

4.27 Installing circlip to front end of mainshaft

4.28A Installing reverse gear, locking ball and speedometer drive gear to rear end of mainshaft

4.28B Lockplate and mainshaft nut installed to rear end of mainshaft

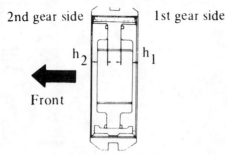

Fig. 6.25 1st./2nd. synchro. unit installation diagram

h1 is less than h2

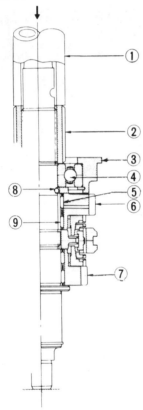

Fig. 6.26 Part sectional view of mainshaft rear bearing and adjacent components

1 Press tool
2 Reverse gear hub
3 Bearing retainer
4 Bearing
5 Needle roller bearing
6 1st. gear
7 2nd. gear
8 Lock ball
9 Spacer

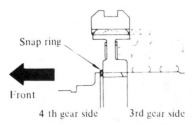

Fig. 6.27 3rd./4th. synchro. unit installation diagram

5 Input shaft - servicing

1 From the front end of the shaft extract the circlip and thrust washer.
2 Using a suitable puller or press, remove the bearing from the shaft.
3 Examine the gearteeth and splines for wear or damage and check the bearing. Renew components as necessary.
4 Reassembly is a reversal of dismantling but select a circlip from those available which will provide the minimum endfloat between the face of the spacer and the circlip groove. (photo)

0.0587 to 0.0610 in. (1.49 to 1.55 mm)
0.0614 to 0.0638 in. (1.56 to 1.62 mm)
0.0638 to 0.0661 in. (1.62 to 1.68 mm)
0.0661 to 0.0685 in. (1.68 to 1.74 mm)
0.0685 to 0.0709 in. (1.74 to 1.80 mm)
0.0709 to 0.0732 in. (1.80 to 1.86 mm)
0.0732 to 0.0756 in. (1.86 to 1.92 mm)

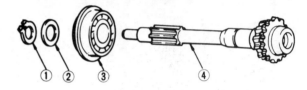

Fig. 6.28 Exploded view of the input shaft

1 Circlip
2 Spacer
3 Bearing and outer circlip
4 Input shaft

5.4 Input shaft bearing, thrust washer and circlip

6 Countershaft and gear assembly - servicing

1 Any wear or damage found in the countergear assembly will necessitate renewal of the complete assembly.
2 The needle roller bearings and thrust washers can be renewed separately.
3 When renewing a countershaft, it is normal to renew the corresponding mainshaft gears as matched sets.

7 Reverse gear assembly - servicing

1 Examine the gears for wear or chipped teeth.
2 Inspect the idler shaft for wear or distortion and renew as appropriate, also the shaft needle roller bearings. (photo)

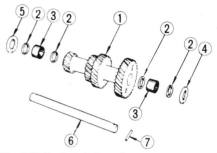

Fig. 6.29 Exploded view of countergear assembly

1 Countergear
2 Washers
3 Needle bearings
4 and 5 Thrust washers
6 Countershaft
7 Pin

7.2 Reverse idler shaft needle roller bearings

8 Selector mechanism - servicing

1 Inspect the selector rods for wear or distortion. Examine the detent notches particularly carefully for wear.
2 Examine the shift forks. Any excessive wear at the synchro. ring engagement surfaces of the forks will necessitate their renewal.

9 Oil seals - renewal

1 Whenever the gearbox has been dismantled for major overhaul, always renew the front cover oil seal and the rear extension housing oil seal.
2 These are simply drifted out and the new ones tapped squarely in, making sure that the lips face the correct way.

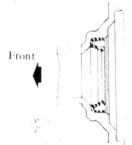

Fig. 6.30 Correct installation of front cover oil seal

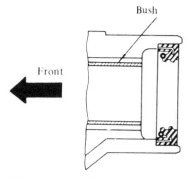

Fig. 6.31 Correct installation of rear extension oil seal

10 Gearbox - reassembly

1 Using a soft faced mallet, tap the input shaft into the front of the gearbox casing. (photos)
2 Install the pilot bearing and then insert the mainshaft assembly from the rear of the gearbox. (photo)
3 Insert and tighten the mainshaft rear bearing retainer bolts.
4 Install the reverse idler shaft so that the identification mark is towards the rear of the gearbox. (photo)
5 Assemble the thrust washer and the helical type idler gear and secure it with its circlip (at the front end of the shaft). (photo)
6 Now insert an 0.0039 in. (0.1 mm) feeler gauge between the helical type gear and its thrust washer. Push the idler shaft fully rearwards and install the thrust washer and spur type gear to the rear end of the idler shaft. Secure the gear with a circlip from available thicknesses:

   0.0413 to 0.0453 in. (1.05 to 1.15 mm)
   0.0453 to 0.0492 in. (1.15 to 1.25 mm)
   0.0492 to 0.0531 in. (1.25 to 1.35 mm)
   0.0531 to 0.0571 in. (1.35 to 1.45 mm)
   0.0571 to 0.0610 in. (1.45 to 1.55 mm)

so that when the feeler gauge is withdrawn from between the helical gear and its thrust washer the correct endfloat of between 0.0039 and 0.0118 in. (0.10 and 0.30 mm) will be established. Note that the reverse idler shaft thrust washers must be installed so that the sides with the oil grooves are towards the gears. (photo)
7 Stick the countershaft thrust washers into position in the interior of the gearcase using a dab of thick grease. Make sure that they are securely held by their lock tabs and that the smaller washer is at the rear. (photo)
8 Using a dummy countershaft or rod, inserted through the countergear, install the needle rollers and washers at both ends of the countergear again using thick grease to retain them (21 needle rollers at each end). (photo)
9 Place the countergear assembly into position and then insert the countershaft so that it displaces the dummy shaft or rod without dislodging the needle rollers or thrust washers. (photo)
10 Now check the countergear endfloat. This should be between 0.0020 and 0.0059 in. (0.05 and 0.15 mm) otherwise change the rear thrust washer for one of different thickness from those available:

   0.0925 to 0.0945 in. (2.35 to 2.40 mm)
   0.0945 to 0.0965 in. (2.40 to 2.45 mm)
   0.0965 to 0.0984 in. (2.45 to 2.50 mm)
   0.0984 to 0.1004 in. (2.50 to 2.55 mm)
   0.1004 to 0.1024 in. (2.55 to 2.60 mm)

11 Drive in a new retaining pin (if removed at dismantling). (photo)
12 Move the synchro. sleeves to mesh the gears and lock the mainshaft and then tighten the mainshaft nut to the specified torque and bend up the lockplate. (photo)
13 Return the synchro. sleeves to the neutral position.
14 Engage the 1st/2nd and 3rd/4th shift forks with the sleeve

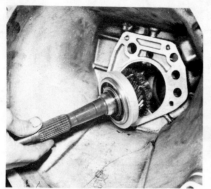
10.1A Installing input shaft

10.1B Connection of mainshaft and input shaft showing needle roller pilot bearing

10.2 Installing mainshaft assembly from rear end of gearbox

10.4 Correct installation of reverse idler shaft and thrust washer

10.5 Reverse idler gear and securing circlip at front end of shaft

10.6 Reverse gear and circlip at rear end of shaft

10.7 Countershaft thrust washer showing locating tag

10.8 Countershaft needle rollers

10.9 Installing countergear

10.11 Correct alignment of countershaft tension pin

10.12 Tighten mainshaft nut

10.14 Installing shift forks to synchro. sleeve grooves
1 3rd/4th   2 1st/2nd

grooves of the respective synchro. units. (photo)

15 Install the 1st/2nd selector rod so that it passes through the shift fork and then secure the fork to the rod with a new tension pin. (photo)

16 With the 1st/2nd selector rod in the neutral mode, insert the interlock plunger and then install the 3rd/4th selector rod and secure the 3rd/4th shift fork to it using a new tension pin. (photo)

17 Set the 3rd/4th selector rod in the neutral mode and insert the second interlock plunger.

18 Install the reverse selector rod and shift fork. The slot in the reverse selector rod must be positioned as shown. (photos)

19 Insert the detent balls, springs and plugs. Apply gasket sealant to the threads of the plugs before installing them. (photos)

20 Check the operation of the selectors and gear engagement making sure it is smooth and positive.

21 Set the gears in neutral and then position a new gasket on the

rear face of the gear casing.

22 Install the rear extension housing making sure that before it is pushed fully home, the remote control rod engages correctly with the selector shaft dogs. (photo)

23 Insert and tighten the extension housing bolts to the specified torque.

24 Install the front cover making sure that the gasket and countershaft roll pin are correctly aligned and the oil seal is not damaged as it passes over the splines of the input shaft. Tighten the securing bolts to the specified torque. (photos)

25 Install the release bearing, withdrawal lever and dust excluder, applying grease to the points indicated. (photo) Now is the time to renew the release bearing and the clutch components if they are worn (see Chapter 5).

26 Invert the gearbox and install the bottom cover plate using a new gasket. (photo)

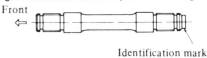

Fig. 6.32 Reverse idler shaft installation diagram

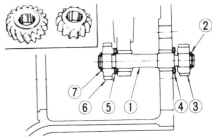

Fig. 6.33 Correct assembly of reverse idler gear components

1 Idler shaft
2 Circlip
3 Spur gear
4 Thrust washer
5 Thrust washer
6 Helical gear
7 Circlip

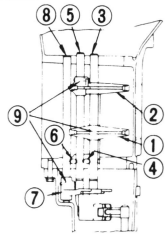

Fig. 6.35 Location of selector rods and shift forks

1 1st./2nd. shift fork
2 3rd./4th. shift fork
3 1st./2nd. selector rod
4 Interlock plunger
5 3rd./4th. selector rod
6 Tension pin
7 Reverse shift fork
8 Reverse selector rod
9 Tension pin

Fig. 6.34 Bending over mainshaft nut locking plate

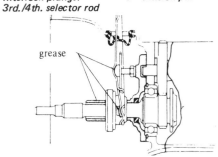

Fig. 6.36 Clutch withdrawal mechanism grease application points

10.15 Securing 1st./2nd. shift fork to selector rod

10.16 Inserting an interlock plunger between 1st./2nd. and 3rd./4th selector rods

10.18A Installing reverse selector fork

10.18B Correct alignment of reverse selector rod

10.19A Inserting a detent ball

10.19B Inserting detent springs

10.19C Installing detent plugs

10.22 Remote control rod correctly engaged with selector shaft dogs

10.24A Front cover gasket and counter-shaft tension pin correctly aligned

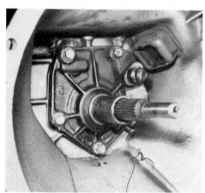
10.24B Front cover installation. Note clutch lever pivot bolt

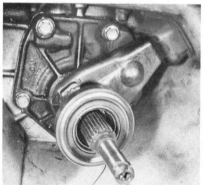
10.25 Clutch release bearing and withdrawal lever correctly installed

10.26 Installing gearbox bottom cover plate

11 Fault diagnosis - manual gearbox

Symptom	Reason/s
Weak or ineffective synchromesh	Synchro. cones worn or damaged Baulk rings worn Defective synchro. unit
Jumps out of gear	Worn interlock plunger Worn detent ball Weak or broken detent spring Worn shift fork or synchro sleeve groove Worn gear
Excessive noise	Incorrect oil grade Oil level too low Worn gear teeth Worn mainshaft bearings Worn thrust washers Worn input or mainshaft splines
Difficult gear changing or selection	Incorrect clutch free movement

Chapter 6 Part 2: Automatic transmission

Contents

Specifications

Type	3N71B, three forward speeds and reverse, three element torque converter with planetary geartrain.	
Model code	X2401 - 16B (1974)	X2402 - 16B (1975)

Ratios

1st	2.458 : 1
2nd	1.458 : 1
3rd	1.000 : 1
Reverse	2.182 : 1

Engine idling speed	650 rpm in 'D' (800 rpm with air conditioning system)
Stall speed	2000 to 2200 rpm
Fluid capacity	5 7/8 US qts (5.5 litres)

Torque wrench settings

	lb/ft	kg/m
Driveplate to crankshaft bolts	100	13.8
Driveplate to torque converter	35	4.8
Torque converter housing to engine	35	4.8
Transmission casing to converter housing	40	5.5
Transmission casing to rear extension	20	2.8
Fluid cooler connection to transmission	35	4.8
Selector range lever nut	25	3.5

12 General description

The automatic transmission unit is the type 3N71B and may be optionally specified on the 710 series only.

The unit provides three forward ratios and one reverse. Changing of the forward gear ratios is completely automatic in relation to the vehicle speed and engine torque input and is dependent upon the vacuum pressure in the manifold and the vehicle road speed to actuate the gearchange mechanism at the precise time.

The transmission has six selector positions:

P - parking position which locks the output shaft. This is a safety device for use when the vehicle is parked on an incline. The engine may be started with "P" selected and this position should always be selected when adjusting the engine while it is running. Never attempt to select "P" when the vehicle is in motion.

R - reverse gear.

N - neutral. Select this position to start the engine or when idling in traffic for long periods.

D - drive, for all normal motoring conditions.

2 - locks the transmission in second gear for wet road conditions or steep hill climbing or descents. The engine can be over revved in this position.

1 - the selection of this ratio above road speeds of approximately 25 mph (40 mph) will engage second gear and as the speed drops below 25 mph (40 kph) the transmission will lock into first gear. Provides maximum retardation on steep descents.

Due to the complexity of the automatic transmission unit,

any internal adjustment or servicing should be left to a main Datsun agent. The information given in this chapter is therefore confined to those operations which are considered within the scope of the home mechanic. An automatic transmission should give many tens of thousands of miles service provided normal maintenance and adjustment is carried out. When the unit finally requires major overhaul, consideration should be given to exchange the old transmission for a factory reconditioned one, the removal and installation being well within the capabilities of the home mechanic as described later in this chapter. The hydraulic fluid does not require periodic draining or refilling but the fluid level must be regularly checked and maintained as described in the next Section.

Periodically clean the outside of the transmission housing as the accumulation of dirt and oil is liable to cause overheating of the unit under extreme conditions.

Adjust the engine slow running as specified.

14 Automatic transmission - removal and installation

1 Removal of the engine and automatic transmission as a combined unit is described in Chapter 1 of this manual. Where it is decided to remove the transmission as a combined unit is described in Chapter 1 of this manual. Where it is decided to remove the transmission leaving the engine in position in the vehicle, proceed as follows:
2 Disconnect the battery negative lead.
3 Drain the fluid from the transmission unit, retaining it in a clean container if required for further use.
4 Jack the car to an adequate working height and support on stands or blocks. Alternatively position the vehicle over a pit.
5 Disconnect the exhaust downpipe from the catalytic converter (where fitted) and remove the shield. On vehicles without a catalytic converter, disconnect the exhaust downpipe from the manifold and from the rear exhaust system.

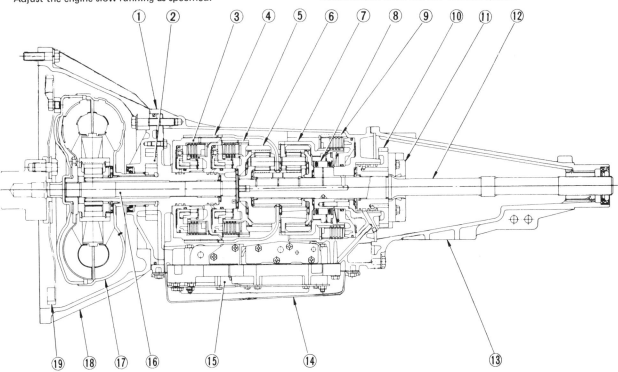

Fig. 6.37 Sectional view of automatic transmission unit

1 Transmission housing	5 Rear clutch	9 Low/reverse brake	13 Rear extension	17 Torque converter
2 Oil pump	6 Front planetary gear	10 Oil distributor	14 Oil pan	19 Converter housing
3 Front clutch	7 Rear planetary gear	11 Governor	15 Control valve	19 Drive plate
4 Brake band	8 One way clutch	12 Output shaft	16 Input shaft	20 Rear extension oil seal

13 Fluid level checking

1 Run the vehicle on the road until normal operating temperature is attained. This will normally take a minimum of 6 miles (9.7 km) to achieve.
2 With the engine idling, select each gear position in turn and then place the speed selector lever in "P"
3 Allow the engine to continue to idle and after a period of two minutes, withdraw the dipstick, wipe it on a piece of clean non-fluffy rag and re-insert it, quickly withdrawing it and reading off the oil level.
4 Top-up as necessary but do not overfill.
5 Switch off the engine.
6 The need for frequent topping-up indicates a leak either in the transmission unit itself or from the fluid cooler or connecting pipes.

6 Disconnect the leads from the starter inhibitor switch.
7 Disconnect the wire from the downshift solenoid.
8 Disconnect the vacuum pipe from the vacuum capsule which is located just forward of the downshift solenoid.
9 Separate the selector lever from the selector linkage.
10 Disconnect the speedometer drive cable from the rear extension housing.
11 Disconnect the fluid filler tube. Plug the opening.
12 Disconnect the fluid cooler tubes from the transmission casing and plug the openings.
13 Mark the edges of the propeller shaft rear driving flange and the pinion flange (for exact refitting), remove the four retaining bolts and withdraw the propeller shaft from its connection with the transmission rear extension housing.
14 Support the engine sump with a jack and use a block of wood to prevent damage to the surface of the sump.
15 Remove the rubber plug from the lower part of the engine rear plate. Mark the torque converter housing and drive plate in

relation to each other for exact replacement.

16 Unscrew and remove the four bolts which secure the torque converter to the drive plate. Access to each of these bolts, in turn is obtained by rotating the engine slowly, using a spanner on the crankshaft pulley bolt.

17 Unbolt and withraw the starter motor.

18 Support the transmission with a jack (preferably a trolley type).

19 Detach the rear transmission mounting from the transmission housing and the vehicle body frame.

20 Unscrew and remove the transmission to engine securing bolts.

21 Lower the two jacks sufficiently to allow the transmission unit to be withdrawn from below and to the rear of the vehicle. The help of an assistant will probably be required due to the weight of the unit.

22 Refitting is a reversal of removal but should the torque converter have been separated from the main assembly, ensure that the notch on the converter is correctly aligned with the corresponding one on the oil pump. To check that the torque converter has been correctly installed, the dimension "A" should exceed 0.846 in. (21.5 mm).

23 Tighten all bolts to the specified torque settings and refill the unit with the correct grade and quantity of fluid.

24 Check the operation of the inhibitor switch and the selector linkage and adjust, if necessary, as described later in this Chapter.

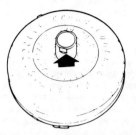

Fig. 6.39 Torque converter alignment notch

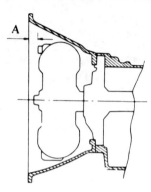

Fig. 6.40 Torque converter installation diagram

15 Selector linkage - adjustment

1   Release the locknuts at the hand control end of the connecting rod.

2   Place the range selector lever on the side of the transmission casing in "N".

3   Place the hand control lever in 'N'' and then adjust the locknuts to provide a clearance (C) at the hand control of 0.040 in. (1.0 mm).

4   Check for correct engagement at all selector positions.

5   A clearance 'B' should always be maintained (between the gate and the gate pin) of between 0.0040 and 0.4331 in. (0.1 and 1.1 mm). This can be adjusted by turning the pushrod after removal of the hand control knob.

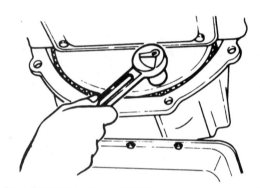

Fig. 6.38 Unscrewing a driveplate to torque converter bolt

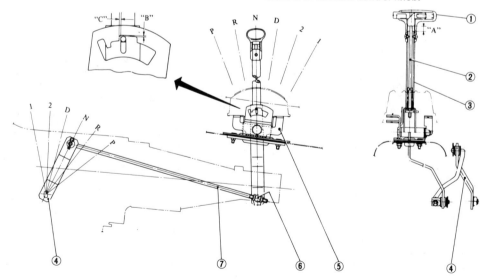

Fig. 6.41 Automatic transmission speed selector linkage

| 1 | Knob | 3 | Control lever | 5 | Bracket | 7 | Rod |
| 2 | Pushrod | 4 | Range selector lever | 6 | Trunnion | | |

(A = 0.43 to 0.47 in - 11.0 to 12.0 mm B = 0.004 to 0.433 in - 0.1 to 1.1 mm C = 0.04 in - 1.0 mm)

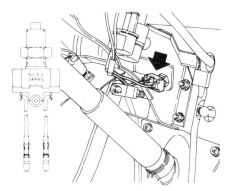

Fig. 6.41A Location of 'kick-down switch'

16 Selector linkage - removal and installation

1 Remove the two small screws which secure the knob to the speed sleector lever. Remove the knob.
2 Remove the console from the transmission tunnel.
3 Unbolt the selector lever bracket and the lever on the side of the transmission and withdraw the complete selector linkage.
4 Installation is a reversal of removal but adjust the linkage as described in the preceding Section.

17 'Kick-down' switch and downshift solenoid - checking

1 If the kick-down facility fails to operate or operates at an incorrect change point, first check the security of the switch on the accelerator pedal arm and the wiring between the switch and the solenoid.
2 Turn the ignition key so that the ignition and oil pressure lamps illuminate but without operating the starter motor. Depress the accelerator pedal fully and as the switch actuates, a distinct click should be heard from the solenoid. Where this is absent, drain 2½ Imp pints, 3 US pints, 1.4 litres of fluid from the transmission unit unscrew the solenoid and fit a new one. Replenish the transmission fluid.

18 Starter inhibitor and reverse lamp switch - testing and adjustment

1 Check that the starter motor operates only in "N" and "P" and the reversing lamps illuminate only with the selector lever in "R".

2 Any deviation from this arrangement should be rectified by adjustment, first having checked the correct setting of the selector linkage.
3 Detach the range selector lever (9) from the selector rod which connects it to the hand control. Now move the range selector lever to the "N" position, (slot in shaft vertical).
4 Connect an ohmmeter to the black and yellow wires of the

inhibitor switch. With the ignition switch on, the meter should indicate continuity of circuit when the range select lever is within 3 degrees (either side) of the "N" and "P" positions.
5 Repeat the test with the meter connected to the red and black wires and the range lever in "R".
6 Where the switch requires adjusting to previde the correct moment of contact in the three selector positions, move the range level to "N" and then remove the retaining nut (6), the two inhibitor switch securing bolts and the screw located below the switch.
7 Align the hole, from which the screw was removed, with the pinhole in the manual shaft (2). A thin rod or piece of wire may be used to do this. Holding this alignment, fit the inhibitor switch securing bolts and tighten them. Remove the alignment rod and refit the screw.
8 Refit the remaining switch components and test for correct operation as previously described. If the test procedure does not prove positive, renew the switch.

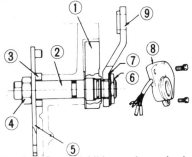

Fig. 6.42 Starter inhibitor and reversing lamp switch

1	Switch	6	Wasner
2	Shaft	7	Nut
3	Washer	8	Switch (detached)
4	Nut	9	Range select lever
5	Plate		

19 Rear extension oil seal - renewal

1 After a considerable mileage, leakage may occur from the seal which surrounds the shaft at the rear end of the automatic transmission extension housing. This leakage will be evident from the state of the underbody and from the reduction in the level of the hydraulic fluid.
2 Remove the propeller shaft as described in Chapter 7.
3 Taking care not to damage the splined output-shaft and the alloy housing, prise the old oil seal from its location. Drive in the new one using a tubular drift.
4 Should the seal be very tight in its recess, then support the transmission on a jack and remove the rear mounting. Unbolt the rear extension housing from the transmission casing.
5 Pull the extension housing straight off over the output shaft and governor assembly.
6 Using a suitable drift applied from the interior of the rear extension housing, remove the old oil seal. At the same time check the bush and renew it if it is scored or worn.
7 Refitting is a reversal of removal, but always use a new gasket between the rear extension and main housing.

Fault diagnosis overleaf

20 Fault diagnosis - automatic transmission

In addition to the information given in this Chapter, reference should be made to Chapter 3 for the servicing and maintenance of the emission control equipment fitted to models equipped with automatic transmission.

Symptom	Reason/s
Engine will not start in "N" or "P"	Faulty starter or ignition circuit Incorrect linkage adjustment Incorrectly installed inhibitor switch
Engine starts in selector positions other than "N" or "P"	Incorrect linkage adjustment Incorrectly installed inhibitor switch
Severe bump when selecting "D" or "R" and excessive creep when handlebar released	Idling speed too high Vacuum circuit leaking
Poor acceleration and low maximum speed	Incorrect oil level Incorrect linkage adjustment

The most likely causes of faulty operation are incorrect oil level and linkage adjustment. Any other faults or mal-operation of the automatic transmission unit must be due to internal faults and should be rectified by your Datsun dealer. An indication of a major internal fault may be gained from the colour of the oil which under normal conditions should be transparent red. If it becomes discoloured or black then burned clutch or brake bands must be suspected.

Chapter 7 Propeller shaft

Contents

Specifications

Propeller shaft

Type:

2 section	Tubular steel with two universal joints and sliding sleeve at front end
3 section	Tubular steel with three universal joints, centre support bearing and sliding sleeve at front end
Maximum permissible out of round	less than 0.024 in. (0.6 mm)
Maximum out of balance at 5800 rpm	0.49 in. oz (35.0 gr. cm)

Torque wrench settings

	lb/ft	kg/m
Rear driving flange bolts	23	3.2
Centre flange locknut (3 section shaft)	150	20.7
Centre flange bolts (3 section shaft)	23	3.2
Centre bearing clamp inner bolts (3 section shaft)	20	2.8
Centre bearing clamp outer bolts (3 section shaft)	35	4.8

1 General description

On models with a rigid rear axle (140J and 710 series) the propeller shaft is of one piece tubular steel construction having a universal joint at each end and a splined sliding sleeve at the front to compensate for the up and down movement of the rear axle due to the deflection of the road springs.

On the 160JSSS which has independent type rear suspension, a propeller shaft of three joint design is used and a centre bearing is also incorporated.

The propeller shaft is finely balanced during manufacture and it is recommended that an exchange unit is obtained rather than dismantle the universal joints when wear is evident. However, this is not always possible and provided care is taken to mark each individual yoke in relation to the one opposite then the balance will usually be maintained. Do not drop the assembly during servicing operations.

2 Universal joints - testing for wear

1 Wear in the needle roller bearings is characterized by vibration in the transmission, 'clonks' on taking up the drive, and in extreme cases of lack of lubrication, metallic squeaking and ultimately grating and shrieking sounds as the bearings break up.

2 It is easy to check if the needle roller bearings are worn with the propeller shaft in position, by trying to turn the shaft with one hand, the other hand holding the rear axle flange when the rear universal joint is being checked, and the front half coupling when the front universal joint is being checked. Any movement between the propeller shaft and the front half couplings, and round the rear half couplings, is indicative of considerable wear.

3 If wear is evident, either fit a new propeller shaft assembly complete or renew the universal joints, as described later in this Chapter.

4 A final test for wear is to attempt to lift the shaft and note any movement between the yokes of the joints.

3 Propeller shaft - removal and installation

1 Jack-up the rear of the car, or position the rear of the car over a pit.

2 If the rear of the car is jacked-up, supplement the jack with support blocks so that danger is minimized should the jack collapse.

3 If the rear wheels are off the ground, place the car in gear and apply the handbrake to ensure that the propeller shaft does not turn when an attempt is made to loosen the four bolts securing the propeller shaft to the rear axle.

4 The propeller shaft is carefully balanced to fine limits and it is important that it is replaced in exactly the same position it was in prior to removal. Scratch marks on the propeller shaft and rear axle flanges to ensure accurate mating when the time comes for installation.

5 Unscrew and remove the four bolts and spring washers which hold the flange on the propeller shaft to the flange on the rear axle.

6 On propeller shafts which have a centre bearing, unscrew and

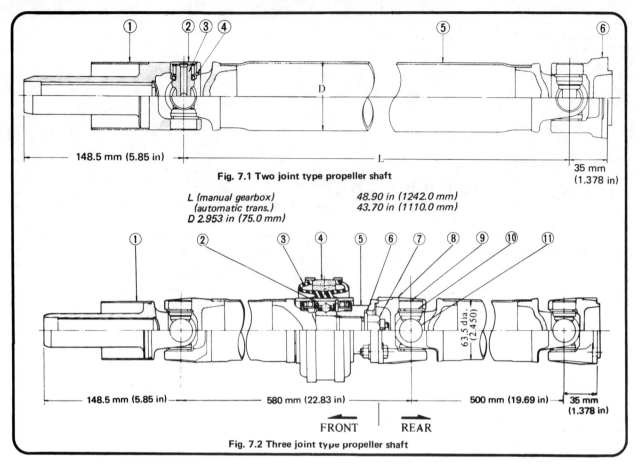

Fig. 7.1 Two joint type propeller shaft

L (manual gearbox)   48.90 in (1242.0 mm)
  (automatic trans.)   43.70 in (1110.0 mm)
D 2.953 in (75.0 mm)

FRONT   REAR

Fig. 7.2 Three joint type propeller shaft

remove the bolts which secure the bearing carrier to the body-frame.

7 Slightly push the shaft forward to separate the two flanges, then lower the end of the shaft and pull it rearwards to disengage it from the gearbox mainshaft splines.

8 Place a large can or tray under the rear of the gearbox extension to catch any oil which is likely to leak past the oil seal when the propeller shaft is removed.

9 Installation is a reversal of removal but ensure that the rear flange marks are in alignment and tighten all securing bolts to the specified torque. Check the oil level in the transmission unit and top-up if necessary.

4 Centre bearing - dismantling and reassembly

1 With the propeller shaft removed as already described, disconnect the rear section of the shaft from the front section by unbolting the flanges which are located just to the rear of the centre bearing, (mark the flange alignment first).

2 Relieve the staking on the locknut which is now exposed and unscrew and remove the locknut. This nut will be very tight and the best method of holding the shaft still while it is unscrewed is to pass two old bolts through two of the flange holes and secure them in a vice. Alternatively, a special flange securing wrench can be used.

3 Mark the relative positions of the centre bearing assembly to the clamp/support and the bearing and clamp/support to the propeller shaft itself.

4 Unbolt and remove the bearing clamp/support and draw off the centre bearing complete with insulator.

5 Commence reassembly by inserting the centre bearing into its insulator. If a new bearing is being fitted, do not lubricate it as it is of grease sealed type.

6 Fit the bearing/insulator to the propeller shaft making sure to align the marks made before dismantling or in the case of new components, locate them in similar relative positions.

7 Install the washer and locknut and tighten to the specified torque. Stake the nut into the shaft groove using a punch.

8 Reconnect the propeller shaft flanges, tightening the securing bolts to the specified torque.

9 Fit the clamp/support to the centre bearing, aligning it correctly and tighten the inner bolts to the specified torque.

5 Universal joints - servicing

1 Clean away all dirt from the ends of the bearings on the yokes so that the circlips may be removed using a pair of contracting circlip pliers or a small screwdriver. If they are very tight, tap the end of the bearing cup (inside the circlip) with a drift and hammer to relieve the pressure.

2 Once the circlips are removed, tap the universal joints at the yoke with a wooden or plastic faced hammer and the bearings and cups will come out of the housing and can be removed easily.

3 If they are obstinate they can be gripped in a self-locking wrench for final removal provided they are to be renewed.

4 Once the bearings are removed from each opposite journal the trunnion can be easily disengaged.

5 Replacement of the new trunnions and needle rollers and cups is a reversal of the removal procedure.

6 Place the needle in each cup and fill the cup one-third full with grease prior to placing it over the trunnion, and tap each bearing journals after three have been fitted should be removed before fitting the fourth cup.

7 Replace the circlips ensuring they seat neatly in the retaining grooves.

8   In cases of extreme wear or neglect, it is conceivable that the bearing housings in the propeller shaft, sliding sleeve or rear flange have worn so much that the bearing cups are a slack fit in them. In such cases it will be necessary to replace the item affected as well. Check also that the sliding sleeve splines are in good condition and not a sloppy fit on the gearbox mainshaft.

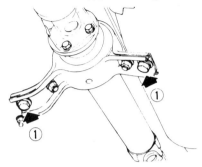

Fig. 7.3 Centre bearing support to bodyframe bolts (1)

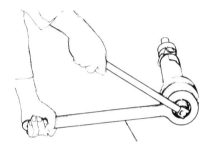

Fig. 7.4 Unscrewing centre flange locknut (three joint type shaft). Flange securing wrench (arrowed)

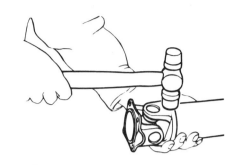

Fig. 7.6 Dismantling a universal joint

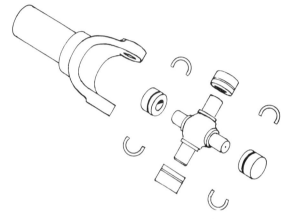

Fig. 7.7 Exploded view of a universal joint

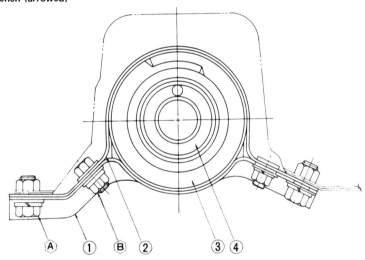

Fig. 7.5 Front view of propeller shaft centre bearing (three joint type shaft)

1 Support	2 Clamp	3 Rubber insulator	4 Bearing
A support to bodyframe bolts		B clamp to support bolts	

6   Fault diagnosis - propeller shaft

Symptom	Reason/s
Vibration when vehicle running on road	Out of balance or distorted propeller shaft
	Backlash in splines shaft
	Loose flange securing bolts
	Worn universal joint bearings
	Worn centre bearing

Chapter 8 Part 1: Rigid type rear axle

Contents

Specifications

Type ... ... Semi-floating, rigid with hypoid gear

Construction ... ... Axle casing pressed steel, differential carrier cast-iron

Application

Model 140J ... ... Type H165

710 series ... ... Type H165B

Ratios

	140J	710 series to 1975	710 series 1975 on
Manual gearbox	4.11 : 1	3.89 : 1	3.70 : 1
Automatic transmission		4.11 : 1	3.70 : 1

Oil capacity ... ... 2¼ Imp. pts. 2¾ U.S. pts 1.3 litres

Torque wrench settings

	lb/ft	kg/m
Shock absorber lower mounting bolt	16	2.2
Spring 'U' bolt nut	35	4.8
Diff. carrier to axle casing nut	20	2.8
Propeller shaft flange bolt	23	3.2
Drain and filter plugs	40	5.5
Drive pinion nut (initial torque)	100	13.8
Side bearing cap bolt	43	5.9

1 General description

The rear axle is of the semi-floating type and is held in place by two semi-elliptic springs. These provide the necessary lateral and longitudinal support for the axle.

The banjo type/casing carries the differential assembly which consists of a hypoid crownwheel and pinion and the two star pinion differential bolted in the carrier to the cast-iron nose piece.

All repairs can be carried out to the component parts of the rear axle without removing the axle casing from the car. It will be found simpler in practice to fit a guaranteed second-hand axle from a car breakers yard rather than dismantle the differential unit which calls for special tools which very few garages will have.

As an alternative a replacement differential carrier assembly can be fitted which means that the axle can be left in position and dismantling is reduced to a minimum.

2 Axle-shaft, bearing and oilseal - removal and refitting

1 Jack-up the rear of the vehicle and support the rear axle and

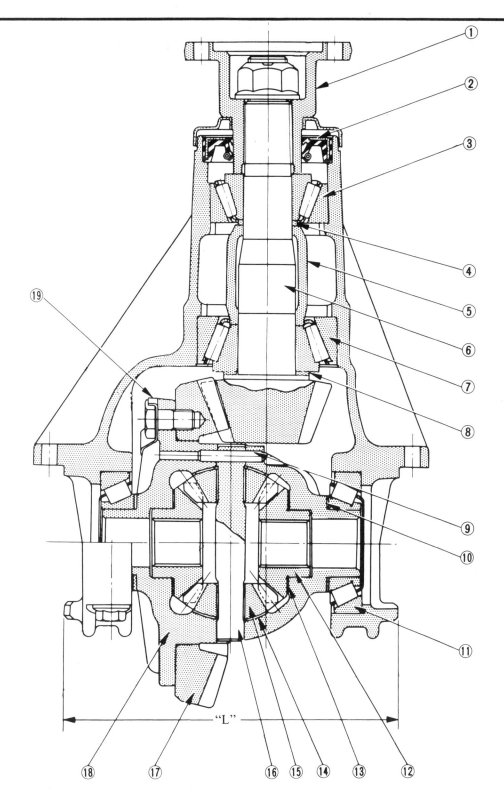

Fig. 8.1 Sectional view of differential carrier (type H165 rigid axle)

1	Pinion coupling	7	Pinion rear bearing	11	Side bearing	16 Pinion shaft
2	Pinion oil seal	8	Pinion height adjusting	12	Side gear	17 Crownwheel
3	Pinion front bearing		washer	13	Thrust washer	18 Differential case
4	Bearing thrust washer	9	Lock pin	14	Thrust washer	19 Lockplate
5	Spacer	10	Side bearing	15	Pinion gear	
6	Drive pinion		adjusting shim			

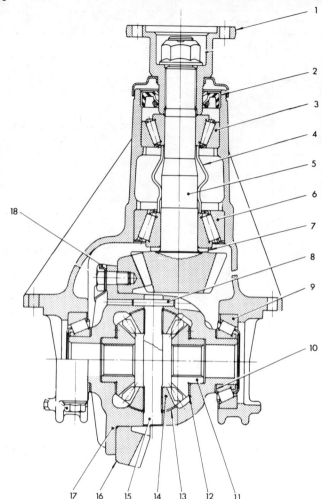

Fig. 8.2 Sectional view of differential carrier (type H165B rigid
axle)

1 Pinion coupling flange	10 Side bearing adjusting shim
2 Pinion oil seal	11 Side gear
3 Pinion front bearing	12 Thrust washer
4 collapsible spacer	13 Thrust washer
5 Drive pinion	14 Pinion gear
6 Pinion rear bearing	15 Pinion shaft
7 Pinion height adjusting washer	16 Crownwheel
8 Lock pin	17 Differential case
9 Side bearing	18 Lockplate

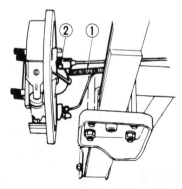

Fig. 8.3 Handbrake cable return spring (1) and clevis (2)

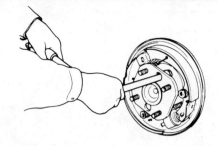

Fig. 8.4 Unscrewing a rear brake backplate nut

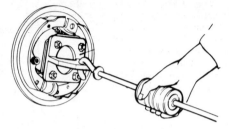

Fig. 8.5 Using a slide hammer to remove an axle-shaft

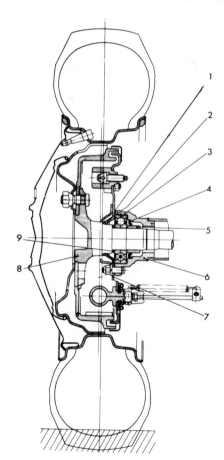

Fig. 8.6 Sectional view of a rear hub

1 Bearing adjusting shim
2 Oil slinger
3 Bearing
4 Oil seal
5 Collar
6 Axle casing
7 Brake backplate
8 Axle-shaft
9 Spacer

the bodyframe securely on stands.

2   Remove the rear roadwheel.

3   Disconnect the handbrake rod spring and then remove the clevis pin to disconnect the control rod at the brake backplate.

4   Disconnect the brake pipe at the wheel cylinder union and plug the pipe to prevent the entry of dirt and loss of hydraulic fluid. In order to prevent loss of fluid from the hydraulic system, the fluid reservoir cap can be removed and a piece of plastic film placed over the opening and the cap refitted. This will cause a vacuum to be created and prevent the fluid running from the disconnected pipe.

5   Remove the brake drum.

6   Pass a socket through the hole in the axle-shaft end flange and unscrew each of the four backplate securing nuts in turn.

7   A slide hammer must now be attached to the wheel studs and the axle-shaft removed complete with brake assembly and backplate. It is quite useless to attempt to pull the axle-shaft from the axle casing. Where a slide hammer is not available, an old road wheel can be bolted onto the axle flange and its inner rims struck simultaneously at two opposite points.

8   Always renew the oil seal in the end of the axle casing whenever the axle-shaft is removed. Prise it from its seat with a screwdriver and tap the new one squarely into position.

9   Oil seepage into the rear brake drums is an indication of failure of the axle housing oil seals. Where oil contamination is observed, always check that this is not, in fact, hydraulic brake fluid leaking from a faulty wheel operating cylinder.

10 The removal and fitting of axle-shaft bearings and spacer/collars is best left to a service station having suitable extracting and pressing equipment. Where the home mechanic has such facilities available, proceed as follows.

11 With the axle-shaft removed, as previously described, secure it in a vice fitted with jaw protectors.

12 Using a sharp cold chisel, make several deep cuts in the collar at equidistant points. The collar can then be easily withdrawn from the axle-shaft. Take great care not to damage or distort the axle-shaft during this operation.

13 Using a suitable extractor, remove the bearing from the axle shaft and finally the bearing spacer.

14 Press wheel bearing grease into the bearing and then locate the spacer, new bearing and new collar in position on the shaft. Press the components into position on the axle-shaft using a suitable press to bear on the end of the collar. Note that the sealed side of the bearing is towards the roadwheel.

15 Pass the axle-shaft carefully through the oil seal, keeping the shaft quite parallel with the axle casing tube. When the splines on the end of the shaft engage with those in the differential unit carefully tap the shaft right home. Using a straight edge and feeler gauge, check that the front face of the bearing does not project more than 0.0039 in (0.1 mm) above the endface of the axle casing. If it does then a bearing adjusting shim must be obtained and fitted, to the endface of the axle casing flange.

16 Tighten the brake backplate bolts and reconnect the handbrake linkage. Install the brake drum.

17 Reconnect the brake pipe and bleed the hydraulic system (see Chapter 9).

18 Refit the roadwheel and lower the vehicle to the ground.

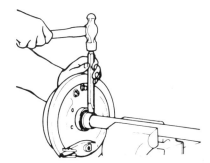

Fig. 8.7 Cutting a bearing retaining collar from an axle-shaft

3   Pinion oil seal (up to 1974) - renewal

1   On models produced before 1974, the pinion oil seal can be renewed with the differential carrier in position in the vehicle.

2   Jack-up the rear of the vehicle and support the axle on stands.

3   Remove the propeller shaft, as described in Chapter 7.

4   Hold the drive pinion coupling flange quite still while the pinion nut is unscrewed and removed. This nut will be very tight and the flange must be secured by inserting two old bolts through two of the flange holes and then passing a long rod or bar between them as a lever, or alternatively using a special ring wrench.

5   Withdraw the coupling using a suitable extractor.

6   Remove the defective oil seal by drifting in one side of it as far as it will go in order to force the opposite side from the housing.

7   Tap the new seal squarely into position and apply some grease to the seal lips.

8   Fit the pinion coupling and tighten the nut to a torque of 110 lb/ft (15.2 kg/m) keeping the coupling quite still.

9   Install the propeller shaft and top-up the rear axle oil level.

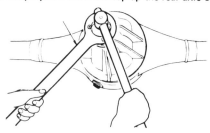

Fig. 8.8 Unscrewing the pinion nut (pinion coupling flange wrench arrowed)

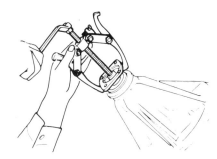

Fig. 8.9 Withdrawing the drive pinion coupling

4   Pinion oil seal (1974 onwards) - renewal

1   The pinion oil seal cannot be renewed with the differential carrier still in position in the vehicle. This is due to the use of a collapsible type spacer, between the pinion bearings, which must be renewed if the pinion adjustment is disturbed by removal of the pinion nut.

2   Remove the differential carrier, as described in the next Section.

3   Unbolt and remove the side bearing caps.

4   Withdraw the differential case assembly.

5   Unscrew and remove the drive pinion nut and coupling. Extract the pinion oil seal.

6   Withdraw the pinion to the rear and the front pinion bearing race to the front.

7   Extract the collapsible spacer.

8   Insert a new collapsible spacer onto the pinion and fit the front bearing race.

9   Tap a new oil seal into position and grease its lips.

10 Install pinion coupling and screw on the pinion nut finger-tight.

11 Now tighten the pinion nut (coupling flange held quite still) until any endfloat in drive pinion is just eliminated.

12 The pinion nut should now be tightened a fraction at a time until with a spring balance attached to one of the coupling flange bolt holes, the force required to turn it (preload) is between 4½ and 6½ lbs (2.0 and 2.9 kg). Turn the pinion in both directions during the tightening process to settle the bearings. As a guide to tightening, tighten the pinion nut initially to 100 lb/ft (14 kg/m).

13 Refit the differential case assembly and side bearing caps and install the carrier to the axle casing, as described in the next Section.

Fig. 8.10 Withdrawing the differential case assembly

---

5   Differential carrier - removal and installation

1 The overhaul of the rear axle differential unit is not within the scope of the home mechanic due to the specialized gauges and tools which are required. Where the unit requires servicing or repair due to wear or excessive noise it is most economical to exchange it for a factory reconditioned assembly and this Section is limited to a description of the removal and refitting procedure.

2 Drain the oil from the rear axle.

3 Jack-up the axle, remove the roadwheels and partially withdraw the axle-shafts, as described in Section 2, of this Chapter.

4 Disconnect and remove the propeller shaft as previously described.

5 Unscrew, evenly and in opposite sequence, the nuts from ten differential unit securing studs. Pull the differential unit from the axle casing.

6 Although only of academic interest, the new exposed crownwheel teeth should show a pinion contact pattern as shown, on Fig. 8.10A, provided that the differential unit was correctly set up originally.

7 Scrape all trace of old gasket from the mating surface of the axle casing. Position a new gasket on the axle casing having first smeared it on both sides with jointing compound.

8 Install the differential carrier so that the pinion assembly is at the lowest point. Tighten the securing nuts to the specified torque.

9 Refit the axle-shafts and the propeller shaft.

10 Refit the roadwheels and lower the jack.

11 Fill the differential unit to the correct level with oil of the specified grade.

Fig. 8.10A Correct crownwheel to pinion contact pattern

---

6   Rear axle - removal and installation

1 Remove the hub caps from the rear roadwheels and loosen the wheel nuts.

2 Jack-up the bodyframe at the rear of the vehicle and support it securely on stands.

3 Place a jack under the centre of the rear axle casing and raise the axle sufficiently to take its weight.

4 Disconnect the propeller shaft from the rear axle pinion driving flange, as described in Chapter 7.

5 Disconnect the handbrake cables by withdrawing the clevis pins at the axle casing pivots. Disconnect the brake pipe and plug the openings.

6 Disconnect the shock absorber lower mountings.

7 Unscrew and remove the spring 'U' bolt nuts and detach the lower plates.

8 Lower the axle jack until the axle casing is separated from the road springs and then withdraw the complete rear axle assembly sideways through the space between the spring and the bodyframe.

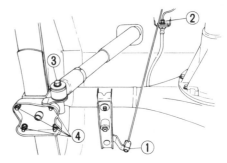

Fig. 8.11 Rear axle handbrake cable pivot (1) rigid to flexible brake pipe union (2) shock absorber lower mounting (3) and spring 'U' bolts (4)

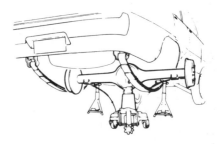

Fig. 8.12 Withdrawing rigid type rear axle assembly from the side of the vehicle

7 Fault diagnosis - rigid axle

Symptom	Reason/s
Noise on drive, coasting or overrun	Shortage of oil Incorrect crownwheel to pinion mesh Worn pinion bearings Worn side bearings Loose bearing cap bolts
Noise on turn	Differential side gears worn, damaged or tight
Knock on taking up drive or during gearchange	Excessive crownwheel to pinion backlash Worn gears Worn axle-shaft splines Pinion bearing preload too low Loose drive coupling nut Loose securing bolts or nuts within unit Loose roadwheel nuts or elongated wheel nut holes
Oil leakage	Defective gaskets or oil seals possibly caused by clogged breather or oil level too high

Chapter 8   Part 2:
Independent suspension type rear axle

Contents

Specifications

Type	Hypoid, independently mounted, driving through universal jointed open type driveshafts to roadwheels
Construction	Cast-iron
Application Model 160JSSS	Type R 160
Ratio	3.90 = 1
Oil capacity	1.3/8 Imp pts, 1.5/8 US pts, 0.8 litres

Torque wrench settings

	lb/ft	kg/m
Drive pinion nut	140	19.4
Side flange securing bolt	20	2.8
Rear cover plate bolts	20	2.8
Rear cover to crossmember locknut	50	6.9
Differential carrier to front crossmember bolt	50	6.9
Driveshaft inner flange bolts	40	5.5
Rear crossmember self-locking nuts	70	9.7
Pinion coupling flange bolts	23	3.2
Oil drain and filler plugs	40	5.5
Rear hub bearing locknut	180 to 240	24.9 to 33.2
Driveshaft outer flange bolts	40	5.5

8 General description

The differential carrier incorporates a hypoid pinion supported on one ball and two tapered roller bearings. The differential case is supported by two tapered roller bearings. The crownwheel is bolted to the differential case.

The differential is mounted at its front face and rear upper edge by flexibly anchored support corssmembers. Power from the differential is transmitted to the roadwheels through two open type driveshafts which incorporate a universal joint at each end and a sliding centre section.

9 Driveshaft - removal, servicing and installation

1   Jack-up the rear of the vehicle and support the bodyframe sidemembers on axle stands.

2   Unscrew and remove the bolts from the drive flanges at both ends of the driveshaft and then withdraw the driveshaft.

3   Lubrication of the ball spline is the only servicing operation which can be carried out and this should be done every 48,000 miles (77,000 km).

4   Disconnect the universal joint at the differential end of the driveshaft by removing the circlips, bearing cups and spider in a similar manner to that for propeller shaft universal joints, as described in Chapter 7.

5   Extract the (now exposed) circlip from the sleeve yoke plug.

6   Compress the driveshaft so that the stop plate is exposed and then extract the circlip from it.

7   Remove the stop plate, peel back the rubber boot from the sleeve yoke and then separate the driveshaft sections retaining carefully all the balls and spacers.

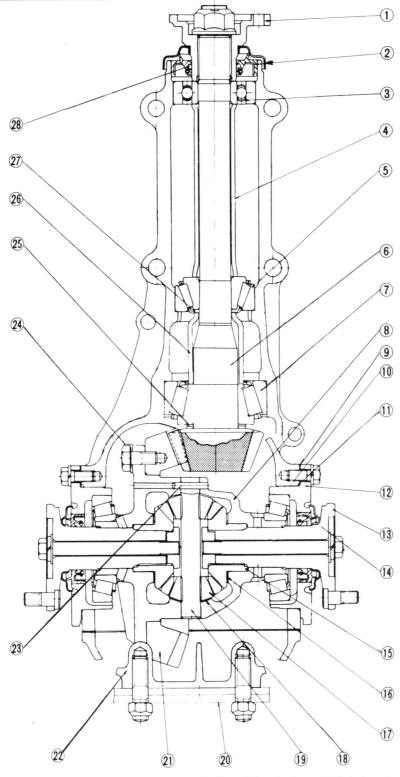

Fig. 8.13 Sectional view of differential carrier (type R160, independent rear suspension)

1	Pinion coupling flange	9	Side retainer adjusting shim	16	Thrust washer
2	Dust deflector	10	Side bearing	17	Pinion gear
3	Front pilot bearing	11	'O' ring	18	Thrust washer
4	Spacer	12	Side retainer	19	Pinion shaft
5	Pinion front bearing	13	Side flange	20	Rear mounting
6	Drive pinion	14	Oil seal	21	Crownwheel
7	Pinion rear bearing	15	Side gear	22	Rear cover plate
8	Differential case				

23	Lock pin
24	Lockplate
25	Pinion height adjusting washer
26	Pinion bearing spacer
27	Adjusting washer
28	Oil seal

8   Reassembly is a reversal of dismantling but ensure that the balls and spacers are correctly located in their grooves.
9   Apply multi-purpose grease to the grooves of the driveshaft, and to the balls and spacers: also pack some around the driveshaft stop plate.

10 Installation is a reversal of removal but tighten the (four bolt) type flanges to 40 lb/ft (5.5 kg/m).
11 Any wear which occurs in the driveshaft components can only be rectified by renewing the driveshaft complete, no individual components being available.

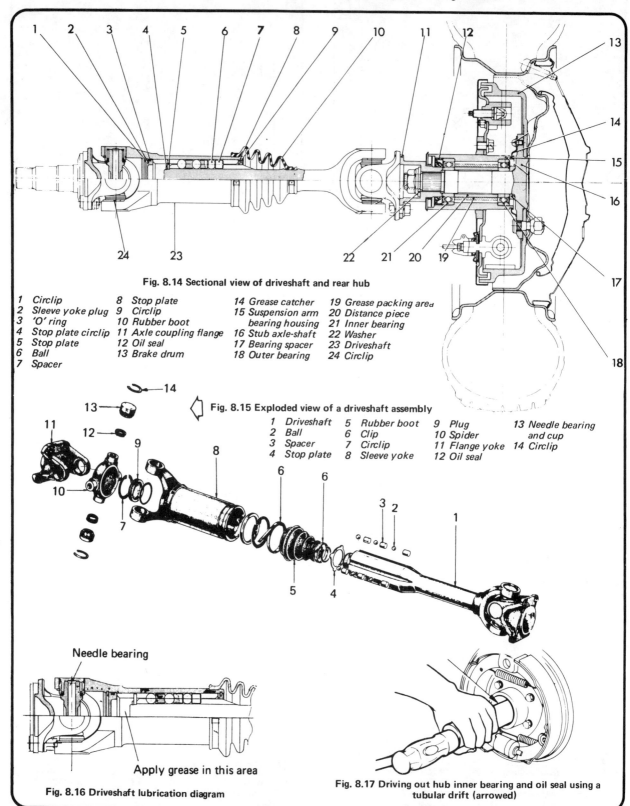

Fig. 8.14 Sectional view of driveshaft and rear hub

1 Circlip	8 Stop plate	14 Grease catcher	19 Grease packing area
2 Sleeve yoke plug	9 Circlip	15 Suspension arm	20 Distance piece
3 'O' ring	10 Rubber boot	bearing housing	21 Inner bearing
4 Stop plate circlip	11 Axle coupling flange	16 Stub axle-shaft	22 Washer
5 Stop plate	12 Oil seal	17 Bearing spacer	23 Driveshaft
6 Ball	13 Brake drum	18 Outer bearing	24 Circlip
7 Spacer			

Fig. 8.15 Exploded view of a driveshaft assembly

1 Driveshaft	5 Rubber boot	9 Plug	13 Needle bearing
2 Ball	6 Clip	10 Spider	and cup
3 Spacer	7 Circlip	11 Flange yoke	14 Circlip
4 Stop plate	8 Sleeve yoke	12 Oil seal	

Needle bearing

Apply grease in this area

Fig. 8.16 Driveshaft lubrication diagram

Fig. 8.17 Driving out hub inner bearing and oil seal using a tubular drift (arrowed)

10 Rear axle stub, bearing and oil seal - dismantling and re-assembly

1 Jack-up the rear of the car and remove the roadwheel. Support the bodyframe and the suspension securely.
2 Unscrew and remove the four bolts which secure the driveshaft flange at the wheel hub end; move the driveshaft to one side out of the way.
3 Temporarily refit the roadwheel and lower the jacks. Apply the handbrake fully and then unscrew the wheel bearing locknut. This nut is very tight and will require leverage from a socket having an operating arm extension of from two to three feet (0.60 to 0.90 metres).
4 Jack-up the car again, remove the brake drum and using a slide hammer extract the rear axle shaft stub. This will come out complete with outer bearing.
5 Remove the inner flange, distance piece and the bearing washer.
6 Using a tubular drift, drive out the inner bearing and oil seal. Extract the grease caliper form the axle stub.
7 Examine the condition of the outer bearing/oil seal. If the seal face is cracked or the bearing is rough or noisy in operation, it must be pressed off and a new one fitted to the axle stub so that the side of the bearing with the seal will be facing the roadwheel.
8 Drive in the inner bearing and new oil seal. Make sure that the sealed side of the inner bearing faces the differential unit.
9 Pack general purpose grease into the bearings and into the space between them and then fit the distance piece. Should the ends of the distance piece be deformed it should be renewed after reference to the grading mark stamped on it (this is repeated on the bearing housing).
10 Insert the axle stub and the inner flange, taking care not the damage the oil seal.
11 Fit the thrust-washer and bearing locknut. Tighten the locknut to 180 lb/ft (24.8 kg/m) after having temporarily refitted the roadwheel and brakedrum and lowered the car to the ground. Raise the car again and remove the roadwheel. Attach a spring balance to a roadwheel stud and check the point at which the hub will rotate. This should be at a reading on the spring balance not exceeding 1.8 lb (0.8 kg). Where this condition is not met, tighten the locknut progressively up to 240 lb/ft (33.2 kg/m) testing each increase in torque tightening until the preload is correct. When the preload is correctly set, the endfloat of the rear axle shaft stub should not exceed 0.0057 in. (0.15 mm).
12 Securely stake the bearing locknut, refit the driveshaft, brake drum and roadwheel and lower the car.

11 Differential unit - servicing general

1 Due to the need for special gauges and tools, it is not recommended that the unit is dismantled.
2 Operations should be limited to the renewal of oil seals which are the only components likely to require renewal after a high mileage.
3 A full description is given to enable the unit to be removed from the car so that it can be renewed on an exchange basis or taken to a specialist repairer.

12 Pinion oil seal - renewal

1 Drain the oil from the differential unit.
2 Raise the rear of the vehicle to obtain access to the unit and support the bodyframe and differential securely.
3 Disconnect the rear end of the propeller shaft and move it to one side.
4 Attach a spring balance to one of the bolt holes in the pinion coupling flange and exert a pull, noting the reading on the balance. This indicates the bearing preload, and it should be

between 5 and 7 lbs (2.3 and 3.2 kg).
5 Hold the pinion coupling flange quite still by placing two bolts through two of the holes in the pinion coupling flange and passing a long rod or bar between them as a lever, or alternatively using a special ring wrench.
6 Unscrew the self-locking type pinion nut and remove the coupling flange.
7 Remove the defective oil seal by drifting in one side of the seal from the housing. The opposite side of the seal will then be ejected.
8 Refit the new oil seal first having greased the mating surfaces of the seal and the axle housing. The lips of the oil seal must face inwards. Using a piece of brass or copper tubing of suitable diameter, carefully drive the new oil seal into the axle housing recess until the face of the seal is flush with the housing. Make sure that the end of the pinion is not knocked during this operation.
9 Refit the coupling flange and thrust-washer and screw on the pinion nut.
10 Again holding the pinion coupling flange quite still with the two bolts and lever, tighten the pinion nut to 120 lb/ft (16.6 kg/m).
11 Check the bearing preload by the spring balance method and if necessary tighten the nut by increases in the torque wrench setting of 5 lb/ft (0.7 kg/m) until the reading on the spring balance matches that which applied before dismantling.
12 Refit the propeller shaft.
13 Lower the vehicle to the ground and check and top-up the differential oil level.

13 Differential side bearing oil seals - renewal

1 Unbolt the driveshaft inner universal joint flange from the differential carrier side flange.
2 Unscrew and remove the single bolt which retains the side flange and then withdraw the flange.
3 Extract the oil seal.
4 Drive in the new oil seal squarely and apply multi-purpose grease to the oil seal lips.
5 Reassembly is a reversal of removal and dismantling but renew the side flange centre bolt 'O' ring if it has deteriorated and tighten all bolts to specified torque.

14 Differential unit - removal and installation

1 Jack-up the rear of the car and support the bodyframe on axle stands or blocks.
2 Place a jack (preferably trolley type) beneath the differential carrier.
3 Disconnect the propeller shaft from the differential pinion drive flange, as described in Chapter 7.
4 Disconnect the driveshaft inner universal joint flanges from the differential side flanges.
5 Unscrew and remove the nuts from the ends of the rear upper differential carrier mounting support.
6 Unscrew and remove the four bolts which secure the front face of the differential unit to the crossmember.
7 Lower the jack under the differential until the unit can be withdrawn to the rear from under the car.
8 While the differential unit is removed, support the centre of the front mounting crossmember on an axle stand to prevent distortion of the flexible bushes and insulators.
9 Installation is a reversal of removal but note the fitting of the front crossmember spacer.
10 Tighten all bolts and nuts to specified torque and when the car has been lowered to the ground, refill the unit with the correct grade and quantity of oil.

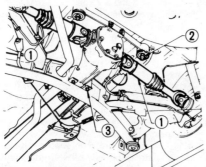

Fig. 8.18 Differential carrier mountings

1 *Driveshaft*
2 *Rear mounting*
   attachment bolt
3 *Front mounting bolts*

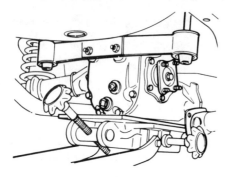

Fig. 8.19 Withdrawing differential unit using a trolley jack

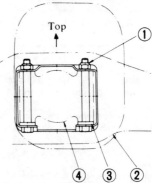

Fig. 8.20 Installation diagram for front mounting crossmember spacer

1 *Nut*
2 *Suspension crossmember*
3 *Spacer*
4 *Differential carrier*

15 Fault diagnosis - driveshafts and differential unit

A noisy differential unit will necessitate its removal and overhaul or its exchange for a reconditioned unit. Before taking this action, check the following components, as it is possible for sounds to travel and mislead the owner as to the source of the trouble.

Check for:

Loose driveshaft flange
Tyres out of balance
Dry or worn rear hub bearings
Worn differential flexible mountings
Damaged or worn driveshaft universal joint
Worn or seized driveshaft ball grooves
Loose roadwheel nuts
Worn rear shock absorber mountings
Coil road spring incorrectly installed and seated

Chapter 9 Braking system

Contents

Specifications

System type	Front disc, rear drum, dual hydraulic circuit with servo assistance. Handbrake mechanical on two rear wheels

Disc brakes

Diameter of disc	9.134 in. (232.0 mm)
Minimum (regrind) thickness	0.331 in. (8.4 mm)
Pad dimensions	3.386 x 1.563 x 0.354 in. (86.0 x 39.7 x 9.0 mm)
Minimum pad lining material thickness	0.040 in. (1.0 mm)

Drum brakes

Inside diameter of drum	9.0 in. (228.6 mm)
Maximum (regrind) diameter	9.055 in. (230.0 mm)
Lining dimensions	8.642 x 1.575 x 0.177 in. (219.5 x 40.0 x 4.5 mm)
Minimum shoe lining material thickness	0.06 in. (1.5 mm)

Master cylinder internal diameter	¾ in. (19.05 mm)
Disc caliper cylinder internal diameter	2.0 in. (50.8 mm)
Rear wheel cylinder internal diameter	13/16 in. (20.64 mm)
Brake pedal height	7.283 in. (185.0 mm)
Brake pedal free-play	0.04 to 0.20 in. (1.0 to 5.0 mm)

Torque wrench settings	lb ft	kg/m
Brake pedal pivot bolt	30	4.1
Caliper securing bolts	60	8.3
Disc to hub bolts	35	4.8
Rear brake backplate bolts	20	2.8

1 General description

The braking system is hydraulic and operates on all four wheels. A dual circuit system is employed with a tandem master cylinder so that failure of either (a) the front brakes or (b) the rear brakes will still leave the remaining circuit unaffected.

The front brakes are of single cylinder caliper disc type while the rear brakes are of leading-trailing drum type.

The handbrake is mechanically operated on the rear wheels only.

A pressure regulating valve is incorporated in the hydraulic circuit and prevents the rear wheels locking before the front ones.

All models incorporate vacuum servo assistance and some versions are fitted with one or both of the following devices:

Handbrake 'on' switch and indicator lamp.

Hydraulic circuit pressure differential warning switch and indicator lamp.

2 Rear drum brakes - adjustment

1 Fully release the handbrake.

2 Depress the footbrake pedal hard several times to centralize the brake shoes.

3 Jack-up the rear of the vehicle until the roadwheels are clear of the ground.

4 Turn each of the brake adjusters (in the same direction as the roadwheel would turn if the vehicle was moving forward), until the brake shoes begin to drag when the roadwheel is turned.

5 Now slacken each of the adjusters until the shoe lining just ceases to be in contact with the drum.

6 Lower the jack and apply the handbrake.

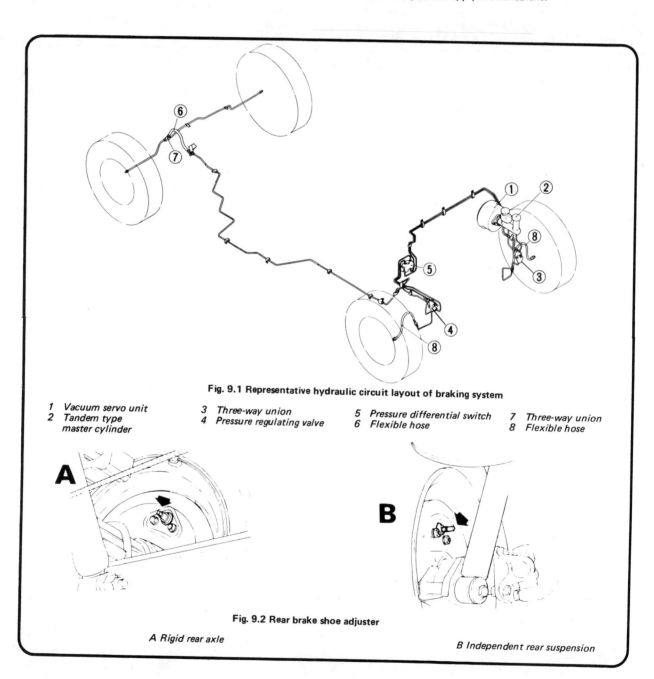

Fig. 9.1 Representative hydraulic circuit layout of braking system

1 Vacuum servo unit
2 Tandem type
   master cylinder
3 Three-way union
4 Pressure regulating valve
5 Pressure differential switch
6 Flexible hose
7 Three-way union
8 Flexible hose

Fig. 9.2 Rear brake shoe adjuster

A Rigid rear axle

B Independent rear suspension

3   Disc pads - inspection and renewal

1   Due to the design of the caliper the pad to disc clearance is automatically adjusted.

2   To check the pad lining thickness, chock the rear wheels, jack-up the front of the car and support on firmly based stands. Remove the roadwheels.

3   Carefully remove the anti-rattle clip from the caliper plate and inspect the lining thickness. When the lining has worn down to 0.04 in. (1 mm) or less the pad must be renewed.

4   To remove the pads ease the caliper plate outwards away from the engine compartment so as to allow the piston to retract into its bore by approximately 0.157 in. (4 mm).

5   The outer pad may now be withdrawn using a pair of long nose pliers. (photo)

6   Move the caliper plate inward towards the engine compartment and withdraw the inner pad and anti-squeal shim (if fitted). (photo)

7   Carefully clean all traces of dirt or rust from the recesses in the caliper in which the pads lie, and the exposed face of the piston.

8   Use a piece of wood or screwdriver to fully retract the piston within the caliper cylinder.

9   Pads must always be renewed in sets of four and not singly. Also pads must not be interchanged side to side.

10 Fit new friction pads and secure with the anti-rattle clip. The clip must be fitted the correct way round as indicated by the sticker on the outer face of the clip.

11 Refit the roadwheels and lower the car. Tighten the wheel nuts securely and replace the wheel trim.

12 To correctly seat the pads pump the brake pedal several times and finally top up the hydraulic fluid level in the master cylinder reservoir as necessary.

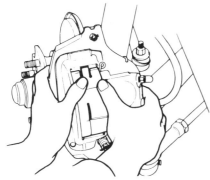

Fig. 9.3 Removing a disc pad anti-rattle clip

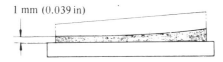

1 mm (0.039 in)

Fig. 9.4 Disc pad wear limit diagram

4   Rear drum brake shoes - inspection and renewal

1   Jack-up the axle casing (rigid rear axle) or the suspension member (independent rear suspension).

2   Remove the roadwheel and chock the front roadwheels.

3   Fully release the handbrake and the drum adjuster.

4   Remove the brake drum. If it is hard to remove, either tap it off using a block of hardwood as an insulator or screw in two bolts (8 mm) into the threaded holes to force off the drum. (photo)

5   Brush all accumulated dust from the shoes and the interior of

3.5 Removing outer disc pad

3.6 Removing inner disc pad

the drum and then inspect the thickness of the friction lining material. If they are worn down to (or very nearly to) the level of the securing rivets, the shoes must be renewed. With bonded type linings, if they are worn down to 3/64 (1.2 mm) then renew the shoes. It is not worth attempting to reline shoes yourself but rather exchange them for factory reconditioned ones.

6   Remove the cup washers from the shoe steady posts. To do this, grip the edges of the water with a pair of pliers and depress it against the coil spring and then turn the washer through 90° and release it. The 'T' shaped head of the steady post will now pass through the slot in the washer and the washer and spring can be withdrawn. (photo)

7   Pull one brake shoe from engagement with the slots in the wheel cylinder piston and the wedge adjuster. (photo)

8   Pull the shoe forward slightly and then release it so that it moves towards the centre of the wheel hub and the opposite shoe can then be released.

9   Before separating the shoes and return springs, note the holes in the shoes webs in which the return springs engage, also the position of the shoes with regard to leading the trailing ends.

10 Before installing the new shoes, clean the brake backplate and apply a smear of high melting point grease to the sliding surfaces on the backplate, also to the slots of the wheel cylinder.

11 Lay out the new brake shoes on the bench and engage the

return springs in their correct holes.

12 Maintain slight outward pressure on the shoes and then engage one shoe with the slots of the adjuster (fully released) and the wheel cylinder. Now pull the opposite shoe over and into engagement with the slots.

13 Refit the shoe steady posts, springs and cup washers.

14 Install the brake drum and adjust the shoes as described in Section 2. The closest adjustment cannot be expected until the linings have had a chance to bed down.

15 Refit the roadwheel and lower the jack.

16 Repeat the operations on the opposite rear brake.

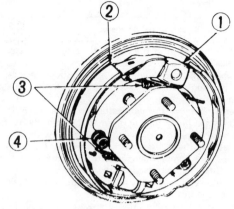

Fig. 9.6 Rear brake assembly with drum removed

1   Adjuster
2   Shoe
3   Shoe return springs
4   Shoe steady

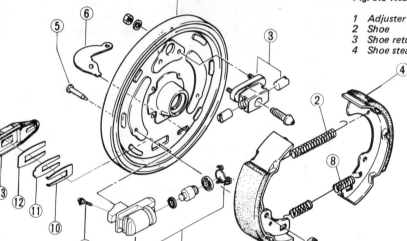

**Fig. 9.5 Exploded view of a rear
          drum brake**

1   Backplate
2   Shoe return spring
3   Adjuster
4   Leading shoe
5   Shoe steady post
6   Bleed nipple
7   Wheel cylinder
8   Shoe return spring
9   Bleed nipple
10 11 and 12 Wheel cylinder
    lockplates
13 Dust cover
14 Trailing shoe
15 Shoe steady spring

4.4 Using bolts to extract a rear brake drum

4.6 Removing a shoe steady post washer

4.7 Removing rear brake shoes

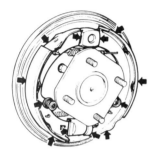

Fig. 9.7 Grease application points on rear brake assembly

5 Front disc caliper - removal and installation

1 Jack-up the front roadwheel and remove it.
2 Remove the disc pads, as described in Section 3.
3 Unscrew the cap from the master cylinder front circuit reservoir and place a piece of plastic film over the opening and then refit the cap. This will prevent loss of fluid when the brake pipe is disconnected.
4 Disconnect the flexible pipe from the rigid brake line at the support bracket (see Section 12). If the caliper is to be moved aside for the purpose of giving attention to the hub or disc then there is no need to disconnect the hydraulic line but simply tie the caliper up out of the way (when it is removed) so as not to strain the flexible hose.
5 Unscrew and remove the bolts which secure the caliper to its support bracket.
6 Installation is a reversal of removal but if the brake hose was disconnected, the hydraulic system must be bled, as described in Section 11.

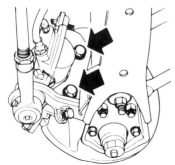

Fig. 9.8 Caliper securing bolts

6 Front disc caliper - servicing

1 Remove the caliper, as described in the preceding section.
2 Extract the cotter pins from the spring loaded holddown pin and the pivot pin. Unscrew and remove the nuts.
3 Disengage the caliper plate from the mounting bracket.
4 Brush all dust and dirt from the external surfaces of the caliper body and then prise off the torsion spring and detach the caliper body from the plate.
5 Apply air pressure at the fluid inlet union and eject the piston. Hold the finger over the end of the piston during this operation to prevent the piston flying out and being damaged.
6 Remove the wiper seal and the seal retainer.
7 At this stage, examine the surfaces of the piston and the cylinder bore. If they are scored or any 'bright' wear areas are evident, renew the caliper unit complete.Where the components are in good order, wash them in clean brake fluid or methylated spirit, discard all rubber seals and obtain a repair kit. When extracting the piston seal from its groove in the cylinder. take great care not to scratch or score the bore.

8 Install the new piston seal using the fingers only to manipulate it into position.
9 Dip the piston in clean hydraulic fluid and enter it squarely (closed end first) into the cylinder so that the cut-away portion on the rim is at the bottom.
10 Fit the new wiper seal and the retainer.
11 Install the caliper body to the plate and assemble the holddown and pivot pins and their springs, tighten the nuts fully and insert new cotter pins.
12 Install the caliper and bleed the brakes, as described in the preceding Section.

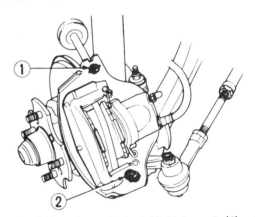

Fig. 9.9 Caliper plate spring-loaded hold down pin (1) and pivot pin (2)

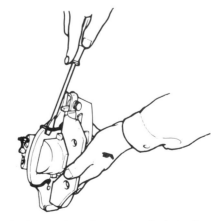

Fig. 9.10 Removing caliper plate to body torsion spring

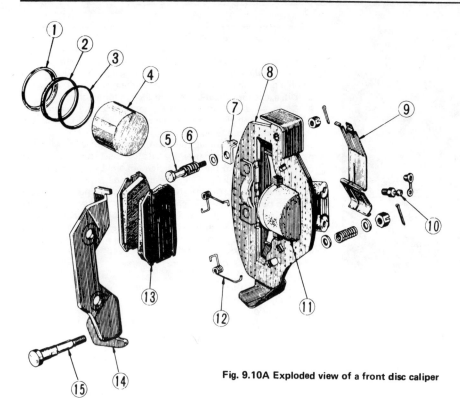

Fig. 9.10A Exploded view of a front disc caliper

1   Retainer
2   Dust excluding seal
3   Piston seal
4   Piston
5   Hold down pin
6   Spring
7   Support bracket
8   Plate
9   Anti-rattle clip
10 Bleed nipple
11 Cylinder body
12 Torsion spring
13 Friction pads
14 Mounting bracket
15 Pivot pin

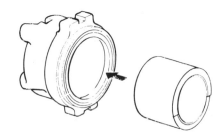

Fig. 9.11 Relationship of caliper piston to cylinder body

7   Front brake disc - inspection and servicing

1   Jack-up the front of the car and remove the roadwheel.
2   Examine the surface of the disc for deep scoring or grooving. Light scoring is normal and should be ignored.
3   The discs can be skimmed professionally, provided their thickness will not be reduced below 0.331 in (8.4 mm).
4   Disc run-out (buckle or out of true) must not exceed 0.005 in (0.12 mm). This can only be satisfactorily measured with a dial gauge applied at the centre of the disc pad contact area. Where the disc is out of true, renew it.
5   To remove the brake disc first remove the caliper (Section 5) then prise off the grease cap from the end of the front hub, remove the split pin and unscrew the castellated nut.
6   Pull the hub/disc assembly towards you and catch the thrust-washer and outer bearing.
7   Withdraw the hub/disc assembly.
8   Unscrew and remove the four setscrews which secure the brake disc to the hub. It will prevent the disc rotating if the assembly is dropped into a roadwheel used as a support and mounting.
9   If required, the backplate-shield may be unbolted from the suspension leg.

10   Refitting is a reversal of dismantling but tighten the disc bolts to a torque of 35 lb/ft (4.8 kg/m) and the backpalte-shield bolts to only 3 lb/ft (0.4 kg/m). The front hub should be adjusted as described in Chapter 11. Bleed the hydraulic system (Section 11).

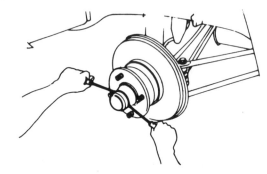

Fig. 9.12 Removing front hub grease cap

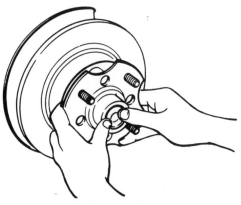

Fig. 9.13 Withdrawing front hub/disc assembly

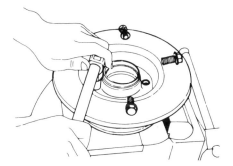

Fig. 9.14 Unbolting front brake disc from hub

8 Rear brake wheel cylinder - removal, servicing and refitting

1 Remove the brake shoes, as described in Section 4.
2 Remove the cap and filter from the rear circuit reservoir of the master cylinder and place a piece of polythene sheeting over the reservoir opening and secure it with a tightly fitting rubber band. This will create a vacuum and prevent loss of fluid when the hydraulic pipe is disconnected.
3 Disconnect the handbrake cable from the lever on the wheel cylinder.
4 Disconnect the fluid pipe by unscrewing the union on the wheel cylinder.
5 Peel off and remove the rubber dust excluder.
6 Drive out the forked lockplate towards the front of the car and then remove the wedge plate rearwards.
7 The wheel cylinder can now be removed.
8 Should the brake backplate need to be removed, the rear stub axle will first have to be withdrawn as described in Chapter 8 or the axle half-shaft according to type, before the backplate can be unbolted from the suspension arm, or the rigid type axle casing.
9 Remove the spring clip and dust cover from the wheel cylinder and extract the piston.
10 Examine the surfaces of the piston and cylinder bores. If they are scored or show evidence of 'bright' wear areas, renew the wheel cylinder complete. Where these components are in good order, discard the piston cup seal and obtain a repair kit.
11 Manipulate the new seal into position using the fingers only.
12 Dip the piston in clean brake fluid and enter it into the cylinder. Fit the dust excluder and spring clip.
13 Refitting is a reversal of removal but apply high melting point grease to the sliding surfaces of the wheel cylinder and backplate. It is essential for the wheel cylinder to slide on the backplate to ensure maximum braking efficiency and even wear of the two shoe linings.
14 The wheel cylinder lockplates should be driven into position in the sequence A-B-C as shown, according to type. 'A' is positioned next to the brake backplate.

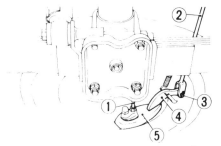

Fig. 9.15 Rear wheel cylinder connections (rigid axle)

1 Hydraulic pipe
2 Handbrake cable
3 Clevis pin
4 Handbrake lever
5 Dust cover

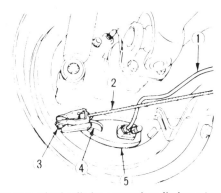

Fig. 9.16 Rear wheel cylinder connections (independent rear suspension)

1 Hydraulic pipe   4 Handbrake lever
2 Handbrake cable   5 Dust cover
3 Clevis pin

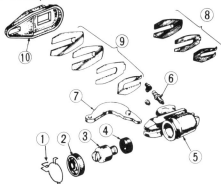

Fig. 9.17 Exploded view of rear wheel cylinder

1 Circlip   6 Bleed nipple
2 Dust excluder   7 Handbrake operating lever
3 Piston   8 Wheel cylinder lockplates
4 Cup seal   9 Alternative lockplates
5 Cylinder   10 Dust excluder

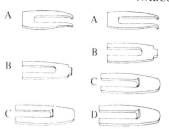

Fig. 9.18 Rear brake wheel cylinder lockplates

9 Brake drum - inspection and renovation

1 Inspect the interior friction surfaces of the rear brake drum. If they are deeply grooved or scored, the drum must either be renewed or turned on a lathe, provided the inner diameter of the drum will not exceed 9.055 in (230.0 mm). Ovality of the drum must also be corrected by one of these methods.

10 Master cylinder - removal, servicing and refitting

1 The master cylinder is mounted on the front face of the vacuum servo unit on the engine compartment rear bulkhead. (photo)
2 Disconnect the brake pipes from the master cylinder and allow the fluid to drain into a container.
3 Unscrew and remove the flange securing nuts and remove the master cylinder from the vacuum servo unit.

4 Drain the fluid from the reservoirs.
5 Remove the stop bolts.
6 Remove the circlip and extract the primary piston assembly followed by the secondary piston assembly.
7 Remove the non-return valves and bleed nipples.
8 Examine the surfaces of the pistons and cylinder bores. If they are scored or any 'bright' wear areas are evident, renew the master cylinder complete.
9 Where the components are in good order, wash them thoroughly in clean brake fluid or methylated spirit and obtain a repair kit. This will include complete primary and secondary piston/cup seal assemblies; the cup seals are not supplied separately.
10 Reassembly is a reversal of dismantling, but dip each components in clean brake fluid before assembly and observe absolute cleanliness to avoid any dirt or grit entering the unit.
11 Refitting is a reversal of removal but when installation is complete, bleed the hydraulic system (Section 11).
12 Check the foot pedal height and adjust if necessary, as described in Section 18.

10.1 Location of brake master cylinder

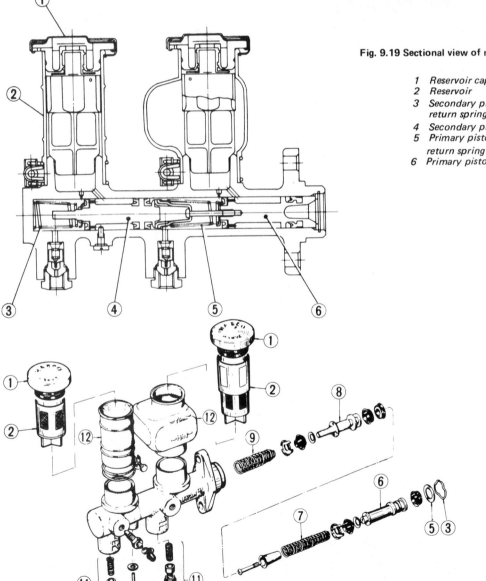

Fig. 9.19 Sectional view of master cylinder

1 Reservoir cap
2 Reservoir
3 Secondary piston return spring
4 Secondary piston
5 Primary piston return spring
6 Primary piston

Fig. 9.20 Exploded view of the brake master cylinder

1 Reservoir cap
2 Filter
3 Circlip
4 Stop bolt
5 Stop ring
6 Primary piston
7 Primary piston return spring
8 Secondary piston
9 Secondary piston return spring
10 Plug
11 Non-return valve
12 Reservoir

11 Hydraulic system - bleeding

1 Removal of all the air from the hydraulic system is essential to the correct working of the braking system, and before undertaking this, examine the fluid reservoir cap to ensure that both vent holes, one on top and the second underneath but not in line, are clear; check the level of fluid and top-up if required.

2 Check all brake line unions and connections for possible seepage, and at the same time check the condition of the rubber hoses, which may be perished.

3 If the condition of the wheel cylinders is in doubt, check for possible signs of fluid leakage.

4 If there is any possibility of incorrect fluid having been put into the system, drain all the fluid out and flush through with methylated spirit. Renew all piston seals and cups since these will be affected and could possible fail under pressure.

5 Gather together a clean jar, a length of tubing which fits tightly over the bleed nipples, and a tin of correct brake fluid.

6 Depress the brake pedal several times in order to destroy the vacuum in the servo system.

7 As the front and rear circuits are independent, it will be obvious that only one circuit need be bled if only one hydraulic line has been disconnected.

8 Clean dirt from around the bleed nipples on the master cylinder and bleed one or both as necessary. To do this, fit the rubber tube to the nipple and immerse its open end in a little brake fluid contained in the jar. Keep the open end of the tube submerged throughout the operation.

9 Open the bleed nipple about one half of a turn and then have an assistant depress the brake pedal fully. The foot should then be removed quickly from the pedal so that it returns unobstructed. Pause and then repeat the operation until no more air bubbles can been seen emerging from the end of the bleed nipple (do not force it) when the pedal is held in the fully depressed position.

10 Now bleed the calipers and wheel operating cylinders working on the principle of bleeding the unit first which is furthest from the master cylinder then the next furthest away, and so on, in sequence.

11 It is vital that the reservoir supplying the circuit with is being bled, is kept topped-up throughout the operation with clean hydraulic fluid which has been stored in an airtight container and has remained unshaken for the previous 24 hours.

Always discard fluid which is expelled into the jar - never use if for topping-up.

12 Flexible hoses - inspection, removal and refitting

1 Inspect the condition of the fleixlbe hydraulic hoses. If they are swollen, perished or chafed, they must be renewed.

2 To remove a flexible hose, hold the flats on its end-fitting in an open-ended spanner and unscrew the union nut which couples it to the rigid brake line.

3 Disconnect the flexible hose from the rigid line and support bracket and then unscrew the hose from the caliper or wheel cylinder circuit as the case may be.

4 Refitting is a reversal of removal. The flexible hoses may be twisted not more than one quarter turn in either direction if necessary to provide a 'set' to ensure that they do not rub or chafe against any adjacent component.

5 Bleed the hydraulic system on completion.

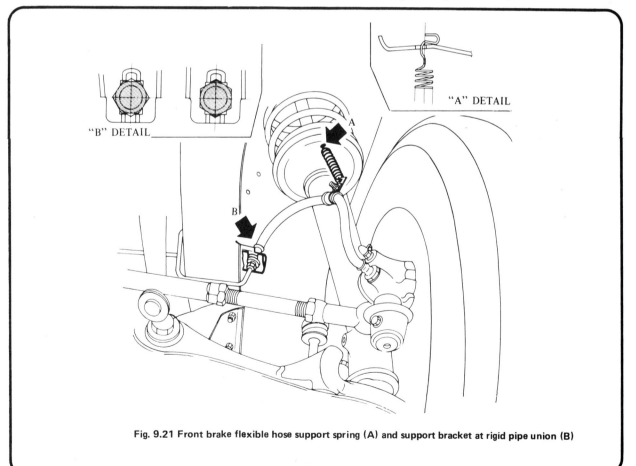

Fig. 9.21 Front brake flexible hose support spring (A) and support bracket at rigid pipe union (B)

13 Rigid brake lines - inspection, removal and refitting

1 At regular intervals wipe the steel brake pipes clean and examine them for signs of rust or denting caused by flying stones.

2 Examine the securing clips which are plastic coated to prevent wear to the pipe surface. Bend the tongues of the clips if necessary to ensure that they hold the brake pipes securely without letting them rattle or vibrate.

3 Check that the pipes are not touching any adjacent components or rubbing against any part of the vehicle. Where this is observed, bend the pipe gently away to clear.

4 Although the pipes are galvanized, any section of pipe may become rusty through chafing and should be renewed. Brake pipes are available to the correct length and fitted with end unions from most Datsun dealers and can be made to pattern by many accessory suppliers. When installing the new pipes use the old pipes as a guide to bending and do not make any bends sharper than is necessary.

5 The system will of course have to be bled when the circuit has been reconnected.

14 Handbrake (rigid type rear axle) - adjustment

1 Adjust the rear brakes, as described in Section 2.

2 At the centre lever swing arm, release the primary cable locknut and turn the adjusting nut until all the slack is removed from the handbrake cables. (photo)

3 The handbrake should be fully applied after it has passed over three or four notches of the lever ratchet.

4 Release the handbrake control fully and check that the rear brakes are not binding and that there is a clearance between the swing arm and its bracket as shown.

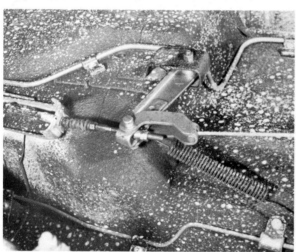

14.2 Handbrake centre swing lever

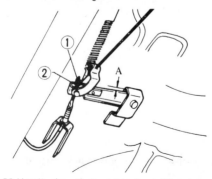

Fig. 9.22 Handbrake adjustment locknut (1) and nut (2) on vehicles with rigid rear axle

15 Handbrake (independent rear suspension) - adjustment

1 Adjust the rear brakes, as described in Section 2.

2 Adjust the handbrake primary cable (nut and locknut) so that with the handbrake fully off the distance 'A' between the endface of the locknut and the edge of the centre lever is as specified.

3 Now adjust the turn buckle on the secondary (rear) cable until all slack is removed.

4 The rear brakes should be fully applied when the handbrake lever has passed over three or four notches of its ratchet.

5 Fully release the handbrake and check that the rear brakes are not binding and that the levers on the wheel cylinders have fully returned to their released position.

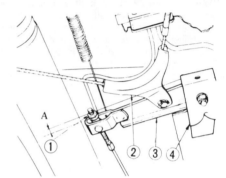

Fig. 9.23 Handbrake adjustment diagram (independent rear suspension)

1 Locknut
2 Equalizer
3 Centre lever
4 Bracket
A = 0.20 in (5.0 mm)

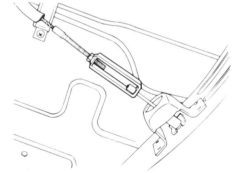

Fig. 9.24 Handbrake secondary (rear) cable adjuster (independent suspension)

16 Handbrake cable (rigid rear axle) - renewal

1 Remove the centre console from within the vehicle.

2 Disconnect the lead from the handbrake warning switch (where fitted). (photo)

3 Unscrew and remove the four bolts which secure the handbrake lever to the floor.

4 Disconnect the primary cable from the centre swing arm and remove the cable and hand control lever.

5 Disconnect the primary cable from the control lever.

6 Unhook the return springs at the centre swing lever and at the rear brake cross rod.

7 Remove the clevis pins from the ends of the secondary cable and detach the cable from the centre swing arm and the rear balance lever.

8 Installation of the new cables is a reversal of removal but adjust, as described in Section 14.

16.2 Location of handbrake warning light switch

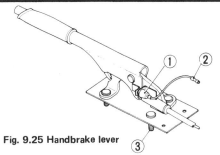

Fig. 9.25 Handbrake lever

1 Handbrake 'ON' switch
2 Snap connector
3 Securing bolt

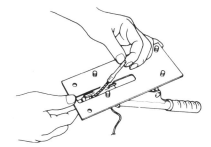

Fig. 9.26 Detaching handbrake primary cable from handbrake lever

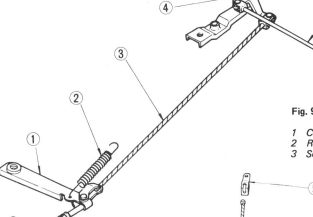

Fig. 9.27 Handbrake cable and rod layout (rigid rear axle)

1 Centre lever   4 Balance lever
2 Return spring   5 Rod
3 Secondary (rear) cable 6 Rod return spring

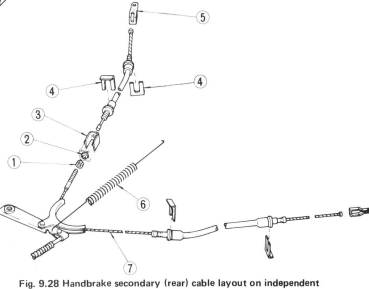

Fig. 9.28 Handbrake secondary (rear) cable layout on independent rear suspension type vehicles

1 Locknut	3 Turnbuckle	5 Clevis	7 Secondary cable
2 Adjusting nut	4 Lockplate	6 Return spring	

17 Handbrake cables (independent rear suspension) - renewal

1 Carry out operations 1 to 5, of Section 16.
2 Unhook the return spring from the centre lever.
3 Disconnect the secondary cable at the turnbuckle adjuster.
4 Remove the handbrake cable lockplates at the rear suspension members.
5 Remove the clevis pins which connect the cable ends to the wheel cylinder levers.
6 Draw the end of the cable through the groove of the equalizer.
7 Installation of the new cables is a reversal of removal but adjust, as described in Section 15.

18 Brake pedal - adjustment, removal and installation

1 Check the installation of the stop lamp switch. Make sure that the end face of the switch bolt is flush with the front face of the locknut and that the locknut is fully tightened.
2 Adjust the pedal stop bolt until the upper surface of the pedal pad is 7.3 in (185.0 mm) above the floor. Tighten the stop bolt locknut.
3 Now adjust the length of the pushrod, after releasing the locknut at the clevis fork so that the pedal has a free-movement of between 0.04 and 0.20 in (1.0 and 5.0 mm). Tighten the locknut.
4 To remove the brake pedal, detach the pedal arm return spring, remove the cotter pin from the pushrod clevis pin and disconnect the pushrod from the pedal arm.
5 Withdraw the pivot bolt to the right, after unscrewing it in a clockwise direction.
6 Renew any worn bushes and other components.
7 Reassembly is a reversal of removal and dismantling but apply grease to the points indicated and then check the pedal height, as described earlier in this Section.

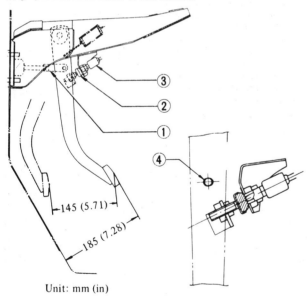

Unit: mm (in)

Fig. 9.29 Brake pedal setting diagram and sectional view of stop lamp switch

1 Pushrod clevis
2 Pedal stop
3 Switch
4 Clevis pin

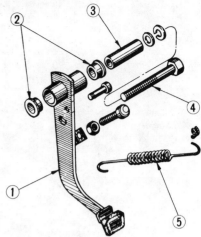

Fig. 9.30 Exploded view of the brake pedal

1 Pedal
2 Bushes
3 Sleeve
4 Pivot pin
5 Return spring

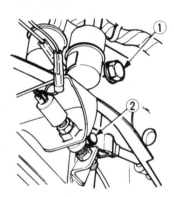

Fig. 9.31 Brake pedal pivot bolt (1) and pushrod clevis pin (2)

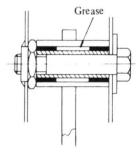

Grease

Fig. 9.32 Brake pedal pivot grease application area

19 Vacuum servo unit - description and testing

1 A vacuum servo unit is fitted into the brake hydraulic circuit in series with the master cylinder, to provide assistance to the driver when the brake pedal is depressed. This reduces the effort required by the driver to operate the brakes under all braking conditions.
2 The unit operates by vacuum obtained from the induction manifold and comprises basically a booster diaphragm and non-return valve. The servo unit and hydraulic master cylinder are connected together so that the servo unit piston rod acts as the

master cylinder pushrod. The driver's braking effort is transmitted through another pushrod to the servo unit piston and its built-in control system. The servo unit piston does not fit tightly into the cylinder, but has a strong diaphragm to keep its edges in constant contact with the cylinder wall, so assuring an air tight seal between the two parts. The forward chamber is held under vacuum conditions created in the inlet manifold of the engine and, during periods when the brake pedal is not in use, the controls open a passage to the rear chamber so placing it under vacuum conditions as well. When the brake pedal is depressed, the vacuum passage to the rear chamber is cut off and the chamber opened to atmospheric pressure. The consequent rush of air pushes the servo piston forward in the vacuum chamber and operates the main pushrod to the master cylinder.

3 The controls are designed so that assistance is given under all conditions and, when the brakes are not required, vacuum in the rear chamber is established when the brake pedal is released. All air from the atmosphere entering the rear chamber is passed through a small air filter.

4 Under normal operating conditions the vacuum servo unit is very reliable and does not require overhaul except at very high mileages. In this case it is far better to obtain a service exchange unit, rather than repair the original unit. Servicing procedures are however described for those wishing to carry out this work.

5 It is emphasised, that the servo unit assists in reducing the braking effort required at the foot pedal and in the event of its failure, the hydraulic braking system is in no way affected except that the need for higher pedal pressures will be noticed.

6 To test the efficiency of the vacuum servo unit, a vacuum gauge should be connected in the line between the non-return valve and the servo unit.

7 Start the engine and run it until the vacuum gauge shows a reading of 19.7 in Hg (500 mm Hg). Switch off the engine and wait 15 seconds without touching the brake pedal. The pressure should not rise by more than 0.98 in Hg (25.0 mm Hg). If it does then this will probably be due to one of the following faults:

Insecure or split connecting pipes.
Faulty or worn pushrod seals.
Faulty sealing between main valve body and seal.
Faulty sealing of main valve plunger seat.

8 Repeat the operation but this time wait 15 seconds with the brake pedal fully applied. Again, the pressure should not rise by more than 0.98 in Hg (25.0 mm Hg). If it does, it will be probably be due to one of the following faults:

Damaged diaphragm.
Loose or displaced reaction disc.

Faulty non-return valve or leaking connections.
Poppet assembly not seating to provide airtight seal.

9 Even where the servo unit is performing satisfactorily, it is recommended that it is overhauled at two-yearly intervals.

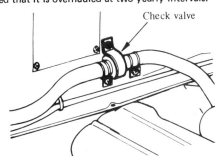

Fig. 9.34 Location of brake servo unit non-return valve

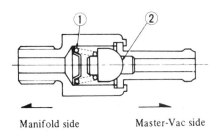

Fig. 9.35 Sectional view of brake servo non-return valve

20 Vacuum servo unit - removal and installation

1 Disconnect the pushrod from the arm of the brake pedal by withdrawing the split pin and clevis pin.
2 Disconnect the brake pipes from the master cylinder.
3 Remove the master cylinder from the servo unit.
4 Disconnect the vacuum pipe from the servo unit.
5 Unscrew and remove the four securing nuts from the mounting studs of the vacuum servo unit and withdraw the unit from the engine compartment rear bulkhead.
6 Installation is a reversal of removal but bleed the hydraulic system on completion (see Section 11).

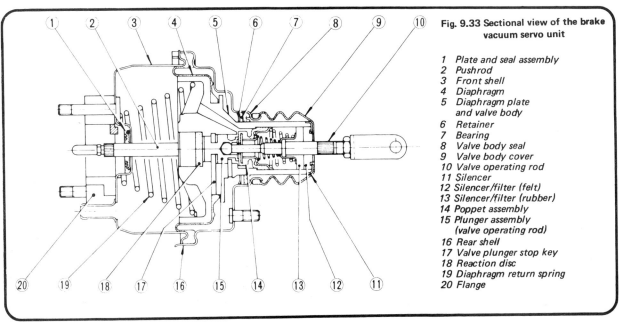

Fig. 9.33 Sectional view of the brake
vacuum servo unit

1 Plate and seal assembly
2 Pushrod
3 Front shell
4 Diaphragm
5 Diaphragm plate
   and valve body
6 Retainer
7 Bearing
8 Valve body seal
9 Valve body cover
10 Valve operating rod
11 Silencer
12 Silencer/filter (felt)
13 Silencer/filter (rubber)
14 Poppet assembly
15 Plunger assembly
   (valve operating rod)
16 Rear shell
17 Valve plunger stop key
18 Reaction disc
19 Diaphragm return spring
20 Flange

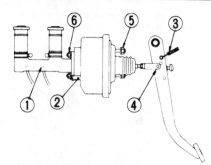

Fig. 9.36 Installation diagram of servo unit, master cylinder and brake pedal

1 Master cylinder
2 Servo unit
3 Pedal return spring
4 Pushrod clevis
5 Servo mounting stud
6 Master cylinder mounting stud

21 Vacuum servo unit - servicing

1   Remove all external dust and accumulated dirt.
2   Make alignment marks on the front and rear shells to facilitate reassembly.
3   Secure the studs which are located on the front face of the servo unit (and are used to mount the master cylinder), in the jaws of a vice but take care not to damage the threads of the studs or to distort them.
4   Remove the clevis fork (1) locknut (2) and the valve protective cover (3).
5   A tool will now have to be made up which can be slipped over the mounting studs of the servo unit to enable the rear shell to be slightly depressed and then released by turning it in an anticlockwise direction.
6   Remove the pushrod from the diaphragm plate.
7   Detach the valve body and the diaphragm from the rear shell.
8   Use a screwdriver to detach the retainer, bearing and seal from the rear shell.
9   Pull the diaphragm from its groove in the diaphragm plate.
10 Prise off the air silencer retainer carefully using a screwdriver applied at several points around its edge.
11 Depress the valve operating rod so that the keyhole opening faces downwards and then shake until the valve plunger stop key is ejected.
12 Withdraw the valve operation rod assembly and air silencer filter from the valve body and diaphragm plate.
13 Push out the reaction disc from the direction of the valve body.
14 Unscrew and remove the nuts which secure the master cylinder mounting flange to the front shell.
15 Examine all components for wear or deterioration and renew as required. If it is a routine overhaul, use the components supplied as a repair kit.
16 Reassembly is a reversal of dismantling but apply silicone grease, sparingly to the seal at its contact face with the rear shell, to the lip of the poppet, to both faces of the reaction disc, to the edges of the diaphragm, to the plate and seal assembly and to the end of the pushrod. A pack of specified grease is supplied in the kit provided for repair purposes.
17 Insert the valve operation rod, holding it vertically and depressing it so that the stop key can be slid into position from the side.
18 Fit the retainer to the rear shell using a piece of tubing as a drift.
19 Position the servo unit so that the pushrod (at the master cylinder mounting flange end) is vertical and then adjust its length (locknut and sleeve) so that the measurement between the face of the mounting flange and the end of the pushrod is between 0.384 and 0.394 in (9.75 and 10.00 mm).

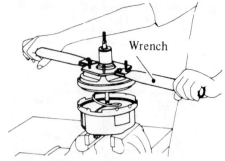

Fig. 9.37 Removing the brake servo rear shell

Fig. 9.38 Removing retainer from servo rear shell

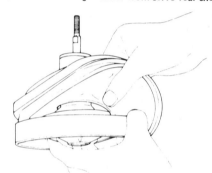

Fig. 9.39 Removing servo diaphragm from diaphragm plate

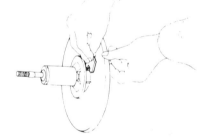

Fig. 9.40 Removing the valve plunger stop key

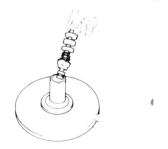

Fig. 9.41 Withdrawing valve operating rod assembly

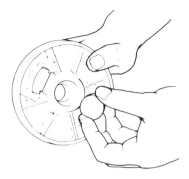

Fig. 9.42 Removing servo reaction disc

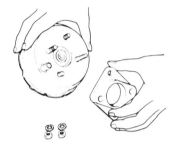

Fig. 9.43 Removing master cylinder mounting flange from face of servo front shell

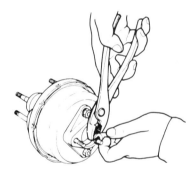

Fig. 9.44 Adjusting servo pushrod length

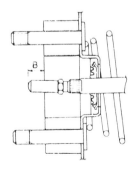

Fig. 9.45 Servo pushrod setting diagram B = 0.384 to 0.394 in (9.75 to 10.00 mm)

22 Pressure regulating valve - testing and renewal

1 The purpose of the pressure regulating valve is to prevent the rear brakes locking in advance of the front brakes.
2 To test the valve, drive the car in a straight line at 31 mph (50 kph) and apply the brakes hard to lock the wheels. The skid marks for the front wheels should be longer than those for the rear, indicating that the front wheels locked first.
3 Where the test proves the valve to be faulty, renew it as an assembly.
4 Disconnect the hydraulic pipes from the valve body and unscrew and remove the valve mounting bolts.
5 When installing the new valve, make sure that the fluid ports are correctly connected by reference to the appropriate (LHD or RHD steering) diagram.
6 Bleed the hydraulic system.

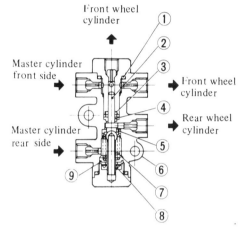

R.H. Drive Model

Fig. 9.46 Sectional view of pressure regulating valve (R.H.D.)

1 'O' ring	6 Body
2 Plunger	7 Spring
3 Support ring	8 Cup seal
4 and 5 Seals	9 Spring retainer

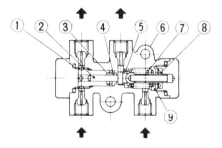

L.H. Drive Model

Fig. 9.47 Sectional view of pressure regulating valve (L.H.D.)

1 'O' ring	6 Body
2 Plunger	7 Spring
3 Support ring	8 Cup seal
4 and 5 Seals	9 Spring retainer

23 Pressure differential warning switch

1   With dual circuit hydraulic braking systems, a switch is fitted
to the engine bulkhead to monitor any drop in pressure in either
of the circuits.

2   The switch is essentially a piston which is kept in balance
when the pressure in the front and rear hydraulic circuits is
equal. Should a leak occur in either circuit then the piston is
displaced by the greater pressure existing in the non-leaking
circuit and makes an electrical contact to illuminate a warning
lamp on the vehicle facia.

3   In the event of the warning lamp coming on, check
immediately to establish the source of fluid leakage. This may be
in the rigid or flexible pipes or more likely, at the wheel
operating cylinders, master cylinder or caliper units.

4   When the faulty component has been repaired or renewed,
bleed the brakes as described in Section 11 of this Chapter when
the pressure differential switch piston will automatically return
to its 'in balance' position.

5   In the event of a fault developing in the switch itself, renew it
as an assembly.

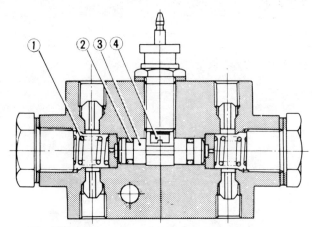

Fig. 9.48 Sectional view of pressure differential switch

1   *Valve spring*
2   *'O' ring*
3   *Valve*
4   *Terminal*

24 Fault diagnosis - braking system

Symptom	Reason/s
Pedal travels almost to floor before brakes operate	Brake fluid level too low Caliper leaking Wheel cylinder leaking Master cylinder leaking (bubbles in master cylinder fluid) Brake flexible hose leaking Brake line fractured Brake system unions loose Pad or shoe linings over 75% worn
Brake pedal feels "springy"	New linings not yet bedded-in Brake discs or drums badly worn or cracked Master cylinder securing nuts loose
Brake pedal feels "spongy" and "soggy"	Caliper or wheel cylinder leaking Master cylinder leaking (bubbles in master cylinder reservoir) Brake pipe line or flexible hose leaking Unions in brake system loose Blocked reservoir cap vent hole
Excessive effort required to brake car	Pad or shoe linings badly worn New pads or shoes recently fitted - not yet bedded-in Harder linings fitted than standard causing increase in pedal pressure Linings and brake drums contaminated with oil, grease or hydraulic fluid Servo unit inoperative or faulty Scored drums or discs
Brakes uneven and pulling to one side	Linings and discs or drums contaminated with oil, grease or hydraulic fluid Tyre pressures unequal Radial ply tyres fitted at one end of the car only Brake caliper loose Brake pads or shoes fitted incorrectly Different type of linings fitted at each wheel Anchorages for front suspension or rear suspension loose Brake discs or drums badly worn, cracked or distorted Incorrect front wheel alignment Incorrectly adjusted front wheel bearings
Brakes tend to bind, drag or lock-on	Air in hydraulic system Wheel cylinders seized Handbrake cables too tight Weak shoe return springs Incorrectly set foot pedal or push-rod Master cylinder seized Front disc distorted (excessive run-out) Rear brakes over-adjusted

Chapter 10 Electrical system

Contents

Specifications

System type	12 volt negative earth
Battery	60 amp/hr.

Alternator

	140J	160J SSS	710 except Canada	710 Canada
Type	LT135-13	LT150-05	LT150-13	LT160-24
Rating	12V 35A	12V 50A	12V 50A	12V 60A
Output current	28A (14V 2500 rpm)	37.5A (14V 2500 rpm)	37.5A (14V 2500 rpm)	45A (14V 2500 rpm)

Voltage regulator
Type:

140J	TL IZ - 57
160J and 710 (up to 1974)	TL IZ - 58
710 (1974 on)	TL IZ - 82
Regulating voltage (with fully charged battery)	14.3 to 15.3V at 68°F (20°C)
Voltage coil resistance	10.5 ohms at 68°F (20°C)
Core gap	0.024 to 0.039 in. (0.6 to 1.0 mm)
Points gap	0.012 to 0.016 in. (0.3 to 0.4 mm)

Cut-out

Release voltage	4.2 to 5.2V at 'N' terminal
Voltage coil resistance	37.8 ohms at 68°F (20°C)
Core gap	0.032 to 0.039 in. (0.8 to 1.0 mm)
Points gap	0.016 to 0.024 in. (0.4 to 0.6 mm)

Starter

	140J 160J SSS	710 (up to 1975) Manual	710 (up to 1975) Automatic	710 (1975 on) Manual	710 (1975 on) Automatic
Make	Hitachi pre-engaged				
Type	5114-103P	5114-103P	5114-126M	5114-170	540A(5V)
Output	1.0 kw	1.0 kw	1.2 kw	1.2 kw	1.2 kw
Starting current	less than 480A (6V)	less than 480A(6V)	less than 540A(5V)	less than 540A(5V)	less than 500A(5V)
No load current	less than 60A(12V)				
No load speed	in excess of 7000 rpm	in excess of 7000 rpm	in excess of 6000 rpm	in excess of 7000 rpm	in excess of 6000 rpm
No. of pinion teeth	9				
No. of flywheel (or driveplate) ring gear teeth	120				

Fuses

Rating	1 x 5A; 6 x 10A; 3 x 20A

Bulbs (wattage)

	710 series	140J/160J SSS
Headlamp (outer)	37.5/50 (sealed beam)	40/45 (bulb)
Headlamp (inner)	37.5 (sealed beam)	40 (bulb)
Front lamp (direction/parking)	27/8.3	21
		5
Side marker lamp (or side flasher)	8	5
Licence plate lamp	7.5	5
Rear stop/tail lamp	27/8.3	21/5
Rear direction indicator lamp	27	21
Reversing lamp	27	21
Tail (Hardtop)	10	—
Interior (front) lamp	10	10
Interior (rear) lamp - wagon	10	—
Knob illumination lamp	3.4	3.4
Auto. transmission speed selector indicator	3.4	—
Clock illumination lamp	—	3.4
Hazard warning switch	—	2.6
Rear window demister indicator lamp	—	1.5 wedge base
Main beam indicator lamp (140J)	—	3.4
(160J SSS)	—	1.7
Ignition (charge) warning lamp (140J)	—	3.4
(160J SSS)	—	1.7
Cigar lighter lamp	—	1.7
All other indicator and warning lamps	3.4 (wedge base)	3.4 (wedge base)

1 General description

The electrical system is of 12 volt negative earth type. The major components comprise the battery, a belt driven alternator and a pre-engaged starter motor.

The battery supplies a steady current to the ignition system and for the operation of the electrical accessories.

The alternator maintains the charge in the battery and the voltage regulator adjusts the charging rate according to the demands of the battery. Silicon diodes within the alternator rectify the alternating current produced into direct current. A cut-out prevents the battery discharging to earth when the engine is switched off or when it is running at tick-over speed and the ignition warning lamp is on.

2 Battery - removal and installation

1 The battery is located within the engine compartment.
2 Always disconnect the lead from the battery negative terminal first, then disconnect the lead from the positive terminal.
3 Remove the battery securing frame and lift out the battery, taking care not to spill any electrolyte on the paintwork. (photos)
4 Installation is a reversal of removal but clean any corrosion from the terminals or ends of the leads and after reconnection, smear the terminals with petroleum jelly.

3 Battery - maintenance and inspection

1 Keep the top of the battery clean by wiping away dirt and moisture.
2 Remove the plugs or lid from the cells and check that the electrolyte level is just above the separator plates. If the level has fallen, add only distilled water until the electrolyte level is just above the separator plates.
3 As well as keeping the terminals clean and covered with petroleum jelly, the top of the battery, and especially the top of the cells, should be kept clean and dry. This helps prevent corrosion and ensures that the battery does not become partially discharged by leakage through dampness and dirt.
4 Once every three months, remove the battery and inspect the battery securing bolts, the battery clamp plate, tray and battery leads for corrosion (white fluffy deposits on the metal which are brittle to touch). If any corrosion is found, clean off the deposits with ammonia and paint over the clean metal with an anti rust/

anti-acid paint.

5 At the same time inspect the battery case for cracks. If a crack is found, clean and plug it with one of the proprietary compounds marketed for this purpose. If leakage through the crack has been excessive then it will be necessary to refill the appropriate cell with fresh electrolyte as detailed later. Cracks are frequently caused to the top of the battery cases by pouring in distilled water in the middle of winter *after* instead of *before* a run. This gives the water no chance to mix with the electrolyte and so the former freezes and splits the battery case.

6 If topping-up the battery becomes excessive and the case has been inspected for cracks that could cause leakage, but none are found, the battery is being over-charged and the voltage regulator will have to be checked and reset.

7 With the battery on the bench at the three monthly interval check, measure its specific gravity with a hydrometer to determine the state of charge and condition of the electrolyte. There should be very little variation between the different cells and if a variation in excess of 0.025 is present it will be due to either:

  a) *Loss of electrolyte from the battery at some time caused by spillage or a leak, resulting in a drop in the specific gravity of electrolyte when the deficiency was replaced with distilled water instead of fresh electrolyte.*

  b) *An internal short circuit caused by buckling of the plates or a similar malady pointing to the likelihood of total battery failure in the near future.*

8 The specific gravity of the electrolyte for fully charged conditions at the electrolyte temperature indicated, is listed in Table A. The specific gravity of a fully discharged battery at different temperatures of the electrolyte is given in Table B.

Table A
Specific Gravity - Battery Fully Charged

1.268 at 100°F or 38°C electrolyte temperature
1.272 at 90°F or 32°C electrolyte temperature
1.276 at 80°F or 27°C electrolyte temperature
1.280 at 70°F or 21°C electrolyte temperature
1.284 at 60°F or 16°C electrolyte temperature
1.288 at 50°F or 10°C electrolyte temperature
1.292 at 40°F or 4°C electrolyte temperature
1.296 at 30°F or-1,5°C electrolyte temperature

Table B
Specific Gravity - Battery Fully Discharged

1.098 at 100°F or 38°C electrolyte temperature
1.102 at 90°F or 32°C electrolyte temperature
1.106 at 80°F or 27°C electrolyte temperature
1.110 at 70°F or 21°C electrolyte temperature
1.114 at 60°F or 16°C electrolyte temperature
1.118 at 50°F or 10°C electrolyte temperature
1.112 at 40°F or 4°C electrolyte temperature
1.126 at 30°F or-1.5°C electrolyte temperature

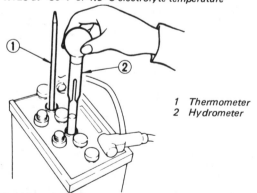

1 Thermometer
2 Hydrometer

Fig. 10.1 Measuring battery specific gravity and electrolyte temperature

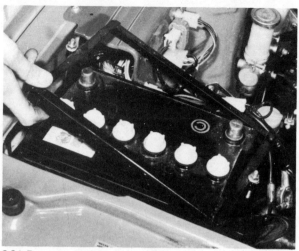

2.3A Removing battery securing frame

2.3B Lifting battery from engine compartment

4 Electrolyte replenishment

1 If the battery is in a fully charged state and one of the cells maintains a specific gravity reading which is 0.025 or more lower than the others, and a check of each cell has been made with a voltage meter to check for short circuits (a four to seven second test should give a steady reading of between 1.2 to 1.8 volts), then it is likely that electrolyte has been lost from the cell with the low reading at some time.

2 Top up the cell with a solution of 1 part sulphuric acid to 2.5 parts of water. If the cell is already fully topped up draw some electrolyte out of it with a pipette.

3 When mixing the sulphuric acid and water **never add water to sulphuric acid** - always pour the acid slowly onto the water in a glass container. **If water is added to sulphuric acid it will explode.**

4 Continue to top-up the cell with the freshly made electrolyte and then recharge the battery and check the hydrometer readings.

5 Battery charging

1   In winter time when heavy demand is placed upon the battery, such as when starting from cold, and much electrical equipment is continually in use, it is a good idea to occasionally have the battery fully charged from an external source at the rate of 3.5 or 4 amps (see Section 7).

2   Continue to charge the battery at this rate until no further rise in specific gravity is noted over a four hour period.

3   Alternatively, a trickle charger at the rate of 1.5 amps can be safely used overnight.

4   Specially rapid 'boost' charges which are claimed to restore the power of the battery in 1 to 2 hours are most dangerous as they can cause serious damage to the battery plates.

6 Alternator - general description and maintenance

1   Briefly, the alternator comprises a rotor and stator. Current is generated in the coils of the stator as soon as the rotor revolves. This current is three-phase alternating which is then rectified by positive and negative silicon diodes and the level of voltage required to maintain the battery charge is controlled by a regulator unit.

2   Maintenance consists of occasionally wiping away any oil or dirt which may have accumulated on the outside of the unit.

3   No lubrication is required as the bearings are grease sealed for life.

4   Check the drivebelt tension periodically to ensure that its specified deflection is correctly maintained, as described in Chapter 1, Section 47.

5   There are minor differences between the types of alternator fitted to the various models but the procedure described in this Chapter applies to all versions.

7 Alternator - special precautions

Take extreme care when making circuit connections to a vehicle fitted with an alternator and observe the following. When making connections to the alternator from a battery always match correct polarity. Before using electric-arc welding equipment to repair any part of the vehicle, disconnect the connector from the alternator and disconnect the positive battery terminal. Never start the car with a battery charger connected. Always disconnect both battery leads before using a main charger. If boosting from another battery, always connect in parallel using heavy cable.

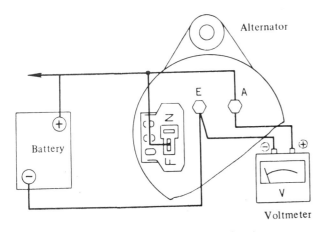

Fig. 10.2 Alternator test circuit

8 Alternator - testing in position in the vehicle

1   Where a faulty alternator is suspected, first ensure that the battery is fully charged; if necessary charge from an outside source.

2   Obtain a 0 to 30 voltmeter.

3   Disconnect the leads from the alternator terminals.

4   Connect a test probe from the voltmeter positive terminal to the 'N' to 'BAT' terminal of the alternator. Connect the voltmeter negative terminal to earth and check that the voltmeter indicates battery voltage (12 volts).

5   Switch the headlamps to main beam.

6   Start the engine and gradually increase its speed to approximately 1100 rev/min and check the reading on the voltmeter. If it registers over 12.5 volts then the alternator is in good condition, if it registers below 12.5 volts then the alternator is faulty and must be removed and repaired.

9 Alternator - removal and refitting

1   Loosen the alternator mounting bracket bolts and strap, push the unit towards the engine block sufficiently to enable the fan belt to be slipped off the alterator pulley. (photos)

2   Remove the cable connectors from the alternator and withdraw the mounting bracket bolts. Lift away the alternator.

3   Replacement is a reversal of removal procedure but ensure that the connections are correctly made and that the fan belt is adjusted, as described in Chapter 1, Section 47. (photo)

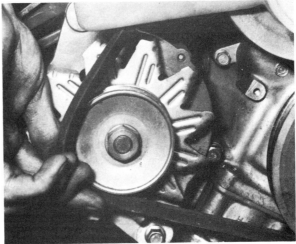

9.1A Removing alternator drivebelt

9.1B Alternator adjustment strap and bolt

9.3 Alternator upper mounting bracket attachment

10 Alternator - brush renewal

1   These are the most likely components to require renewal, and their wear should be checked at 50,000 mile (80,000 km) intervals or whenever the alternator is suspected of being faulty (indicated by a discharged battery).
2   Remove the brush holder cover securing screws and withdraw the cover.

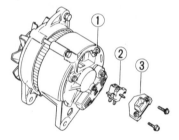

Fig. 10.3 Alternator 'N' terminal (1) brush holder (2) and cover (3)

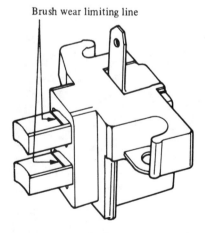

Brush wear limiting line

Fig. 10.4 Alternator brush wear limit marks

3   Remove the brush holder complete with brushes. Do not disconnect the 'N' terminal from the stator coil lead.
4   If the brushes have worn down to the limit line marked on them, renew them.
5   Check that the brushes move smoothly in their holders otherwise clean the holders free from any dust or dirt.
6   Reassembly of the brush mechanism is a reversal of removal and dismantling.

11 Alternator - dismantling, servicing and reassembly

1   Components of any alternator have a very long life and apart from the brushes, any malfunction is most economically overcome by fitting an exchange unit. For those who prefer to overhaul the original unit however, the following procedure will apply.
2   Clean dirt, dust and oil from the external surfaces.
3   From the front of the alternator, remove the nut, pulley and fan.
4   Remove the brush holder assembly, as described in the preceding Section.
5   Unscrew and remove the tie-bolts.
6   Separate the front cover (complete with rotor) from the rear cover and stator, by gently tapping the front mounting bracket with a soft faced mallet.
7   Remove the bearing retainer setscrews from the front face of the front cover and separate the rotor from the front cover.
8   If necessary, remove the rear bearing from the rotor shaft with a suitable puller.
9   Remove the diode cover fixing screw and withdraw the cover.
10 Disconnect the three stator coil leads from the diode terminals using a soldering iron.
11 Unscrew the alternator 'A' terminal nut and the diode assembly securing nut and withdraw the assembly.
On type LT 160/24 alternators: before the diode assembly can be remvoed, the connecting wires between the diodes must also be unsoldered and then the stator coils pulled carefully from the rear cover.
12 The diode assembly can then be removed from the rear cover.
13 To avoid unnecessary expense in the purchase of sound components, carry out the following tests.
14 Using an ohmmeter, test the rotor coils for continuity. Apply the probes of the meter to the slip rings when the meter should indicate 4.4 ohms. If there is no reading then there is probably a break in the field coils and the rotor must be renewed.
15 Next test the rotor for insulation breakdown by placing the probes, one on the slip ring and one on the rotor core. If the meter shows any reading then the slip ring or rotor coil is earthing, probably due to faulty insulation.
16 Check the stator for continuity by connecting the meter probes to the stator coil terminals. If no reading is indicated on the meter then the coil wiring is broken.
17 Now connect one probe to each of the stator coil terminals in turn. No reading should be indicated otherwise the insulation of the coil has broken down.
18 Reassembly is a reversal of dismantling but observe the following special requirements. Localise the heat and work quickly when soldering the stator coil leads to the diode terminals. Make sure that the diode 'A' terminal is correctly assembled with insulating bush and tube.

12 Voltage regulator and cut-out - description, testing and adjustment

1   The voltage regulator and cut-out are located on the right-hand side within the engine compartment.
2   The voltage regulator controls the output from the alternator depending upon the state of the battery and the demands of the vehicle electrical equipment and it ensures that the battery is not overcharged. The cut-out is virtually an automatic switch which completes the charging circuit as soon as the alternator starts to

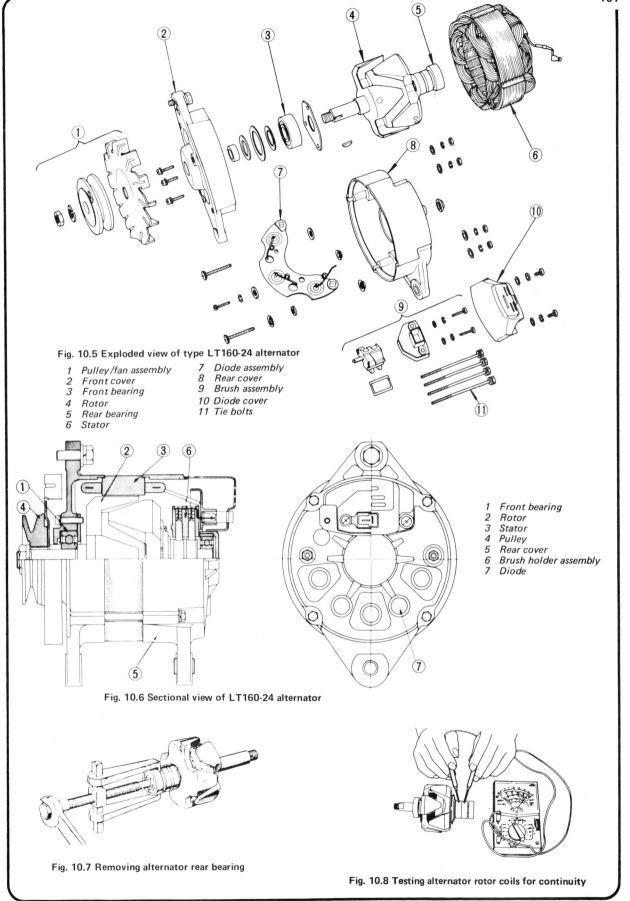

Fig. 10.5 Exploded view of type LT160-24 alternator

1 Pulley/fan assembly
2 Front cover
3 Front bearing
4 Rotor
5 Rear bearing
6 Stator
7 Diode assembly
8 Rear cover
9 Brush assembly
10 Diode cover
11 Tie bolts

Fig. 10.6 Sectional view of LT160-24 alternator

1 Front bearing
2 Rotor
3 Stator
4 Pulley
5 Rear cover
6 Brush holder assembly
7 Diode

Fig. 10.7 Removing alternator rear bearing

Fig. 10.8 Testing alternator rotor coils for continuity

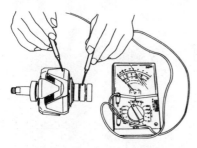

Fig. 10.9 Testing alternator rotor for insulation breakdown

Fig. 10.10 Testing alternator stator for continuity

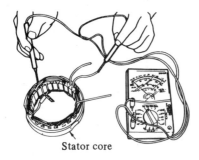

Stator core

Fig. 10.11 Testing alternator stator for insulation breakdown

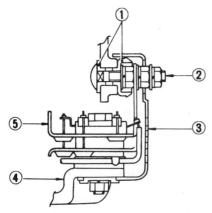

Fig. 10.12 Correct assembly of alternator diode and 'A' terminal

1   *Insulating bush*
2   *'A' terminal bolt*
3   *Diode cover*
4   *Rear cover*
5   *Diode assembly*

rotate and isolates it when the engine stops so that the battery cannot be discharged to earth through the alternator. One visual indication of the correct functioning of the cut-out is the ignition warning lamp. When the lamp is out, the system is charging.

3   **Before testing, check that the alternator drivebelt is not broken or slack and that all electrical leads are secure.**

4   Test the regulator voltage with the unit still installed in the vehicle. If it has been removed make sure it is positioned with the connector plug hanging downward. Carry out the testing with the engine compartment cold and complete the test within one minute to prevent the regulator heating up and affecting the specified voltage readings.

5   Establish the ambient temperature within the engine compartment, turn off all vehicle electrical equipment and ensure that the battery is in a fully charged state. Connect a DC (15 to 30v) voltmeter, a DC (0 to 10 amp) ammeter and a 0.25 ohm 100 watt resistor, as shown.

6   Start the engine and immediately detach the short circuit wire. Increase the engine speed to 2500 rpm and check the voltmeter reading according to the pre-determined ambient temperature table below.

7   If the voltage does not conform to that specified, continue to run the engine at 2500 rpm for several minutes and then with the engine idling check that the ammeter reads below 5 amps. If the reading is above this, the battery is not fully charged and must be removed for charging as otherwise accurate testing cannot be carried out.

Ambient temperature		Rated regulating voltage
^{o}C	(^{o}F)	(V)
−10	(14)	14.75 to 15.75
0	(32)	14.60 to 15.60
10	(50)	14.45 to 15.45
20	(68)	14.30 to 15.30
30	(86)	14.15 to 15.15
40	(104)	14.00 to 15.00

8   Switch off the engine, remove the cover from the voltage regulator and inspect the surfaces of the contacts. If, these are rough or pitted, clean them by drawing a strip of emery cloth between them.

9   Using feeler gauges, check and adjust the core gap if necessary, to between 0.024 and 0.040 in (0.6096 and 1.0160 mm).

10   Check and adjust the contact point gap if necessary, to between 0.012 and 0.16 in (0.3048 and 0.4064 mm).

11   By now the voltage regulator will have cooled down so that the previous test may be repeated. If the voltage/temperature is still not compatible, switch off the engine and adjust the regulator screw. Do this by loosening the locknut and turning the screw clockwise to increase the voltage reading and anti-clockwise to reduce it.

12   Turn the adjuster screw only fractionally before retesting the voltage charging rate gain with the unit cold. Finally tighten the locknut.

13   If the cut-out is operating incorrectly, first check the fan belt and the ignition warning lamp bulb. Connect the positive terminal of a moving coil voltmeter to the 'N' socket of the regulator connection plug and the voltmeter negative terminal to earth as shown.

14   Start the engine and let it idle. Check the voltmeter reading. If the reading is zero volts check for continuity between the 'N' terminals of the regulator unit and the alternator. If the reading is below 5.2 volts and the ignition warning lamp remains on, check and adjust the core gap to between 0.032 and 0.040 in (0.8 and 1.0 mm) and the points gap to 0.016 and 0.024 in (0.4 and 0.6 mm). Remember that this time the adjustments are carried out to the cut-out not the voltage regulator although the procedure is similar.

15   If the reading is over 5.2 volts with the ignition warning lamp on the core and points gap are correctly set, the complete regulator unit must be renewed.

16 The cut-out is operating correctly if the voltmeter shows a reading of more than 5.2 volts (ignition lamp out).

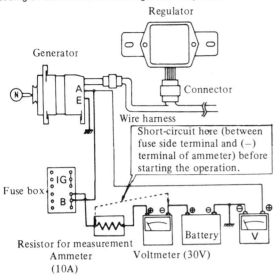

Fig. 10.13 Voltage regulator test circuit

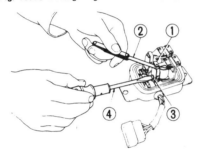

Fig. 10.14 Checking and adjusting voltage regulator core gap

    1 Contacts   3 Adjusting screw
    2 Feeler blade   4 Screwdriver

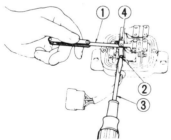

Fig. 10.15 Checking and adjusting voltage regulator points gap

    1 Feeler blade   3 Screwdriver
    2 Adjusting screw 4 Upper contact

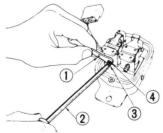

Fig. 10.16 Adjusting voltage regulating screw on voltage regulator

    1 Spanner   3 Adjusting screw
    2 Screwdriver 4 Locknut

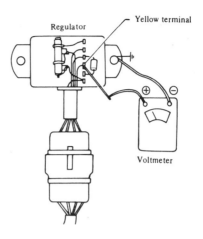

Fig. 10.17 Test circuit for cut-out (charge relay)

13 Starter motor - general description

1 This type of starter motor incorporates a solenoid mounted on top of the starter motor body. When the ignition switch is operated, the solenoid moves the starter drive pinion, through the medium of the shift lever, into engagement with the flywheel or driveplate starter ring gear. As the solenoid reaches the end of its stroke and with the pinion by now partially engaged with the flywheel ring gear, the main fixed and moving contacts close and engage the starter motor to rotate the engine.

This fractional pre-engagement of the starter drive does much to reduce the wear on the flywheel ring gear associated with inertia type starter motors.

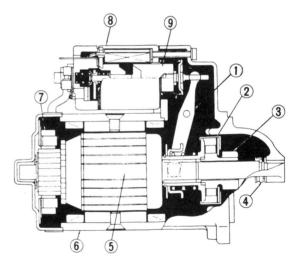

Fig. 10.18 Sectional view of Hitachi type S114 - 103P stater motor

    1 Shift lever
    2 Over-running clutch
    3 Pinion
    4 Pinion stop
    5 Armature
    6 Yoke
    7 Brush
    8 Solenoid
    9 Plunger

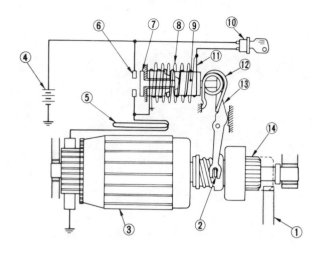

Fig. 10.19. Starting circuit

1 Flywheel ring gear	8 Shunt coil
2 Shift lever guide	9 Plunger
3 Armature	10 Ignition switch
4 Battery	11 Series coil
5 Field coil	12 Torsion spring
6 Stationary contact	13 Shift lever
7 Moving contact	14 Pinion

14 Starter motor - removal and installation

1 Disconnect the cable from the battery negative terminal.
2 Disconnect the black and yellow wire from the S terminal on the solenoid and the black cable from the 'B' terminal also on the end cover of the solenoid.
3 Unscrew and remove the two starter motor securing bolts, pull the starter forward, tilt it slightly to clear the motor shaft support from the flywheel ring gear and withdraw it.
4 Refitting is a reversal of removal.

15 Starter motor - dismantling, servicing and reassembly

1 Disconnect the lead from the 'M' terminal of the solenoid.
2 Remove the solenoid securing screws and withdraw the solenoid from the starter motor.
3 Remove the dust cover, the 'E' ring and the two thrust washers (S114-170/180 starter motors only).
4 Unscrew and remove the two screws which secure the brush holder.
5 Unscrew and remove the two tie-bolts and the rear cover.
6 Using a length of wire with a hook at its end, remove the brushes by pulling the brush springs aside.
7 Remove the brush holder.
8 Withdraw the yoke assembly and extract the armature assembly and shift lever. Push the pinion stop towards the pinion to expose the circlip. Extract the circlip and then withdraw the stop and clutch assembly.

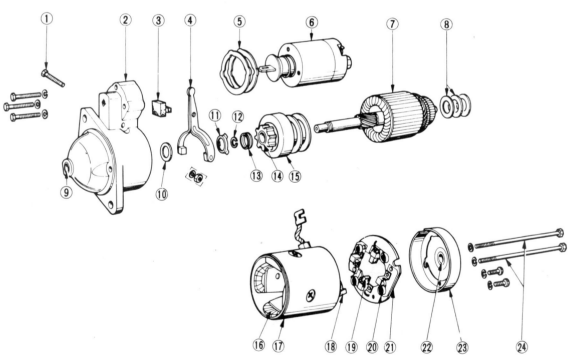

Fig. 10.20. Exploded view of type S114-103 starter motor

1 Shift lever pivot pin	7 Armature	13 Pinion stop	19 Brush (−)
2 Front housing	8 Thrust washer	14 Pinion	20 Brush spring
3 Dust excluder	9 Bush	15 Over-running clutch	21 Brush holder assembly
4 Shift lever	10 Thrust washer	16 Field coil	22 Bush
5 Dust cover	11 Stop washer	17 Yoke	23 Rear cover
6 Solenoid	12 Circlip	18 Brush (+)	24 Tie bolts

9 Check the brushes for wear. If their length is less than 0.472 in (12.0 mm), renew them.

10 If an ohmmeter is available, test the field coil for continuity. To do this, connect one probe of the meter to the field coil positive terminal and the other to the positive brush holder. If no reading is indicated then the field coil circuit has a break in it.

11 Connect one probe of the meter to the field coil positive lead and the other one to the yoke. If there is little or no resistance then the field coil is earthed due to a breakdown in insulation. When this fault is discovered, the field coils should be renewed by an automotive electrician as it is very difficult to remove the field coil securing screws without special equipment. In any event, it will probably be more economical to exchange the complete starter motor for a reconditioned unit.

12 Undercut the mica separators of the commutator using an old hacksaw blade ground to suit. The commutator may be polished with a piece of very fine glass paper - never use emery cloth as the carborundum particles will become embedded in the copper surfaces.

13 The armature may be tested for insulation breakdown again using the ohmmeter. To do this, place one probe on the armature shaft and the other on each of the commutator segments in turn. If there is a reading indicated at any time during the test then the armature must be renewed.

14 Wash the components of the drive gear in paraffin and inspect for wear or damage, particularly to the pinion teeth and renew as appropriate. Refitting is a reversal of dismantling but stake a new stop washer in position and oil the sliding surfaces of the pinion assembly with a light oil, applied sparingly.

15 Reassembly of the remaining components of the starter motor is a reversal of dismantling.

16 When the starter motor has been fully reassembled, actuate the solenoid which will throw the drive gear forward into its normal flywheel engagement position. Do this by connecting jumper leads between the battery negative terminal and the solenoid 'M' terminal and between the battery positive terminal and the solenoid 'S' terminal. Now check the gap between the

end face of the drive pinion and the mating face of the thrust washer. This should be between 0.012 and 0.059 in (0.3 to 1.5 mm) measured either with a vernier gauge or feelers. Adjusting washers are available in different thicknesses.

Fig. 10.22 Removal of dust cover, E ring and thrust washer from types S114 - 170/180 starter motors

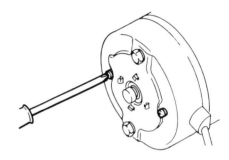

Fig. 10.23 Removing starter motor brush holder screws

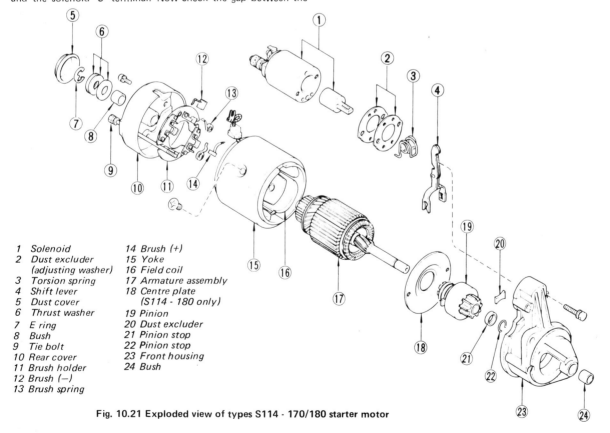

1   Solenoid
2   Dust excluder
    (adjusting washer)
3   Torsion spring
4   Shift lever
5   Dust cover
6   Thrust washer
7   E ring
8   Bush
9   Tie bolt
10 Rear cover
11 Brush holder
12 Brush (−)
13 Brush spring
14 Brush (+)
15 Yoke
16 Field coil
17 Armature assembly
18 Centre plate
    (S114 - 180 only)
19 Pinion
20 Dust excluder
21 Pinion stop
22 Pinion stop
23 Front housing
24 Bush

Fig. 10.21 Exploded view of types S114 - 170/180 starter motor

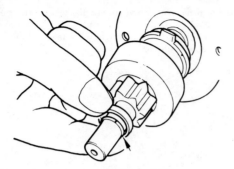

Fig. 10.24 Removing starter motor pinion stop circlip (arrowed)

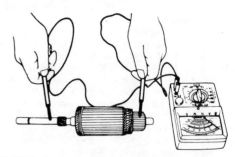

Fig. 10.28 Testing starter motor armature for insulation breakdown

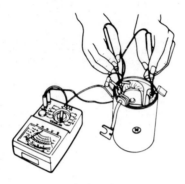

Fig. 10.25 Testing starter motor field coil for continuity

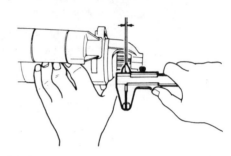

Fig. 10.29 Testing starter motor solenoid (actuated) clearance

Fig. 10.26 Testing starter motor field coil for insulation breakdown

16 Fuses and fusible link

1   The fuse block is located just below the instrument panel.
2   A fusible link is incorporated in the battery to alternator wiring harness within the engine compartment. Its exact location is dependent upon the vehicle model and date of production and it provides an additional protection for the starting and charging circuits.
3   In the event of a fuse or fusible link blowing, always establish the cause before fitting a new one. This is most likely to be due to faulty insulation somewhere in the wiring circuit. Always carry a spare fuse for each rating and never be tempted to substitute a piece of wire or a nail for the correct fuse as a fire may be caused or, at least, the electrical component ruined.

17 Electrical relays - description and testing

1   On 710 series vehicles, the later the date of production, the greater the number of relays incorporated in the electrical system.
2   The relays (with the exception of the ignition relay - see Section 25) are grouped on a bracket which is located on the right-hand side of the engine compartment.
3   Apart from checking the security of connecting plugs and wiring, any fault can only be rectified by renewal of the sealed unit concerned.
4   On 140J models, the relays are limited to horn and lighting. (photo)

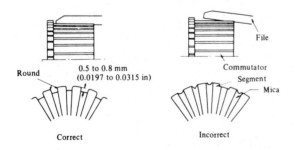

Round   0.5 to 0.8 mm
         (0.0197 to 0.0315 in)

File

Commutator
Segment
Mica

Correct   Incorrect

Fig. 10.27 Starter motor commutator undercutting diagram

18 Hazard warning and direction indicator units

1   Both units are located next to each other adjacent to the pedal bracket under the instrument panel.
2   If the flasher unit fails to operate, or works very slowly or rapidly, check out the flasher indicator circuit as detailed below,

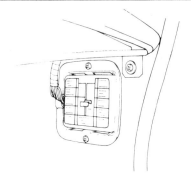

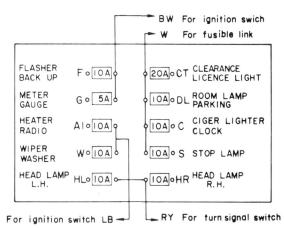

Fig. 10.30 Location of fuse block and circuit protection diagram

In the diagram:

BW For ignition swich
W For fusible link

FLASHER BACK UP	F ○ 10A ○	20A ○ CT	CLEARANCE LICENCE LIGHT
METER GAUGE	G ○ 5A ○	10A ○ DL	ROOM LAMP PARKING
HEATER RADIO	A ○ 10A ○	10A ○ C	CIGER LIGHTER CLOCK
WIPER WASHER	W ○ 10A ○	10A ○ S	STOP LAMP
HEAD LAMP L.H.	HL ○ 10A ○	10A ○ HR	HEAD LAMP R.H.

For ignition switch LB →

→ RY For turn signal switch

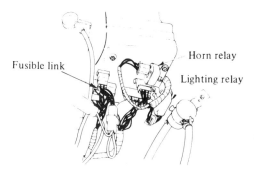

Fig. 10.31 Location of fusible link (140J model)

Fusible link

Horn relay

Lighting relay

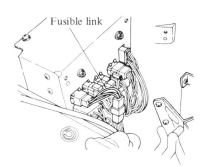

Fig. 10.32 Location of fusible link (710 series up to 1975)

Fusible link

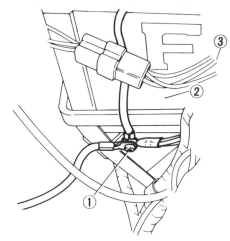

Fig. 10.33 Location of fusible link (710 series, 1975 onwards)

1 Earth connection
2 Battery
3 Fusible link

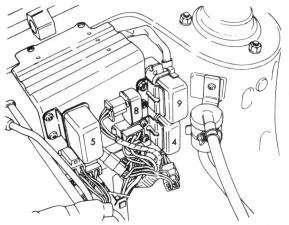

Fig. 10.34 Relay identification (710 series up to 1975)

3 Neutral relay (auto. transmission)
4 Lighting relay
5 Automatic choke relay
8 Horn relay
9 Interlock relay

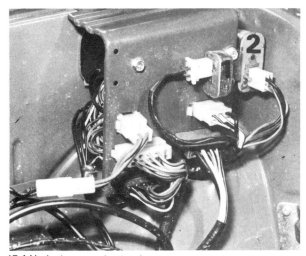

17.4 Under bonnet relay bracket
1 Horn relay   2 Lighting relay

before assuming that there is a fault in the unit:

a) *Examine the direction indicator bulbs both front and rear for broken filaments.*

b) *If the external flashers are working but either of the internal flasher warning lights have ceased to function, check the filaments in the warning light bulbs and replace with a new bulb if necessary.*

c) *If a flasher bulb is sound but does not work, check all the flasher circuit connections with the aid of the wiring diagram found at the end of this Chapter.*

3 With these tests completed, the fault must lie in the respective flasher unit. To renew it, disconnect the lead from the battery negative terminal, disconnect the leads from the flasher unit and pull the unit from its spring clip.

19 Fuel gauge and transmitter unit

1 The unit is fitted to the fuel tank by means of a bayonet coupling.

2 In the event of no reading being shown on the fuel gauge when it is known that there is fuel in the tank, first check the fuses in case they have blown.

3 Check the wiring connections for security, also the wiring for chafing of the insulation and earthing to the bodyframe.

4 The transmitter unit comprises a float which as it moves up and down according to the level of fuel in the tank, alters the amount of current supplied to the fuel gauge by means of variable resistance.

5 The fuel gauge itself is of bimetallic coil type and the indicator needle is actuated by the amount of current received from the transmitter unit.

6 If necessary, both units should be removed from their locations and tested with a circuit tester.

20 Water temperature gauge and transmitter

1 The water temperature transmitter is screwed into the left-hand side of the cylinder head. It is connected to the gauge on the instrument panel and the circuit incorporates a voltage stabilizer.

2 In the event of the water temperature and fuel gauges becoming faulty at the same time, then the voltage stabilizer should be suspected.

3 If unsatisfactory gauge readings are being obtained, the thermal transmitter may be tested by detaching the lead from the transmitter and connecting the end of the lead to a good earth. Switch on the ignition and observe the gauge needle. If the needle moves to the 'Hot' position, the transmitter is faulty.

4 If the needle does not move at all, then the connecting cable or the gauge itself will be at fault.

5 Renewal of the transmission unit can be carried out after partially draining the cooling system.

21 Oil pressure switch, lamp or gauge

1 The oil pressure lamp will come on when the ignition key is turned to the 'IGN' position and should go out almost as soon as the engine fires and the oil pressure rises above 6 p.s.i. (0.4 kg/cm^2).

2 Failure of the bulb to illuminate, may be due to a blown bulb or defective connections.

3 If the lamp comes on during normal engine operational speeds, stop at once and check for low oil level or a severely restricted filter. If the engine is known to be in good condition and the other items have been checked satisfactorily then the fault will probably lie in the switch itself which is screwed into the crankcase just above the oil filter.

4 *On 160J SSS models* an oil gauge is fitted as an alternative to the warning lamp. The gauge is of bi-metal type and incorporates in its circuit, a voltage regulator and variable resistance sensor.

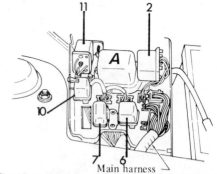

Main harness

Fig. 10.35 Relay identification (710 series 1975 on)

2 *Automatic choke relay*   10 *Seat belt warning relay*
6 *Lighting relay*   11 *Starter interlock relay*
7 *Horn relay*   *A is voltage regualtor*

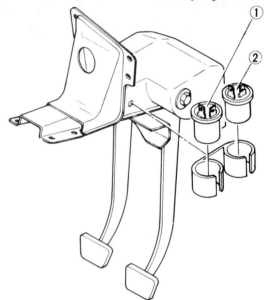

Fig. 10.36 Location of flasher units

1 *Hazard warning*   2 *Direction indicator*

Tank unit   Fuel tank

Fig. 10.37 Fuel tank transmitter unit

transmitter

Fig. 10.38 Location of water temperature transmitter. Thermal transmitter switch to right-hand side is component of E.G.R. (exhaust gas recirculation) system on 710 series vehicles

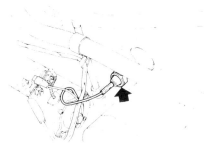

Fig. 10.39 Location of oil pressure switch

22 Instrument panel and instruments (140J and 710 series) - removal and installation

1 Disconnect the negative lead from the battery terminal.
2 Remove the upper and lower steering column shrouds (four screws).
3 The following operations will be made easier if the steering wheel is removed (Chapter 11) and the direction indicator switch withdrawn (Section 24, this Chapter).
4 Pull off the knobs from the windshield wiper switch and the instrument panel light switch. Unscrew the two switch retaining ring nuts.
5 Unscrew and remove the two securing screws from the switch panel (10) and withdraw the panel.
6 Withdraw the ashtray and then disconnect the four instrument harness connectors.

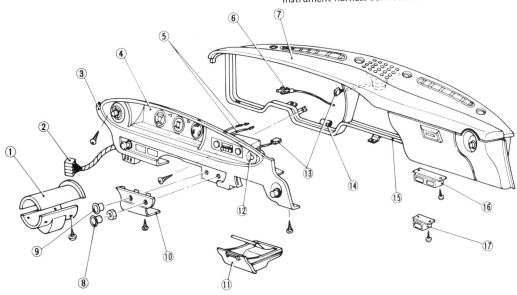

Fig. 10.40 Instrument panel components

1 Steering column upper shrouds
2 Wiring harness
3 Instrument panel
4 Combined gauge assembly
5 Light projection tubes
6 Speedometer cable
7 Crash pad
8 Wiper/washer knob
9 Illumination intensity control knob
10 Lower switch panel
11 Ashtray
12 Clock
13 Speaker harness
14 Bulbs
15 Fascia panel
16 Catalytic converter and floor temperature warning lamps (California only)
17 E.G.R. system warning lamp

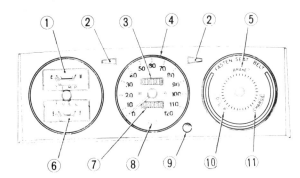

Fig. 10.41 Instrument panel (L.H.D.) on 140J and 710 series vehicles

1 Water temperature gauge
2 Direction indicator warning lamps
3 Trip recorder
4 Speedometer
5 Handbrake warning lamp
6 Fuel gauge
7 Odometer
8 Main beam warning lamp
9 Trip mileage re-set control
10 Oil pressure warning lamp
11 Ignition (charge warning lamp)

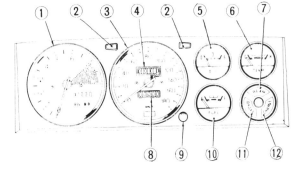

Fig. 10.42 Instrument panel on 160J SSS model

1 Tachometer
2 Direction indicator warning lamp
3 Speedometer
4 Trip recorder
5 Oil pressure gauge
6 Water temperature gauge
7 Main beam warning lamp
8 Odometer
9 Trip mileage re-set control
10 Fuel gauge
11 Handbrake warning lamp
12 Ignition (charge warning lamp)

7 Unscrew and remove the ten screws which secure the instrument panel (do not forget the two screws located at the ashtray cover).
8 Disconnect the speedometer cable, the radio speaker leads and the aerial lead.
9 Disconnect the leads from the panel light switch, and the tachometer.
10 To remove the combined gauge assembly, remove the trip knob from the speedometer.
11 Remove the six screws which secure the lower housing to the gauge assembly and remove the housing.
12 The individual instruments are retained to the lower housing by two or three screws and once these are removed, the instruments may be withdrawn.
13 Refitting is a reversal of dismantling and removal.

23 Instrument panel and instruments (160J SSS) - removal and installation

1 The procedure is as described for the 140J and 710 series vehicles in the preceding Section, except that the leads to the additional instruments must first be disconnected.

24 Direction indicator switch - removal and refitting

1 Disconnect the lead from the battery negative terminal.
2 Remove the steering wheel, as described in Chapter 11.
3 Remove the steering column upper shrouds (four screws).
4 Disconnect the leads to the switch and then remove the two switch securing screws.
5 Refitting is a reversal of removal but make sure that the locking tab of the switch engages in the hole in the steering column jacket.

25 Ignition switch and relay - removal and refitting

1 On all models, the ignition and starting switch is located in the base of the steering column lock.
2 Disconnect the negative battery lead and remove the steering column upper shrouds.
3 Disconnect the leads from the ignition switch.
4 Unscrew and remove the small securing screw and withdraw the ignition switch from the steering column lock housing.
5 Refitting the switch is a reversal of removal.
6 On late models, an ignition relay is incorporated in the circuit and this is located above the fuse block under the instrument panel.
7 Any fault which developes in the relay can only be rectified by renewal of the sealed unit.

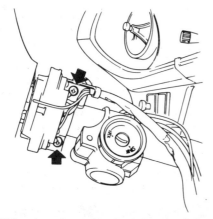

Fig. 10.43 Steering column direction indicator switch securing screws

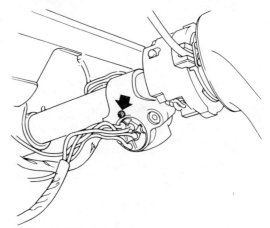

Fig. 10.44 Location of ignition/starter switch

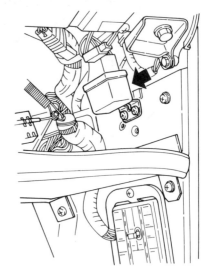

Fig. 10.45 Location of ignition relay (late model vehicles)

26 Lighting switch - removal and installation

1 Disconnect the lead from the battery negative terminal.
2 Depress the switch knob, turn it anticlockwise and then pull it from the switch.
3 Unscrew the switch retaining bezel nut.
4 Reach up under the instrument panel and disconnect the switch leads at the connector plug.
5 Disconnect the switch knob illumination tube from the lamp cap and withdraw the switch assembly.
6 Refitting is a reversal of removal.

27 Hazard warning lamp switch - removal and installation

1 The procedure is similar to that described for the lighting switch in the preceding Section, except that the switch is retained in position by two body side clips.

28 Courtesy lamp switch - removal and installation

1 Courtesy lamp (interior) switches are located on both sides of the centre pillar.
2 To remove a switch, first disconnect the lead from the battery negative terminal and then pull the rubber mounted

switch from its location.

3 Withdraw the switch far enough to be able to disconnect the leads at the connector plugs.

4 Installation is a reversal of removal.

5 The left and right-hand switches are not interchangeable as they have a different number of connecting leads.

29 Tailgate switch (wagon) - removal and installation

1 This switch is of plunger type and complets the circuit to the interior rear compartment lamp when the tailgate is opened.

2 To remove the switch, first disconnect the lead from the battery negative terminal.

3 Remove the right-hand hinge cover (three screws) and pull the switch from its bracket.

4 Disconnect the switch leads at the connector plug.

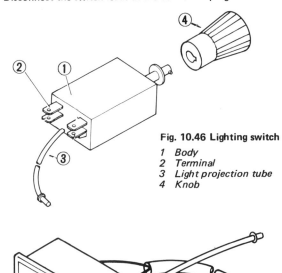

Fig. 10.46 Lighting switch

1 Body
2 Terminal
3 Light projection tube
4 Knob

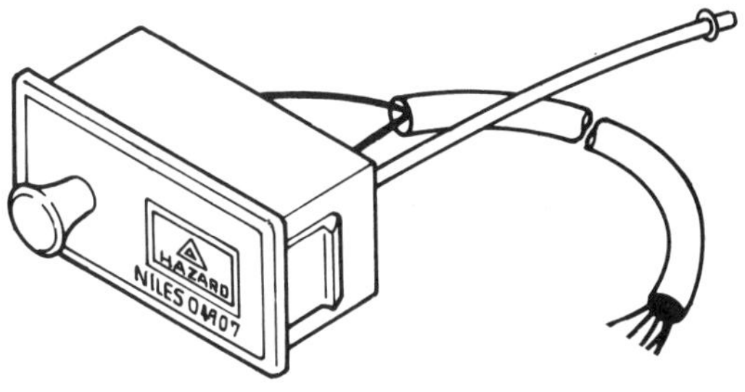

Fig. 10.47 Hazard warning switch. Lift projection tube (arrowed)

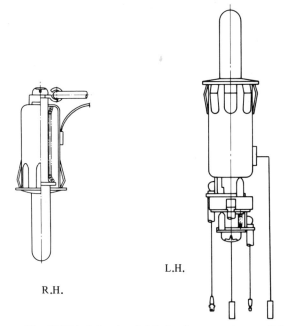

L.H.

R.H.

Fig. 10.49 Left-hand and right-hand courtesy lamp switches

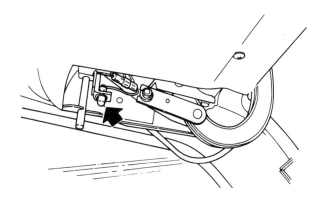

Fig. 10.50 Location of wagon tailgate switch

30 Control knob; illumination intensity switch - removal and refitting

1 This switch is of the variable resistor type and is removed and refitted in a similar manner to that described in Section 26 for the lighting switch.

31 Headlamps (140J and 160J SSS) - bulb renewal

1 Remove the radiator grille (Chapter 12).

2 Loosen (do not remove) the three headlamp retaining screws and then turn the retaining ring in a clockwise direction. On no account disturb the adjusting screws.

3 Withdraw the light unit from the mounting ring and disconnect the leads at the connector plug.

4 Peel back the dust excluder which is fitted at the rear of the bulb holder and remove the holder by turning it in a clockwise direction.

5 Renew the bulb for one of similar wattage and rating and reassemble the components making sure that the word 'TOP' on the headlamp lens is correctly placed.

Fig. 10.48 Courtesy lamp door pillar switch

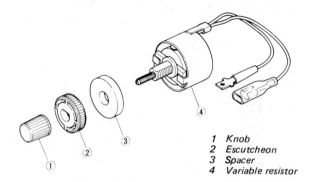

1 Knob
2 Escutcheon
3 Spacer
4 Variable resistor

Fig. 10.51 Control knob illumination intensity switch

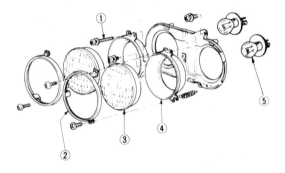

Fig. 10.52 Headlamp assembly (140J and 160J SSS)

1 Adjusting screw
2 Retaining ring
3 Lens unit
4 Mounting ring
5 Bulb

32 Headlamps (140J, 160J SSS and 710 series) - sealed beam unit renewal

1 The procedure is similar to that described in the preceding Section except that the complete light unit must be renewed by removing the rim retaining screws. (photo)
2 Always renew the sealed beam light unit for one of similar wattage and rating and never interchange inner or outer ones. (photo)

33 Headlamps - adjustment

1 It is strongly recommended that the headlamps are adjusted on optical beam setting equipment at a service station.
2 In an emergency, horizontal and vertical adjustment screws are accessible from the front of the headlamp rim. (photo)

34 External lamps - bulb renewal

1 Most of the lamp bulbs are accessible after removal of the lens securing screws and lens.
2 The bulbs on some rear lamp units are accessible after removal of the bulb holder from within the luggage boot. (photo)
3 Reference to the appropriate illustration will provide full guidance.
4 Always renew a bulb with one of similar wattage and rating and check and renew if necessary the lens sealing gasket to prevent entry of water.

32.1 Sealed beam headlamp retaining ring screws (arrowed)

32.2 Removing a sealed beam headlamp unit

33.2 Adjusting a headlamp

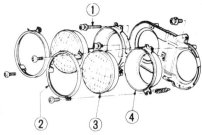

Fig. 10.53 Headlamp assembly (710 series)

1 *Adjusting screw*
2 *Retaining ring*
3 *Sealed beam unit*
4 *Mounting ring*

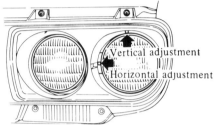

Fig. 10.54 Location of headlamp adjusting screws

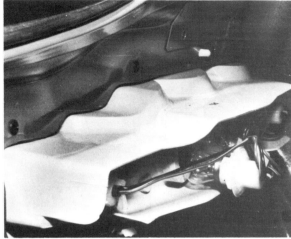

34.2 Rear lamp cluster bulbs accessible
from within luggage boot

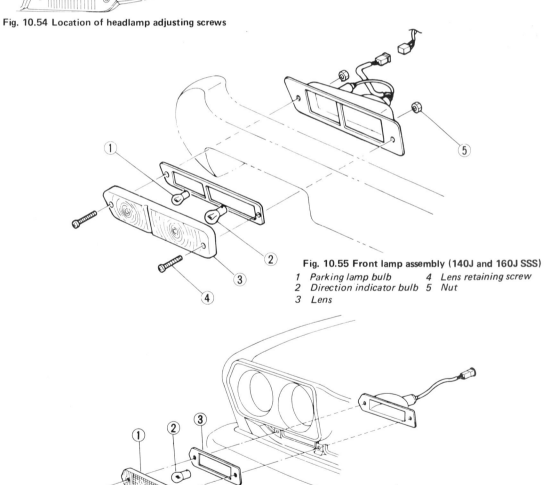

Fig. 10.55 Front lamp assembly (140J and 160J SSS)

1 *Parking lamp bulb*   4 *Lens retaining screw*
2 *Direction indicator bulb* 5 *Nut*
3 *Lens*

Fig. 10.56 Front lamp assembly (710 series)

1 *Lens*   2 *Dual filament bulb*   3 *Gasket*

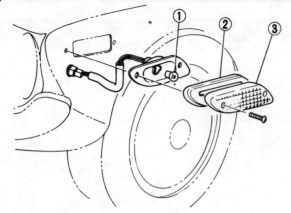

Fig. 10.57 Side flasher (140J and 160J SSS) or side marker (710 series) lamp

1 *Bulb*
2 *Gasket*
3 *Lens*

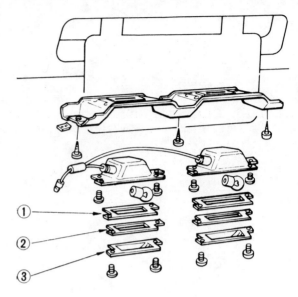

Fig. 10.60 Number plate lamp (140J and 160J SSS)

1 *Gasket*
2 *Lens*
3 *Lens frame*

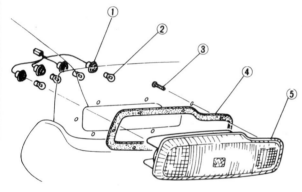

Fig. 10.58 Rear lamp (140J, 160J SSS and 710 series saloons)

1 *Bulb holder*
2 *Bulb*
3 *Screw*
4 *Gasket*
5 *Lens/body*

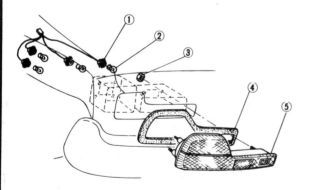

Fig. 10.59 Rear lamp (160J SSS and 710 series hardtop)

1 *Bulb holder*
2 *Bulb*
3 *Nut*
4 *Gasket*
5 *Lens/body*

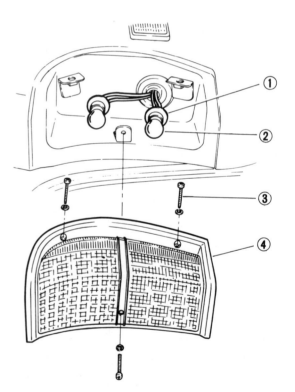

Fig. 10.61 Rear lamp (wagon)

1 *Bulb holder*
2 *Bulb*
3 *Securing scrw*
4 *Lens*

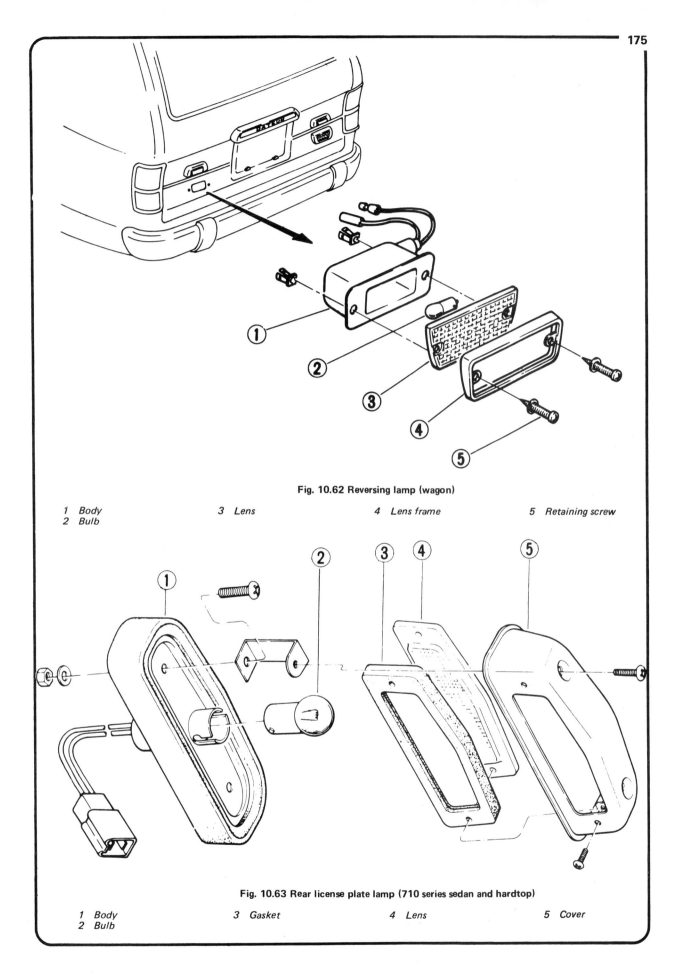

Fig. 10.62 Reversing lamp (wagon)

1	Body	3	Lens	4	Lens frame	5	Retaining screw
2	Bulb						

Fig. 10.63 Rear license plate lamp (710 series sedan and hardtop)

1	Body	3	Gasket	4	Lens	5	Cover
2	Bulb						

35 Interior lamps - bulb renewal

1   To renew the festoon type bulb in the interior front compartment lamp, squeeze the side of the lens so that it can be withdrawn from the lamp body.
2   Pull the bulb from the spring contacts and renew it with one of similar wattage and rating.
3   *On 710 series* station wagon models, the rear compartment interior lamp bulb is renewed in a similar way.
4   *On 710 series* vehicles equipped with automatic transmission, the speed selector indicator lamp can be renewed in the following way.
5   Remove the centre console.
6   Unscrew the retaining screws from the selector speed position indicator assembly and pull it up the control lever until the bulb is visible and can be removed from its socket.
7   On all models, the bulbs for instrument illumination and indicator and warning lamps are of wedge-base type and they can be removed simply by twisting the holders in an anticlockwise direction and then extracting the bulbs from their holders.
8   *On late models,* the knobs of the wiper and lighting switches are illuminated by means of internally reflective light projection tubes which are attached to the cap of the knob illumination lamp.
9   To renew the bulb in the light source, simply reach up under the instrument panel and pull out the bulb holder from the back of the lamp.

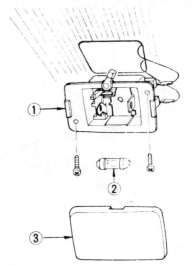

Fig. 10.66 Rear interior lamp (710 series wagon)

1   *Body*
2   *Bulb*
3   *Lens*

36 Windscreen wipers and washer - description

1   The wiper system comprises a two-speed motor, the connecting linkage and the necessary leads and switch.
2   The washer comprises a tank in which is incorporated the washer electric pump, two spray jets and the interconnecting tubing. The washer should not be operated for periods in excess of 30 seconds, nor when the fluid tank is empty. (photo)

37 Wiper blade and arm - removal and refitting

1   The wiper blade should be renewed whenever they fail to wipe the screen clean.
2   To remove the wiper blade, raise the locking tab and slide the blade from the end of the wiper arm. (photo)
3   To remove a wiper arm, pull the arm away from the windscreen until it locks in position at about 90° to the screen. Unscrew and remove the nut which secures the arm to the driving spindle and then pull the arm assembly from the splines of the spindle. (photo)
4   Installation is a reversal of removal but ensure that the arms are set on the splined driving spindles so that their blades will be parallel with the bottom frame of the screen. Make sure that the wipe mechanism is in the parked position before fitting the arms.

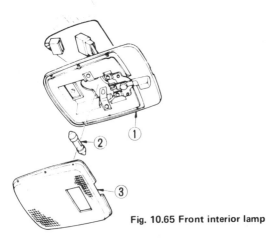

Fig. 10.65 Front interior lamp

1   *Body*
2   *Bulb*
3   *Lens*

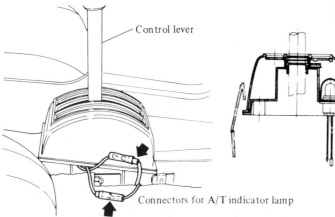

Fig. 10.67 Auto. transmission selector lever indicator lamp

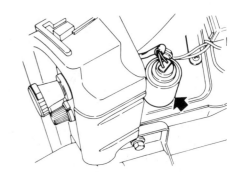

Fig. 10.68 Wiper and lighting switch knob illumination light source

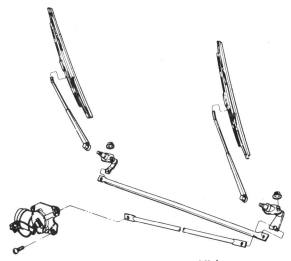

Fig. 10.69 Windscreen wiper motor and linkage

37.3 Wiper arm removal

36.2 Windscreen washer motor at base of tank

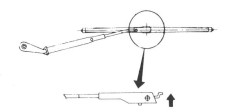

Fig. 10.70 Wiper blade removal

38 Wiper motor and linkage - removal and refitting

1   Remove the wiper arm and blade as described in the preceding Section.
2   Raise the bonnet and disconnect the wiper lead connector plug.
3   Unscrew and remove the screws which retain the heater air intake grille. Remove the grille (see Chapter 12, Section 18).
4   Unscrew and remove the screws which secure each of the spindle housing plates in position.
5   Disconnect the linkage from the wiper motor crankarm.
6   Withdraw the linkage.
7   Remove the four wiper motor mounting bolts and remove the motor.
8   Refitting is a reversal of removal.

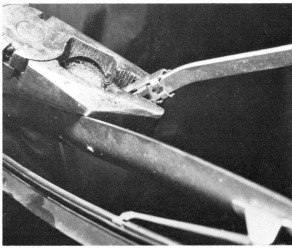

37.2 Raising wiper blade locking tab

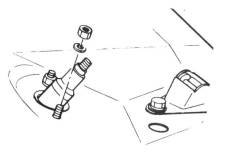

Fig. 10.71 Wiper arm drive spindle attachment

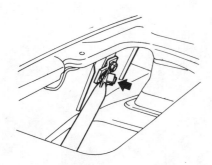

Fig. 10.72 Wiper linkage to motor crankarm connection

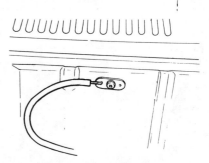

Fig. 10.73 Windscreen washer attached to engine compartment rear bulkhead

38.2 Wiper motor location

39 Wiper motor and linkage - servicing

1 It is not recommended that the wiper motor is overhauled byond renewing the brushes if they are badly worn. Always check the fuses in the circuit before dismantling needlessly.
2 Check for wear in the linkage and renew any worn bushes. Slackness in these components can cause the wiper blades to strike or ride over the windscreen frame surround at the ends of the arc of travel of the arm.
3 When reassembling the linkage, apply a little grease to the swivel bushes.

40 Windscreen washer - servicing

1 Normally the windscreen washer requires no maintenance other than keeping the reservoir topped-up with water to which some screen cleaning fluid has been added.
2 If the washer jets are incorrectly aligned to provide satisfactory coverage of the glass, they can be adjusted (only a fraction at a time) by using a pair of long nosed pliers inserted through the heater air intake grille.
3 If the washer reservoir or electric pump have to be renewed individually, they may be separated after disconnecting the connecting pipes and leads.
4 When reconnecting the pump to the base of the reservoir, warm the reservoir by immersing it in hot water and use a solution of soapy water to lubricate the neck of the pump opening in the reservoir.

41 Horn - maintenance and adjustment

1 The horn is located behind the radiator grille.
2 Normal maintenance consists of checking the security of the connecting leads.
3 If the horn does not operate at all, check that the fuse has not blown. If the horn itself is found to be working (by connecting it directly to the battery) and all the leads and connections are secure, then the relay has probably failed and must be tested and renewed (see Section 17).
4 If the horn sounds continuously, check that the horn switch springs have not broken. If they are satisfactory, it is probably the relay which is at fault.
5 Adjustment to the note of the horn can be made by loosening the locknut on the rear of the horn and turning the screw until satisfactory tone and volume are obtained.

41.1 Location of horn

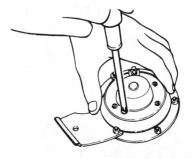

Fig. 10.74 Adjusting the horn note

42 Heated rear window

1 The heated rear window is controlled from an illuminated type switch mounted on the instrument panel.
2 The system is wired in conjunction with the ignition switch and ignition relay to prevent the heater element being left on when the vehicle is parked.
3 The filament is printed inside on the glass surface and repairs can be made by your Datsun dealer using special conductive silver compound.

43 Anti-theft device

1 This device is fitted in conjunction with the combined ignition/steering column lock and comprises a door switch (part of the courtesy light switch) and a buzzer, mounted behind the speedometer under the instrument panel.
2 The system is designed to operate when the driver's door is opened and the key is still in the ignition lock.
      This serves to remind him to at least remove the key before leaving the vehicle.

44 Starter interlock system

1 This sytem is installed on cars destined for operation in North America (excluding Canada) and is designed to prevent operation of the car unless the front seat belts are fastened and the gear lever is in the neutral position (manual gearbox). On cars with automatic transmission, the speed selector lever must be in 'N' or 'P'.
2 Components of the system include a seat switch, a safety belt switch, interlock relay, interlock unit, warning buzzer and lamp. On cars with a manual gearbox, a neutral switch is incorporated in the gearbox and on cars with automatic transmission, the standard starter inhibitor switch is utilised in the circuit but an additional relay is located within the engine compartment.
3 In the event of a fault developing in the system, check all the interconnecting wiring and connector plugs for security. Use a test lamp to check for continuity when the seat or safety belt switches are closed.
4 None of the components is repairable and in the event of a fault they must be renewed.
5 An overriding switch is located within the engine compartment on the right-hand side. On cars with air conditioning, the switch is positioned on the vacuum tank bracket. The purpose of the switch is to enable the engine to be started and the car moved if a fault should develop in the interlock system.
6 Should the engine stall under normal driving conditions, the engine can be restarted without the interlock system being actuated provided the ignition key remains in the 'ON' position and the driver remains seated.
7 For tuning and repair work, the vehicle engine can be started by reaching in through a front window and turning the ignition/ starter key. The system will be inoperative as no weight is upon either front seat.

45 Cigar lighter - removal and installation

1 Withdraw the heater element unit from the housing.
2 Unscrew and remove the small switch mounting panel from the lower edge of the instrument panel.
3 Disconnect the three electrical leads.
4 Unscrew and remove the large retaining nut on the end of the housing and withdraw the lamp cover and the nut.
5 The casing may be removed from the front of the instrument panel noting that it is an interference fit in its panel hole.
6 Installation is a reversal of removal.

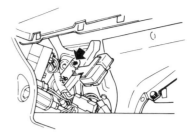

Fig. 10.75 Location of anti-theft device warning buzzer

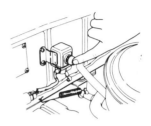

Fig. 10.76 Starter interlock system emergency engine starting switch

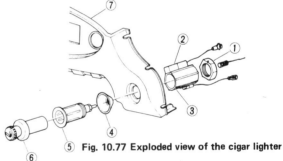

Fig. 10.77 Exploded view of the cigar lighter

1 Retaining nut
2 Illuminating lamp housing
3 Cover
4 Escutcheon
5 Casing
6 Heater element
7 Instrument panel

46 Clock - removal and installation

1 Remove the instrument panel, as described in Section 22 or 23.
2 Disconnect the electrical leads from the clock and then unscrew and remove the two clock securing screws and remove it.
3 Installation is a reversal of removal.

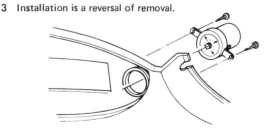

Fig. 10.78 Clock location and mounting

47 Radio equipment - removal and installation

1   Remove the instrument panel, as described in Sections 22 or 23, of this Chapter.
2   Unscrew and remove the four radio securing screws and remove it.
3   The speaker can be removed after withdrawing the two screws which secure it to the fascia panel.
4   Installation of the radio receiver and speaker is a reversal of removal.
5   The aerial can be removed after withdrawing the two screws which secure the feeder base.
6   The aerial feeder cable is easily removed by pulling it through the hole in the front pillar after first having disconnected it from the receiver and removed the cable clamps.

48 Radio aerial trimming and interference suppression

1   Whenever new components or equipment has been installed, adjust the aerial trimmer. To do this, extend the aerial fully and tune the receiver to the weakest station between 1200 and 1600 Hz.
2   Using a very thin screwdriver inserted in the trimmer hole, turn the trimmer screw slowly to left and right until maximum sensitivity is obtained.
3   Interference from the vehicle electrical equipment can be a problem if a new radio receiver has been installed. Its occurrence with existing radio equipment will indicate a failure of one of the capacitors installed or a breakdown in the HT suppressed type leads.
4   The interference tracing table at the end of this Chapter will assist in the diagnosis of electrical interference and its suppression.

49 Auxiliary lamps - guide to installation

1   The following remarks are intended to provide the reader with a guide to the selection and fitting of auxilary driving lamps and are not intended to be precise instructions.
2   Decide on the type of lamps required - two fog, two spot or one of each.
3   Check the available space at the front of the car and try and purchase lamps which are slim enough to be protected by the projection of the bumper bar.
4   Check local regulations regarding the minimum mounting height and the distance between the lamp centres.
5   Try and buy lamps which are supplied either with a universal mounting bracket or one specifically designed for the car.
6   Whether the lamps are wired for operation with the ignition key on or off, is a matter of personal preference but in any event wire them through the fuse box of the car and use cable of adequate section to carry the current needed for the high wattage bulbs employed.

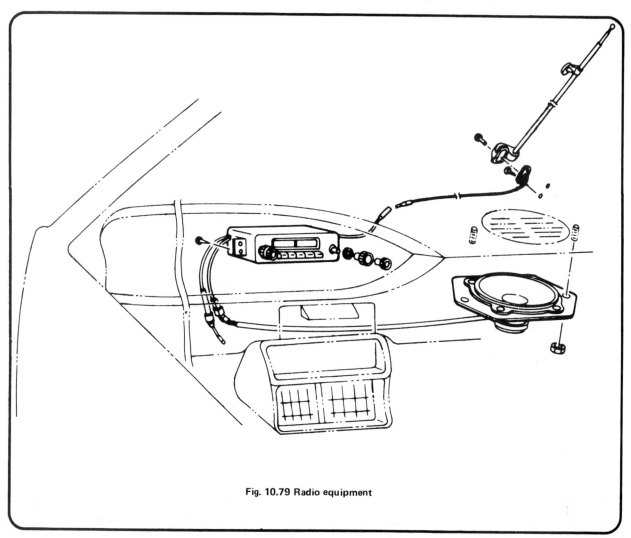

Fig. 10.79 Radio equipment

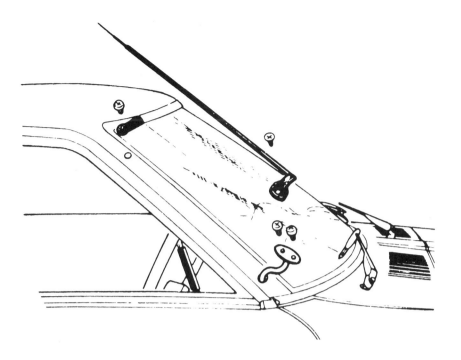

Fig. 10.80 Aerial installation

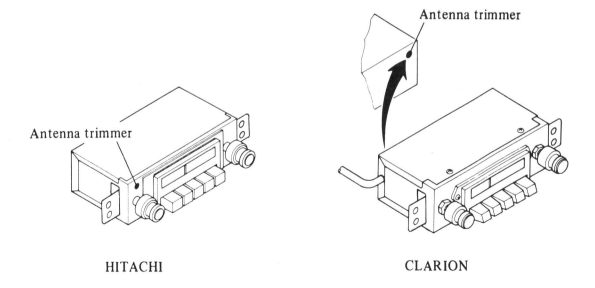

Antenna trimmer

Antenna trimmer

HITACHI

CLARION

Fig. 10.81 Aerial trimmer screw locations

50 Fault diagnosis - electrical system (general)

Symptom	Reason/s
Starter fails to turn engine	Battery discharged
	Battery defective internally
	Battery terminal leads loose or earth lead not securely attached to body
	Loose or broken connections in starter motor circuit
	Starter motor switch or solenoid faulty
	Starter motor pinion jammed in mesh with flywheel gear ring
	Starter brushes badly worn, sticking, or brush wires loose
	Commutator dirty, worn or burnt
	Starter motor armature faulty
	Field coils earthed
Starter turns engine very slowly	Battery in discharged condition
	Starter brushes badly worn, sticking or brush wires loose
	Loose wires in starter motor circuit
Starter spins but does not turn engine	Starter motor pinion sticking on the screwed sleeve
	Pinion or flywheel gear teeth broken or worn
	Battery discharged
Starter motor noisy or excessively rough engagement	Pinion or flywheel gear teeth broken or worn
	Starter motor retaining bolts loose
Battery will not hold charge for more than a few days	Battery defective internally
	Electrolyte level too low or electrolyte too weak due to leakage
	Plate separators no longer fully effective
	Battery plates severely sulphated
	Drive belt slipping
	Battery terminal connections loose or corroded
	Alternator not charging
	Short in lighting circuit causing continual battery drain
	Regulator unit not working correctly
Ignition light fails to go out, battery runs flat in a few days	Drive belt loose and slipping or broken
	Alternator brushes worn, sticking, broken or dirty
	Alternator brush springs weak or broken
	Internal fault in alternator
	Regulator incorrectly set
	Cut-out incorrectly set
	Open circuit in wiring of cut-out and regulator unit

Failure of individual electrical equipment to function correctly is dealt with alphabetically, item-by-item, under the headings listed below

Horn

Horn operates all the time	Horn push either earthed or stuck down
	Horn cable to horn push earthed
Horn fails to operate	Cable or cable connection loose, broken or disconnected
	Horn has an internal fault
Horn emits intermittent or unsatisfactory noise	Cable connections loose
	Horn incorrectly adjusted

Lights

Lights do not come on	If engine not running, battery discharged
	Wire connections loose, disconnected or broken
	Light switch shorting or otherwise faulty
Lights come on but fade out	If engine not running battery discharged
	Light bulb filament burnt out or bulbs or sealed beam units broken
	Wire connections loose, disconnected or broken
	Light switch shorting or otherwise faulty
Lights give very poor illumination	Lamp glasses dirty
	Lamps badly out of adjustment

Lights work erratically - flashing on and off, especially over bumps	Battery terminals or earth connection loose Lights not earthing properly Contacts in light switch faulty

Wipers

Wiper motor fails to work	Blown fuse Wire connections loose, disconnected or broken Brushes badly worn Armature worn or faulty Field coils faulty
Wiper motor works very slowly and takes excessive current	Commutator dirty, greasy or burnt Armature bearings dirty or unaligned Armature badly worn or faulty
Wiper motor works slowly and takes little current	Brushes badly worn Commutator dirty, greasy or burnt Armature badly worn or faulty
Wiper motor works but wiper blades remain static	Wiper motor gearbox parts badly worn

51 Fault diagnosis - radio interference

Noise	Source	Remedy
'Machine gun' rattle when engine running	Ignition system coil or HT lead	Renew HT leads Install 0.5 uF capacitor to + (switch) terminal of ignition coil
Undulating whine according to engine speed	Alternator	Install 0.5 uF capacitor to alternator terminal A
Crackle when accelerator pedal depressed or released	Voltage regulator	Install 0.5 uF capacitor to 'IGN' terminal of voltage regulator

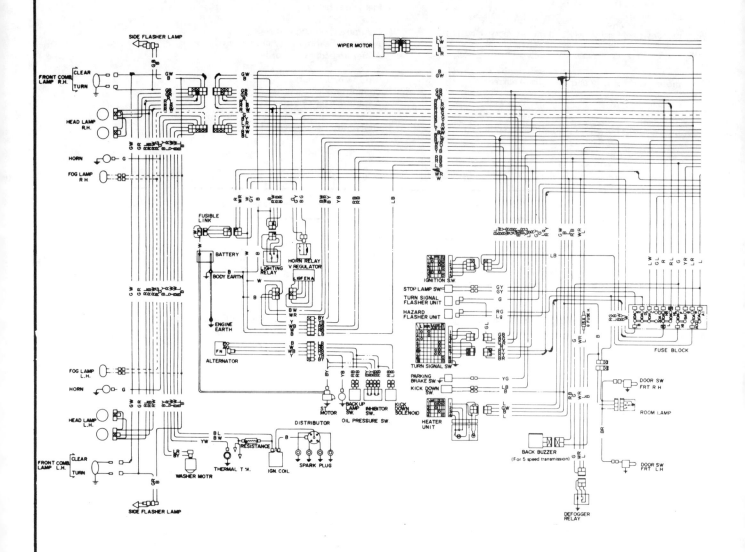

Wiring diagram for 140J and 160J SSS

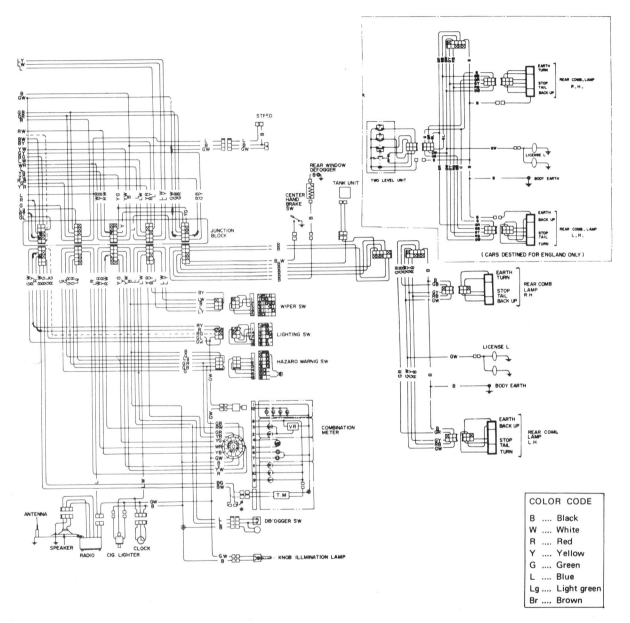

(CARS DESTINED FOR ENGLAND ONLY)

COLOR CODE	
B	.... Black
W	.... White
R	.... Red
Y	.... Yellow
G	.... Green
L	.... Blue
Lg	.... Light green
Br	.... Brown

* In case of optional tachometer connection

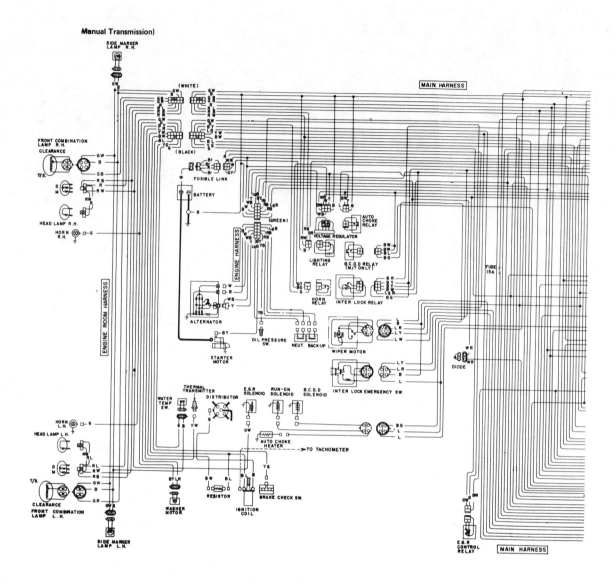

Wiring diagram for 710 Series (North America except Canada)
Manual gearbox up to 1975

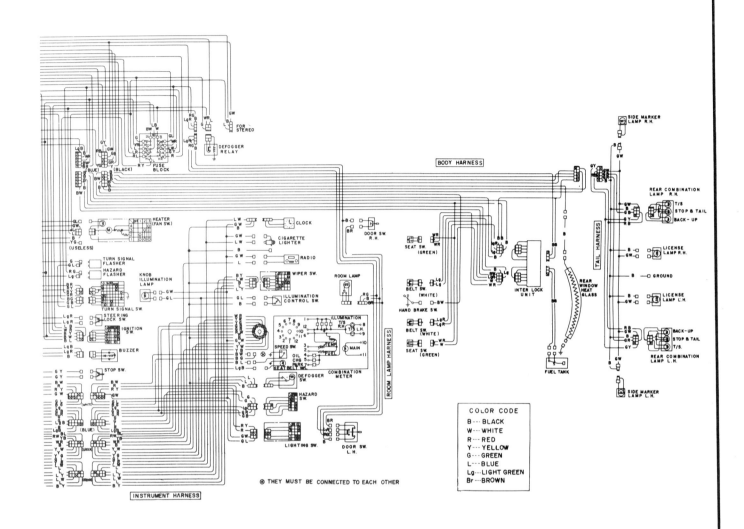

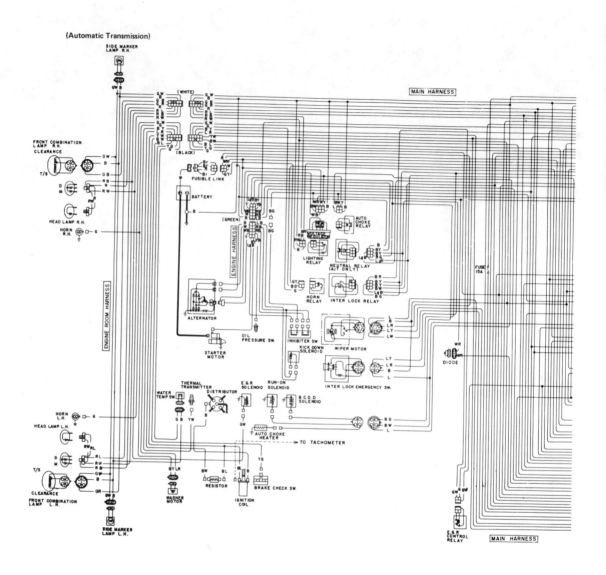

Wiring diagram for 710 Series (North America except Canada)
Automatic transmission up to 1975

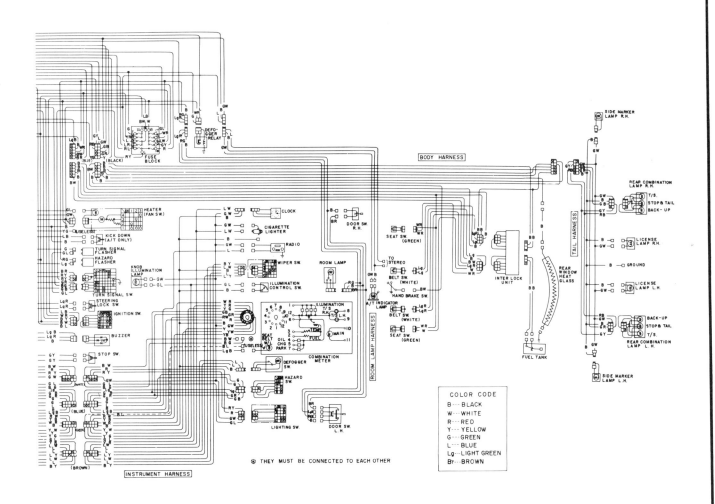

For CANADA (Manual Transmission)

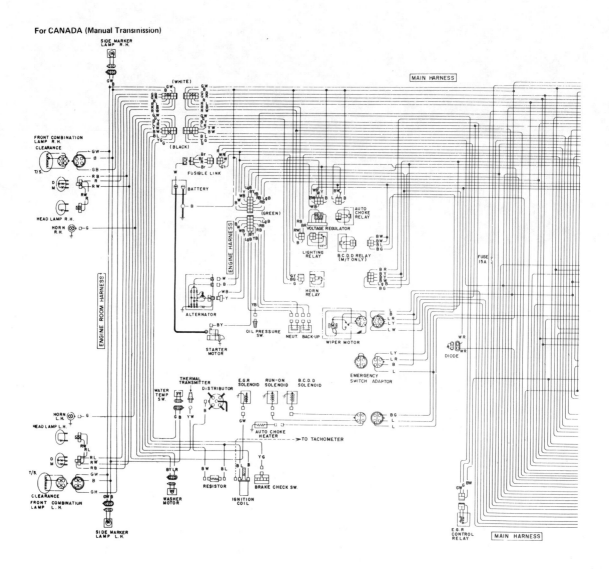

Wiring diagram for 710 Series (Canada) Manual gearbox up to 1975

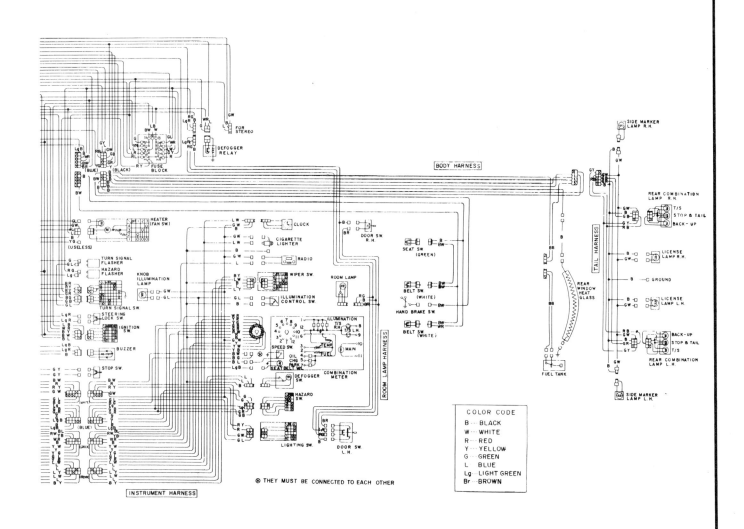

THEY MUST BE CONNECTED TO EACH OTHER

COLOR CODE
B — BLACK
W — WHITE
R — RED
Y — YELLOW
G — GREEN
L — BLUE
Lg — LIGHT GREEN
Br — BROWN

For CANADA (Automatic Transmission)

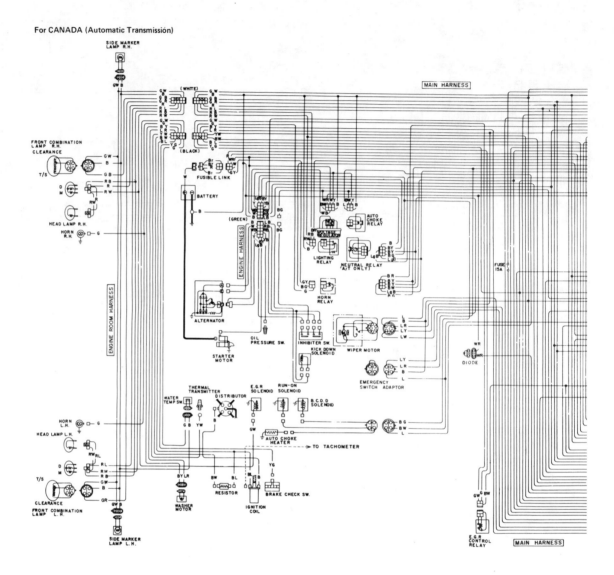

Wiring diagram for 710 Series (Canada)
Automatic transmission up to 1975

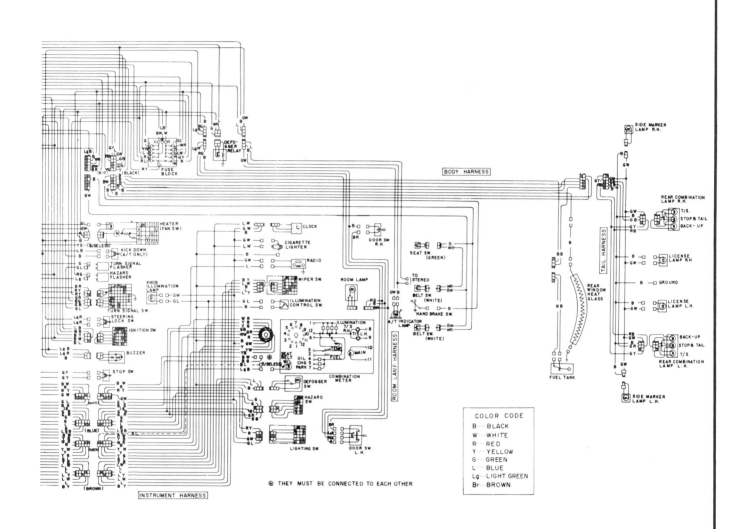

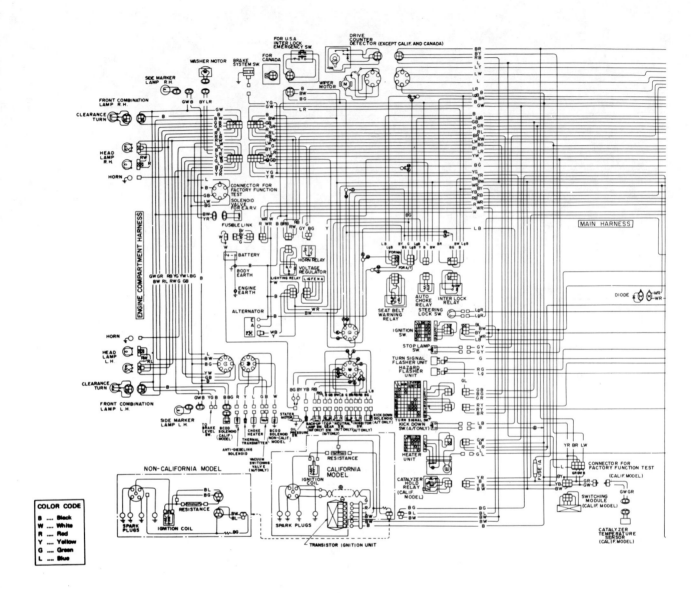

Wiring diagram for 710 Series 1975 onwards

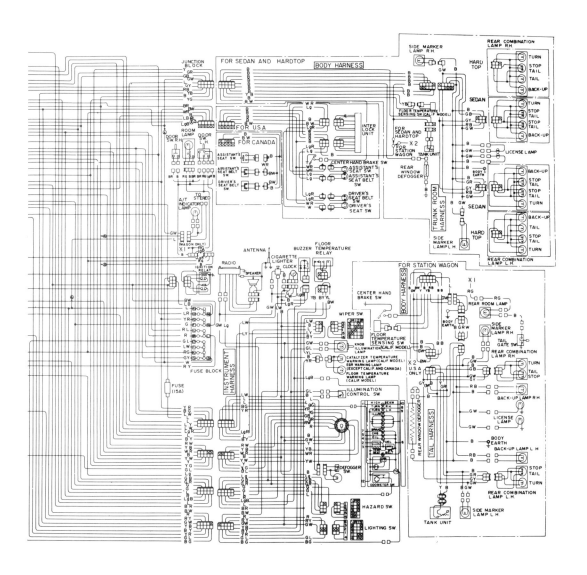

Chapter 11 Suspension and steering

Contents

Specifications

Front suspension

Type	MacPherson hydraulic strut with coil spring. Stabilizer bar
Front coil spring:	
Wire diameter	0.492 in. (12.5 mm)
Coil diameter	5.12 in. (130.0 mm)
No. of coil turns	8 (7.75 for 160J SSS)
Free length:	
140J	14.5 in. (369.0 mm)
160J SSS	13.0 in. (330.0 mm)
710 series	16.0 in. (406.5 mm)

Rear suspension

Type:	
140J and 710 series	Semi-elliptic leaf springs with double-acting hydraulic shock absorbers
160J SSS	Independent with coil springs and suspension arm (wishbone). Double-acting hydraulic shock absorber
Leaf spring dimensions (except wagon)	47.2 in long x 2.36 in. wide (1200 mm long x 60.0 mm wide)
4 leaves	0.236 in. (6.0 mm) thick
1 leaf	0.197 in. (5.0 mm) thick
Leaf spring dimensions (station wagon)	47.2 in. (1200 mm) long x 2.36 in. (60.0 mm) wide
6 leaves	0.236 in. (6.0 mm) thick
Coil spring dimensions (160J SSS):	
Wire diameter	0.571 in. (14.5 mm)
No. of coil turns	11
Free length:	
RH	12.6 in. (321.0 mm)
LH	12.1 in. (307.0 mm)

Steering

Type	Worm and nut, recirculating ball. Collapsible steering column
Ratio:	
140J and 160J SSS	15 : 1
710 series	16.48 : 1

Steering angle (lock):				
Inner wheel	37° to 38°			
Outer wheel	30° 42′ to 32° 42′			
No. of turns of steering wheel (lock-to-lock)	3.3			
Turning circle	34.2 ft (10.4 m)			
Steering angles (vehicle unladen):	**Camber**	**Castor**	**Steering axis inclination**	**Toe-in**
140J and 160J SSS	1° 10′ to 2° 40′	55′ to 2° 55′	6° 40′	0.32 to 0.43 in. (8.0 to 11.0 mm)
710 series	1° 25′ to 2° 55′	1° 10′ to 2° 40′	6° 25′	0.32 to 0.43 in. (8.0 to 11.0 mm)

Wheels and tyres

Wheel type and size	Pressed steel: 4½J - 13
Tyre type and size	Radial: 165SR - 13
Tyre pressures	28 lbs/in^2 (2.0 kg/cm^2) front and rear

Torque wrench settings

	lb/ft	kg/m
Front suspension		
Stabilizer bar end nuts	15	2.1
Stabilizer bar bracket bolts	15	2.1
Radius rod end nut	35	4.8
Radius rod to track control arm	40	5.5
Radius rod bracket to bodyframe	50	6.9
Balljoint to track control arm	20	2.8
Balljoint to steering arm	50	6.9
Suspension strut upper mounting nuts	25	3.5
Steering arm to suspension strut	70	9.7
Suspension strut piston self-locking nut	50	6.9
Track control arm pivot bolts	45	6.2
Front crossmember bolts	35	4.8
Rear suspension (rigid axle)		
Rear spring U bolts:		
Saloon/Hardtop	35	4.8
Wagon	45	6.2
Shock absorber lower mounting:		
Saloon/Hardtop	16	2.2
Wagon	35	4.8
Shock absorber upper mounting	12	1.6
Brake backplate bolts	20	2.8
Roadspring front pivot bolt:		
Saloon/Hardtop	50	6.9
Wagon	45	6.2
Roadspring rear shackle bolts:		
Saloon/Hardtop	45	6.2
Wagon	45	6.2
Damper (roadspring) nuts	10	1.4
Steering		
Drop arm nut	100	13.8
Rear cover bolts	20	2.8
Top cover bolts	20	2.8
Adjusting screw locknut	25	3.5
Steering box to bodyframe bolts	55	7.6
Idler to bodyframe bolts	44	6.1
Balljoint taper pin nuts	60	8.3
Track rod end locknuts	60	8.3
Steering wheel nut	36	5.0
Flexible coupling pinch bolt	35	4.8
Flexible coupling securing bolts	20	2.8
Steering column upper clamp bolts	15	2.1
Wheels		
Securing nut	60	8.3

1 General description

The front suspension on all models is of independent MacPherson strut type. A stabilizer bar is incorporated. The rear suspension of 140J and 710 series models is of semi-elliptic type utilizing leaf springs and telescopic type hydraulic shock absorbers.

The rear suspension of 160J SSS models is of independent type, the layout comprising a suspension wishbone, a suspension member, coil springs and telescopic hydraulic shock absorbers.

The steering system is of worm and nut recirculating ball type incorporating an idler, relay and outer trackrods. The steering column is of collapsible telescopic design.

Fig. 11.1 Sectional view of one side of the front suspension

1 Insulator
2 Rebound rubber
3 Dust excluder
4 Coil spring
5 Suspension strut
6 Tyre
7 Hub bearings
8 Hub
9 Roadwheel
10 Lower balljoint
11 Stabilizer bar
12 Radius rod
13 Track control arm
14 Crossmember

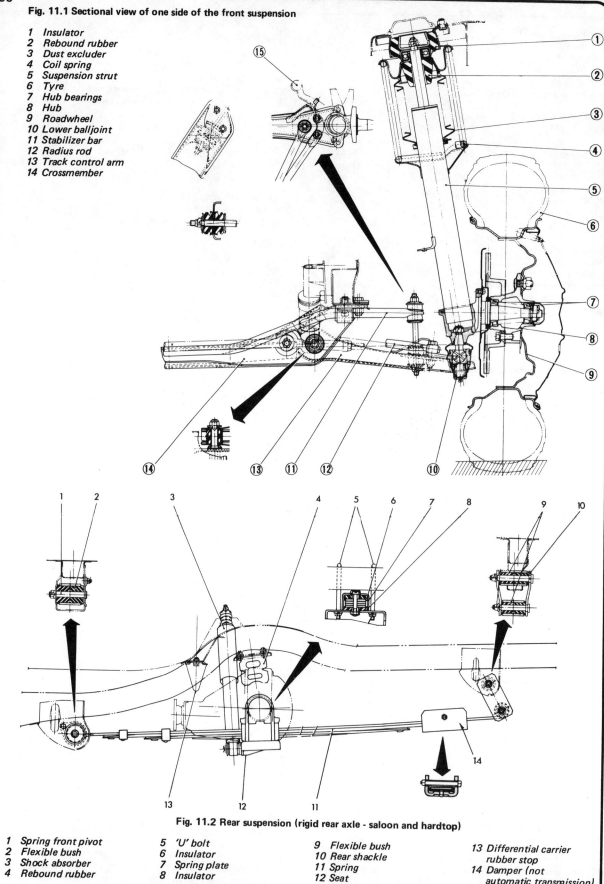

Fig. 11.2 Rear suspension (rigid rear axle - saloon and hardtop)

1 Spring front pivot
2 Flexible bush
3 Shock absorber
4 Rebound rubber

5 'U' bolt
6 Insulator
7 Spring plate
8 Insulator

9 Flexible bush
10 Rear shackle
11 Spring
12 Seat

13 Differential carrier
   rubber stop
14 Damper (not
   automatic transmission)

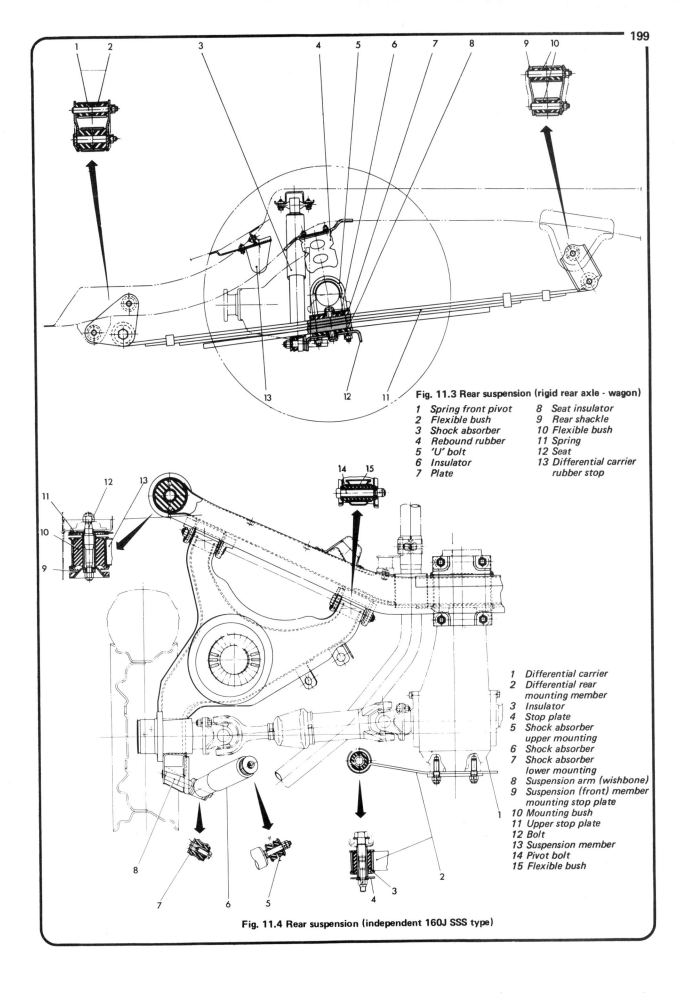

Fig. 11.3 Rear suspension (rigid rear axle - wagon)

1	Spring front pivot	8	Seat insulator
2	Flexible bush	9	Rear shackle
3	Shock absorber	10	Flexible bush
4	Rebound rubber	11	Spring
5	'U' bolt	12	Seat
6	Insulator	13	Differential carrier
7	Plate		rubber stop

1 Differential carrier
2 Differential rear
  mounting member
3 Insulator
4 Stop plate
5 Shock absorber
  upper mounting
6 Shock absorber
7 Shock absorber
  lower mounting
8 Suspension arm (wishbone)
9 Suspension (front) member
  mounting stop plate
10 Mounting bush
11 Upper stop plate
12 Bolt
13 Suspension member
14 Pivot bolt
15 Flexible bush

Fig. 11.4 Rear suspension (independent 160J SSS type)

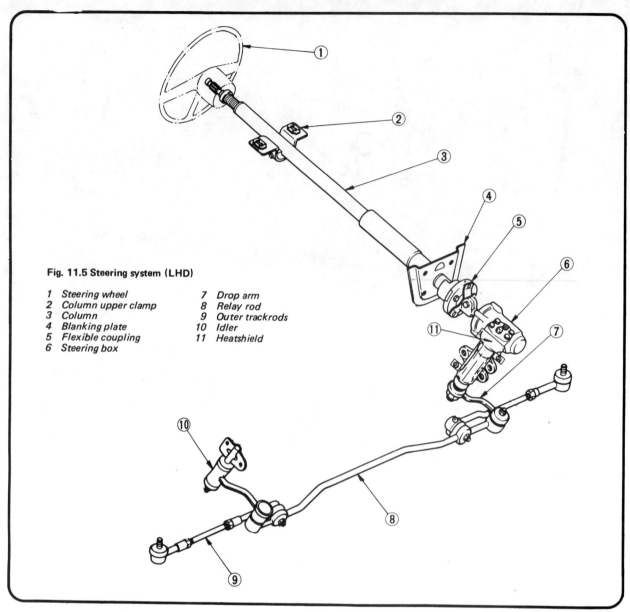

Fig. 11.5 Steering system (LHD)

1 Steering wheel
2 Column upper clamp
3 Column
4 Blanking plate
5 Flexible coupling
6 Steering box

7 Drop arm
8 Relay rod
9 Outer trackrods
10 Idler
11 Heatshield

2 Maintenance and inspection

1 Inspect regularly the condition of all rubber dust excluders and ball joint covers for splits and deterioration. Renew them as necessary after reference to the appropriate Section of this Chapter.
2 Check the security of the trackrod-end locknuts, also the ball-pin nuts.
3 Examine the condition of all suspension link rubber bushes. If they are perished, or permit movement of the adjacent components due to elongation of their holes, then they must be renewed.
4 Every 30,000 miles (48,000 km) remove the plugs from the ball joints, screw in a grease nipple and recharge the ball joint with multi-purpose grease.
5 At the same mileage interval, dismantle the front hubs, clean out the old grease and repack with fresh, as described in Section 8, of this Chapter.
6 On 160J SSS models, the rear hubs will require dismantling and repacking with grease in conjunction with the lubrication of the driveshafts at 48,000 miles (77,000 km) service intervals, as

described in Chapter 8, Sections 9 and 10.
7 *On 140J and 710 series vehicles,* no maintenance of the rear suspension is required except to periodically inspect the rubber bushes for wear and to check the security of the attachment bolts.

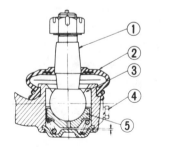

1 Taper pin
2 Dust excluder
3 Seat
4 Plug
5 Spring seat

Fig. 11.6 Sectional view of balljoint

3 Shock absorbers - removal, testing and refitting

1 Any sign of oil on the outside of the rear shock absorber bodies will indicate that the seals have started to leak and the units must be renewed as assemblies. Where the shock absorber has failed internally, this is more difficult to detect although rear axle patter or tramp, particularly on uneven road surfaces may provide a clue. When a shock absorber is suspected to have failed, remove it from the vehicle and holding it in a vertical position operate it for the full length of its stroke eight or ten times. Any lack of resistance in either direction will indicate the need for renewal.

2 Removal and installation of a rear shock absorber is simply a matter of disconnecting the upper and lower mountings which differ according to vehicle type and model as shown.

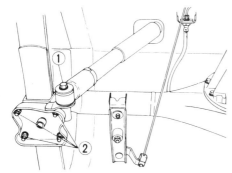

Fig. 11.7 Shock absorber lower mounting (1) and upper mounting (2) on rigid rear axle (saloon and hardtop)

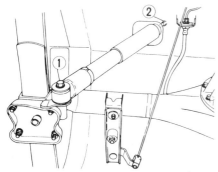

Fig. 11.8 Removing a rear shock absorber (wagon)

1   *Lower mounting*
2   *Upper mounting bolts*

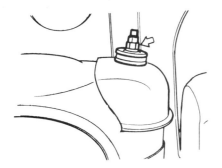

Fig. 11.9 Rear shock absorber mounting (160J SSS)

4 Front stabilizer bar and radius rod - removal and installation

1 Jack-up the front of the car and support it securely on stands.
2 Remove the roadwheel.
3 Remove the nut (1) which secures the end of the radius rod to the bracket.
4 Unscrew and remove the bolts (2) which secure the radius rod to the track control arm.
5 Remove the radius rod.
6 Unscrew and remove the nut (3) which secures the end of the stabilizer bar to the track control arm.
7 Unscrew and remove the radius rod brackets from the body-frame and then remove the stabilizer bar brackets and the rubber insulators. Withdraw the stabilizer bar.
8 Installation is a reversal of removal but check that the clearance between the stabilizer bar and the radius rod on both sides is equal. Tighten all bolts to the specified torque making sure that the radius rod bolts are tightened first.

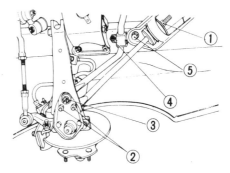

Fig. 11.10 Radius rod and stabilizer bar attachment points

1   *End nut*
2   *Drag strut to track control arm bolts*
3   *Stabilizer bar to track control arm nut*
4   *Stabilizer bar bracket bolt*
5   *Radius rod bracket bolt*

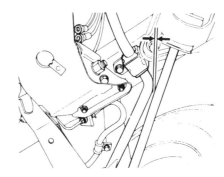

Fig. 11.11 Stabilizer bar to radius rod clearance

5 Front suspension strut - removal, servicing and installation

1 Jack-up the front of the vehicle and support the bodyframe securely on stands.
2 Disconnect the flexible brake hose from the rigid line at the support bracket, as described in Chapter 9.
3 Remove the disc caliper unit also, as described in Chapter 9.
4 Unscrew and remove the bolts which connect the base of the strut to the steering arm.

5 Disconnect the steering arm from the base of the strut by levering the components apart.

6 Place a jack under the strut to support its weight and then working within the engine compartment, unscrew and remove the three strut upper mounting nuts.

7 Lower the jack and withdraw the strut assembly, complete with hub and coil spring, from under the front wing. Remove the disc/hub assembly and the backplate.

8 A coil spring compressor must now be used to compress the spring until the top mounting assembly can be turned by hand.

9 Unscrew and remove the self-locking nut from the top face of the mounting. The mounting must be held stationary to do this and the way to do it is to pass a long bar between two of the mounting studs. Protect the threads of the studs to prevent damage.

10 Withdraw the top mounting insulator, the bearing and the upper spring seat.

11 The coil spring complete with compressor may now be withdrawn from the suspension strut. If the original spring is to be refitted, there is no need to remove the compressor.

12 Inspect the suspension strut for oil leakage from around the piston gland. Hold the strut vertically and fully extend and depress the piston rod several times. Unless there is a definite resistance with smooth operation in both directions, the unit must be renewed.

13 It is not recommended that the strut is dismantled due to the special tools required and the difficulty of obtaining individual components. Either renew the complete strut or obtain one of the sealed cartridge type repair units which are available. If the latter course is adopted then the upper gland nut and 'O' ring will have to be unscrewed, the internal components withdrawn from the strut outer casing and the new cartridge fitted in accordance with the maker's instructions.

14 Before installing the suspension strut, bleed it of any air which may have accumulated while it has been stored in a horizontal position. This is carried out in exactly the same manner as described for testing the unit earlier in this Section. Check all mounting components for wear.

15 Locate the coil spring (in its compressed state) on the suspension strut so that its lower coil fits correctly into the spring pan.

16 Fit the upper spring seat, the bearing (packed with multi-purpose grease) and the insulator. Fit the protective cap. (photo)

17 Screw on the self-locking nut to a torque of 50 lb/ft (6.9 kg/m).

18 Release the coil spring compressor gently and then refit the suspension leg, disc, caliper and hub in the reverse manner to removal. Tighten all nuts and bolts to the specified torque settings (see Specifications). Adjust the front hub, as described in Section 8. Reconnect the hydraulic line and bleed the brakes (Chapter 9).

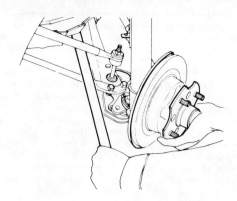

Fig. 11.13 Levering steering arm from base of suspension strut

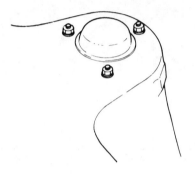

Fig. 11.14 Suspension strut upper mounting nuts

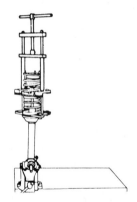

Fig. 11.15 Suspension strut coil spring compressed

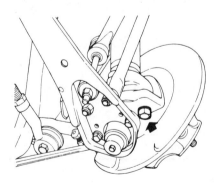

Fig. 11.12 Suspension strut to steering arm bolts

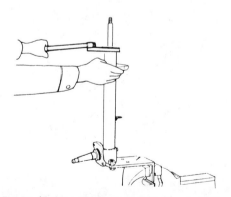

Fig. 11.16 Unscrewing suspension strut gland nut

Fig. 11.17 Withdrawing suspension strut internal components

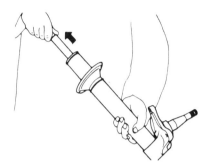

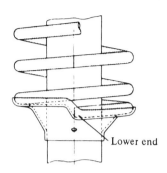

Fig. 11.19 Front suspension coil spring installation diagram

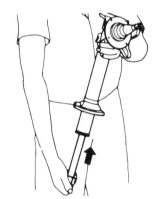

Fig. 11.18 Bleeding air from a suspension strut prior to installation

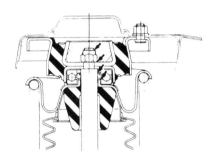

Fig. 11.20 Sectional view of suspension strut upper mounting and lubrication points (arrowed)

6 Front coil spring - removal and installation

1   Removal of a coil spring using a compressor is described in the preceding Section. An alternative method which can be used when the original spring is to be refitted, is to use clips.
2   Have an assistant sit on the top of the front wing to compress the front suspension leg and spring. Use a minimum of three clips to engage over three or four coils and then secure them in position with a strap or large worm drive clip.
3   Once the suspension strut is removed, the spring can be detached after the upper mounting has been withdrawn.
4   Installation is a reversal of removal. Remove the strap and clips after the weight of an assistant has again compressed the spring.

7 Track control arm and lower balljoint - removal, servicing and refitting

1   Jack-up the front of the vehicle and support it on stands. Remove the roadwheel.
2   Remove the under engine splash shield.
3   Disconnect the trackrod-end balljoint (see Section 15) from the steering arm.
4   Disconnect the steering arm from the base of the suspension strut (two bolts).
5   Remove the radius rod and stabilizer bar, as described in Section 4.
6   Disconnect the track control arm from the suspension cross-member after first removing the pivot pin nuts. With the track control arm removed, unbolt the track control arm from the balljoint housing.

5.16 Suspension strut upper mounting cap

7 Check the balljoint for wear by gripping the taper pin and pushing and pulling it to test for seat movement. Now move it sideways in several different directions. There must be a stiff resistance during the complete arc of movement. If the rubber dust cover is split or has perished, renew it. The balljoint should be lubricated, as described in Section 2.

8 Examine the rubber bonded type bush of the track control arm. If this has perished or is deformed it must be renewed using a press and this is a job best left to your Datsun dealer who will have the necessary removal and installation tools.

9 Refitting is a reversal of removal but tighten all nuts and bolts to the specified torque.

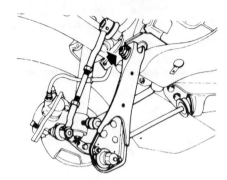

Fig. 11.21 Removing track control arm (pivot arrowed)

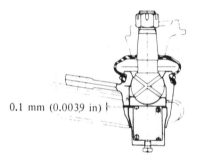

0.1 mm (0.0039 in)

Fig. 11.22 Sectional view of suspension lower swivel balljoint

8 Front hub bearings - adjustment, lubrication and renewal

1 Adjustment of the front hub bearings must be carried out if they develop an excessive amount of 'play', whenever the hub components have been dismantled and reassembled or the bearings repacked with grease (see Section 2). Every 3,000 miles (4,800 km) jack-up the front of the car and grip the top and bottom of the roadwheel. Rock it backwards and forwards and if there is a perceptible amount of 'play', check the adjustment in the following manner.

2 Remove the roadwheel and withdraw the disc pads (Chapter 9).

3 Remove the dust cap from the end of the hub, using two screwdrivers as levers or tapping it off with a small cold chisel and hammer.

4 Remove the cotter pin from the nut retainer and withdraw the nut retainer.

5 To adjust the hub bearings, tighten the hub nut to a torque of 22 lb/ft (3.0 kg/m). Turn the hub a few turns in both directions to settle the bearings and then check the torque setting.

6 Unscrew the nut 60° (one sixth of a turn) fit the retainer and insert a new cotter pin but do not bend over the ends at this stage. Using a spring balance attached to one of the wheel studs check the rotational torque which should be about 1.7 lbs if the original bearings are being used or 3.3 lbs if new bearings are installed. Adjust the nut if necessary and refit the retainer and cotter pin and bend over the ends of the pin neatly.

7 To lubricate or renew the hub bearings, remove the dust cap, split pin, nut retainer and nut as previously described. Unbolt the brake caliper and tie it up out of the way to prevent straining the flexible hose.

8 Withdraw the hub/disc assembly from the stub axle catching the outer bearing and thrust-washer.

9 Where the bearings are only to be replaced with grease, wipe all the old grease from the bearings and from the space inside the hub between the two bearings. Examine the condition of the oil seal and if there is evidence of leakage of grease, renew it by levering out the old one and driving in a new one with a piece of tubing used as a drift.

10 Repack the intervening space between the wheel bearing with fresh grease and also fill the dust cap not more than quarter full.

11 Where the bearings are slack and defy adjustment then they are worn and must be renewed. Use a drift to drive out the inner and outer bearing tracks and drive in the new ones using a piece of tubing for the purpose. The oil seal will of course have to be renewed whenever the inner bearing track is removed and refitted. If both front hubs are being serviced at the same time, do not mix the new bearings up but keep them in their packets until required as the roller cages and outer tracks are matched in production.

12 Reassembly of the front hub is a reversal of removal and dismantling but adjust the bearings as described earlier in this Section.

9 Front crossmember - removal and installation

1 Jack-up the front of the vehicle and support the body side-frame members securely on stands.

2 Remove the roadwheels and under engine shield.

3 Disconnect both the track controls arms from the cross-member.

4 Using a suitable hoist, raise the engine just enough to take its weight off the front mountings.

5 Disconnect the engine mountings from the crossmember and then unbolt the crossmember from the bodyframe.

6 Installation is a reversal of removal.

10 Rear leaf spring - removal, servicing and refitting

1 Jack-up the rear of the vehicle and support the bodyframe sidemembers securely on stands.

2 Disconnect the shock absorber at its lower mounting.

3 Unscrew and remove the 'U' bolt nuts and detach the spring lower plate.

4 Jack-up the rear axle casing under the differential housing until the casing is separated from the road spring.

5 Disconnect the spring rear shackle.

6 Disconnect the spring front pivot bolt or plate according to vehicle type. Remove the spring.

7 A broken spring can be replaced as a complete unit or the individual leaf can be renewed. If the leaf only is being replaced new spring clips, rivets and inserts will be required to reassemble the leaves. A replacement unit can usually be found at a breaker's and this is the simplest and cheapest way to go about it.

8 Examine the condition of the shackle bushes and bolts and renew them if they are worn. Bush renewal is best left to a service station, but they can be removed and refitted by using a threaded rod, nuts, washers and a tubular distance piece as an extractor.

9 When refitting a road spring, note that the centre bolt is offset toward the front.

10 When refitting the spring to the hangers it is usually easier to fit the front end first. Then replace the shackle pins and bushes. Replace the nuts but do not tighten them yet. Then lower the axle and position it so that it locates correctly onto the spring and put the 'U' bolts and clamp plate in position. Tighten the 'U' bolt nuts only moderately.

11 The shock absorber should next be fitted to the lower mountings.

12 The car should then be lowered to the ground, bounced a few times to settle the bushes and then all the nuts tightened to the specified torque.

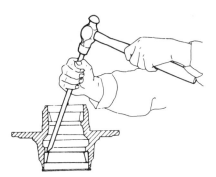

Fig. 11.27 Removing wheel bearing track

Fig. 11.23 Tightening a front wheel hub bearing nut

Fig. 11.24 Hub retainer and cotter pin

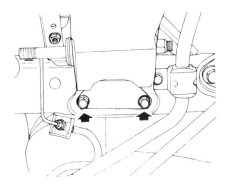

Fig. 11.28 Crossmember mounting bolts

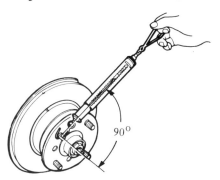

Fig. 11.25 Measuring front hub bearing preload

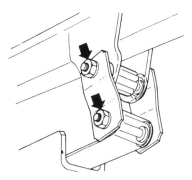

Fig. 11.29 Rear spring shackle bolts

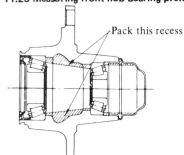

Fig. 11.26 Front wheel grease packing diagram

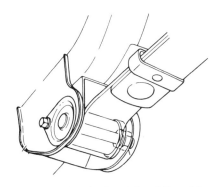

Fig. 11.30 Rear road spring front pivot (all models except wagon)

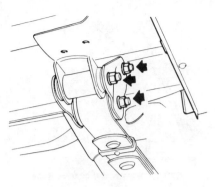

Fig. 11.31 Rear road spring front pivot (wagon)

11 Rear coil springs (160J SSS) - removal and refitting

1 Jack-up the rear of the car and support the bodyframe side-members securely on stands.
2 Remove the roadwheel.
3 Disconnect the handbrake cables at the adjusting turnbuckle and detach the return spring.
4 Disconnect the driveshaft flange (at the roadwheel end).
5 Unscrew the rebound stop securing nut.
6 Disconnect the flexible brake hose from the rigid line at the suspension arm support bracket.
7 Jack-up the suspension arm slightly to relieve the tension on the shock absorber and then disconnect the shock absorber at its lower mounting.
8 Carefully lower the jack until the spring, spring seat and rebound stop can all be withdrawn.
9 Refitting is a reversal of removal but ensure that the flat face of the coil spring is located at the top.
10 Tighten all the bolts to specified torque.

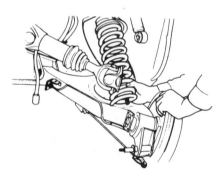

Fig. 11.32 Removing a coil spring (independent rear suspension)

12 Rear suspension assembly (160J SSS) - removal and installation

1 Jack-up the rear of the car and support it securely under the bodyframe sidemembers.
2 Remove the rear roadwheel and disconnect the handbrake cable at the adjuster turnbuckle and disconnect the return spring.
3 Remove the rear exhaust pipe section and silencer.
4 Remove the propeller shaft, as described in Chapter 7.
5 Disconnect the rear brake hoses at the suspension arms.
6 Raise the suspension arms slightly so that the shock absorbers can be disconnected at their lower mountings.

7 Disconnect the suspension member from the body by removing the two end bolts.
8 Disconnect the differential (rear) mounting member by removing the two end bolts.
9 The complete suspension/differential assembly can now be withdrawn from under the rear of the car, preferably on a trolley type jack.
10 If on inspection, the suspension member or mounting member rubber bushes are worn or have deteriorated, then they must be removed on a press and new ones installed.
   Disconnection of the suspension member is described in the next Section.
11 Installation of the complete assembly is a reversal of removal but tighten all bolts to the specified torque.

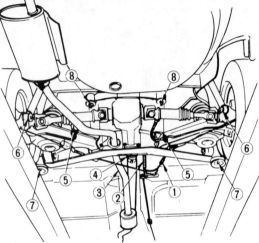

Fig. 11.33 Independent rear suspension removal points

1 Handbrake cable turnbuckle
2 Return spring
3 Rear exhaust
4 Propeller shaft flange
5 Rear brake hoses
6 Shock absorber lower mountings
7 Suspension member bolts
8 Suspension rear member mounting bolts

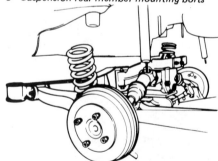

Fig. 11.34 Removing complete independent rear suspension

13 Suspension member (160J SSS) - removal and refitting

1 The suspension member supports the front end of the differential unit and the suspension lower wishbone front pivots.
2 Remove the complete suspension/differential assembly, as described in the preceding Section.
3 Disconnect the front face of the differential from the suspension member (four bolts).
4 Disconnect the wishbone front pivots from the suspension member by withdrawing the pivot bolts.
5 Refitting is a reversal of removal but the wishbone pivot bolts must not be tightened to their specified torque until the jacks have been lowered and the weight of the car is upon them.

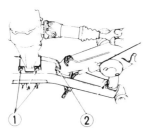

Fig. 11.35 Differential to suspension member bolts (1) and suspension wishbone pivot bolts (2) - independent type rear suspension

14 Suspension wishbone (160J SSS) - removal and installation

1   Jack-up the rear of the car and support the bodyframe side-members securely on stands.
2   Remove the roadwheel and the brake drum.
3   Disconnect the dirveshaft at its outer universal joint flange.
4   Disconnect the handbrake cable from the wheel cylinder operating lever.
5   Disconnect the flexible brake hose at its union with the rigid pipeline and then disconnect the rigid line from the wheel cylinder.
6   Unscrew and remove the wheel bearing locknut, using a special wrench to hold the axle flange still or by temporarily refitting the roadwheel and lowering the car, as described in Chapter 8, Section 10.
7   Extract the axle stub, bearings and oil seal; again, as described in Chapter 8.
8   Unscrew and remove the four bolts which secure the brake backplate and then withdraw the brake assembly.
9   Remove the rubber rebound stop securing nut.
10 Place a jack under the suspension wishbone and raise the jack just enough to relieve the tension on the shock absorber then disconnect the shock absorber lower mounting.
11 Gently lower the jack under the suspension arm until the coil spring, spring seat and rebound stop can be removed.
12 Unscrew and remove the pivot bolts which secure the suspension wishbone to the suspension member.
13 Renewal of the suspension arm bushes can be carried out using a suitable press or a long bolt, nut and a distance piece of suitable outside diameter.
14 Installation is a reversal of removal but tighten all nuts and bolts to the specified torque. Tighten the suspension wishbone pivot bolts when the weight of the car is on the suspension and always renew the self locking nuts.
15 Refer to Chapter 8 for details of rear hub reassembly.
16 When installation is complete, bleed the brake hydraulic system, as described in Chapter 9

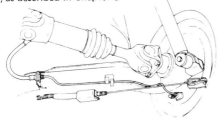

Fig. 11.36 Rear brake hose unions (independent rear suspension)

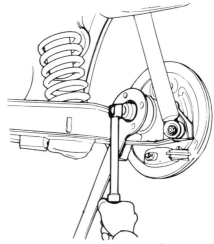

Fig. 11.37 Unscrewing bearing locknut (independent rear suspension)

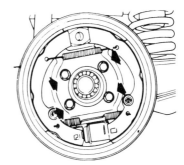

Fig. 11.38 Rear brake backplate securing bolts (independent rear suspension)

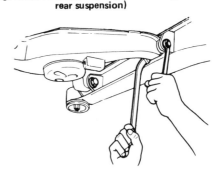

Fig. 11.39 Removing the suspension wishbone pivot bolts

15 Steering linkage - inspection, dismantling and reassembly

1   Wear in the steering gear and linkage is indicated when there is considerable movement in the steering wheel without corresponding movement at the roadwheels. Wear is also indicated when the car tends to 'wander' off the line one is trying to steer. There are three main steering 'groups' to examine in such circumstances. These are the wheel bearings, the linkage joints and bushes and the steering box itself.
2   First jack up the front of the car and support it on stands under the side frame members so that both front wheels are clear of the ground.
3   Grip the top and bottom of the wheel and try to rock it. It will not take any great effort to be able to feel any play in the wheel bearing. If this play is very noticeable it would be as well to adjust it straight away as it could confuse further examinations. It is also possible that during this check play may be

discovered also in the lower suspension track control arm ball-joint (at the foot of the suspension strut). If this happens the balljoint will need renewal.

4   Next grip each side of the wheel and try rocking it laterally. Steady pressure will, of course, turn the steering but an alternated back and fourth pressure will reveal any loose joint. If some play is felt it would be easier to get assistance from someone so that while one person rocks the wheel from side to side, the other can look at the joints and bushes on the track rods and connections. Excluding the steering box itself there are eight places where the play may occur. The two outer balljoints on the two outer track rods are the most likely, followed by the two inner joints on the same rods there they join the centre relay rod. Any play in these means renewal of the balljoint. Next are the two swivel bushes, one at each end of the centre relay rod. Finally check the steering box drop arm balljoint and the one on the relay or idler arm which supports the centre relay rod on the side opposite the steering box. This unit is bolted to the side frame member and any play calls for renewal of the bushes.

5   Finally, the steering box itself is checked. First make sure that the bolts holding the steering box to the side frame member are tight. Then get another person to help examine the mechanism. One should look at, or get hold of, the drop arm at the bottom of the steering box while the other turns the steering wheel a little way from side to side. The amount of lost motion between the steering wheel and the drop arm indicates the degree of wear somewhere in the steering box mechanism. This check should be carried out with the wheels first of all in the straight ahead position and then at nearly full lock on each side. If the play only occurs noticeably in the straight ahead position then the wear is most probably in the worm and/or nut. If it occurs at all positions of the steering then the wear is probably in the rocker shaft bush. An oil leak at this point is another indication of such wear. In either case the steering box will need removal for closer examination and repair.

6   The balljoints on the two outer track rods and the swivel bushes on the centre trackrod are all fitted into their respective

locations by means of a taper pin in a tapered hole and secured by a self-locking or castellated nut. In the case of the four ball-joints (two on each of the outer trackrods) they are also screwed onto the rod and held by a locknut.

7   To remove the taper pin first remove the self-locking nut. On occasion the taper pins have been known to simply pull out. More often they are well and truly wedged in position and a clamp or slotted steel wedges may be driven between the ball unit and the arm to which it is attached. Another method is to place the head of a hammer (or other solid metal article) on one side of the hole in the arm into which the pin is fitted. Then hit it smartly with a hammer on the opposite side. This has the effect of squeezing the taper out and usually works, provided one can get a good swing at it.

8   When the taper pin is free, grip the shank of the joint and back off the locknut. Move this locknut just sufficiently to unlock the shank as its position is a guide to fitting the new joint. Then screw the balljoint off the head.

9   It is most important when fitting new balljoints to first ensure that they are screwed on to the rod the same amount and then, before tightening the locknut, that they are correctly angled. So, after connecting everything up and before tightening the locknuts set the steering in the straight ahead position and see that the socket of the balljoint is square with the axis of the ball taper pin. If this is not done the whole joint could be under extreme strain when the steering is on only partial lock.

10 If the centre track rod bushes require that the trackrod be renewed then it will be necessary to detach the inner balljoints of the outer trackrods from it. The two swivel joints can then be removed from the drop arm and idler arm respectively and the unit removed.

11 Any play in the idler assembly can be remedied by renewal of the rubber bushes. Tighten the idler assembly nut to 30 lb/ft (4.1 kg/m).

12 When any part of the steering linkage is renewed it is advisable to have the alignment of the steering checked at a garage with the proper equipment.

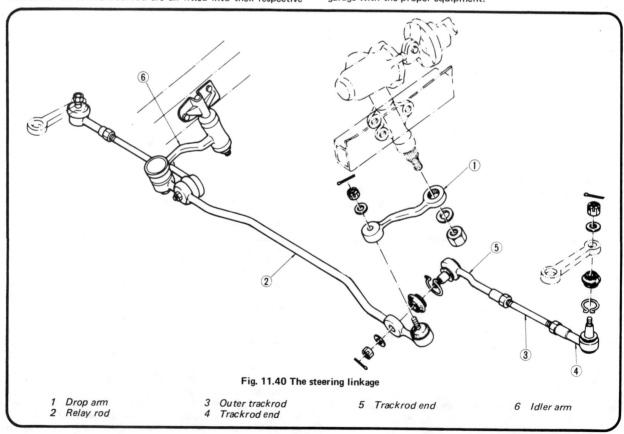

Fig. 11.40 The steering linkage

1 Drop arm	3 Outer trackrod	5 Trackrod end	6 Idler arm
2 Relay rod	4 Trackrod end		

16 Steering wheel - removal and refitting

1 Set the roadwheels in the straight-ahead position.
2 Disconnect the lead from the battery negative terminal.
3 On two spoke steering wheels, push the crash pad upwards and then pull it from its clips.
4 On three spoke steering wheels, simply pull the pad from its securing clips.
5 Unscrew and remove the steering wheel nut.
6 A suitable extractor will now have to be used to pull the wheel from the splines of the steering shaft. Two holes are tapped in the steering wheel as anchor points for an extractor. On no account strike the end of the shaft or the reverse side of the steering wheel in an attempt to jar the wheel free or the collapsible type column may be damaged.
7 Refitting is a reversal of removal but apply a little grease to the shaft splines, align the wheel correctly and tighten the securing nut to the specified torque.

17 Steering column lock - removal and installation

1 This operation will normally only be required in the event of loss of keys or malfunction of the lock.
2 The two securing bolts are of shear head type and they will have to be drilled out after centre punching them. The two halves of the lock can then be withdrawn.
3 Refitting is a reversal of removal but align the tonque of the lock correctly with the hole in the steering column by operating the lock several times before the bolts are fully tightened and their heads sheared.

18 Steering column - removal and installation

1 Set the roadwheels in the straight-ahead position.
2 Remove the pinch bolt which secures the clamp on the wormshaft to flexible coupling.
3 Remove the steering wheel, as described in Section 16.
4 Remove the steering column upper shrouds (four screws).
5 Remove the direction indicator switch (Chapter 10).
6 Remove the four bolts which secure the steering column lower blanking panel.
7 Unbolt the steering column upper clamp from the fascia panel.
8 Withdraw the column into the vehicle interior.
9 If a frontal impact has occurred to the vehicle, check the dimensions 'A' and 'B', as shown in the diagrams. Where the dimensions are less than those specified, renew all components and assemblies.
10 Commence installation by connecting the steering shaft to the worm shaft. Make sure that the punch mark on the end of the shaft is uppermost with the roadwheels still in the straight-ahead position. Tighten the coupling pinch bolt.
11 Bolt the steering column upper clamp to the fascia panel tightening them to the specified torque.
12 Release the lower blanking panel column clamp and push the panel fully down into contact with the bulkhead. Tighten the blanking panel bolts.
13 Tighten the blanking panel to column clamp bolt.
14 Refit the shrouds, direction indicator switch and steering wheel.

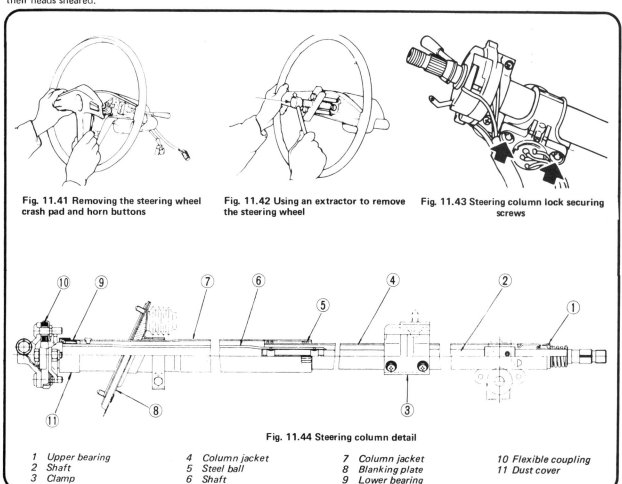

Fig. 11.41 Removing the steering wheel crash pad and horn buttons

Fig. 11.42 Using an extractor to remove the steering wheel

Fig. 11.43 Steering column lock securing screws

Fig. 11.44 Steering column detail

1 Upper bearing	4 Column jacket	7 Column jacket	10 Flexible coupling
2 Shaft	5 Steel ball	8 Blanking plate	11 Dust cover
3 Clamp	6 Shaft	9 Lower bearing	

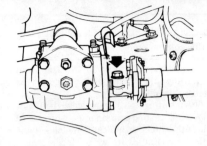

Fig. 11.45 Flexible coupling

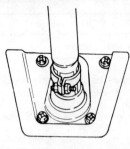

Fig. 11.46 Steering column blanking panel bolts

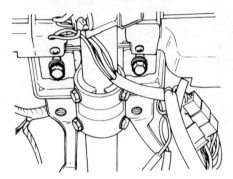

Fig. 11.47 Steering column upper clamp bolts

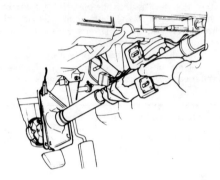

Fig. 11.48 Withdrawing steering column into vehicle interior

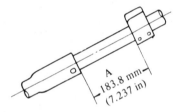

Fig. 11.49 Correct dimension of steering column (lower jacket tube to column upper clamp)

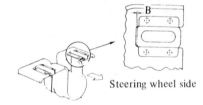

Fig. 11.50 Correct dimension of undamaged column upper clamp

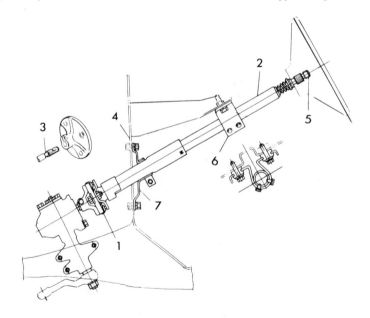

Fig. 11.51 Steering column installation diagram

1 Flexible coupling	3 Worn shaft	5 Shaft	7 Blanking panel
2 Steering column	4 Bulkhead	6 Column clamp	

19 Steering gear - removal and installation

1 Remove the heat sheild securing bolts (710 series).
2 Unscrew and remove the flexible coupling pinch bolt.
3 Remove the nut which secures the drop arm to the end of the sector shaft, mark the relationship of the drop arm to the sector shaft and then extract the drop arm.
4 Unscrew and remove the three bolts which secure the steering gear housing to the bodyframe sidemember. Withdraw the steering gear from the engine compartment.
5 Installation is a reversal of removal but align the drop arm to the sector shaft and the coupling to the worm shaft using the mating marks and punch mark.
6 Tighten all bolts to the specified torque.
7 If the steering gear has been dismantled, refill the steering box to the correct level with oil.

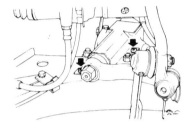

Fig. 11.52 Removing heat shield

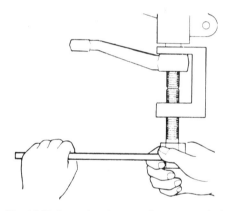

Fig. 11.53 Removing drop arm from sector shaft

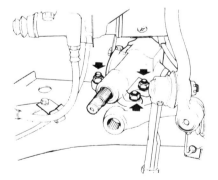

Fig. 11.54 Steering box securing bolts

20 Steering gear - dismantling and reassembly

1 Remove the filler plug and drain the oil from the steering box.

2 Secure the steering box in a vice and then loosen the locknut from the adjusting screw on the top cover and unscrew the adjuster two or three turns.
3 Unscrew the top cover bolts and remove the cover and the gasket.
4 To release the cover from the adjuster screw, turn the slot in the end of the screw. Withdraw the sector shaft.
5 Remove the rear cover (three bolts) followed by the bearing adjusting shims and the worm assembly. Do not remove the nut from the worm neither allow the nut to run from end to end of the worm or the ball guides will be damaged.
6 Inspect all components for wear or damage and renew as necessary. If the sector shaft needle bearings are worn, do not remove them but renew the steering gear housing complete.
7 Always renew both oil seals at time of major overhaul.
8 Clean all components and lubricate them prior to reassembly.
9 Insert the worm assembly into the steering box.
10 Install the rear cover with 'O' ring and bearing shims, (thicker shims to steering box side). If new components have been fitted, the worm bearing pre-load must be checked and adjusted. To do this attach a spring balance to a piece of cord wrapped round the splines of the worm pinion and check the starting torque which should be between 3 and 5 lbs. Add or remove shims as necessary from the following shim thicknesses which are available.
0.002 in (0.050 mm)   0.005 in (0.127 mm)
0.010 in (0.254 mm)   0.030 in (0.762 mm)
11 Insert the adjusting screw into the T-shaped groove in the sector shaft. Using a feeler blade, check the play between the bottom of the groove and the lower face of the adjusting screw. Use shims if necessary to provide an endplay of between 0.0004 and 0.0012 in (0.01 and 0.03 mm). Shims are available in the following thicknesses:
0.057 to 0.058 in   (1.450 to 1.475 mm)
0.059 to 0.060 in   (1.500 to 1.525 mm)
0.060 to 0.061 in   (1.525 to 1.550 mm)
0.061 to 0.062 in   (1.550 to 1.575 mm)
0.062 to 0.063 in   (1.575 to 1.600 mm)
12 Turn the worm shaft by hand until the nut is in the centre of its travel then install the sector shaft complete with adjusting screw. Make sure that the centre tooth of the sector shaft engages with the centre groove of the nut. Take great care not to cut or damage the lips of the oil seals during these operations.
13 Install the top cover using sealant between the gasket faces. Turn the adjusting screw in an anticlockwise direction (in order to fit the cover to the steering box mating faces) by means of the screwdriver slot.
14 With the top cover bolts tightened to torque, turn the adjusting screw clockwise with finger pressure only and then tighten the locknut temporarily.
15 Temporarily engage the drop arm onto the sector shaft splines and move the sector shaft over its complete arc of travel in both directions to check for smooth operation.
16 Move the drop arm to the steering straight-ahead position (in alignment with worm pinion) and after releasing the top cover adjusting screw locknut, turn the adjusting screw until any sector shaft end-float just disappears. Turn the adjusting screw a further 1/6th. of a turn and fully tighten the locknut.

21 Front wheel alignment and steering angles

1 Accurate front wheel alignment is essential for good steering and slow tyre wear. Before considering the steering angle, check that the tyres are correctly inflated, that the front wheels are not buckled, the hub bearings are not worn or incorrectly adjusted and that the steering linkage is in good order, without slackness or wear at the joints.
2 Wheel alignment consists of four factors:
Camber, is the angle at which the front wheels are set from the vertical when viewed from the front of the car. Positive camber is the amount (in degrees) that the wheels are tilted outwards at the top from the vertical).

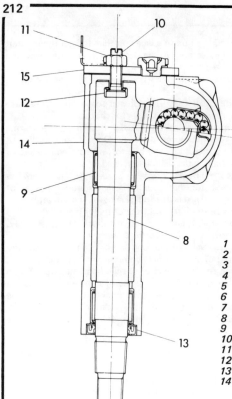

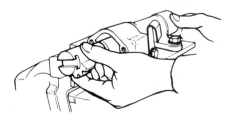

1 Worm shaft
2 Ball nut
3 Worm *bearing*
4 Rear cover
5 Bearing adjustment shim
6 'O' ring
7 Oil seal
8 Sector shaft
9 Sector shaft bearing
10 Adjusting screw
11 Locknut
12 Adjusting
13 Oil seal
14 Steering box

Fig. 11.55 Sectional views of the steering gear

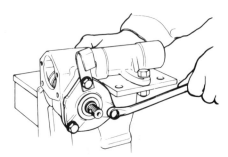

Fig. 11.56 Withdrawing the sector shaft

Fig. 11.57 Removing rear cover bolts

Fig. 11.59 Checking sector shaft groove to adjuster screw clearance

Fig. 11.58 Withdrawing the wormshaft assembly

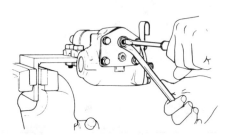

Fig. 11.60 Tighten the adjuster screw locknut

Castor is the angle between the steering axis and a vertical line when viewed from each side of the car. Positive castor is when the steering axis is inclined rearward.

Steering axis inclination is the angle, when viewed from front of the car, between the vertical and an imaginary line drawn between the upper and lower suspension leg pivots.

Toe-in is the amount by which the distance between the front inside edges of the roadwheels (measured at hub height) is less than the diametrically opposite distance measured between the rear inside edges of the front roadwheels

3 Due to the need for special gap gauges and correct weighting of the car suspension it is not within the scope of the home mechanic to check steering angles. Indeed, the steering angles (except toe-in) are all set in production and cannot be altered. They should be checked by a service station however after any part of the steering or the front end of the car has been damaged in an accident. Front wheel tracking (toe-in) checks are best carried out with modern setting equipment but a reasonably accurate alternative and adjustment procedure may be carried out as follows:

4 Place the car on level ground with the wheels in the straight-ahead position.

5 Obtain or make a toe-in gauge. One may be easily made from tubing, cranked to clear the sump and bellhousing, having an adjustable nut and setscrew at one end.

6 Using the gauge, measure the distance between the two inner wheel rims at hub height at the rear of the wheels.

7 Rotate the wheels (by pushing the car backwards or forwards) through 180° (half a turn) and again using the gauge, measure the distance of hub height between the two inner wheel rims at the front of the wheels. This measurement should be between 0.32 to 0.43 in (8.0 to 11.0 mm) less than that previously taken at the rear of the wheel and represents the correct toe-in.

8 Where the toe-in is found to be incorrect, slacken the locknuts on each outer trackrod and rotate each end fitting an equal amount until the correct toe-in is obtained. Tighten the locknuts ensuring that the balljoints are held in the centre of their arc of travel during tightening.

9 If new components have been fitted, set the trackrods as shown in the diagram as a basic setting before commencing adjustment.

22 Steering locks - adjustment

1 The steering angles differ between the inner and outer road-wheels during a turn on full steering lock (see Specifications). These angles can only be satisfactorily measured on turn tables at a service station but in an emergency in order to prevent a tyre rubbing against the inside of a wheel arch, the lockstop bolts can be adjusted.

2 Remove the caps from the bolt heads and loosen the lock-nuts.

3 Turn one or both bolts in or out as necessary to reduce or increase one or both steering locks.

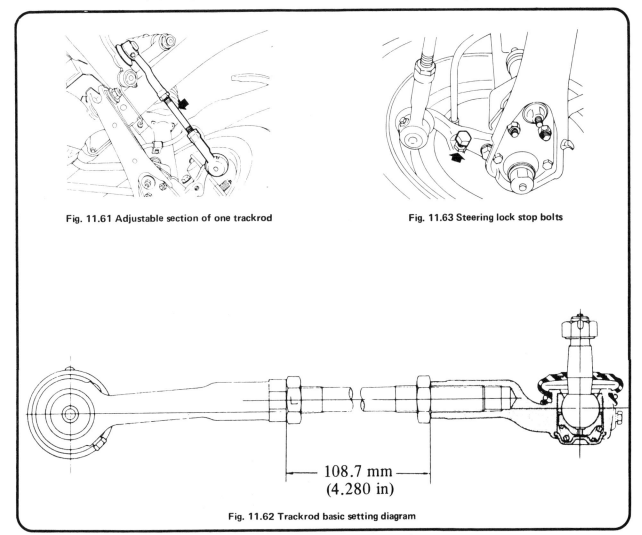

Fig. 11.61 Adjustable section of one trackrod

Fig. 11.63 Steering lock stop bolts

|— 108.7 mm —|
(4.280 in)

Fig. 11.62 Trackrod basic setting diagram

23 Roadwheels and tyres

1 Whenever the roadwheels are removed it is a good idea to clean the insides of the wheels to remove accumulations of mud and in the case of the front ones, disc pad dust.

2 Check the condition of the wheel for rust and repaint if necessary.

3 Examine the wheel stud holes. If these are tending to become elongated or the dished recesses in which the nuts seat have worn or become overcompressed, then the wheel will have to be renewed.

4 With a roadwheel removed, pick out any embedded flints from the tread and check for splits in the sidewalls or damage to the tyre carcass generally.

5 Where the depth of tread pattern is 1 mm or less, the tyre

must be renewed.

6 Rotation of the roadwheels to even out wear is a worthwhile idea if the wheels have been balanced off the car. Do not change radial tyres from one side of the vehicle to the other but only between wheels on the same side.

7 If the wheels have been balanced on the car then they cannot be moved round the car as the balance of wheel, tyre and hub will be upset.

8 It is recommended that wheels are re-balanced halfway through the lift of the tyres to compensate for the loss of tread rubber due to wear.

9 Finally, always keep the tyres (including the spare) inflated to the recommended pressures and always replace the dust caps on the tyre valves. Tyre pressures are best checked first thing in the morning when the tyres are cold.

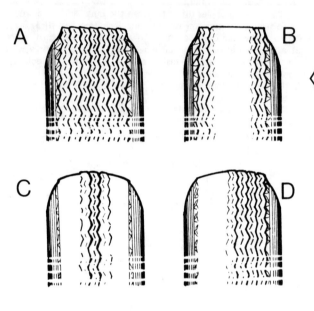

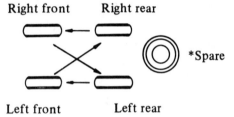

Fig. 11.64 Typical tyre wear abnormalities

A 'Feathering' due to front wheels toeing in or out incorrectly
B Result of over-inflation
C Result of under-inflation
D Uneven wear due to worn or incorrectly adjusted wheel bearings, excessive toe-in or incorrect camber angle (as the result of an accident)

Fig. 11.65 Cross ply tyre rotational diagram

24 Fault diagnosis - suspension and steering

Symptom	Reason/s
Steering feels vague, car wanders and floats at speed	Tyre pressures uneven Shock absorbers worn Spring broken Steering gear balljoints badly worn Suspension geometry incorrect Steering mechanism free play excessive Front suspension and rear axle pick-up points out of alignment
Stiff and heavy steering	Tyre pressures too low No grease in swivel joints No grease in steering and suspension balljoints Front wheel toe-in incorrect Suspension geometry incorrect Steering gear incorrectly adjusted too tightly Steering column badly misaligned
Wheel wobble and vibration	Wheel nuts loose Front wheels and tyres out of balance Steering balljoints badly worn Hub bearings badly worn Steering gear free play excessive Front springs weak or broken Front struts weak

Chapter 12 Body and fittings

Contents

Body dimensions and weights are listed in the Routine Maintenance Section at the front of this manual.

1 General description

The bodyframe and shell are of steel all-welded, unitary construction. Internal and external design varies in detail between the various models, but any differences in removal or installation procedures are described where necessary.

The front wings are detachable after removing the securing bolts; this provides some economy in repair costs when front-end damage occurs.

On late 710 series models, the bumpers are of impact absorbing type being mounted on gas-filled telescopic shock absorbers. A heater and ventilating system are fitted as standard and an air conditioning system can be specified as optional equipment.

2 Maintenance - bodywork and underframe

1 The general condition of a car's bodywork is the one thing that significantly affects its value. Maintenance is easy but needs to be regular. Neglect, particularly after minor damage, can lead quickly to further deterioration and costly repair bills. It is important also to keep watch on those parts of the car not immediately visible, for instance the underside, inside all the wheel arches and the lower part of the engine compartment.
2 The basic maintenance routine for the bodywork is washing - preferably with a lot of water, from a hose. This will remove all the loose solids which may have stuck to the car. It is important to flush these off in such a way as to prevent grit from scratching the finish.

The wheel arches and underbody need washing in the same way to remove any accumulated mud which will retain moisture and tend to encourage rust. Paradoxically enough, the best time to clean the underbody and wheel arches is in wet weather when the mud is thoroughly wet and soft. In very wet weather the underbody is usually cleaned of large accumulations automatically and this is a good time for inspection.
3 Periodically it is a good idea to have the whole of the underside of the car steam cleaned, engine compartment included, so that a thorough inspection can be carried out to see what minor repairs and renovations are necessary. Steam cleaning is available at many garages and is necessary for removal of accumulations of oily grime which sometimes is allowed to cake thick in certain areas near the engine, gearbox and back axle. If steam facilities are not available, there are one or two excellent grease solvents available which can be brush applied. The dirt can then be simply hosed off.
4 After washing paintwork, wipe off with a chamois leather to give an unspotted clear finish. A coat of clear protective wax polish will give added protection against chemical pollutants in the air. If the paintwork sheen has dulled or oxidised, use a cleaner/polisher combination to restore the brilliance of the shine. This requires a little effort, but is usually caused because regular washing has been neglected. Always check that the door and ventilator opening drain holes and pipes are completely clear so that water can drain out. Bright work should be treated the same way as paintwork. Windscreens and windows can be kept clear of the smeary film which often appears if a little ammonia is added to the water. If they are scratched, a good rub with a proprietary metal polish will often clear them. Never use any form of wax or other body or chromium polish on glass.

3 Maintenance - upholstery and carpets

1 Mats and carpets should be brushed or vacuum cleaned regularly to keep them free of grit. If they are badly stained remove them from the car for scrubbing or sponging and make quite sure they are dry before replacement. Seats and interior trim panels can be kept clean by a wipe over with a damp cloth. If they do become stained (which can be more apparent on light coloured upholstery) use a little liquid detergent and a soft nail brush to scour the grime out of the grain of the material. Do not forget to keep the head lining clean in the same way as the upholstery. When using liquid cleaners inside the car do not over-wet the surfaces being cleaned. Excessive damp could get into the seams and padded interior causing stains, offensive odours or even rot. If the inside of the car gets wet accidentally it is worthwhile taking some trouble to dry it out properly particularly where carpets are involved. **Do not** leave oil or electric heaters inside the car for this purpose.

4 Minor body damage - repair

The photograph sequence on pages 222 and 223 illustrates the operations detailed in the following sub-Sections.

Repair of minor scratches in the car's bodywork

If the scratch is very superficial, and does not penetrate to the metal of the bodywork, repair is very simple. Lightly rub the area of the scratch with a paintwork renovator (eg; T-Cut), or a very fine cutting paste, to remove loose paint from the scratch and to clear the surrounding bodywork of wax polish. Rinse the area with clean water.

Apply touch-up paint to the scratch using a thin paint brush, continue to apply thin layers of paint until the surface of the paint in the scratch is level with the surrounding paintwork. Allow the new paint at least two weeks to harden; then, blend it into the surrounding paintwork by rubbing the paintwork, in the scratch area with a paintwork renovator (eg; T-Cut), or a very fine cutting paste. Finally apply wax polish.

An alternative to painting over the scratch is to use Holts "Scratch-Patch". Use the same preparation for the affected area; then simply pick a patch of a suitable size to cover the scratch completely. Hold the patch against the scratch and burnish its backing paper; the patch will adhere to the paintwork, freeing itself from the backing paper at the same time. Polish the affected area to blend the patch into the surrounding paintwork. Where the scratch has penetrated right through to the metal of the bodywork, causing the metal to rust, a different repair technique is required. Remove any loose rust from the bottom of the scratch with a penknife, then apply rust inhibiting paint (eg; Kurust) to prevent the formation of rust in the future. Using a rubber or nylon applicator fill the scratch with bodystopper paste. If required, this paste can be mixed with cellulose thinners to provide a very thin paste which is ideal for filling narrow scratches. Before the stopper-paste in the scratch hardens, wrap a piece of smooth cotton rag around the top of a finger. Dip the finger in cellulose thinners and then quickly sweep it across the surface of the stopper-paste in the scratch; this will ensure that the surface of the stopper-paste is slightly hollowed. The scratch can now be painted over as described earlier in this Section.

Repair of dents in the car's bodywork

When deep denting of the car's bodywork has taken place, the first task is to pull the dent out, until the affected bodywork almost attains its original shape. There is little point in trying to restore the original shape completely, as the metal in the damaged area will have stretched on impact and cannot be reshaped fully to its original contour. It is better to bring the level of the dent up to a point which is about 1/8 inch (3 mm) below the level of the surrounding bodywork. In cases where the dent is very shallow anyway, it is not worth trying to pull it out at all.

If the underside of the dent is accessible, it can be hammered out gently from behind, using a mallet with a wooden or plastic head. Whilst doing this, hold a suitable block of wood firmly against the impact from the hammer blows and thus prevent a large area of bodywork from being 'belled-out'.

Should the dent be in a section of the bodywork which has a double skin or some other factor making it inaccessible from behind, a different technique is called for. Drill several small holes through the metal inside the dent area - particularly in the deeper sections. Then screw long self-tapping screws into the holes just sufficiently for them to gain a good purchase in the metal. Now the dent can be pulled out by pulling on the protruding heads of the screws with a pair of pliers.

The next stage of the repair is the removal of the paint from the damaged area, and from an inch or so of the surrounding 'sound' bodywork. This is accomplished most easily by using a wire brush or abrasive pad on a power drill, although it can be done just as effectively by hand using sheets of abrasive paper. To complete the preparations for filling, score the surface of the bare metal with a screwdriver or the tang of a file, or alternatively, drill small holes in the affected area. This will provide a really good 'key' for the filler paste.

To complete the repair see the Section on filling and respraying.

Repair of rust holes or gashes in the car's bodywork

Remove all paint from the affected area and from an inch or so of the surrounding 'sound' bodywork, using an abrasive pad or a wire brush on a power drill. If these are not available a few sheets of abrasive paper will do the job just as effectively. With the paint removed you will be able to gauge the severity of the corrosion and therefore decide whether to replace the whole panel (if this is possible) or to repair the affected area. Replacement body panels are not as expensive as most people think and it is often quicker and more satisfactory to fit a new panel than to attempt to repair large areas of corrosion.

Remove all fittings from the affected area except those which will act as a guide to the original shape of the damaged bodywork (eg; headlamp shells etc.,). Then, using tin snips or a hacksaw blade, remove all loose metal and any other metal badly affected by corrosion. Hammer the edges of the hole inwards in order to create a slight depression for the filler paste.

Wire brush the affected area to remove the powdery rust from the surface of the remaining metal. Paint the affected area with rust inhibiting paint (eg; Kurust); if the back of the rusted area is accessible treat this also.

Before filling can take place it will be necessary to block the hole in some way. This can be achieved by the use of one of the following materials: Zinc gauze, Aluminium tape or Polyurethane foam.

Zinc gauze is probably the best material to use for a large hole. Cut a piece to the approximate size and shape of the hole to be filled, then position it in the hole so that its edges are below the level of the surrounding bodywork. It can be retained in position by several blobs of filler paste around its periphery.

Aluminium tape should be used for small or very narrow holes. Pull a piece off the roll and trim it to the approximate size and shape required, then pull off the backing paper (if used) and stick the tape over the hole; it can be overlapped if the thickness of one piece is insufficient. Burnish down the edges of the tape with the handle of a screwdriver or similar, to ensure that the tape is securely attached to the metal underneath.

Polyurethane foam is best used where the hole is situated in a section of bodywork of complex shape, backed by a small box section (eg; where the sill panel meets the rear wheel arch - most cars). The unusual mixing procedure for this foam is as follows: Put equal amounts of fluid from each of the two cans provided in the kit, into one container. Stir until the mixture begins to thicken, then quickly pour this mixture into the hole, and hold a piece of cardboard over the larger apertures. Almost immediately the polyurethane will begin to expand, gushing out of any small holes left unblocked. When the foam hardens it can be cut back to just below the level of the surrounding bodywork with a hacksaw blade.

Bodywork repairs - filling and re-spraying

Before using this Section, see the Sections on dent, deep scratch, rust hole, and gash repairs.

Many types of bodyfiller are available, but generally speaking those proprietary kits which contain a tin of filler paste and a tube of resin hardener (eg; Holts Cataloy) are best for this type of repair. A wide, flexible plastic or nylon applicator will be found invaluable for imparting a smooth and well contoured finish to the surface of the filler.

Mix up a little filler on a clean piece of card or board - use the hardener sparingly (follow the maker's instructions on the packet) otherwise the filler will set very rapidly.

Using the applicator, apply the filler paste to the prepared area; draw the applicator across the surface of the filler to achieve the correct contour and to level the filler surface. As soon as a contour that approximates the correct one is achieved, stop working the paste - if you carry on too long the paste will become sticky and begin to 'pick-up' on the applicator. Continue to add thin layers of filler paste at twenty-minute intervals until the level of the filler is just 'proud' of the surrounding bodywork.

Once the filler has hardened, excess can be removed using a Surform plane or Dreadnought file. From then on, progressively finer grades of abrasive paper should be used, starting with a 40 grade production paper and finishing with 400 grade 'wet-and-dry' paper. Always wrap the abrasive paper around a flat rubber, cork, or wooden block - otherwise the surface of the filler will not be completely flat. During the smoothing of the filler surface the 'wet-and-dry' paper should be periodically rinsed in water. This will ensure that a very smooth finish is imparted to the filler at the final stage.

At this stage the dent' should be surrounded by a ring of bare metal, which in turn should be encircled by the finely 'feathered' edge of the good paintwork. Rinse the repair area with clean water, until all of the dust produced by the rubbing-down operation is gone.

Spray the whole repair area with a light coat of grey primer - this will show up any imperfections in the surface of the filler. Repair these imperfections with fresh filler paste or bodystopper, and once more smooth the surface with abrasive paper. If bodystopper is used, it can be mixed with cellulose thinners to form a really thin paste which is ideal for filling small holes. Repeat this spray and repair procedure until you are satisfied that the surface of the filler, and the feathered edge of the paintwork are perfect. Clean the repair area with clean water and allow to dry fully.

The repair area is now ready for spraying. Paint spraying must be carried out in a warm, dry, windless and dust free atmosphere. This condition can be created artificially if you have access to a large indoor working area, but if you are forced to work in the open, you will have to pick your day very carefully. If you are working indoors, dousing the floor in the work area with water will 'lay' the dust which would otherwise be in the atmosphere. If the repair area is confined to one body panel, mask off the surrounding panels; this will help to minimise the effects of a slight mis-match in paint colours. Bodywork fittings (eg; chrome strips, door handles etc.,) will also need to be masked off. Use genuine masking tape and several thicknesses of newspaper for the masking operation.

Before commencing to spray, agitate the aerosol can thoroughly, then spray a test area (an old tin, or similar) until the technique is mastered. Cover the repair area with a thick coat of primer; the thickness should be built up using several thin layers of paint rather than one thick one. Using 400 grade 'wet-and-dry' paper, rub down the surface of the primer until it is really smooth. While doing this, the work area should be thoroughly doused with water, and the 'wet-and-dry' paper periodically rinsed in water. Allow to dry before spraying on more paint.

Spray on the top coat, again building up the thickness by using several thin layers of paint. Start spraying in the centre of the repair area and then, using a circular motion, work outwards until the whole repair area and about 2 inches of the surrounding original paintwork is covered. Remove all masking material 10 to 15 minutes after spraying on the final coat of paint.

Allow the new paint at least 2 weeks to harden fully; then, using a paintwork renovator (eg; T-Cut) or a very fine cutting paste, blend the edges of the new paint into the existing paintwork. Finally, apply wax polish.

5 Major body damage - repair

Where serious damage has occurred or large areas need renewal due to neglect, it means certainly that completely new sections or panels will need welding in and this is best left to professionals. If the damage is due to impact it will also be necessary to completely check the alignment of the bodyshell structure. Due to the principle of construction the strength and shape of the whole can be affected by damage to a part. In such instances the services of a Datsun agent with specialist checking jigs are essential. If a body is left misaligned it is first of all dangerous as the car will not handle properly, and secondly uneven stresses will be imposed on the steering, engine and transmission, causing abnormal wear or complete failure. Tyre wear may also be excessive.

6 Maintenance - hinges and locks

1 Oil the hinges of the bonnet, boot and doors with a drop or two of light oil periodically. A good time is after the car has been washed.
2 Oil the bonnet, release the catch pivot pin and the safety catch pivot pin periodically.
3 Do not over lubricate door latches and strikers. Normally a little oil on the rotary cam spindle alone is sufficient.

7 Doors - tracing rattles and their rectification

1 Check first that the door is not loose at the hinges and that the latch is holding the door firmly in position. Check also that the door lines up with the aperture in the body.
2 If the hinges are loose or the door is out of alignment it will be necessary to reset the hinge positions, as described in Section 15.
3 If the latch is holding the door properly it should hold the door tightly when fully latched and the door should line up with the body. If it is out of alignment it needs adjustment as described. If loose, some part of the lock mechanism must be worn out and requires renewal.
4 Other rattles from the door would be caused by wear or looseness in the window winder, the glass channels and sill strips or the door buttons and interior latch release mechanism.

8 Front grille - removal and installation

1 Open the bonnet lid fully and support it on its stay.
2 Unscrew and remove the six upper securing screws and lift the grille upwards and outwards. (photo)
3 Installation is a reversal of removal but make sure that the locating tabs at the base of the grille engage correctly in the mounting clips of the front apron. (photo)

9 Bumpers (non impact absorbing type) - removal and installation

1 This is simply a matter of unscrewing and removing the bumper bracket attachment bolts from the bodyframe side-members.
2 On the front bumper two additional bolts secure the bumper side brackets to the front wings.
3 Installation is a reversal of removal.

218

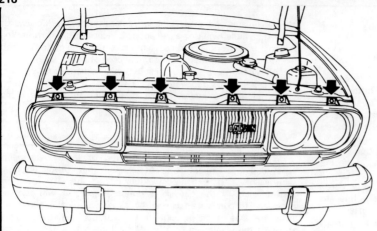

Fig. 12.1 Location of the radiator grille securing screws

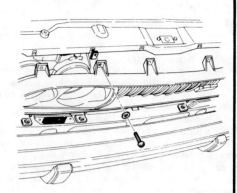

Fig. 12.2 Radiator grille lower mounting clips

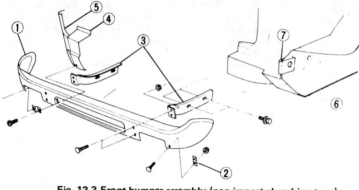

Fig. 12.3 Front bumper assembly (non-impact absorbing type)

1 Bumper bar
2 Side bracket
3 Centre bracket
4 Apron
5 Front wing
6 Body frame
7 Nut

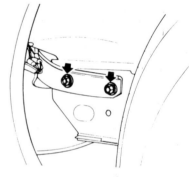

Fig. 12.4 Front bumper (non-impact) centre bracket bolts

Fig. 12.5 Front bumper (non-impact) side bracket bolts

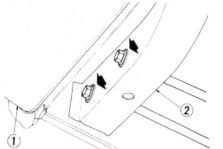

Fig. 12.6 Rear bumper (non-impact) bracket bolts

1 Rear wing
2 Body frame

8.2 Removing front grille

8.3 Front grille lower locating tabs

10 Bumpers (impact absorbing type) - removal and installation

1   The front bumpers are identical for all models but the rear bumpers differ between the saloon and wagon models.

2   *To remove a front bumper*, unscrew and remove the nuts which secure it to the shock absorber flanges.

3   The shock absorbers may now be unbolted from the bodyframe.

4   Do not attempt to dismantle a shock absorber but if it is faulty, renew it as a complete unit.

5   *To remove a rear bumper*, remove the securing nuts and bolts which are located according to vehicle type as shown in the respective illustrations.

6   Installation is a reversal of removal but adjust the bumper height according to the appropriate setting diagram.

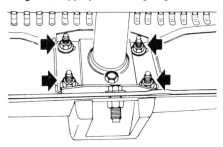

Fig. 12.9 Front bumper (impact type) mounting bolts

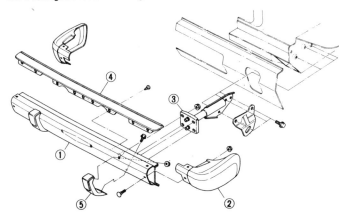

Fig. 12.7 Front bumper (impact absorbing type)

1   *Centre section*
2   *End section*
3   *Shock absorber*
4   *Shield*
5   *Overrider*

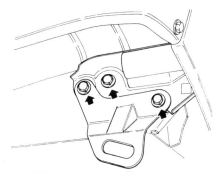

Fig. 12.10 Front bumper shock absorber mounting bolts

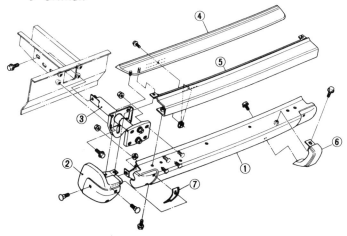

Fig. 12.8 Rear bumper (impact absorbing type) for saloon and hardtop

1   *Centre section*   5   *Upper section*
2   *End section*   6   *Overrider*
3   *Shock absorber*   7   *Insulating strip*
4   *Shield*

Fig. 12.11 Rear bumper (impact type) mounting bolts

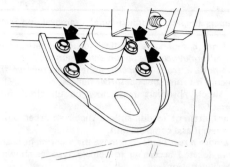

Fig. 12.12 Rear bumper shock absorber mounting bolts
(saloon and hardtop)

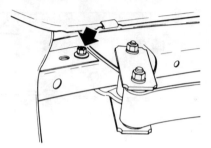

Fig. 12.13 Rear bumper shock absorber mounting bolts (wagon)

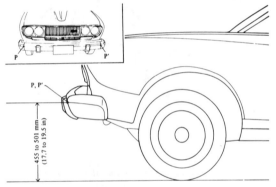

Fig. 12.14 Front bumper (impact absorbing type) height setting
diagram

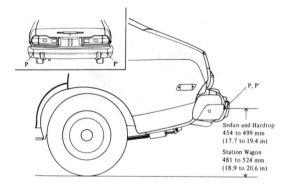

Fig. 12.15 Rear bumper (impact absorbing type) - height setting
diagram

11 Front wing - removal and installation

1 Open the bonnet lid and support it on its stay.
2 Remove the front bumper, as described in the previous Sections.
3 Remove the radiator grille (Section 8).
4 Disconnect and remove the front side and direction indicator lamp assembly.
5 Disconnect and remove the side marker (or flasher repeater) lamp.
6 Unscrew and remove the bolts which secure the front wing to the front apron.
7 Unscrew and remove the screws which secure the front apron to the bonnet lock stay.
8 Remove the windscreen wiper blades and arms, the heater air intake grille, all as described in Chapter 10.
9 Detach the bright trim from the body sill front end.
10 Unscrew and remove the wing securing screws (a) from the top edge (b) from the front end of the body sill and (c) from the cowl top panel.

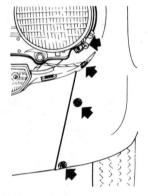

Fig. 12.16 Front wing to apron securing bolts

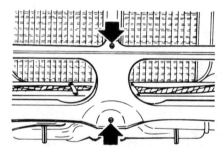

Fig. 12.17 Front apron to bonnet lock stay securing screws

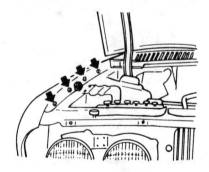

Fig. 12.18 Wing upper edge securing screws

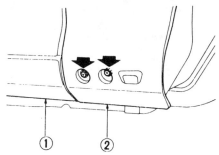

Fig. 12.19 Sill (1) to wing (2) screws

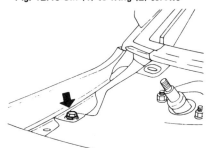

Fig. 12.20 Cowl panel to wing securing bolt

12 Door lock - removal, installation and adjustment

1 Open the door to its fullest extent.
2 Remove the armrest (two screws). (photo)
3 Remove the door interior handle escutcheon (one screw). (photo)
4 On rear doors, remove the ashtray.
5 Using a hooked piece of wire, pull out the spring clip which secures the window regulator handle. Access to this clip is obtained by pressing in the trim panel at the rear of the regulator handle. (photo)
6 Carefully insert a screwdriver between the doorframe and the door interior panel and prise the trim panel securing clips from the holes in the doorframe.
7 Carefully remove the waterproof sheet from the interior of the door.
8 Remove the securing screws from the door interior handle and the bellcrank.
9 Remove the securing screws from the remote control rod and the plunger knob rod.
10 Remove the door exterior handle (two nuts).
11 Detach the remote control rod from the lock cylinder, (front doors only).
12 Unscrew the door lock assembly retaining screws from the edge of the doorframe and withdraw the lock from the door cavity. (photo)
13 Installation is a reversal of removal but carry out the following adjustments.
14 Adjust the clearance between the exterior door lock lever and the nylon nut on the door handle rod to between 0 and 0.04 in. (0 and 1.0 mm).
15 Only partially tighten the control rod bellcrank screws and door interior handle screws and then set the lock plunger knob to the closed position. Move the bellcrank in its elongated holes towards the leading edge of the door until the bellcrank stops. Tighten all securing screws fully.

Fig. 12.21 Window regulator handle securing clip

12.2 Removing armrest

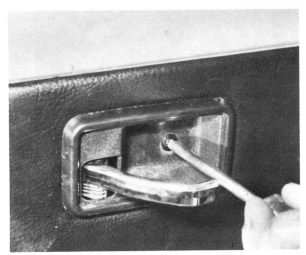

12.3 Removing door interior handle escutcheon

12.5 Window regulator handle and securing clip

This sequence of photographs deals with the repair of the dent and paintwork damage shown in this photo. The procedure will be similar for the repair of a hole. It should be noted that the procedures given here are simplified – more explicit instructions will be found in the text

In the case of a dent the first job – after removing surrounding trim – is to hammer out the dent where access is possible. This will minimise filling. Here, the large dent having been hammered out, the damaged area is being made slightly concave

Now all paint must be removed from the damaged area, by rubbing with coarse abrasive paper. Alternatively, a wire brush or abrasive pad can be used in a power drill. Where the repair area meets good paintwork, the edge of the paintwork should be 'feathered', using a finer grade of abrasive paper

In the case of a hole caused by rusting, all damaged sheet-metal should be cut away before proceeding to this stage. Here, the damaged area is being treated with rust remover and inhibitor before being filled

Mix the body filler according to its manufacturer's instructions. In the case of corrosion damage, it will be necessary to block off any large holes before filling – this can be done with aluminium or plastic mesh, or aluminium tape. Make sure the area is absolutely clean before ...

... applying the filler. Filler should be applied with a flexible applicator, as shown, for best results; the wooden spatula being used for confined areas. Apply thin layers of filler at 20-minute intervals, until the surface of the filler is slightly proud of the surrounding bodywork

Initial shaping can be done with a Surform plane or Dreadnought file. Then, using progressively finer grades of wet-and-dry paper, wrapped around a sanding block, and copious amounts of clean water, rub down the filler until really smooth and flat. Again, feather the edges of adjoining paintwork

The whole repair area can now be sprayed or brush-painted with primer. If spraying, ensure adjoining areas are protected from over-spray. Note that at least one inch of the surrounding sound paintwork should be coated with primer. Primer has a 'thick' consistency, so will find small imperfections

Again, using plenty of water, rub down the primer with a fine grade wet-and-dry paper (400 grade is probably best) until it is really smooth and well blended into the surrounding paintwork. Any remaining imperfections can now be filled by carefully applied knifing stopper paste

When the stopper has hardened, rub down the repair area again before applying the final coat of primer. Before rubbing down this last coat of primer, ensure the repair area is blemish-free — use more stopper if necessary. To ensure that the surface of the primer is really smooth use some finishing compound

The top coat can now be applied. When working out of doors, pick a dry, warm and wind-free day. Ensure surrounding areas are protected from over-spray. Agitate the aerosol thoroughly, then spray the centre of the repair area, working outwards with a circular motion. Apply the paint as several thin coats

After a period of about two weeks, which the paint needs to harden fully, the surface of the repaired area can be 'cut' with a mild cutting compound prior to wax polishing. When carrying out bodywork repairs, remember that the quality of the finished job is proportional to the time and effort expended

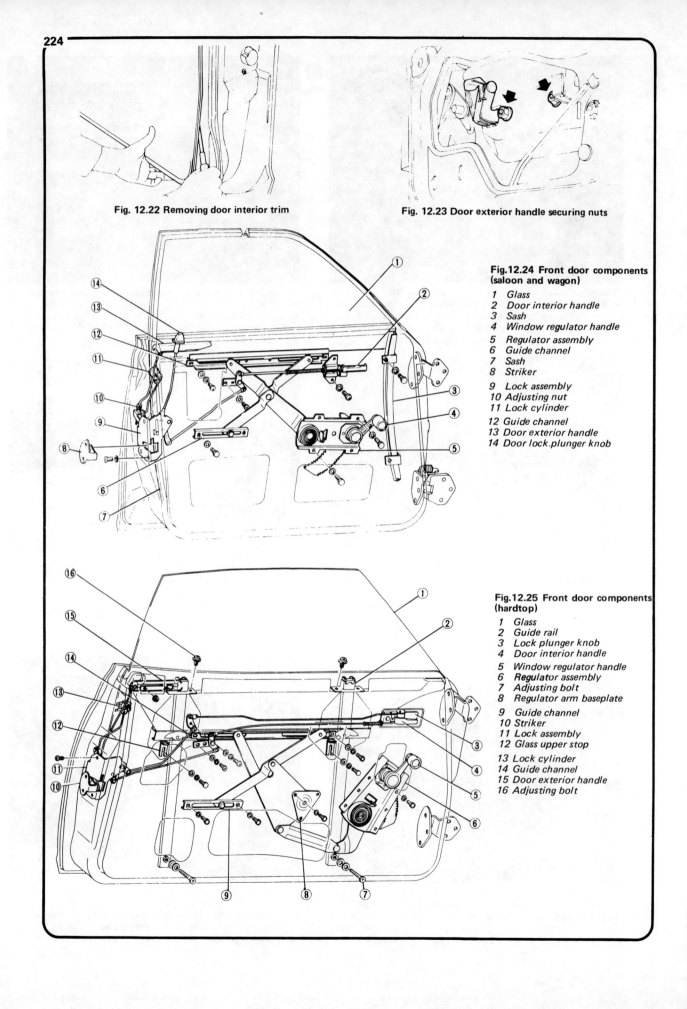

Fig. 12.22 Removing door interior trim

Fig. 12.23 Door exterior handle securing nuts

Fig.12.24 Front door components (saloon and wagon)

1　Glass
2　Door interior handle
3　Sash
4　Window regulator handle

5　Regulator assembly
6　Guide channel
7　Sash
8　Striker

9　Lock assembly
10　Adjusting nut
11　Lock cylinder

12　Guide channel
13　Door exterior handle
14　Door lock.plunger knob

Fig.12.25 Front door components (hardtop)

1　Glass
2　Guide rail
3　Lock plunger knob
4　Door interior handle

5　Window regulator handle
6　Regulator assembly
7　Adjusting bolt
8　Regulator arm baseplate

9　Guide channel
10　Striker
11　Lock assembly
12　Glass upper stop

13　Lock cylinder
14　Guide channel
15　Door exterior handle
16　Adjusting bolt

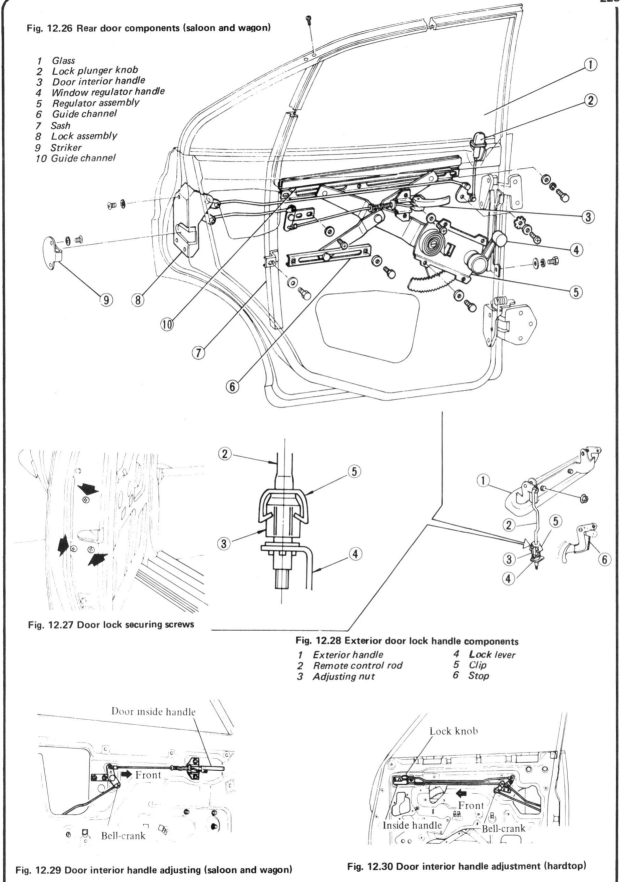

Fig. 12.26 Rear door components (saloon and wagon)

1 Glass
2 Lock plunger knob
3 Door interior handle
4 Window regulator handle
5 Regulator assembly
6 Guide channel
7 Sash
8 Lock assembly
9 Striker
10 Guide channel

Fig. 12.27 Door lock securing screws

Fig. 12.28 Exterior door lock handle components

1 Exterior handle   4 Lock lever
2 Remote control rod   5 Clip
3 Adjusting nut   6 Stop

Door inside handle

Front

Bell-crank

Fig. 12.29 Door interior handle adjusting (saloon and wagon)

Lock knob

Front

Inside handle

Bell-crank

Fig. 12.30 Door interior handle adjustment (hardtop)

12.12 Location of door lock

13 Door winding windows - removal and installation

1   Remove the door interior trim panel, as described in the preceding Section. Wind the glass fully down.
2   Remove the glass exterior weatherstrip and moulding.
3   Unscrew and remove the sash securing screws.
4   Support the glass and remove the screws which retain the guide channel to the glass backplate. In the case of hardtop models, the window will have to be wound up until the glass upper stops are visible and can be removed, then the window wound down again to disconnect the channel from the backplate.
5   The window regulator can be withdrawn from the door cavity after removal of the securing screws.
6   Installation is a reversal of removal but the sashes and guide channels must be adjusted to provide smooth operation of the window and its correct alignment within the upper door frame when it is wound fully up. The sash bolt holes are elongated to provide the necessary adjustment.

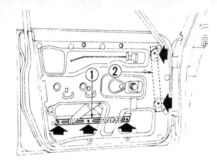

Fig. 12.31 Glass guide channel (1) and sash (2) securing screws on saloon and wagon front door

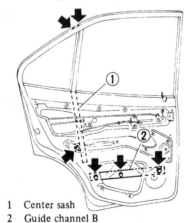

1   Center sash
2   Guide channel B

Fig. 12.32 Sash (1) and guide channel (2) securing screws on saloon and wagon rear door

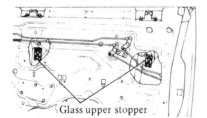

Glass upper stopper

Fig. 12.33 Glass upper stop (hardtop)

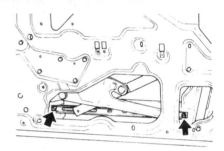

Fig. 12.34 Glass backplate to guide channel securing screws

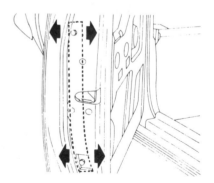

Fig. 12.35 Rear sash adjustment on a front door

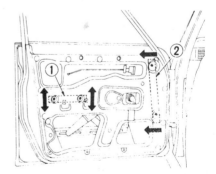

Fig. 12.36 Front sash (2) and guide channel (1) adjustment on a front door

14 Side rear window (hardtop) - removal and installation

1   Remove the rear seat cushion and the seat back.
2   Disconnect the seat belt anchorage.
3   Remove the rear parcels shelf trim strip.
4   Lower fully the window glass.
5   Remove the arm rest, window regulator and trim panel, precise details of which are given in Section 12.
6   Withdraw the waterproof sheet from the door panel.
7   Temporarily refit the window regulator handle and raise the glass until the regulator arm bracket appears in the upper aperture of the door interior panel. Support the glass and remove the nut which secures the regulator arm bracket to the glass backplate.
8   Loosen the locknuts on the upper and lower guide plate adjusting bolts and withdraw the bolts.
9   Raise the glass and withdraw it towards the car interior.
10 Unscrew and remove the four regulator assembly securing screws and withdraw the assembly through the lower aperture of the door interior panel.
11 Installation is a reversal of removal but great care must be taken to carry out the following adjustment procedure.
12 Tighten the guide plate bolts temporarily in the centres of their elongated holes, then unscrew the two upper bolts five turns and the lower bolt eleven turns. Temporarily tighten the locknuts.
13 Now adjust the upper bolts by screwing them in, or out, until a clearance of between 0.32 and 0.40 in. (8.0 to 10.0 mm) is obtained between the outer surface of the glass and the rear wing.
14 Close the door fully and raise both the door and side window glass fully. Re-adjust the guide plate bolts to provide the clearances shown in the two diagrams.

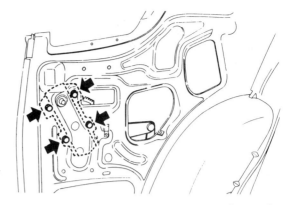

Fig. 12.38 Window regulator assembly bolts (hardtop)

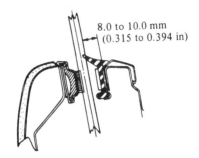

8.0 to 10.0 mm
(0.315 to 0.394 in)

Fig. 12.39 Rear wing to side rear window glass clearance diagram (hardtop)

3.0 to 5.0 mm
(0.1181 to 0.1969 in)

Fig. 12.40 Side rear window glass to weatherstrip clearance diagram (hardtop)

1   Weatherstrip
2   Door glass
3   Side rear window glass

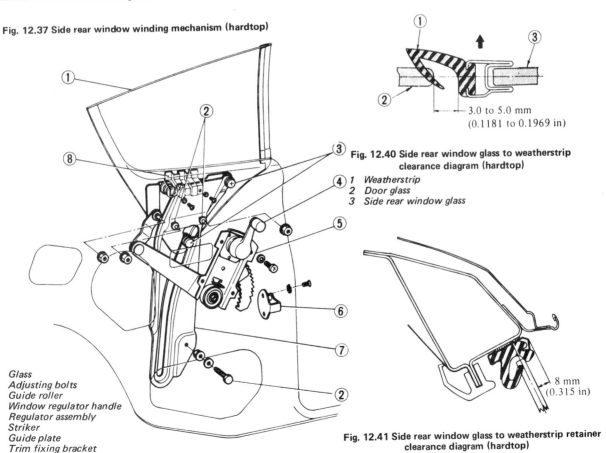

Fig. 12.37 Side rear window winding mechanism (hardtop)

1   Glass
2   Adjusting bolts
3   Guide roller
4   Window regulator handle
5   Regulator assembly
6   Striker
7   Guide plate
8   Trim fixing bracket

8 mm
(0.315 in)

Fig. 12.41 Side rear window glass to weatherstrip retainer clearance diagram (hardtop)

15 Door - removal, installation and adjustment

1   The hinge securing bolts for the rear doors are accessible once the door is fully opened but before those for the front door can be reached, the front wing must be removed, as described in Section 11.
2   Support the door in the fully open position by placing a jack or blocks under the lower edge of the door (protect the door edge with rag).
3   Unscrew and remove the bolts which secure the hinge plates to the body pillar and then lift the door from the bodyframe.
4   Refitting is a reversal of removal. The door must be aligned within the bodyframe by either positioning the hinge plates on the door pillars as originally marked or by moving the door (hinge plate bolts only finger tight), until the door is located centrally within its frame and has an even gap all round. The door striker plate will probably need adjustment to ensure that the door closes securely without rattling. To do this, loosen the striker plate securing screws and slide the plate in the required direction to give the desired result.

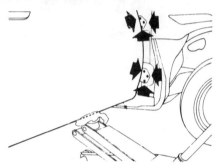

Fig. 12.42 Front door hinge bolts

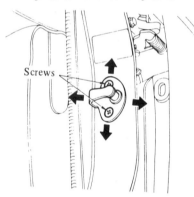

Fig. 12.43 Door striker plate

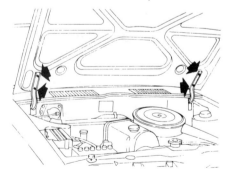

Fig. 12.44 Bonnet hinges

16 Windscreen - removal and installation

The windscreen is set in special self-vulcanizing sealant and for this reason the removal and installation of the windscreen is not within the scope of the home mechanic. Special tools and sealant injection equipment are required.

17 Bonnet - removal, installation and adjustment

1   Open the bonnet and support it on its stay.
2   Using a sharp pencil, mark round the hinges on the bonnet lid for ease of alignment on refitting.
3   With the help of an assistant, remove the bolts and lift the bonnet lid from the vehicle.
4   Installation is a reversal of removal but any adjustment to correct poor alignment should be carried out by loosening the hinge bolts and moving the bonnet lid as necessary.
5   Satisfactory closure of the bonnet lid is accomplished in two ways. Firstly, the dovetail bolt of the bonnet lock must be screwed in or out to provide a positive yet easily released locking action. Any misalignment of the dovetail bolt with the female component of the lock can be corrected by moving the lock within the elongated bolt holes.
6   The two rubber buffers must then be adjusted to eliminate any tendency of the bonnet lid to rattle.
7   Always keep the dovetail bolt and female component well lubricated with grease.

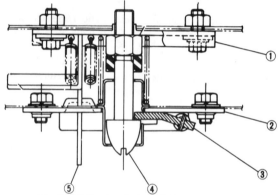

Fig. 12.45 Sectional view of the bonnet lock

1   Mounting plate   4   Dovetail bolt
2   Female component   5   Secondary latch
3   Primary latch

17.6 Bonnet lid buffer

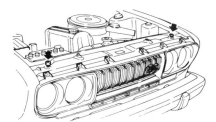

Fig. 12.46 Bonnet lid rubber buffers

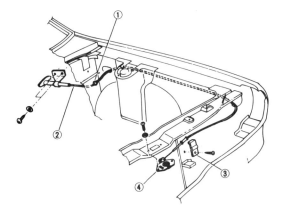

Fig. 12.47 Bonnet lock release cable and control

1 Grommet
2 Cable
3 Clamp
4 Female component

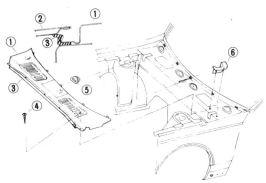

Fig. 12.48 Heater air intake grille

1 Grille
2 Bonnet lid
3 Sealing rubber
4 Screw
5 Cowl top panel cap
6 Baffle plate

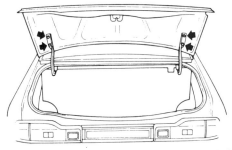

Fig. 12.49 Rear luggage compartment lid hinge bolts

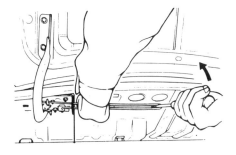

Fig. 12.50 Disengaging luggage compartment lid torsion rods

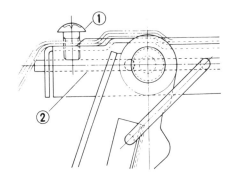

Fig. 12.51 Adjustment diagram for counter balance action of luggage compartment lid torsion rods. (1) adjusting screw (2) torsion rods

18 Heater air intake grille - removal and installation

1 Open the bonnet and support it in its fully open position.
2 Remove the windscreen wiper arms and blades, as described in Chapter 10.
3 Remove the heater air intake grille securing screws and pull the grille forward until it just touches the rear edge of the bonnet lid, it can then be removed in an upward direction.
4 If the bonnet hinges must be removed for any reason, they will now be accessible and can be unbolted from the engine compartment rear bulkhead.

19 Rear luggage compartment lid - removal, installation and adjustment

1 Open the lid fully and mark the position of the hinge plates on the underside of the lid.
2 With the help of an assistant, support the lid and unbolt it from the hinges and then remove it from the car.
3 There is no need to remove the torsion rods for the previously described operation, but where they are to be removed it is best to remove them before withdrawing the lid.
4 To disengage the torsion rods, support the lid in the fully open position and then disengage the rods from their anchorages, using a large screwdriver or bar as a lever. An adjustment screw is provided to increase or decrease the counterbalance action of the lid.
5 Installation is a reversal of removal but align the lid within the body aperture, if necessary, by moving the hinges within the range of the hinge plate elongated bolt holes. Finally, adjust the lock striker to provide smooth and positive closure of the lid.

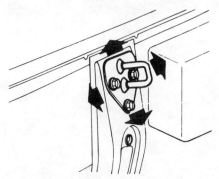

Fig. 12.52 Luggage compartment lid striker plate

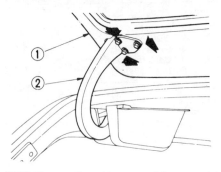

Fig. 12.53 Wagon tailgate hinge bolts (1) tailgate (2) hinge

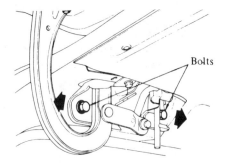

Fig. 12.54 Wagon tailgate fore and aft adjustment

Fig. 12.55 Wagon tailgate stops

20 Tailgate (wagon) - removal, installation and adjustment

1 Open the tailgate to its fullest extent and with the help of an assistant, support it in this position.
2 Mark round the hinge plates on the inner surface of the tailgate to assist in alignment during refitting.
3 If a heated rear window is fitted, disconnect the electrical leads at the element terminals.
4 Disconnect the electrical leads to the license plate lamp and reversing lamps.
5 Unscrew and remove the bolts which secure the hinge plates to the tailgate and lift the tailgate away.
6 Installation is a reversal of removal but alignment of the tailgate within the bodyshell opening is very important to provide positive, weatherproof closure.
7 The tailgate may be moved within the limits of the elongated hinge bolt holes, also the hinge plate bolts (to bodyshell) may be loosened (but not removed with the torsion rods in position) and the tailgate closure pressure adjusted.
8 Once the alignment has been correctly set, the tailgate lock, striker and stops may be adjusted to provide a smooth closure without too much pressure being required but without any tendency to rattle.
9 If for any reason the counterbalancing torsion rods must be removed, open the tailgate fully, remove the rear hinge covers and roof lining panel and then while supporting the tailgate, lever the rods from their anchor brackets. Use a piece of tubing as a lever and remove the yellow painted rod first. Installation is a reversal of removal, making sure that the yellow painted rod is fitted last.

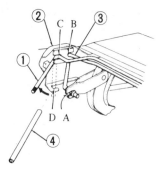

Fig. 12.56 Removing wagon tailgate torsion rods

1 Yellow painted torsion rod
2 Hinge
3 Right-hand torsion rod
4 Tubing used as lever
A/B and C/D Anchor brackets

21 Centre console - removal and refitting

1 The removal and refitting of this assembly is referred to in earlier Chapters as a preliminary operation in order to gain access to the gearshift or spped selector mechanism.
2 The console is secured by self-tapping screws and once these are removed, and the shift control lever knob detached, the assembly can be withdrawn.
3 On vehicles equipped with automatic transmission, the lead to the speed selector indicator lamp must be disconnected.
4 Refitting is a reversal of removal.

22 Heater - general description

The heater/ventilator unit is located at the base of the instrument panel forward of the centre console. When the car is in motion, air enters the intake grille just below the windscreen and passes through the heater matrix which is heated by coolant from the engine cooling system.

When the car is stationary, a multi-speed booster fan can be switched on to suck air into the unit. Demister hoses are fitted behind the instrument panel leading to nozzles which keep the screen free from mist or frost. Control levers are fitted to the panel just above the centre console and provide any desired combination of air direction and temperature.

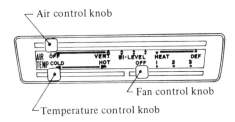

Fig. 12.59 Heater control panel

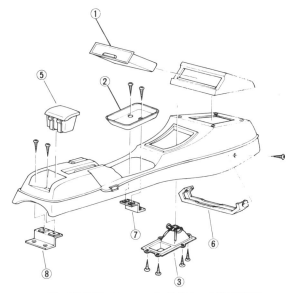

Fig. 12.57 Centre console (140J and 160J SSS)

1 Front compartment
2 Centre blanking plate
3 Gearshift control flexible boot
5 Ashtray
6, 7 and 8 Mounting brackets

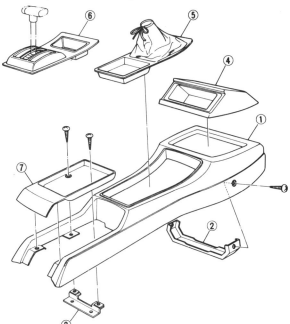

Fig. 12.58 Centre console (710 series)

1 Console   5 Gearshift lever flexible boot
2 Front bracket   6 Speed selector lever indicator assembly
3 Rear bracket   7 Rear blanking plate
4 Front tidy

23 Heater matrix - removal and refitting

1 The heater matrix can be removed independently of the main assembly.
2 Drain the engine coolant and retain it for further use.
3 From the right-hand side of the heater, disconnect the heater hoses from the matrix. Prepare to catch a small quantity of coolant which may be released and damage the carpet. Remove the centre console (Section 21).
4 Remove the matrix retaining clamps.
5 Remove the two clips and four screws which secure the heater grille and withdraw the grille.
6 Release the clip from the demister flap valve cable.
7 Pull the matrix forward and remove it.
8 A leaking matrix is best repaired by professionals or exchanged for a reconditioned unit. A blocked matrix can sometimes be cleared by reverse flushing it with a cold water hose. The use of cleansing compounds is seldom satisfactory as it often releases scale and deposits it elsewhere, blocking the fine tubes of the matrix. Where experience with the heater has shown that the desired temperature cannot be maintained, suspect the engine thermostat or a partially blocked matrix.
9 Refitting and reassembly are reversals of removal.

24 Heater unit - removal and installation

1 Disconnect the lead from the battery negative terminal.
2 Drain the cooling system while the heater controls are in the 'HOT' position.
3 Disconnect the heater hoses from the heater.
4 Working within the vehicle interior, remove the centre console (Section 21).
5 Disconnect the air intake duct and the two demister ducts from the heater unit.
6 Disconnect the heater leads at the connector plugs.
7 Release the snap-on type cable clamps and disconnect the control cables from the air intake housing.
8 Unscrew and remove the three heater unit mounting bolts and withdraw the heater.
9 Installation is a reversal of removal.

25 Heater - dismantling and reassembly

1 In order to renew worn, damaged or faulty components, dismantle the unit in the following sequence.
2 Pull the knobs from the heater control levers.
3 Remove the three screws which secure the centre ventilator to the heater, then disconnect the illumination lamp lead connectors.
4 Withdraw the centre ventilator.
5 Release the four control cable clamps and then disconnect the cables from the air intake flap, the air mixing flap valve, the demister deflector flap valve and the air outlet deflector flap valve.
6 Disconnect the fan switch lead from the main heater wiring harness.

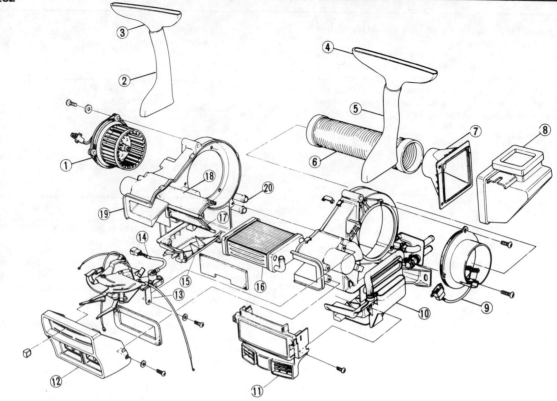

Fig. 12.60 Exploded view of the heater unit

1 Fan and motor	7 Air intake duct
2 Demister duct	8 Air intake housing
3 and 4 demister nozzles	9 Resistor
5 Demister duct	10 Heater housing (section)
6 Air intake hose	11 Grille

12 Centre ventilator	17 Air mixing flap
13 Control panel	18 Air outlet deflector
14 Fan switch	19 Heater housing (section)
15 Demister flap valve	20 Water valve
16 Matrix	

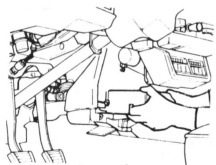

Fig. 12.61 Removing the heater matrix

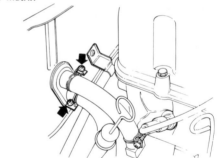

Fig. 12.62 Heater hose connections within the engine compartment

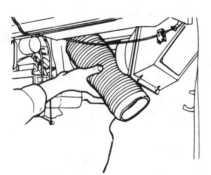

Fig. 12.63 Removing heater air intake duct hose

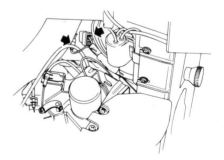

Fig. 12.64 Heater lead connectors

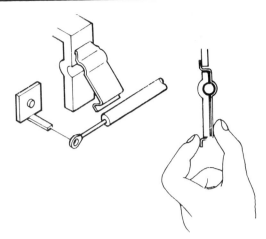

Fig. 12.65 Heater control cable clamp

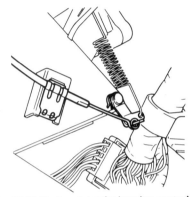

Fig. 12.66 Heater air intake housing control cable

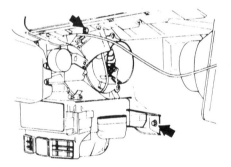

Fig. 12.67 Heater unit securing bolts

the demister flap lever and then clamp the cable without altering the position of the components.

15 Connect the cable to the lever on the air outlet deflector flap and clamp the cable.

16 Move the 'TEMP' lever to the extreme left and then connect the cable to the air mixing flap and clamp the cable. Check all controls for smooth operation over their complete range of travel.

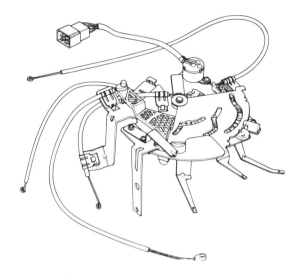

Fig. 12.68 Heater control panel

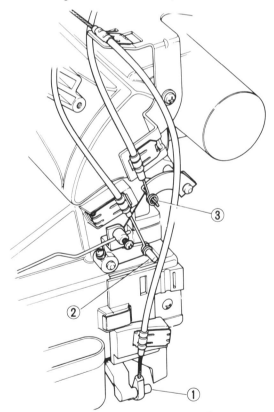

Fig. 12.69 Heater control cable connections

1 Demister flap valve lever
2 Air deflector flap valve lever (also combines heater water valve control)
3 Air mixing flap valve lever

7   Remove the screws which secure the heater control panel to the heater unit and remove the panel.

8   Remove the air intake housing (one screw).

9   Remove the water control valve (two screws).

10 Remove the air intake duct (three screws) and then withdraw the resistor (two screws).

11 The fan and motor can be withdrawn from the heater box after removing the three securing screws.

12 Reassembly is a reversal of dismantling but the control cables must be set and adjusted in the following way.

13 Move 'AIR' lever to 'OFF', connect cable end to air intake flap lever and then clamp the cable without altering the position of the components.

14 Now move the 'AIR' lever to 'DEF', connect the cable end to

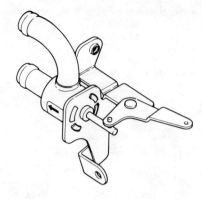

Fig. 12.70 The heater water control valve

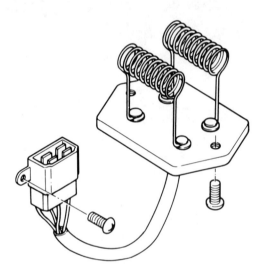

Fig. 12.71 The heater resistor

26 Air conditioning system - description and maintenance

1   An air conditioning system is optionally available on 710 series models. The system incorporates a heater and refrigeration unit with blower assembly.

2   The refrigeration section comprises an evaporator mounted to the rear and below the instrument panel a belt-driven compressor installed in the engine compartment and a condenser mounted just in front of the radiator.

3   Due to the nature of the refrigeration gases employed in the system, no servicing can be undertaken by the home mechanic other than a few maintenance tasks which are described later in this Section. Where any part of the refrigeration circuit must be disconnected to facilitate other repair work, then the system must be discharged (and later re-charged) by professional refrigeration engineers having the necessary equipment.

4   Maintenance tasks which can be carried out safely include checking of the compressor driving belt tension. There should be a total deflection of ½ in. (12.7 mm) of the driving belt at a point midway between the compressor pulley and the idler pulley. The tension is adjusted by moving the position of the idler pulley (see Chapter 1, Section 47).

5   Examine all the hose connections of the system. Any trace of oil at these points indicates leakage of refrigerant and the joint connections should be tightened.

6   Where the car is seldom used, the engine must be run at approximately 1500 rev/min at least once a month to keep the compressor and the system generally in good working order.

7   If it is suspected that the amount of refrigerant in the system is incorrect, start the engine and hold it at a steady speed of 1500 rev/min. Set the 'AIR' lever in the 'A/C' position and switch on the blower to maximum speed. Check the sight glass after an interval of about five minutes. The sight glass is located on the receiver drier. If a continuous stream of bubbles or mist is observed, then there is very little refrigerant left in the system. Where some bubbles are seen at intervals of 1 or 2 seconds then there is insufficient refrigerant in the system. The system is correctly charged when conditions within the sight glass are almost transparent with a few bubbles appearing if the engine speed is raised or lowered. If the system required recharging, this must be carried out professionally.

8   Periodically, draw the air filter (installed between the evaporator and air intake housing) down and clean it either with a soft brush or by careful washing in water to which detergent has been added.9

9   Refer to Chapter 3, for details of adjusting the fast idle actuator which is fitted to all vehicles equipped with an air conditioning system.

Fig. 12.72 Removing the heater fan/motor assembly

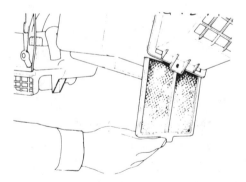

Fig. 12.74 Removing the air conditioning system filter for cleaning

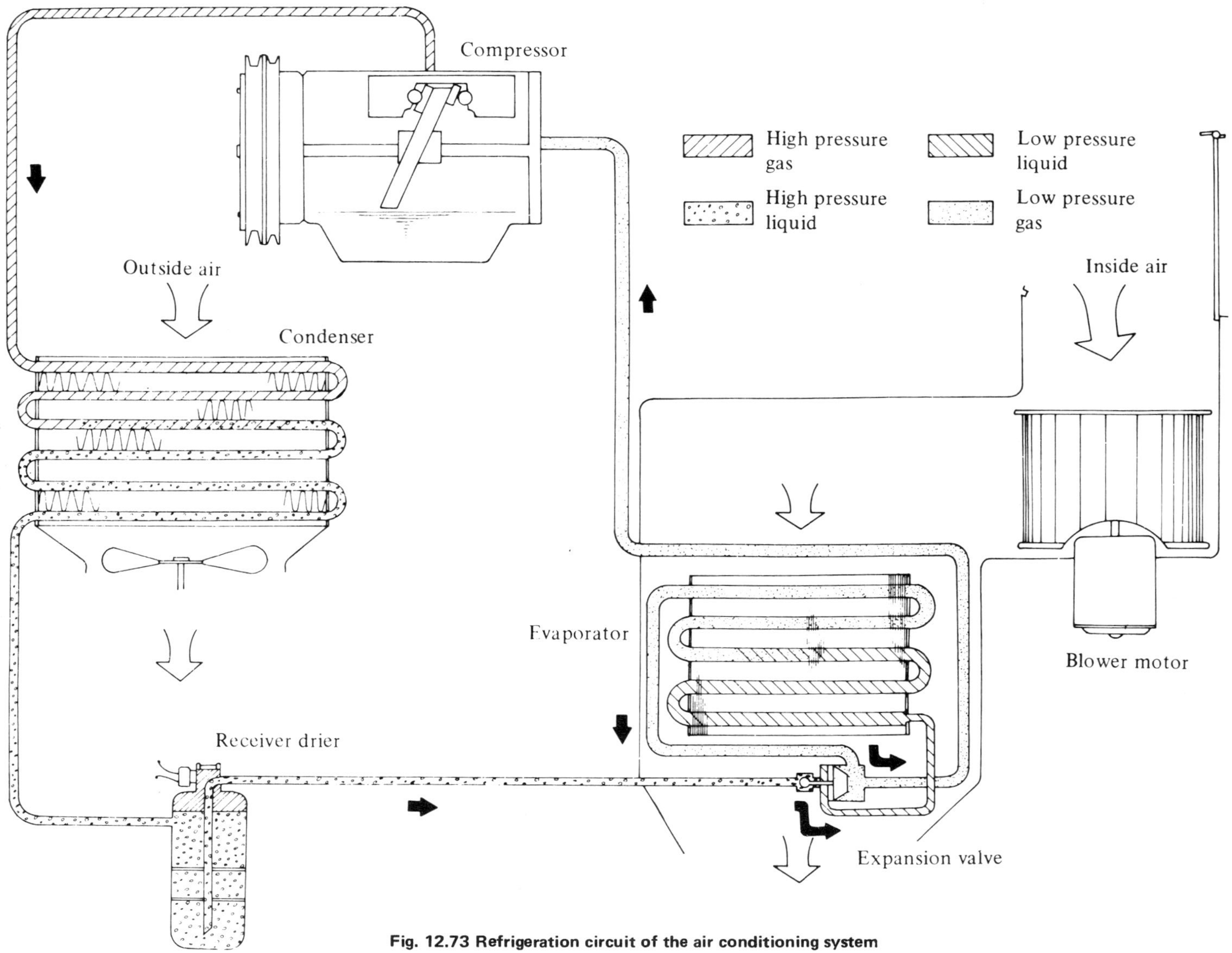

Inside air

Low pressure
liquid

Low pressure
gas

High pressure
gas

High pressure
liquid

Blower motor

Expansion valve

Evaporator

Compressor

Condenser

Outside air

Receiver drier

Fig. 12.73 Refrigeration circuit of the air conditioning system

1977 140J/160J Saloon (UK Specification)

Chapter 13 Supplement

Contents

A Introduction

The 140J and 160J SSS Coupe have now been introduced in Mk 2 versions. From April 1976 the 160J SSS Coupe is fitted with a five speed gearbox. Since the introduction of the Mk2 versions, a 160J Saloon has been introduced, which is identical to the 140J Mk 2 but is fitted with a single carburettor 1595 cc (97.3 cu in) engine. Components and procedures described in this Supplement are intended to cover any not already detailed in the previous Chapters. Any component or procedure, not described in this Supplement, is covered fully in the relevant Chapter elsewhere in this manual.

The 710 Series continued virtually unchanged during this period except for small mechanical and trim changes which are explained where necessary in the Supplement.

B Specifications

The specifications listed in this Section are revised or supplementry to those given at the beginning of each Chapter of this manual. The original specifications apply, unless alternative figures are quoted.

Fuel system

Carburettor (710 Models, 1976)

	Primary	Secondary
Type ... ... Downdraught, dual barrel, fixed jet		
Identification number		
Non-Californian Models		
Manual transmission ... ... DCH 340-43A		
Automatic transmission ... ... DCH 340-44A		
Californian models		
Manual transmission ... ... DCH 340-41A		
Automatic transmission ... ... DCH 340-42B		
Diameter of outlet	1.181 in (30.0 mm)	1.339 in (34.0 mm)
Diameter of venturi	0.945 in (24.0 mm)	1.220 in (31.0 mm)
Main jet		
DCH 340-43A	99	160
DCH 340-44A	99	160
DCH 340-41A	101	160
DCH 340-42B	101	160
Main air bleed	70	60
Slow jet		
DCH 340-43A	48	100
DCH 340-44A	48	100
DCH 340-41A	48	80
DCH 340-42B	48	80
Power valve		
DCH 340-43A	43	
DCH 340-44A	43	
DCH 340-41A	40	
DCH 340-42B	40	

Idling speed
Manual transmission ... ...   750 rpm
Automatic transmission ... ...   650 rpm (in 'D')

CO level 2%

Carburettor (710 Models, 1977 onwards)
Type ... ...   Downdraught, dual barrel, fixed jet
Identification number
Non-Californian or Canadian models
Manual transmission ... ...   DCH 340-51A
Automatic transmission ... ...   DCH 340-52A
Californian models
Manual transmission ... ...   DCH 340-41B
Automatic transmission ... ...   DCH 340-42C
Canadian models
Manual transmission ... ...   DCH 340-43B
Automatic transmission ... ...   DCH 340-44B

	Primary	Secondary
Diameter of outlet	1.18 in (30.0 mm)	1.34 in (34.0 mm)
Diameter of venturi	0.91 in (23.0 mm)	1.18 in (30.0 mm)
Diameter of venturi (Canada and California)	0.94 in (24.0 mm)	1.22 in (31.0 mm)

Main jet
DCH 340-51A	105	165
DCH 340-52A	105	165
DCH 340-41B	101	160
DCH 340-42C	101	160
DCH 340-43B	99	160
DCH 340-44B	99	160
Main air bleed	60	60
Main air bleed (Canada and California)	70	60

Slow jet
DCH 340-51A	48	100
DCH 340-52A	48	100
DCH 340-41B	48	80
DCH 340-42C	48	80
DCH 340-43B	48	100
DCH 340-44B	48	100

Power valve
DCH 340-51A   43
DCH 340-52A   43
DCH 340-41B   40
DCH 340-42C   40
DCH 340-43B   43
DCH 340-44B   43

Idling speed
DCH 340-51A ... ...   600 rpm
DCH 340-52A ... ...   600 rpm (in 'D')
DCH 340-41B ... ...   600 rpm
DCH 340-42C ... ...   600 rpm (in 'D')
DCH 340-43B ... ...   750 rpm
DCH 340-44B ... ...   650 rpm (in 'D')

Spark plugs

Type
L20B (1976 models)
Californian ... ...   BP6ES-11 or L45-PW-11
Non-Californian ... ...   BP6ES or L45PW
L20B (1977 models)
USA ... ...   BP6ES-11 or L45-PW-11
Canada BPR6ES

Spark plug gap
L20B (1976 models)
Californian ... ...   0.039 - 0.043 in (1.0 - 1.1 mm)
Non-Californian ... ...   0.031 - 0.035 in (0.8 - 0.9 mm)

L20B (1977 models)
USA ... ...   0.039 - 0.043 in (1.0 - 1.1 mm)
Canada ... ...   0.031 - 0.035 in (0.8 - 0.9 mm)

Transmission (5 Speed gearbox)

Gearbox type	FS5 W63A - five forward speeds and one reverse
Synchromesh	Warner type on all forward speeds
Application	160 J SSS Coupe (1976 onwards)

Gear ratios

1st	3.382 : 1
2nd	2.013 : 1
3rd	1.312 : 1
4th	1.000 : 1
5th	0.854 : 1
Reverse	3.570 : 1

Speedometer drive ratio	17/5
Final drive ratio	4.111

Endfloat

1st gear	0.0126 - 0.0165 in (0.32 - 0.42 mm)
2nd gear	0.0087 - 0.0126 in (0.22 - 0.32 mm)
3rd gear	0.0020 - 0.0059 in (0.05 - 0.15 mm)
5th gear	0.0020 - 0.0059 in (0.05 - 0.15 mm)
Reverse idler	0.0059 - 0.0157 in (0.15 - 0.40 mm)

Backlash (all gears)	0.0020 - 0.0079 in (0.05 - 0.20 mm)
Baulk ring to gear cone clearance	0.047 - 0.062 in (1.2 - 1.6 mm)
Oil capacity	3 Imp pts, 3 5/8 US pts, 1.7 litres

Torque wrench settings	lbf ft	kgf m
Clutch bellhousing to engine bolts	35	4.8
Clutch operating cylinder bolts	22	3.0
Crossmember to bodyframe bolts	20	2.8
Mainshaft nut	120	16.6
Centre bracket bolts	35	4.8
Filler plug	25	3.5
Drain plug	25	3.5

Braking system

Disc brakes

Diameter of disc	9.65 in (245 mm)
Pad dimensions	1.622 x 0.394 x 2.417 in (41.2 x 10 x 61.4 mm)
Minimum pad lining material thickness	0.080 in (2 mm)
Disc caliper internal diameter	2.012 in (51.10 mm)

Suspension and steering

Steering ratio (Mk 2 models)	16.5 : 1

Steering angle (lock)

Inner wheel (710 series)	32° to 33°
Outer wheel (710 series)	29° 30' to 31° 30'

Number of turns from lock to lock (Mk 2 models)	3.6

Steering angles (vehicle unladen)

	Camber	Castor	Steering axis inclination	Toe-in
140J and 160J	50' - 2° 20'	55' - 2° 25'	6° 40'	0.118 - 0.197 in (3 - 5 mm)
710 series	1° 15' - 2° 45'	1° 05' - 2° 35'	6° 15'	0.16 - 0.24 in (4 - 6 mm)

C Carburation and exhaust emission control

1 Air cleaner

The air cleaner fitted to certain USA models has been modified, and has more hoses to compensate for the addition of a Combined Air Control (CAC) valve.

For disassembly and servicing refer to Chapter 3, Section 3.

2 Emission control systems

Air injection system

The air injection system is basically as described in Chapter 3, Section 25, but the Emergency Air Relief (EAR) valve, and the air pump relief valve, have been replaced on some USA models, by a Combined Air Control (CAC) valve. The CAC valve performs the functions of both the EAR valve, and the air pump relief valve.

1 To remove the CAC valve, undo the relevant hose clips and pull off the hoses. Remove the two retaining screws and lift the unit clear.

2 Refitting is the reverse of the removal procedure.

3 The CAC valve is of the non-repairable type, and to inspect the valve involves the use of a vacuum pump. If the valve is suspect it is best to have your Datsun agent inspect it.

Exhaust Gas Recirculation (EGR) System

4 All 1977 models are now fitted with a BPT valve which monitors the exhaust pressure activating the EGR control valve. A vacuum delay valve which prevents rapid vacuum pressure drop in the EGR control line is also fitted.

5 To remove the BPT valve, remove the two vacuum tubes, and remove the two screws which secure the valve to the bracket.

6 After the valve has been removed, the control tube can be disconnected.

7 To inspect the BPT valve involves the use of a water gauge, so it is wise to entrust this work to your Datsun agent.

8 The vacuum delay valve is positioned between the BPT valve and the thermal vacuum valve. To remove this valve simply pull it from its hoses. When refitting the vacuum delay valve, ensure that the brown coloured face is connected to the thermal vacuum valve side.

9 Check the vacuum delay valve by blowing air through it from the EGR control valve side. A good flow of air indicates a serviceable valve. Blowing air through the unit from the opposite port should result in much more resistance. If it is thought that no air is passing through the valve, dip the port into a receptacle filled with water, and look for air bubbles.

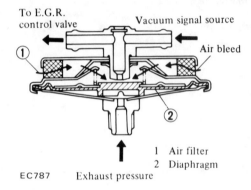

Fig. 13.2. Cross-sectional view of a BPT valve

Fig. 13.1. Air cleaner (710 series type 1977)

1   Air inlet
2   Vacuum capsule
3   Air control valve
4   Hot air inlet
5   Air hose for AIS system
     From CAC valve - California models
     From air control valve - non-California models
6   Air relief valve for air pump
     (Non-California models)
7   Air hoses for altitude compensator
     (California models)
8   Vacuum pipe from intake manifold
9   Vacuum pipe from carbon canister
10 Air inlet for AB valve
11 Filter
12 Hose
13 Idle compensator
14 Altitude compensator (California models)
15 Air hose for TCS system - M/T only
     (From vacuum switching valve)
16 Temperature sensor assembly
17 Air hole for BCDD
     (Non-California models)

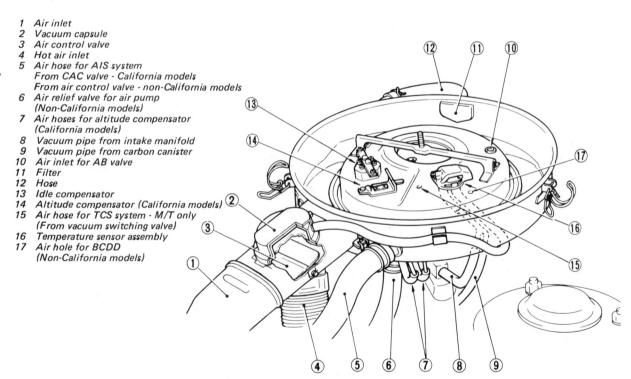

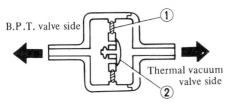

Fig. 13.3. Cross-sectional view of a vacuum delay valve

1   Disc   2   Umbrella valve

Fig. 13.4. Disconnecting control tube (Do not use a spanner on nut A)

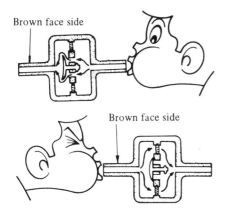

Fig. 13.5. Checking a vacuum delay valve

D Transmission (5-speed gearbox)

1   General description

The gearbox fitted to the 160J SSS Coupe from 1976 onwards, has five forward speeds and one reverse, with synchromesh on all forward gears. The characteristics of this unit are generally the same as those described in Chapter 6 of this manual, comprising three main transmission case parts, namely the transmission case with clutch bellhousing, an adaptor plate to which all gears and shafts are fitted, and a rear extension cover. There is no adaptor plate on the four-speed gearbox.

Fig. 13.6. Sectional view of 5-speed gearbox

*1   Input shaft
2   Front cover
3   Baulk ring
4   Synchro sleeve
5   Shift key
6   Synchronizer hub
7   5th gear
8   3rd gear
9   Adaptor plate
10 2nd gear
11 Bearing retainer
12 1st gear
13 Reverse gear
14 Selector fork
15 Selector rod
16 Rear extension
17 Mainshaft
18 Speedometer drive gear
19 Reverse idler shaft
20 Reverse idler gear
21 1st counter gear
22 Counter gear
23 Counter gear bearing shim
24 Transmission case*

Torque wrench settings:
A   101 to 123 lbf ft (14 to 17 kgf m)
B   18 to 25 lbf ft (2.5 to 3.5 kgf m)
C   9.4 to 13 lbf ft (1.3 to 1.8 kgf m)

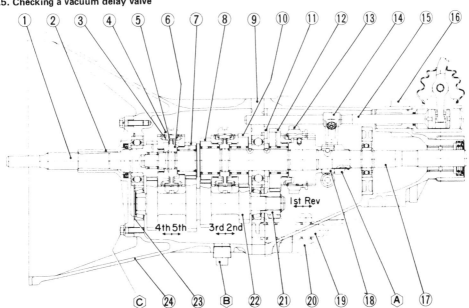

2 Gearbox - removal and refitting

1 Preferably place the vehicle over an inspection pit, or if a pit is not available, raise the vehicle and support it securely on axle stands. Ensure that enough height is gained to allow the bellhousing to pass under the lowest point of the bodyframe when removing the gearbox unit.

2 Disconnect the lead from the battery negative terminal.

3 Place a suitable container under the gearbox, and drain the oil into it.

4 Where applicable, disconnect the sensor wiring harness from the catalytic converter and remove the harness shield.

5 From inside the vehicle, remove the centre console.

6 Place the gear lever in the neutral position, remove the E-clip, push out the pin, and remove the gear lever.

7 Where applicable, remove the shield from the lower side of the catalytic converter, and disconnect the exhaust pipe from the converter.

8 On all other models, disconnect the exhaust downpipe from the exhaust manifold, and from the rest of the exhaust system.

9 Disconnect the accelerator linkage between the accelerator pedal and the carburettor.

10 Remove the wires from the reverse lamp switch.

11 Disconnect the speedometer drive cable.

12 Unbolt the clutch operating cylinder from the clutch bellhousing and tie it up out of the way. There is no need to disconnect the hydraulic system, but ensure that the clutch pedal is not depressed after removing the operating cylinder as this will result in the operating piston coming out of its cylinder, causing a loss of hydraulic fluid.

13 Disconnect the propeller shaft and remove it, as described in Chapter 7.

14 Support the engine under the sump by using a suitable jack and a wooden insulating block, to prevent any damage to the sump.

15 Remove the rear mounting from the transmission and body frame.

16 Disconnect the wires to the starter motor, unbolt it and remove it from the vehicle.

17 Unbolt and remove the two rear reinforcement plates.

18 Support the gearbox unit with a trolley jack.

19 Unscrew and remove the bolts which secure the bellhousing to the engine.

20 Carefully lower the jack supporting the gearbox until the gearbox can be withdrawn from the engine. Here it is wise to seek assistance, as it is most important that the weight of the gearbox does not hang on the input shaft, whilst the latter is still engaged with the engine, or damage to the input shaft could result.

21 Refitting is a reversal of the removal sequence, but apply a smear of high melting point grease to the splines of the input shaft.

22 When refitment is complete, check the clutch pedal adjustment (Chapter 5).

23 Refill the gearbox with the correct grade and quantity of oil.

3 Gearbox - dismantling into major assemblies

1 Before commencing a major stripdown of the gearbox assembly it is fair to point out to the owner that some special tools will be needed. It is best to ensure that these tools can be acquired from your local Datsun dealer, either on a loan or hire basis. Bearing in mind that such tools are expensive to manufacture, your Datsun dealer may not be prepared to do this. Where special tools are required the text will quote the Datsun tool number. If the special tools are not available, it is best to entrust the work to your local Datsun dealer.

2 Before work commences, thoroughly clean all external surfaces of the unit with a suitable cleaning agent.

3 Drain the oil from the gearbox (if this was not carried out prior to removal).

4 Remove the dust excluding boot from the clutch bellhousing,

then extract the clutch withdrawal lever and release bearing.

5 Unbolt and remove the reverse lamp switch.

6 Remove the speedometer pinion and housing assembly by taking off the lock plate.

7 Unbolt and remove the front cover.

8 Remove the countershaft front bearing shim.

9 Using circlip pliers, remove the input shaft bearing circlip.

10 Unbolt and remove the reverse select return plug, spring and plunger from the rear extension.

11 Remove the securing bolts from around the rear extension. To remove the rear extension use a standard puller and extract the rear extension backwards, away from the bellhousing.

12 Using a soft faced hammer, separate the transmission case from the adaptor plate.

13 Mount the adaptor plate and gear assembly in a suitable vice. It is preferable to make up a holding plate, which will lift the assembly clear of the vice jaws, but providing the adaptor plate is held firmly in protected jaws (two pieces of suitably sized wood between the vice jaws and the adaptor plate), work can now commence on this assembly.

14 Drive out the retaining pins from each selector rod with a suitably sized drift.

15 Unbolt and remove the three detent ball plugs located in the side of the adaptor plate. Lightly tap the selector rods out of the adaptor plate. Ensure that the three balls and two interlock plungers are not lost in this operation. With the selector rods removed, it is likely that the shift forks will fall out of their synchro sleeves. Try to prevent this happening, in case of damage occurring to the shift forks.

16 Lift out the reverse idler gear together with the shaft.

17 At this stage check all the gears for backlash and endfloat. Note any dimensions that are outside the specifications, for correction when reassembly commences. With a dial test indicator check that the specified backlash is evident. With feeler gauges check all gear endfloats. Specifications for both backlash and endfloat are given at the beginning of this Supplement under gearbox specifications.

18 Remove the circlip from the mainshaft end bearing, and using bearing puller number ST 22460001 draw out the bearing. Remove the circlip that is behind the mainshaft end bearing.

19 Engage 1st and 2nd gears to prevent the mainshaft from turning, and carefully chip out the caulking around the mainshaft nut.

20 Undo and remove the mainshaft nut, take out the speedometer drive gear, the synchrohub with reverse gear and 1st gear together with the needle bearing. Remove the thrust washer. Take great care not to lose the steel ball retaining the speedometer drive gear and the thrust washer.

21 Remove the circlip from the rear end of the 1st counter gear, take off the spacer, and using gear puller number ST 22480000 draw out the 1st counter gear.

22 Using mainshaft puller number ST 22471000 draw out the mainshaft about 0.394 in (10 mm), then lift off the input shaft gear assembly and the counter gear assembly.

23 Pull the mainshaft out of the adaptor plate, leaving the mainshaft bearing in the adaptor plate. Hold the mainshaft in the vertical plane to ensure that the 2nd gear and needle bearing do not fall off of the mainshaft.

24 Remove the thrust washer, steel ball, 2nd gear and needle bearing. Place the steel ball and thrust washer in a safe place, to prevent them from getting lost!

25 With the aid of bearing puller number ST 30031000, press out the 2nd gear sleeve together with the 3rd gear and 2nd and 3rd speed synchronizer.

26 Remove the circlip on the front end of the mainshaft. Remove 4th and 5th speed synchronizer and 5th gear.

27 Now that all the gears and bearings have been removed from the mainshaft, thoroughly wash all the components in a suitable cleaning agent. Check all bearings for wear and roughness when turned. Inspect the gears for cracks, chips and excessive wear. The shaft should be free from cracks and the spline should be undamaged. Check for excessive wear and bending.

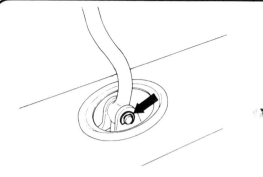

Fig. 13.7. Removing gearshift lever

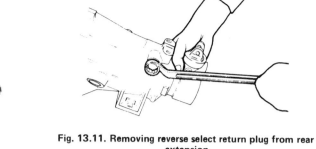

Fig. 13.11. Removing reverse select return plug from rear extension

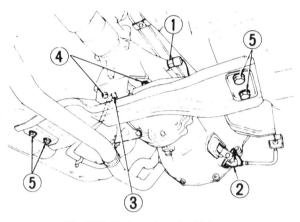

Fig. 13.8. Bottom view of vehicle

1 Reversing lamp switch
2 Clutch operating cylinder
3 Speedometer cable
4 Securing bolts
5 Crossmember mounting bolts

Fig. 13.12. Extracting rear extension with a standard puller

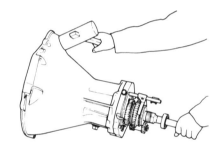

Fig. 13.13. Separating transmission case from adaptor plate

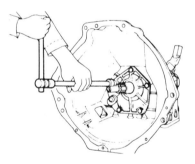

Fig. 13.9. Unbolting gearbox front cover

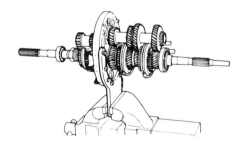

Fig. 13.14. Holding adaptor plate and gear assembly in a vice

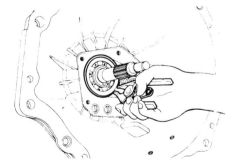

Fig. 13.10. Removing input shaft bearing circlip

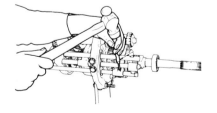

Fig. 13.15. Driving out selector rod retaining pins

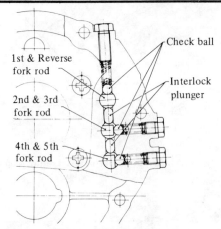

Check ball

1st & Reverse fork rod

Interlock plunger

2nd & 3rd fork rod

4th & 5th fork rod

Fig. 13.16. Sectional view of adaptor plate showing position of selector rods (fork rods), detent balls (check balls) and interlock plungers

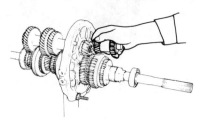

Fig. 13.17. Lifting out reverse idler gear

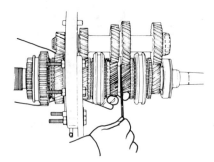

Fig. 13.18. Checking gear endfloat

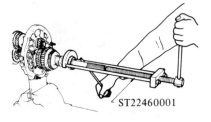

ST22460001

Fig. 13.19. Using puller number ST 22460001 to remove mainshaft end bearing

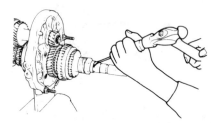

Fig. 13.20. Removing caulking around mainshaft nut

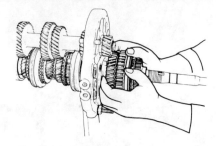

Fig. 13.21. Removing reverse and 1st gear

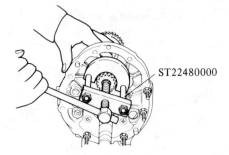

ST22480000

Fig. 13.22. Using gear puller number ST 22480000 to remove 1st counter gear

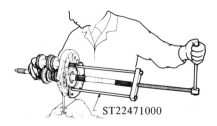

ST22471000

Fig. 13.23. Removing mainshaft gear using gear puller number ST 22471000

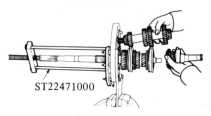

ST22471000

Fig. 13.24. Lifting off counter gear and input shaft gear assemblies

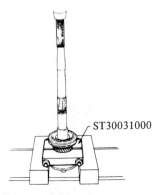

ST30031000

Fig. 13.25. Pressing out the 2nd gear sleeve, 3rd gear and 2nd and 3rd speed synchronizer

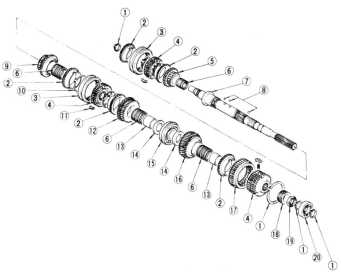

Fig. 13.27. Exploded view of mainshaft assembly

1	Circlip	6	Needle bearing	11	Shifting key
2	Baulk ring	7	Mainshaft	12	2nd speed gear
3	Coupling sleeve	8	Steel ball	13	Sleeve
4	Synchronizer hub	9	3rd speed gear	14	Thrust washer
5	5th speed gear	10	Spread spring	15	Mainshaft bearing

16	1st speed gear
17	Reverse gear
18	Speedometer drive gear
19	Nut
20	Mainshaft end bearing

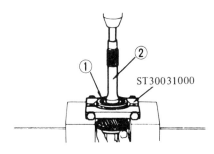

Fig. 13.26. Removing circlip to free synchronizer and 5th gear

4 Input shaft drive gear - servicing

1   Remove the circlip and the spacer.

2   Using bearing puller number ST 30031000, or suitable sizes of metal tubing, press out the input shaft drive bearing. Hold the gear while the shaft is being pressed out, to ensure that the gear is not dropped onto the floor.

3   Check the input shaft bearing for roughness when turned, and the gear for damage. If there is any doubt regarding the condition of the components, it is best to renew them.

4   To assemble, reverse the disassembly procedure. It is recommended that the circlip is renewed. There is bound to be wear on a circlip after many thousands of miles. It is also wise to purchase some circlips with oversize thicknesses as it may be necessary to use one of these to eliminate any end play. The oversize circlips available are:

0.0587 to 0.0610 in (1.49 to 1.55 mm)
0.0614 to 0.0638 in (1.56 to 1.62 mm)
0.0638 to 0.0661 in (1.62 to 1.68 mm)
0.0661 to 0.0685 in (1.68 to 1.74 mm)
0.0685 to 0.0709 in (1.74 to 1.80 mm)
0.0709 to 0.0732 in (1.80 to 1.86 mm)
0.0732 to 0.0756 in (1.86 to 1.92 mm).

5 Counter gear - servicing

1   With the aid of bearing puller number ST 22730000 and adaptor number ST 22471040, press out the counter gear front bearing.

2   Invert the assembly, and using the bearing puller mentioned in the preceding paragraph, press out the rear bearing. Take care not to drop the counter gear.

3   Thoroughly clean the bearings and check for rough running and wear. Inspect the gear for any chips, cracks or wear. Check the shaft for bending, cracks, or worn bearing surfaces.

4   Reassembly is the reverse of disassembly.

Fig. 13.28. Removing input shaft bearing

1   Input shaft bearing   2   Input shaft drive gear

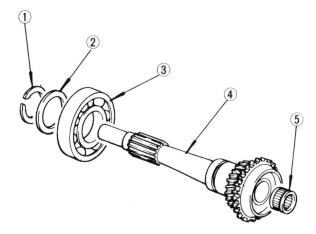

Fig. 13.29. Exploded view of input shaft gear assembly

1	Circlip	4	Input shaft drive gear
2	Spacer	5	Pilot bearing
3	Input shaft bearing		

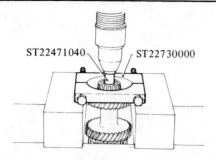

Fig. 13.30. Pressing out counter gear front bearing

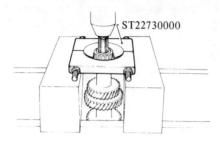

Fig. 13.31. Pressing out counter gear rear bearing

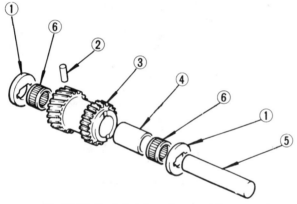

Fig. 13.32. Exploded view of reverse idler gear

1   Thrust washer   4   Needle bearing spacer
2   Retaining pin   5   Reverse idler shaft
3   Reverse idler gear   6   Needle bearing

---

6   Synchronizer hubs - servicing

Refer to Chapter 6, Section 4, mainshaft servicing.

---

7   Adaptor plate - servicing

1   Remove the bearing retainer by undoing the four screws, a sharp tap on the end of the screwdriver will help here, as the four screws are secured with a locking compound.
2   Press out the mainshaft bearing from the rear extension side.
3   To remove the outer race of the counter gear shaft rear bearing, use a brass drift on the race side surface and tap it out with a hammer.
4   Assemble in the reverse of disassembly. Torque the bearing retainer screws to 6 to 10 lbf ft (0.8 to 1.3 kgf m). With a pointed punch stake each screw in two places.

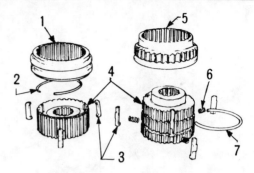

Fig. 13.33. Components of synchro. hub

1   Sleeve   5   Reverse gear
2   Spring   6   Synchro spring
3   Shift key   7   Ring
4   Hub

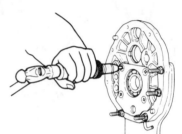

Fig. 13.34. Removing bearing retainer screws from adaptor plate

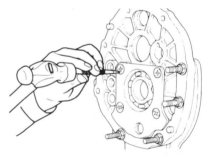

Fig. 13.35. Locking bearing retainer screws (adaptor plate)

---

8   Rear extension - servicing

1   Remove the screw and locating pin from the top side of the rear extension.
2   Undo and tap out the cotter pin from the shift rod lever. The shift rod and lever can now be removed.
3   Inspect the shift rod for undue wear or damage. Check the casing for any cracks, which could cause an oil loss. If the rear extension bush is cracked or worn the rear extension housing will have to be renewed.
4   Reassembly is the reverse of removal but it is usual to renew the oil seal in the rear of the casing. Apply multi-purpose grease to the O-ring and plunger grooves in the shift rod.

---

9   Mainshaft - reassembly

1   Before commencing reassembly ensure that all components are clean. It is advisable to read this Section through, to establish the correct sequence of gears and bearings to be assembled, and to lay them out in respective order on a clean sheet of paper.

2   Position the 5th gear needle bearing, 5th speed gear, baulk ring, together with 4th and 5th speed synchronizer to the front of the mainshaft.

3   To retain the components described in the preceding paragraph, fit a circlip to the circlip groove. Choose a circlip that will eliminate excessive endplay, from the following list of sizes.

  0.0551 to 0.0571 in (1.40 to 1.45 mm)
  0.0571 to 0.0591 in (1.45 to 1.50 mm)
  0.0591 to 0.0610 in (1.50 to 1.55 mm)
  0.0610 to 0.0630 in (1.55 to 1.60 mm)
  0.0630 to 0.0650 in (1.60 to 1.65 mm)

4   Fit the 3rd gear needle roller bearing, 3rd gear, 3rd gear baulk ring, 2nd and 3rd speed synchronizer. Using a suitable base, press on the 2nd gear sleeve and mainshaft bearing thrust washer. Fit the 2nd gear baulk ring, needle bearing, 2nd gear, steel ball and the thin thrust washer. Ensure that the 2nd and 3rd speed synchronizer is fitted facing the correct direction.

Fig. 13.39. Fitting the mainshaft circlip

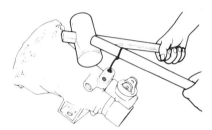

Fig. 13.36. Removing locating pin from rear extension

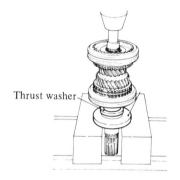

Thrust washer

Fig. 13.40. Assembling 2nd gear sleeve

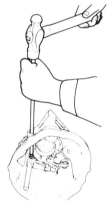

Fig. 13.37. Pushing out cotter pin from shift lever

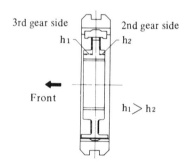

3rd gear side   2nd gear side
      h_1 h_2

Front $h_1 > h_2$

Fig. 13.41. 1st/2nd synchro. unit. Refitment diagram

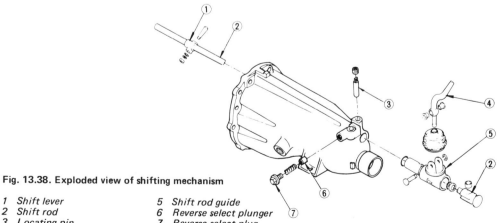

Fig. 13.38. Exploded view of shifting mechanism

1   Shift lever   5   Shift rod guide
2   Shift rod   6   Reverse select plunger
3   Locating pin   7   Reverse select plug
4   Control lever

10 Shafts to adaptor plate - reassembly

1   Place the adaptor plate into a vice, preferably on a holding plate. Slide the mainshaft through the mainshaft bearing in the adaptor plate, screw on the mainshaft nut finger tight.

2   Pull the mainshaft assembly into the adaptor plate, with the aid of the mainshaft puller, number ST 22471000, the bearing puller, number ST 22460001, and the adaptor, number ST 22471040. Leave a clearance of 0.394 in (10 mm) between the thrust washer and the bearing.

3   Position the baulk ring on the coned surface of the input drive gear, and fit the pilot needle bearing to the mainshaft. Assemble the input drive gear assembly to the front of the mainshaft. Locate the countergear assembly into the adaptor plate, and let it rest along the mainshaft gear, locating into the mainshaft gears and the input drive gear.

4   Pull the mainshaft assembly into the adaptor plate together with the input drive gear assembly and the countergear assembly.

5   Using a drift, number ST 22360002, and the adaptor, number ST 22471040, press the 1st countergear onto the countershaft.

6   Place the spacer on the rear end of the 1st countergear and secure it with a new circlip.

7   Assemble the following parts to the rear of the mainshaft, in the order listed. Steel ball, thick thrust washer, 1st gear sleeve, needle bearing, 1st gear, 1st gear baulk ring, 1st synchronizer together with reverse gear, steel ball, speedometer drive gear and the mainshaft nut.

8   Engage 1st and 2nd gears together and tighten the mainshaft nut to 101 to 123 lbf ft (14 to 17 kgf m).

9   Using a pointed punch and a hammer, stake the mainshaft nut to the groove in the mainshaft.

10   With feeler gauges check that all the endfloats are within specifications.

11   Fit a 0.0473 in (1.1 mm) thick circlip to the front side of the mainshaft end bearing.

12   Using a suitable piece of tube, install the mainshaft end bearing by tapping it into position. Fit a suitable sized circlip to the rear side of the mainshaft bearing to eliminate endplay. Oversizes of circlip are available in the following sizes:

      0.0433 in (1.1 mm)
      0.0472 in (1.2 mm)
      0.0512 in (1.3 mm)
      0.0551 in (1.4 mm)

13   Fit the reverse idler gear assembly.

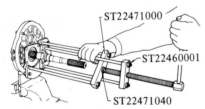

Fig. 13.42. Refitting the mainshaft to the adaptor plate

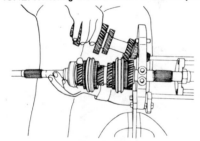

Fig. 13.43. Locating the input drive gear and counter gear assembly

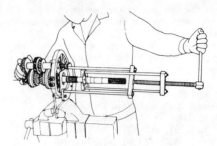

Fig. 13.44. Fitting the mainshaft, input shaft, and the counter gear assembly

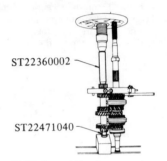

Fig. 13.45. Assembling 1st counter gear

Fig. 13.46. Tightening the mainshaft nut

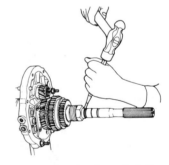

Fig. 13.47. Staking the mainshaft nut

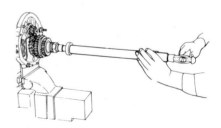

Fig. 13.48. Refitting the mainshaft end bearing

11 Shift forks and selector rods - assembly

1 Place the three shift forks in the locating grooves of their respective coupling sleeves.
2 Locate 1st and reverse selector rod through 1st and reverse shift fork and adaptor plate. Secure the fork to the selector rod with a new retaining pin.
3 Fit the 1st and reverse detent ball, spring, and plug. Before tightening the plug apply a few drops of locking compound to the threads. Align the detent ball with the notch in the selector rod. Note that the detent ball assemblies for 1st and reverse gears, are longer than the other detent ball assemblies.
4 Assemble the interlock plunger into the adapter plate.
5 Fit the 2nd and 3rd selector rod through the adaptor plate, the 2nd and 3rd shift fork and the 4th and 5th shift fork. Secure with a new retaining pin. Assemble the detent ball, spring and plug. Apply a few drops of locking compound to the threads of the plug. Align the notch in the 2nd and 3rd selector rod with the detent ball.
6 Assemble the interlock plunger into the adapter plate.
7 Locate the 4th and 5th selector rod through the adapter plate and 4th and 5th shift fork, and secure with a new retaining pin. Assemble the detent ball, spring and plug with a few drops of locking compound applied to the threads of the plug.
8 Tighten each detent ball plug to a torque wrench setting of 12 to 16 lbf ft (1.6 to 2.2 kgf m).
9 Apply gear oil to all sliding surfaces and ensure that the selector mechanism operates freely, and that all gears select smoothly.

12 Rear extension to adaptor plate - assembly

1 Ensure that the mating surfaces of the rear extension and the adaptor plate are clean. Apply a smear of sealant to these faces.
2 Set the selector rods in the 5th gear position, and carefully slide the rear extension onto the adaptor plate. Locate the shift arm onto the 4th and 5th selector rod, then fit the selector lever pin into the other fork rods.
3 Check that the shift rods operate freely and correctly.

13 Bellhousing to adapter plate - assembly

1 Clean the mating surfaces of the adaptor plate and the transmission case. Apply a smear of sealant to these faces.
2 Carefully slide the transmission case onto the adaptor plate and lightly tap it into position with a soft faced mallet.
3 With a suitable tube, locate and tap home the input driveshaft bearing, and the countershaft front bearing. Make sure that the input driveshaft rotates freely.
4 Fit the washers and through bolts and tighten them to a

torque wrench setting of 9.4 to 13.0 lbf ft (1.3 to 1.8 kgf m).
5 Fit the input shaft bearing circlip.
6 To select the correct size of shim which is placed against the countershaft bearing, will necessitate the use of setting gauge number ST 22500000.
7 Support the transmission securely, with the bellhousing uppermost. Locate the setting gauge on the countershaft bearing. Turn the gearbox mainshaft a few times to allow the countershaft bearing to settle down. Then, using feeler gauges measure the clearance (B) between the setting gauge and the front end of the transmission case. To establish the shim size (H) use the following formula H = A − B.
   A is the dimension marked on the setting gauge. The following is an example. If A = 0.070 in (1.78 mm) and B = 0.010 in (0.25 mm) then, using the formula H = A − B results in a figure of 0.060 in (1.53 mm) for H. To the figure H must be added 0.005 in (0.127 mm) to arrive at the correct shim thickness. There are eighteen shim sizes available, from 0.0531 in (1.350 mm) to 0.0699 in (1.775 mm) increasing in thickness by 0.001 in (0.025 mm) increments.
8 Clean the surface of the front cover and its adjacent surface on the transmission case. Apply a little grease to the selected shim, to help retain it in position. Smear the faces of the front cover and the transmission case with sealant, and fit the front cover with bolts and washers. Tighten them to a torque wrench setting of 9.4 to 13.0 lbf ft (1.3 to 1.8 kgf m). Apply a few drops of sealant to the threads of the bolts prior to fitting.
9 Grease the reverse select return plunger and refit it in the rear extension housing; followed by the reverse select return springs, and the reverse select return plug. Apply a little sealing compound to the plug and tighten it to a torque wrench setting of 5.8 to 7.2 lbf ft (0.8 to 1.0 kgf m).
10 Assemble the speedometer pinion assembly to the rear extension housing. Make sure that the lock plate is lined up with the groove in the speedometer pinion sleeve. Fit the bolts and tighten them to a torque wrench setting of 2.3 to 3.2 lbf ft (0.32 to 0.44 kgf m).
11 Fit the reversing lamp switch and tighten it to a torque wrench setting of 14.5 to 21.7 lbf ft (2.0 to 3.0 kgf m).
12 Apply a light coat of multi-purpose grease to the clutch withdrawal lever, the release bearing, and the bearing sleeve; then fit them to the clutch bellhousing. After the retaining spring has been assembled, slide the dust excluding cover on to the clutch bellhousing.
13 Fit the gear shift lever temporarily and check for a smooth movement through all the gears.

E Braking system

1 The braking system procedures, of disassembly and reassembly, are the same as those described in Chapter 9. The Mk 2 models have larger discs and disc pads, and a larger vacuum servo unit.

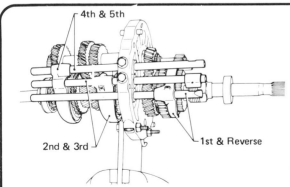

Fig. 13.49. Assembling shift forks and selector rods

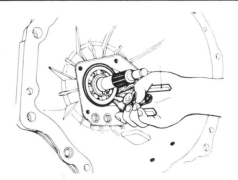

Fig. 13.50. Fitting input drive bearing circlip

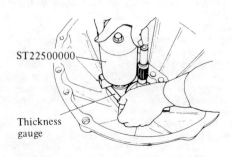

Fig. 13.51. Measuring shim thickness

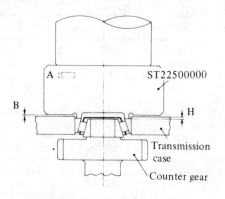

Fig. 13.52. Sectional view of setting gauge in use

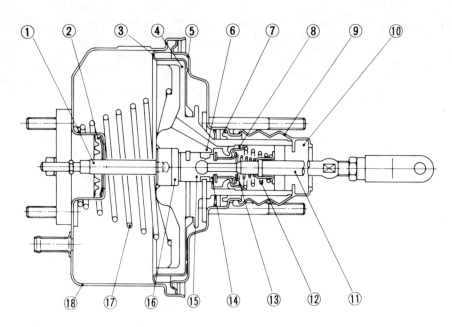

Fig. 13.53. Sectional view of the brake vacuum servo unit (Mk 2 models)

1 Push rod	6 Vacuum valve	11 Valve operating rod	15 Valve plunger
2 Plate and seal	7 Seal	12 Valve return spring	16 Reaction disc
3 Diaphragm	8 Poppet assembly	13 Poppet return spring	17 Diaphragm return spring
4 Diaphragm plate	9 Valve body cover	14 Exhaust valve	18 Front shell
5 Rear shell	10 Air filter		

Wiring diagrams overleaf, pages 252 - 261

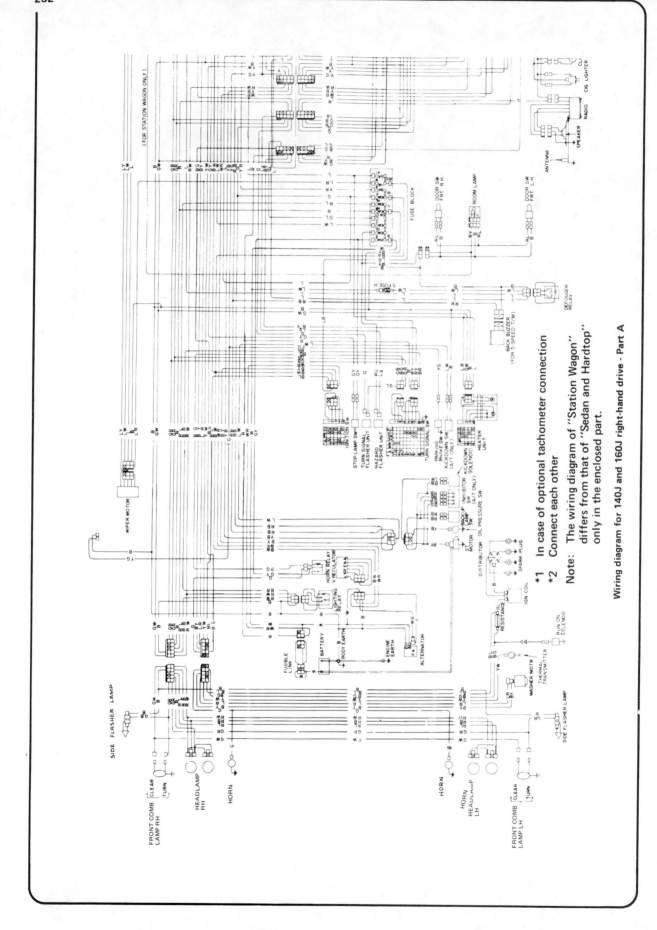

*1   In case of optional tachometer connection

*2   Connect each other

Note: The wiring diagram of "Station Wagon"
differs from that of "Sedan and Hardtop"
only in the enclosed part.

Wiring diagram for 140J and 160J right-hand drive - Part A

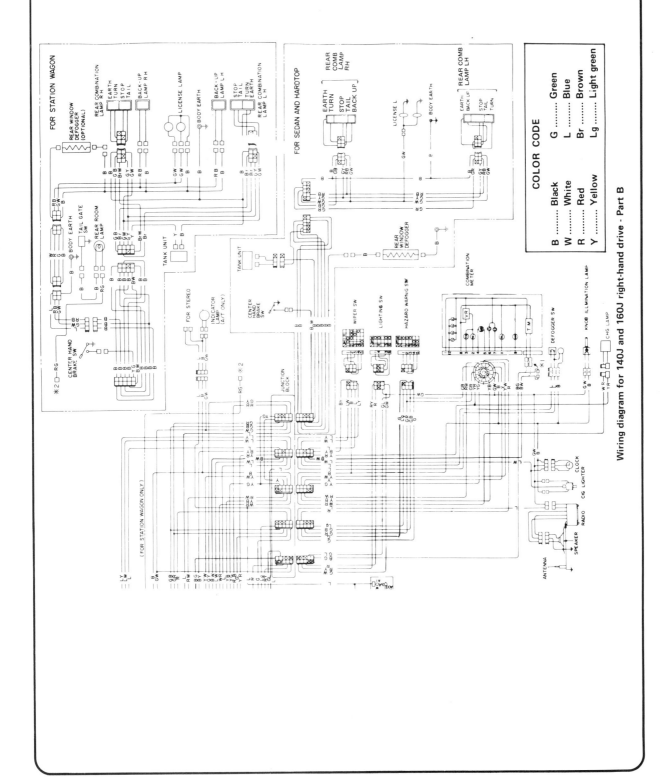

Wiring diagram for 140J and 160J right-hand drive - Part B

COLOR CODE

B	Black	G	Green
W	White	L	Blue
R	Red	Br	Brown
Y	Yellow	Lg	Light green

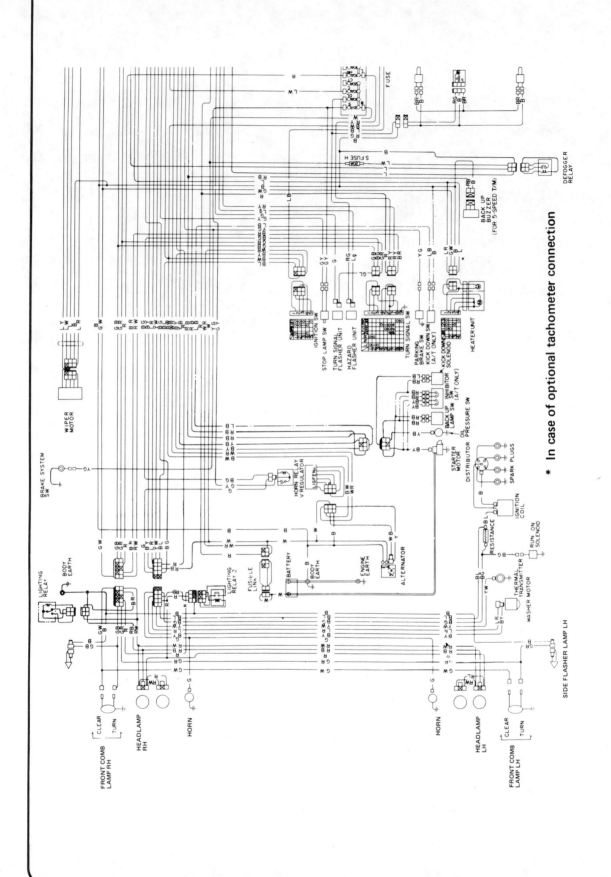

Wiring diagram for 140J and 160J left-hand drive (Europe) - Part A

* In case of optional tachometer connection

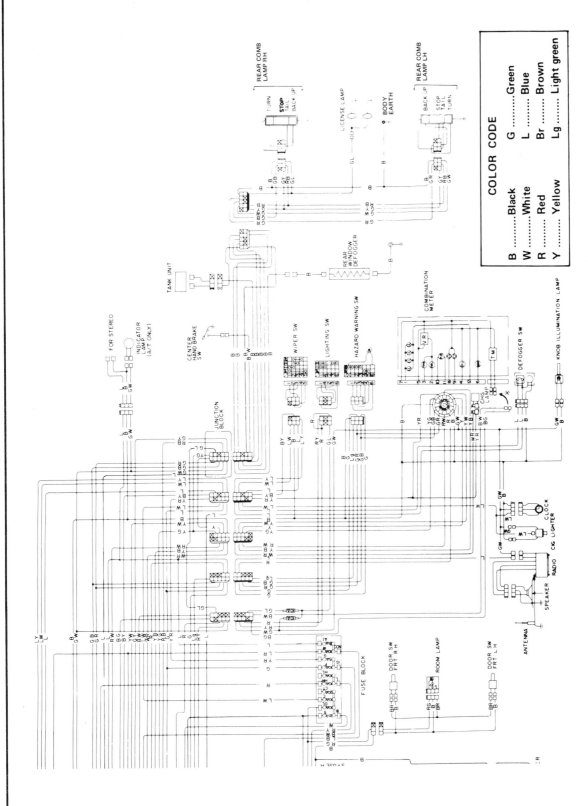

COLOR CODE

B	Black	G	Green
W	White	L	Blue
R	Red	Br	Brown
Y	Yellow	Lg	Light green

Wiring diagram for 140J and 160J left-hand drive (Europe) - Part B

256

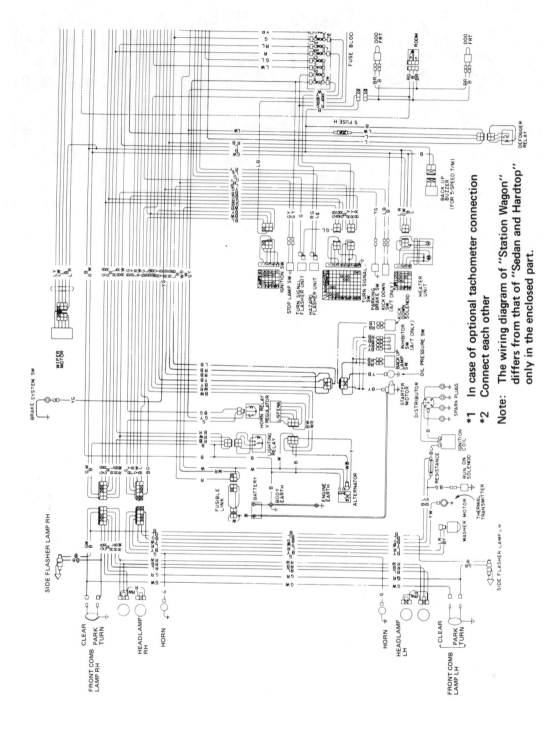

Wiring diagram for 140J and 160J left-hand drive (General) - Part A

Note: The wiring diagram of "Station Wagon" differs from that of "Sedan and Hardtop" only in the enclosed part.

*1 In case of optional tachometer connection
*2 Connect each other

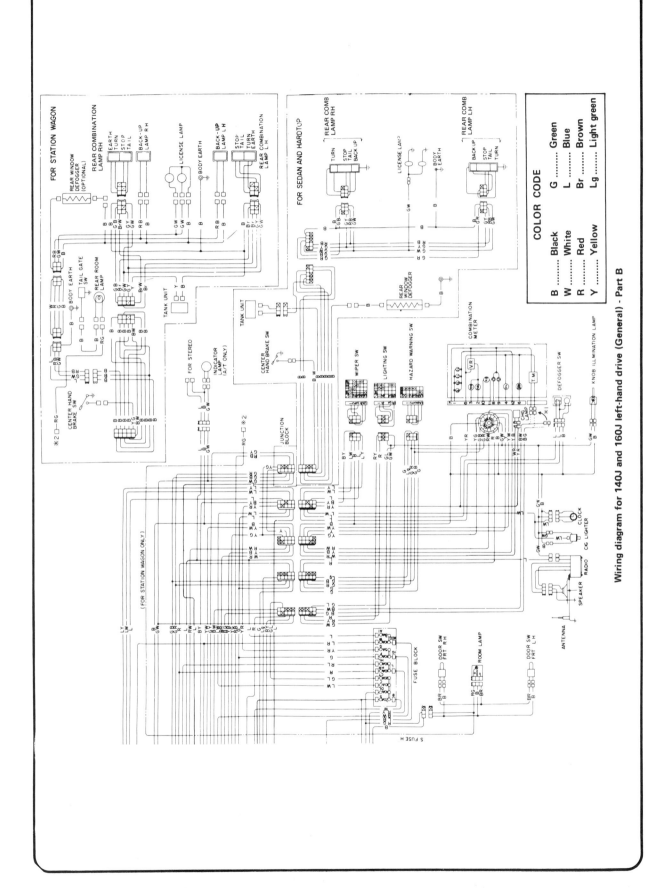

Wiring diagram for 140J and 160J left-hand drive (General) - Part B

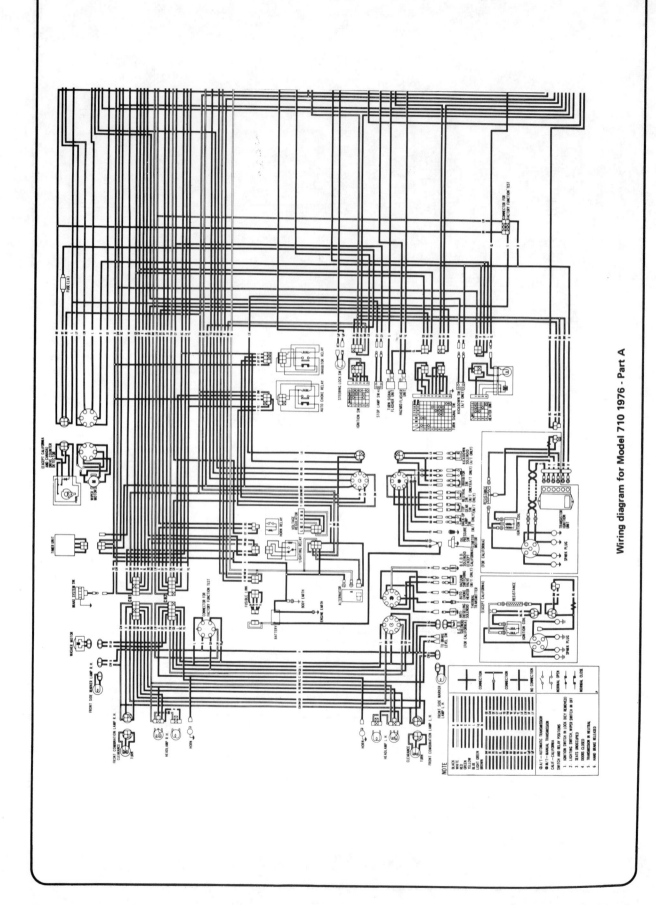

Wiring diagram for Model 710 1976 - Part A

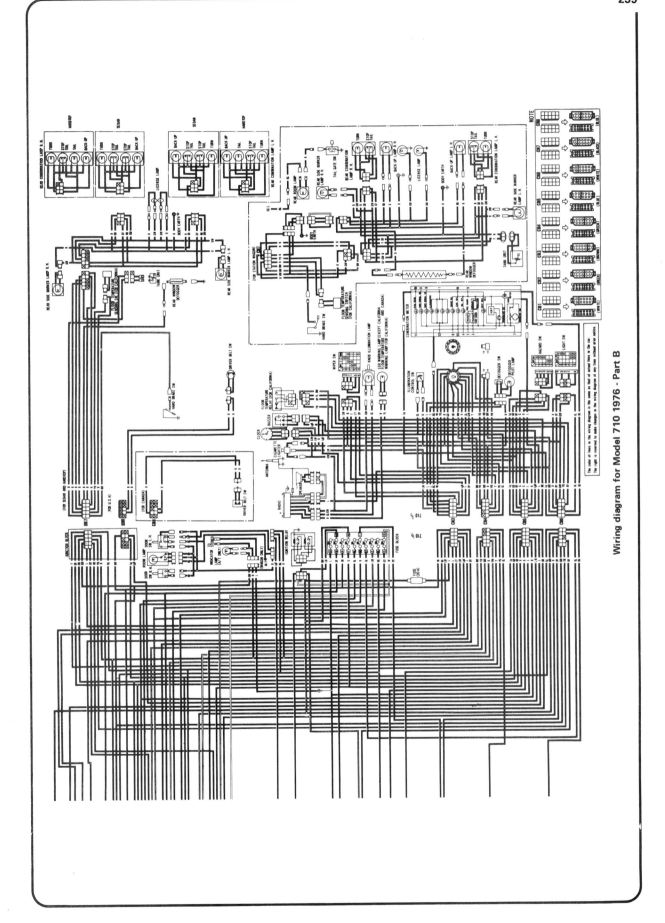

Wiring diagram for Model 710 1976 - Part B

259

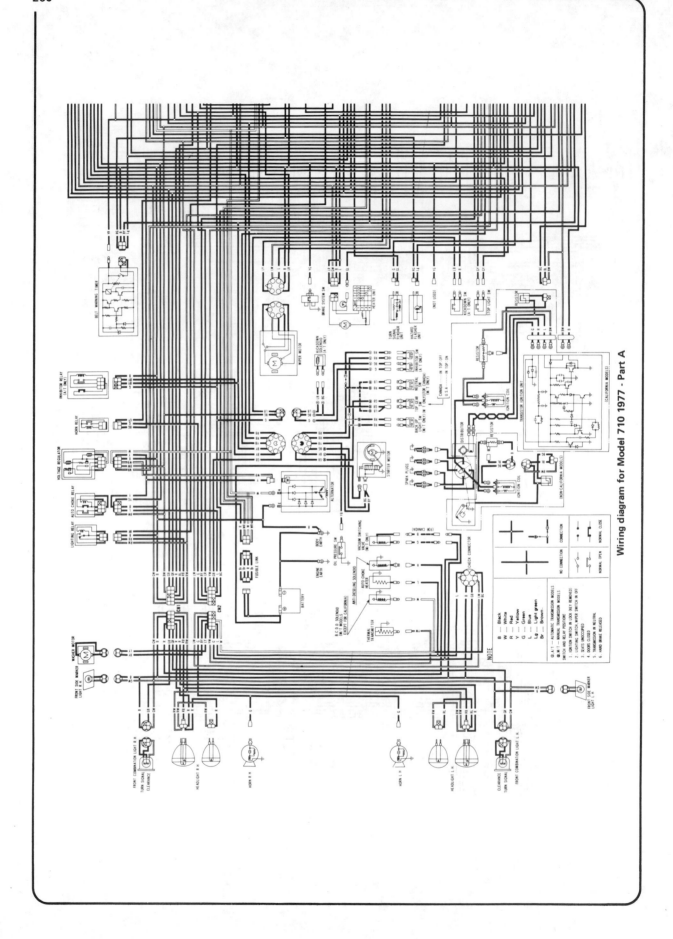

Wiring diagram for Model 710 1977 - Part A

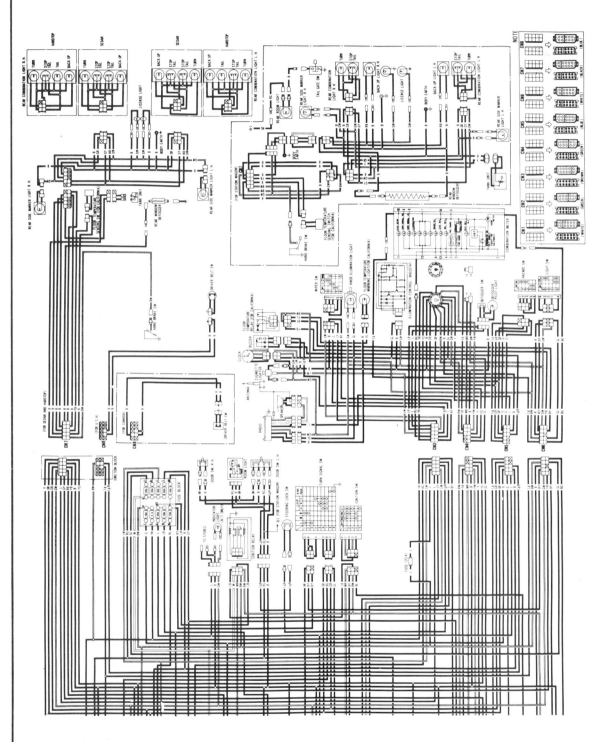

Wiring diagram for Model 710 1977 - Part B

Index

Printed by
J H Haynes & Co Ltd
Sparkford Nr Yeovil
Somerset BA22 7JJ England